D1271065

POLITICAL PRAIRIE FIRE

POLITICAL
PRAIRIE FIRE

The Nonpartisan League, 1915–1922

by Robert L. Morlan

UNIVERSITY OF MINNESOTA PRESS, Minneapolis

To my Mother and Father

Preface

ROCKETING to prominence in the early days of World War I, the Nonpartisan League in North Dakota and adjoining states achieved a measure of political success well beyond that which has been the lot of most movements of protest in the history of the United States. Not only was it to control for some years the government of one state, elect state officials and legislators in a number of midwestern and western states, and send several of its representatives to the Congress—its impact was to help shape the destinies of a dozen states and the political philosophies of an important segment of the nation's voters. Today, almost forty years later, the League continues to exist only in the state of its birth, North Dakota, but its influence has been far-reaching.

The Nonpartisan League was a truly novel experiment on the American political scene—an organization proclaiming public ownership and control as a solution for economic ills, which was in time actually able to put its proposals into practice on a statewide scale. Its technique of operating through the primaries of established political parties rather than as a "third party," and its attempt at the development of a truly nonpartisan spirit—selection of "the best man for the job regardless of party"—could have come only with the establishment of the direct primary. Not only was the League the father of Minnesota's later-to-be-famous Farmer-Labor party and scattered "liberal" movements in other states, but its methods of operation serve not infrequently today as a guide for political action.

The Nonpartisan League during the years covered by this study was a potent political force in both North Dakota and Minnesota and a somewhat lesser power in Montana, Idaho, Wisconsin, and Colorado. In the remainder of the thirteen states in which it was active and in the prairie provinces of Canada it never achieved thorough organization and consequently was of relatively minor importance. The focus of attention is naturally upon those areas in which the League played a major role.

Deeply rooted in the tradition of western "agrarian revolts," the League was nevertheless clearly a product both of its environment and of its times, an element of the tremendous ferment of "reform" so widespread in virtually all aspects of American life during the first two decades of the twentieth century. Throughout most of its active history the League was dominated by the personality and organizing genius of A. C. Townley, one of the great natural leaders of protest movements which this country has produced.

Owing to the nature of the Nonpartisan League's proposals, the methods by which it operated, and the period in which it developed, the League era was one of almost unparalleled ill-feeling in those states in which it was a significant political force. The depth of the emotion on both sides was such that some bitterness still remains, and even today it is impossible to divorce oneself completely from that situation. Virtually all writing pertaining to the League published during its ascendancy reflects extremely biased points of view. In some instances, indeed, it is difficult to be absolutely certain of even noncontroversial facts because of the completely contradictory nature of many existing sources.

Prejudices are deep-seated and rigorously adhered to, and there is also much room for honest and reasoned differences of opinion. Some who are familiar with the events related here will doubtless feel that the treatment of various incidents evidences undue generosity—others that criticism is overly harsh. One can have no illusions as to the possibility of universal satisfaction on a topic so controversial, nor is an attempt at such an objective necessarily desirable. This study is, however, an effort to chronicle with fairness and accuracy the dramatic and swift-moving story of this unique political movement.

Material has been drawn widely from newspapers of both pro-League and anti-League persuasions, and the opinions of a considerable number of persons once prominent in the League or in opposition to it have been secured through personal interviews and correspondence.

Principal though by no means sole reliance has perforce been placed upon representative newspapers, the *Nonpartisan Leader*, official organ of the National Nonpartisan League, the *Grand Forks Herald*, acknowledged chief journalistic spokesman of the anti-League forces in North Dakota, and the *Minneapolis Journal*, one of the leading dailies of the Twin Cities and a vigorous League opponent. Few League leaders or opponents preserved personal papers, and some which were saved have since been accidentally destroyed. Of those available, the National Nonpartisan League Papers, contributed by Henry G. Teigan, and the LeSueur Papers, both in the library of the Minnesota Historical Society, have proved particularly useful.

While I of course assume full responsibility, I wish to express my sincere gratitude for much valuable assistance, information, and opinion to the following: Fred G. Aandahl, former governor of North Dakota and former member of Congress from North Dakota; William A. Anderson, former judge of the District Court of Hennepin County, formerly secretary to the Industrial Commission of North Dakota and attorney for the Bank of North Dakota; John M. Baer, former congressman from North Dakota; A. M. Christianson, former chief justice of the Supreme Court of North Dakota; Joseph Gilbert, former organization manager for the National Nonpartisan League; John N. Hagan, former commissioner of agriculture and labor of North Dakota; Thomas Hall, secretary of state of North Dakota; O. B. Herigstad, prominent I.V.A. attorney and law partner of the late Governor R. A. Nestos; William Lemke, former congressman from North Dakota, former attorney general of North Dakota, and former member of the executive committee of the National Nonpartisan League; Nelson A. Mason, former secretary to Governor Lynn J. Frazier; George Olson, secretary-treasurer of the Nonpartisan League of North Dakota; John R. Steen, former state treasurer and state auditor of North Dakota; A. C. Townley, founder of the Nonpartisan League and president of the organization from 1915 to 1922; Frank A. Vogel, former member of the North Dakota legislature and former manager of the Bank of North Dakota; George E. Wallace, former tax commissioner of North Dakota and former tax commissioner of Minnesota; and Howard R. Wood, former speaker of the House of Representatives of North Dakota and former lieutenant governor of North Dakota. Mr.

and Mrs. Philip Haug of Deering, North Dakota, have extended much assistance and many kindnesses.

The staffs of the libraries of the Minnesota and North Dakota Historical societies, of the library of the University of Minnesota, and of the public libraries of Minneapolis, St. Paul, and Bismarck have been most helpful, as have the staff members of the University of Minnesota Press. The reproducing of illustrations is the work of my wife, Anne Matthews Morlan. To Professors A. N. Christensen of the Department of Political Science and George M. Stephenson of the Department of History of the University of Minnesota my sincere thanks for generous and valuable advice and criticism.

R. L. M.

University of Redlands
February 15, 1955

~~~~~~

Table of Contents

List of Illustrations

POLITICAL PRAIRIE FIRE

Pattern for Conflict

"FIFTY-FIVE million dollars a year is lost to the farmers of North Dakota through unfair practices in the grain trade."[1] The speaker was John H. Worst, president of the North Dakota Agricultural College at Fargo and a veteran crusader for improved marketing practices. His audience, the 1916 convention of the Tri-State Grain Growers Association, received the statement in stony silence—the situation was all too familiar even if the exact figures were not. Convinced that they had been tyrannized for years by the grain combine, the railroads, and the bankers, and smarting under the sense of having too long been treated as "rubes," these farmers were spoiling for action.

North Dakota at this time was an almost purely agricultural state. More than 70 per cent of its population, which totaled a mere 600,000, was rural,[2] while only five communities had more than 5000 inhabitants, the largest, Fargo, boasting a population of something less than 20,000. Approximately 27 per cent of the state's population was foreign-born, with Norwegians predominating among the twenty-five different nationalities represented; an almost equal number were natives born of foreign parents. Of the native residents only a small fraction had been born in North Dakota.[3] The others had come from almost every section of the United States, reflecting the pioneer restlessness still strong in the latter half of the nineteenth century, and the frontier preference for action rather than words was far from dead.

With such a complexion, North Dakota should indeed have been a state run by farmers and concerned primarily with their interests. Yet nothing could have been farther from the truth. North Dakota actually had been dominated for years by a tight little oligarchy largely controlled by the grain and railroad interests, which concerned itself with the problems of the farmer, it appeared, only in the cases where it was in the best interest of these business elements to do so. This ruling power was, moreover, located not in North Dakota but in the Minneapolis and St. Paul banking, milling, and railroad headquarters. North Dakota, weak financially and having virtually a one-crop economy, "always has been, and perhaps always will be in some particulars a province of St. Paul and Minneapolis, rather than an economically and politically independent state." [4]

From almost the beginning of its statehood until 1906 North Dakota had had a boss, the agent of this oligarchy, and the fact was accepted by most of the voters with a rather indifferent resignation. Alex McKenzie had come to North Dakota in the 1870s with the Northern Pacific Railroad as a contractor and had in a few years managed to make himself the political master of the state. He was an adroit and clever manipulator, generous with money and with personal favors, who preferred to persuade rather than command. The railroads provided the free passes and much of the funds necessary for continued power, in return being protected in matters of taxes and rate regulation. McKenzie men had for years held many of the key legislative positions in the state, and his power rested on control of the machinery of the Republican party and its conventions. Lewis F. Crawford, the historian of North Dakota, put the matter this way:

North Dakota had long had a government made up of the executive, legislative, and judicial departments, and also an "invisible government." The source of this invisible government was supposed to reside in a person whom few North Dakotans had ever seen, and perhaps for that very reason his power was exaggerated. A half-whispered reference to the "McKenzie ring" evoked a picture of almost magical power and influence, beside which governors and legislatures were of little consequence. [5]

There had been a short-lived uprising against the McKenzie ring in 1892 when there occurred a fusion of the Democrats, the Populists, and the Farmers' Alliance, which elected Populist Eli Shortridge governor. Not until 1906, however, was real progress made. Influenced greatly by the LaFollette program in Wisconsin and the general passion for "reform" that was then sweeping the country, "Progressive Repub-

4

licans" joined with Democrats to elect the popular John Burke governor and secure control of both houses of the legislature. Burke served until 1912, during which period a number of governmental reforms were put into effect, the most significant being the direct primary.[6] At that time he was succeeded by L. B. Hanna, a well-to-do banker of conservative leanings.

The McKenzie clique was still on the outside, though retaining very real strength, but many a farmer soon began to question the value of political dominance by the Progressives. Thoroughly discontented with the economic conditions with which he was forced to cope, the farmer quite naturally blamed those holding political power, and found it easy to conclude that neither "Stalwarts" nor "Progressives" actually had his interests at heart—that whatever the name the same "old gang" was controlling North Dakota.

This section of the Upper Midwest, with its severe winters and short growing seasons, produced some of the world's finest wheat. This wheat, possessed of superior milling qualities, was in constant demand, and since farms for the most part had been acquired by pre-emption and homesteading and thus represented an insignificant investment for land, the raising of it should have been a highly profitable enterprise. Unfortunately, however, while fortunes were indeed being made from wheat, the average farmer was hard-pressed to provide the bare necessities for his family and keep up the interest on his debts. The profits appeared to be going instead to that familiar bugbear of producers, the "middleman"—in this case an amazing combination of middlemen consisting of line elevators, terminal elevators, commission houses, grain brokers, millers, speculators, and so on.

Nothing reveals the financial straits of these farmers more clearly than the statistics of farm mortgages. In 1910 slightly more than half of the farms of North Dakota were mortgaged (50.9 per cent); only two other states in the nation, with approximately the same figure, had such a high percentage, namely, Iowa and Wisconsin. Even more significant, however, is the fact that ten years earlier only 31.4 per cent had been mortgaged. Furthermore, the average debt of these mortgaged farms had increased over a twenty-year period from $902 to $2493, or 176.4 per cent, though it is true that the valuations had increased by an even higher percentage.[7] The number of farms operated by tenants was likewise on the increase: in 1890, 6.9 per cent; in 1900, 8.5 per cent;

and in 1910, 14.3 per cent. Clearly, all was not well with the midwestern wheat farmers.

The methods by which the Minneapolis Chamber of Commerce,* and to a lesser extent the Duluth Board of Trade, determined the farmers' economic lot are worth more than passing notice. The power of setting prices and determining grades and buying conditions meant virtually complete economic control over the entire area, and on these matters the word of the Chamber was law.

The Chamber of Commerce was an association of the big grain traders, terminal elevators, commission houses, and the like, which completely controlled the Minneapolis exchange, and also controlled its own membership. Consequently, it not only dominated the existing market but also prevented groups likely to endanger its power, such as cooperatives or independent traders, from participating in the exchange activities. Moreover, there was no restriction as to the number of memberships which a large and powerful concern might hold, thus making possible actual control by a few large corporations. Though there appeared to be a great number of concerns holding memberships in the Chamber, investigations showed that holding company combinations in effect made dozens of these organizations one and the same. In a number of cases one company controlled whole chains of elements in the marketing process: line elevators, terminal elevators, commission houses, and mills. These empires frequently were almost staggering in their immensity.[8] Not only did Twin Cities concerns control hundreds of country elevators, although they usually were given a variety of names, but practically all the line elevator companies had iron-clad price-fixing agreements which ruled out any actual competition in buying. The daily prices as determined in the Chamber of Commerce were sent in bulletin form to all line elevators throughout the entire area.[9]

There were no terminal markets in North Dakota, and the farmer was in practice forced to sell through the Minnesota exchanges. Cooperative country elevators were fairly widespread, but their effectiveness was mitigated by the fact that they also had to operate through the exchange, and further by the continuous opposition of both the grain combine and the railroads. The comments of United States Dis-

* The Grain Exchange and not the usual organization of this name. The name was changed January 1, 1947.

6

trict Judge Charles F. Amidon in this connection in 1919 are especially interesting as presenting a reasoned view of the situation:

In the main they [farmers of North Dakota] have made their purchases and sold their products as individuals. Nearly all their livestock and grain is shipped to terminal markets at St. Paul, Minneapolis, and Duluth. There these products pass into the hands of large commission houses, elevator and milling companies, and livestock concerns. These interests are combined not only in corporations, chambers of commerce, boards of trade, and interlocking directorates, but in the millions of understandings which arise among men having common interests and living for long terms of years in the daily intercourse of great cities. These common understandings need not be embodied in articles of incorporation or trust agreements. They may be as intangible as the ancient "powers of the air." But they are as potent in the economic world as those ancient powers were thought to be in the affairs of men. It is the potency of this unity of life of men dwelling together in daily intercourse that has caused all nations thus far to be governed by cities.[10]

When the farmer's crop was harvested and he was ready to sell, he found himself in the grip of an unbeatable combination. Two methods were open to him. He could take it to the elevator in the nearest town or he could ship it himself to a commission firm in Minneapolis and take his chances on the grading and bidding there. It was at the country elevator that the farmer first ran into one of the practices of which President Worst spoke—inaccurate or false grading. The elevator manager, running an experienced hand through the top of the load, would announce that it was, for example, No. 2 or No. 4. This grading, based supposedly on the appearance of the grain, its weight, hardness, and clearness, purported to represent its actual milling qualities and thus determined the price to be paid. Wheat was graded as No. 1 Hard, No. 1 Northern, No. 2, No. 3, No. 4, No Grade, or Rejected, with considerable difference in price between the grades. The farmer, who time after time saw good wheat graded low, had no recourse under this arbitrary system—hence there had been a long-continuing demand for uniform grading laws, with grading scientifically controlled by means of milling and baking tests.

A professional Minneapolis grain grader for thirty-six years, associated with the Equity Cooperative Exchange in 1916, when asked what he thought of the Minnesota grain grades, is reported to have replied vehemently:

Why, they're a joke—that is it would be funny if it wasn't so serious.
Grain is sold here under grades—the Minnesota grades—which are a
system of guess work, more or less good guesses, but they have nothing
to do with the real value of the grain.

Some inspector guesses what grade a sample of grain is, and that's
the grade it must be sold or purchased under. If you don't like his guess
you can call in another guesser, a re-inspector, he is called. He guesses
on it and, chances are, confirms the first guesser, whose guess he is
apprised of beforehand. Then you can call in three more guessers, if
you are still dissatisfied. They call these three the board of appeals. You
must tell them what the other two have guessed and then they confirm
the unanimous opinion of the other two guessers, and there you are . . .
Fair grades will never exist till they are established by milling tests.[11]

He went on to remark that it always seemed astonishingly easier to
get the grade raised on outgoing wheat, and commented on the innu-
merable cases in his experience of wheat purchased at No. 2, dumped
into an outgoing car, and graded as No. 1—it then being the property
of the broker.

The 1915 wheat crop in North Dakota was approximately 140,000,000
bushels. If this were sold on an average of only one grade below its
actual grade, it meant a loss to the farmers from this source alone of
$5,000,000. In fact, the experiments of Dr. Edwin F. Ladd, professor
of chemistry at the state agricultural college and food commissioner
of North Dakota, showed that the wheat in one 100,000,000-bushel crop
was actually worth $5,271,398.23 more than the farmers received for it.[12]

For some years the North Dakota Agricultural Experiment Station
had operated a small experimental mill at which the research staff
milled and baked different grades and kept extensive records of their
findings. Dr. Ladd's publication of the results was most illuminating.
Wheat graded No. 4 was found to make 67.33 per cent flour; No. 3,
69.41 per cent; and No. 1, 70.112 per cent; yet with this minor differential there was a wide spread in the buying price. It was obviously
much more profitable to buy the lower grades, the profits on No. 1
being 33 per cent, on No. 4, 52 per cent, and on "Rejected" 55 per
cent. Furthermore, the experiments showed that No. 1 Hard would
not make as many loaves of bread or as good bread as an equal quantity
of No. 3 or No. 4, because it did not have as much gluten. Though the
housewife's and the baker's standards—quantity and quality of bread
produced—were those by which the miller sold his product, he did not

8

buy it in that way. There was also found to be a better volume of bread from these lower grades; that is, they produced lighter bread, Rejected wheat giving a loaf of 2558 cu. cm. while No. 1 made a loaf of 2347 cu. cm. In loaf color No. 1 was slightly ahead of the others, but all were within 2 per cent of each other, while the texture was essentially the same. Dr. Ladd contended that there would be no need to give such tests to every load of wheat in order to grade it scientifically, since seasonal averages had proved satisfactory to establish fair grades.[13] Publication of these findings did not improve the farmers' estimation of the existing system.

Another source of farmer complaint was what was known as "dockage." When wheat was purchased either at a line elevator or at a terminal point, it was customarily docked so much weight per bushel for impurities, dirt, and other seed, whether or not any were present. Although this dockage was later screened out, and the valuable miscellaneous seed ground and sold as stock feed at about $20 a ton, the farmer received nothing for it and was, moreover, forced to pay the freight on it to the terminal market. From 1907 through 1914 dockage averaged 3.99 per cent, thus amounting on a 100,000,000-bushel crop to a loss of 119,700 tons or approximately $2,394,000.[14]

The *Devils Lake* (N.D.) *Journal* told the story of a local farmer who shipped two cars of wheat to a Minneapolis commission house, after first taking it to a local elevator to have it thoroughly cleaned. Both cars were loaded at the same time from the same bin, yet even though cleaned, one car was docked three pounds and the other four pounds per bushel at Minneapolis.[15]

At any rate, the "impurities" were shipped to Minneapolis at the farmer's expense and later returned and sold to him as "mixed feed" for livestock. In other words he not only did not receive the selling price of the dockage originally, but was forced to pay freight to Minneapolis and back plus commissions and profits for the middlemen in order to get back in only slightly altered form the same produce he had raised.[16]

Nor was the farmer paid for the valuable by-products of his grain. There was an average of 12.7 per cent of bran, representing on a 100,000,000-bushel crop 381,300 tons, or, at $20 a ton, approximately $7,626,000. The average of shorts was 15.15 per cent, representing 450,500 tons, or, at $22 a ton, $9,999,000.[17]

9

Thus the total value of dockage and by-products, for which the farmer was not paid, amounted to $20,019,000 on this one crop. If these items could have been retained in the state and fed to livestock, it was estimated that the profit thereon would not be less than 25 per cent on the value, or $5,000,000. The freight on 955,500 tons—dockage and by-products—at an average carrying charge of $3.25 per ton would be $3,200,000. Furthermore, it was said that these by-products would support 754,400 adult cattle, roughage for which (alfalfa, clover, and corn) could be grown to the advantage of the soil. The value of the manure, according to experiments at the Cornell University Experiment Station, was annually $29.27 per animal, the total approximating $22,373,988.

If to the total of all these calculations, $50,593,000, is added the $5,272,000 which Dr. Ladd previously showed was lost by unfair grading, a grand total of $55,865,000 is reached, representing the amount North Dakota farmers might presumably have saved annually by exporting only flour instead of uncleaned wheat.[18] The necessary costs of handling and processing the grain within North Dakota appear to have been given little attention. While this theorizing seems a bit strained, it is clear that whether or not these specific figures are accepted significant losses were occurring in this manner.

There were two methods of weighing grain at the country elevators, both of which often involved the use of "loaded dice" against the farmer. Under the most common system the wagon was weighed full, the wheat taken out, and then the wagon weighed empty. Would prominent businessmen, "leading citizens," go so far as to use "false weights"? The farmers had been long convinced that they would, but definite proof was not forthcoming until 1919 when weights were checked by state inspectors and condemned by the truckload.[19]

In many elevators the grain was weighed near the top of the elevator instead of on the ground. As it went into the receiving bin and again as it dropped down onto a hopper scale, it passed a spout providing a suction draft which was supposed to remove dirt and chaff and to keep the building free from dust. The suction fan, however, had added attractions in that it was capable of removing a goodly quantity of wheat as well in the course of a season. The records of the Minnesota State Railroad and Warehouse Commission for 1915 showed one elevator, for example, shipping out slightly over 51,000 bushels more than it received during the period and had on hand at the start of the year.[20] At least, after this process, all the impurities should have been out, but the loads were docked just the same.

But let us suppose that the farmer decided to ship his wheat to a Minneapolis commission house to see what the market would bring. Here in all probability was an even more disastrous step, as the grain graders there in effect held office at the pleasure of the Chamber of Commerce and were certainly no more liberal than the elevator men.

The customary practice in selling this wheat was a picture of delightful simplicity. When the market opened at 10 o'clock in the morning, the shipment would usually be purchased immediately by a gentleman representing a terminal elevator company, but the elevator he purchased for was often a part of the same concern as the commission house, though bearing a different name. Thus, in effect, the company sold the grain to itself, not forgetting to charge the shipper the usual one cent per bushel commission, and it was of course sold at the bottom of the market.[21]

In practice it was not uncommon for the shipment to pass through the hands of two or three such agents with a commission exacted each time. During the investigation of the grain trade by the Minnesota House of Representatives committee in 1913, it was alleged by attorney James Manahan, and not denied by the Chamber of Commerce representatives, that half of the Van Dusen-Harrington company's sales daily were made in the first ten minutes of the selling day, and that they were made to subsidiary companies.[22]

It would seem in this case that the farmer was "stuck" even worse than if he had sold to the line elevator because he had had to pay freight charges. The interesting fact is, however, that the farmer paid for shipping in both instances, the line elevator price being the Minneapolis price less freight. There was also an engaging custom of charging the shipper a flat switching fee of $1.50 per car, whether the railroad made such a charge or not, and most of the time it did not. John G. McHugh, secretary of the Minneapolis Chamber of Commerce, freely admitted this in testifying before the committee of the Minnesota House of Representatives investigating the grain trade. Mr. Manahan thereupon asked: "Isn't that crooked?"

"No, I don't think it is crooked."

"Why isn't it—isn't it a fraud upon the shipper?"

McHugh answered lamely that "the rules of the Chamber of Commerce permitted an initial switching charge," and launched into an elaborate discussion of how the practice grew up. He also declared that in some instances the railroads had put in bills of $5 to $6 for switching, but that the shipper had paid only $1.50. Immediately asked if he knew this to be so, "the witness admitted that he did not know this to be a fact." [23]

George S. Loftus of the Equity Cooperative Exchange testified during court attacks on his organization that the Chamber exacted from grain shippers $68,000 more in switching charges during 1912 than its members paid out to the railroads for switching on all their business. At all other exchanges in the country, he said, switching charges were paid by the buyers. [24]

Low grading, as we have seen, was an established practice, but what happened to this low-graded wheat after leaving the farmer's hands? It is hardly a surprise to learn that by some mystical transformation it emerged from the Minneapolis market as No. 1 or No. 2. This bit of magic was accomplished through the instrumentality of the mixing house, sometimes referred to as a "grain hospital." Here carloads of No. 1 were mixed with No. 3, No. 4, or No Grade,* coming out all No. 1 or 2. Heavy wheat could obviously be easily mixed with limited quantities of lighter grades and still pass minimum requirements for No. 1. Twenty-eight of twenty-nine Minneapolis terminal elevators in the years 1911 and 1912 handled 63,000,000 bushels of wheat, of which, on original inspection, 13,927,055 bushels were graded No. 1. After mixing they sold 18,887,777 bushels of No. 1, an increase of 5,057,722 bushels. In the same period they received 20,413,584 bushels of No. 2 and shipped out 22,242,410. Thus there were almost 7,000,000 bushels of No. 1 and No. 2 for which they did not pay as such. Grades No. 3 and No. 4 were purchased at from 2 to 12 cents a bushel cheaper than No. 1 and No. 2. [25] The farmer felt, with considerable logic, that if it was No. 1 when it came out, it was No. 1 when it went in.

The eastern millers complained bitterly about this process, and as early as 1903 the United States Department of Agriculture was receiving complaints from abroad, [26] but because of these buyers' needs for pur-

---

* "No Grade" is good wheat, but not graded because of the presence of too much moisture. It goes to the highest bidder.

chasing in large quantities it was necessary for them to deal with the exchanges.

It would probably be difficult to find a group more conservative on the average than a bankers' association. Yet even the North Dakota Bankers' Association became much disturbed over this general situation, and in 1906 sent a committee to investigate grain marketing practices. Its report was revealing, treating quite plainly most of the above-mentioned abuses. The record of one Duluth elevator which it reported was most enlightening in the matter of mixing: [27]

	Bushels Received	Bushels Shipped
No. 1 Northern	99,711.40	196,288.30
No. 2	141,455.10	467,764.00
No. 3	272,047.20	213,549.30
No. 4	201,267.20	None
No grade	116,021.10	None
Rejected	59,742.30	None
On hand (all grades) ..	12,733.10	

Far from least on the farmer's list of woes was the striking regularity with which he saw wheat prices drop at about the time of year when his crop was ready for harvest and surge upward when the crop was safely in the hands of the dealers. The unending lectures on the subject of supply and demand from the elevator men lost much of their impressive quality when the farmer could read in his newspaper stories of the speculations on the Chicago market and the manner in which grain gamblers could manipulate futures prices through often extremely questionable tactics. It scarcely took a mental giant to deduce that the entire marketing system was rigged against the farmer. It was not pleasant to see his hard labor go so poorly rewarded while others, who made little or no contribution to the public good thereby, reaped huge fortunes through gambling with the product of his labor.

With reference to the speculative system testimony was offered before a committee of the United States House of Representatives to show that for every bushel of actual wheat sold, fifty bushels of "phantom wheat" were dealt in on the floor of the Minneapolis Chamber of Commerce.[28] The speculators were well aware that most farmers were in debt in the fall and that they had no place to store their grain. Since they were thus virtually forced to sell, it was a simple matter to drive the price down at harvest time. Numerous pretenses were used to justify the sudden slumps, and the press was generally helpful in preparing the public mind in advance. In August of 1915, for example, a story was publicized that European orders for two million bushels of wheat had been canceled. This later proved to be completely false, yet on that basis prices dropped several cents and never returned.[29]

The *Devils Lake* (N.D.) *Journal* editorialized on the 1915 situation in heated terms. No elevators in North Dakota or terminal elevators in Chicago, Minneapolis, Duluth, or Kansas City were full, it said. Miles of empty freight cars waited on sidings. No mills had more than a few months' supply. At no place in the United States was the wheat market "glutted." Yet within three weeks the price of wheat was hammered down fifty cents a bushel, which meant, with a crop of 100,000,000 bushels, a loss of $50,000,000 to the farmers of North Dakota alone. The *Journal* concluded: "Does any thinking man believe that the decline in price, before the crop is threshed, aye, even in the shock, is based upon anything except the greed and avarice of the organized gang of robbers who have banded together under the respectable sounding title for the purpose of stealing from the farmers of the Northwest their hard earned profits?"[30]

The already jaundiced eye of the farmer quite naturally fell with extreme displeasure on the statistics of the enormous profits being made by the grain exporters in these early years of the European war. The figures on wheat are for September 1915:

Liverpool: wheat, American, No. 1 Northern, per 100 pounds	$2.70 (11s. 3d.)
Duluth: same grade, 93¢ bu. or per 100 pounds	1.55
Spread between Duluth and Liverpool	$1.15
Handling costs, insurance, ocean freight, elevator charges	.54
Amount taken for profit	$0.61

In other words 39 per cent of the price originally obtained for the wheat was being pocketed—over and above the regular 2 per cent commission and all costs.

The picture on other grains was no more pretty:

Liverpool: American oats,
    per 100 lbs. .... $2.33 (4*s.* 4½ *d.* for 45 lbs.)
Duluth: oats, 33¢ bu. or
    per 100 lbs. 1.03
                      ————

Spread between Duluth
    and Liverpool $1.30
Cost of handling between
    Liverpool and Duluth ...... .54
                      ————

    Amount taken for profit .. $0.76

In this case the traders were taking no less than 73 per cent of the selling price. The farmer felt that if the grains could bring that price abroad, he was the one who should rightfully be getting it. As the September 8 market reports showed shipments of eight million bushels of wheat and ten million bushels of oats per week, the farmers considered themselves cheated to the tune of $4,500,000 a week on this item alone.[31]

In a speech before the United States House of Representatives on February 17, 1916, Congressman George M. Young of North Dakota re-emphasized these facts in pleading for a federal tax on "future" sales of grain, charging repeatedly that though fortunes were being made on the high wartime wheat prices, the bulk was going to the speculators and not the farmers.[32] It is interesting to note in this connection that North Dakota's five representatives in the Congress * were continually working for scientific federal grading laws, a rural credits law, and the like, for some reason seemingly having the interests of their rural constituents more at heart, at least in these regards, than did the majority of the state legislators.

The agricultural college was fast giving the farmers vital facts with which to fight. As Judge Amidon later remarked: "No single factor has contributed as much to that result [understanding the evils of the marketing system] as the scientific investigations of the state's agricultural college and the federal experts connected with that institution."[33]

In 1915, for example, Dr. Ladd examined and analyzed fifty-five kinds of cereal foods sold in packages and purchased by him in North Dakota. His bulletin of results, besides providing much interesting data

* Senators McCumber and Gronna; Representatives Young, Norton, and Helgeson.

on short weights, insignificant food values, and impurities, startled his readers with the announcement that wheat purchased at a maximum price of $1.80 a bushel was being retailed as cereal food at the rate of not less than $27 per bushel. Dr. Ladd wondered if the transformation cost 1500 per cent of the selling price.[34]

One newspaper put the farmer's general view of the marketing situation neatly in the following soliloquy: "Did you ever hear a storekeeper ask a farmer: 'How much are you paying for dried apples and ten-penny nails today?' No, it's the other way around, isn't it? Then why shouldn't the farmers put themselves into position where buyers will have to ask *them*: 'How much are you asking for wheat and hogs today?'"[35]

Or as one prominent farmer commented: "We farmers sell at wholesale and we buy at retail."[36]

Beyond the malpractices in the grain marketing system, however, there were still more grievances plaguing the farmer. Railroad freight rates had not been lowered in North Dakota since the roads were first built, though traffic had increased a hundredfold and other states by legislative enactment had almost without exception forced rates down. In 1915 it cost $32 to ship a car of hogs one hundred miles in North Dakota. The same shipment cost $24 in South Dakota, $16.50 in Iowa, $28.90 in Nebraska, and $20.48 in Minnesota. A 60,000-pound car of wheat might be shipped from Minot to Grand Forks for $91.80; the same car could be taken from Moorhead, Minnesota, to Minneapolis, forty-five miles further, for $61.80. Manufacturers in the Twin Cities, Duluth, and Superior could ship goods to eastern Montana at the same rate paid from Fargo and Grand Forks, though the latter were hundreds of miles nearer to each other. It was common for shippers in Fargo, Grand Forks, and Wahpeton to haul their goods across the river in order to ship at Minnesota rates.[37] At the time it appeared that only by action of the state legislature could these gross inequities be rectified, and this was not likely to occur as long as the railroads retained their powerful influence in that legislature.

Another familiar complaint was unjust demurrage charges against North Dakota shippers and endless laments concerned the quality of cars furnished to grain shippers. Leaky cars jolting several hundred miles to terminals lose anywhere from a few to forty bushels of grain— an approximate average of seven bushels. Yet the shipper is paid on the

basis of the weight on arrival. Though the law required the furnishing
of well-coopered cars, it was rather commonly ignored. If the railroad
refused to fix the cars to suit the shipper, the latter could do the job
himself and recover by suit, but the costs of litigation were usually
more than the cost of repairs, and when cars were short in the busy
season the shippers had no time for such activities.[38] Laws for track
scales at shipping points were continually urged, but without success.

The average North Dakota farmer was almost completely at the
mercy of the local banker, upon whom he was dependent for operating
capital. The great majority lived on credit, getting a loan for living
expenses, seed, and so on, paying it back at harvest time, only to be
forced to get a new loan for the next year, for reasons in part that are
by now obvious. A great many of the farms, as we have seen, also had
heavy mortgages incurred in building, acquiring machinery, buying
livestock, and the like. The bankers commonly charged as much as the
traffic would bear in the way of interest, sometimes such fantastic
amounts as 25 to 50 per cent on loans. Such usury not infrequently
spelled failure for competent farmers who might otherwise have succeeded. It was apparently also standard practice for many merchants,
especially machinery dealers, to charge from 20 to 100 per cent more
than a legitimate profit because of real or imagined risks, thus making
all purchasers cover any possible defaults.[39]

Nationwide interest in excessive loan rates was aroused in the fall of
1915 by a report of John S. Williams, United States comptroller of the
currency, in a speech before the Kentucky Bankers' Association. Williams asserted that on the basis of their reports to his office, nearly one
seventh of the national banks in the country were receiving an average
rate of 10 per cent per year or more on loans, while some reported
rates as high as 40 to 60 per cent. These figures dealt only with the
national banks, and it was quite generally agreed that the practices of
the state and private banks and money lenders were far worse. Only
two states, Texas and Oklahoma, topped North Dakota in the total
number of national banks charging excessive rates.[40]

The Williams report showed that no less than two thirds (96) of the
national banks in North Dakota were charging usurious rates. Though
the law made any rate over 10 per cent usury, many admitted that 10
per cent was the minimum charged on farm loans. On the other hand,
commercial loans customarily ran at a maximum of 6 to 8 per cent.

17

Six per cent was in fact the legal rate in North Dakota, but the laws of that state did not make usury a crime. A man might sue to recover interest or refuse to pay if charged usurious rates, in which case it was possible to collect twice the illegal interest paid, or, if the plea was entered before paying, all the interest might be forfeited. Such action, however, unfailingly resulted in a blacklisting from future loans in any bank, and this the farmer could not risk.[41]

A careful study in 1913 showed the average rate for farm mortgages in North Dakota to be 8 per cent, with the range from 6 or 7 per cent in the eastern counties to 10 or 12 per cent in the west. The average on short-term loans was approximately 11 per cent.[42]

The farmer's viewpoint was given unexpected support in December 1915 by L. J. Bricker, immigration agent of the Northern Pacific Railroad, in a speech before the annual convention of the North Dakota State Federation of Commercial Clubs: "No other business can pay more than 6% for money, how can farmers? They can't. There may be a farmer here and there who can pay big interest and get out from under it, but for the general run of farmers more than 6% interest as a steady diet is fatal. Ten and twelve percent cannot run along with hog cholera, hail or a sick wife without disaster." [43]

Throughout the years of the late nineteenth and early twentieth centuries the farmers had not remained passive under this domination, but the forces they fought were too powerful, and the farmers were either unorganized or insufficiently so. The North Dakota farmer had seen Grangerism and Populism rise and fall, leaving fewer marks than in most midwestern states, and there had also been numerous more localized movements. The most important of these in 1915 was the American Society of Equity, an organization fostering producers' and consumers' cooperatives which had acquired a not inconsiderable strength, despite being fought tooth and nail by the private corporations which denied it access to the regular channels of trade, virtually prevented its obtaining credit, and issued continuous propaganda against it.[44]

The argument which made the greatest impression as a real solution to the marketing problem was the proposal for state-owned terminal elevators advanced by President Worst and Dr. Ladd of the agricultural college and others. It was generally agreed that a constitutional amendment would be required to make such operations possible, but the constitution of North Dakota was admirably constructed to make anything but the most overwhelmingly popular change well-nigh an impossibility. It was necessary for a proposed amendment to pass both houses of two successive legislatures and then be ratified by popular vote, a process consuming at least three or four years. In 1909, however, the demand was so great that an amendment permitting the state to build terminal elevators in Minnesota or Wisconsin passed the legislature. It was passed by the succeeding legislature and ratified by the people in 1912 by a vote of 56,488 to 18,864.

In the meantime agitation had arisen for terminal elevators within the state, including power over inspection, weighing, and grading, and an amendment making this possible went through the process and was ratified in 1914, this time by a vote of 51,507 to 18,483.[45] At last it seemed that relief was in sight. In a land of majority rule the people had twice voted in favor of state-owned elevators by a three to one margin. The mandate was clear. Scattered farmers could not start an effective business system, nor did they have the money to handle such projects in small groups. The state was the only common agency through which to carry out their aims, and if the state could not be used they would have to continue their dealings largely as individuals or in small and relatively ineffective units. The credit of the state was good, and they felt sure that the project would pay for itself in time.

The 1913 legislature had accordingly passed an act levying a special one-eighth mill assessment for the project proposed for Minnesota or Wisconsin and instructed the State Board of Control to report plans and recommendations for construction. After several months of investigation the board issued at the time of the 1915 legislative session a six-hundred-page report consisting in large part of an exhaustive argument against the entire project. Announcing that it had studied terminal elevators in both the United States and Canada and had interviewed government officials, grain dealers, cooperative officials, and others, the board pointed out that elevators in the Twin Cities, Duluth, or Superior would be subject to control by those states and would operate under their grading standards. After citing a number of other reasons, it recommended strongly against erecting new elevators at any time, and suggested that if anything were to be done the state should rent or lease existing terminal elevators and "thereby try out the scheme at the least possible cost." Leasing would permit an immediate start, and if successful perhaps the elevators might be turned over to farmers' organizations. One relatively small structure as currently proposed would have an inconsequential influence on the market and could in no way end the dominance of the Chamber of Commerce, they said.[46]

It was not purely by chance that the North Dakota Union of the American Society of Equity was holding its annual convention in Bismarck while the 1915 legislature was in session. It had hoped to exert a bit of "wholesome influence," and had invited members of the comparatively new Farmers' Union to attend. The farmers had too long been convinced that state-owned elevators were the only answer even to consider proceeding with the caution recommended by the Board of Control. The convention promptly endorsed the terminal elevator bill then before the legislature and drew up other proposals to be presented. Representatives of the city of St. Paul were there to offer aid if the elevator were located in that city, and a special feature was a march to the capitol to present the farmers' demands to the legislature.[47]

Among the speakers at an Equity rally the night before the vote on the elevator issue was George Loftus, the popular and pugnacious sales manager of the Equity Cooperative Exchange and an old hand in the war with "the interests." Loftus was bitter over the report of the Board of Control. Fanning the emotions of the crowd to fever pitch with an impassioned speech, he concluded by calling the roll of the legislature and violently denouncing all those whom he expected to vote against the bill. Not only did he attack the known opponents, but he included those who were still undecided. Many legislators were present seeking information, but when they tried to explain that they were uncertain as to how to vote they were hissed back to their seats. As a result of this uncalled-for abuse many members who might have been won over were antagonized, and the next day the bill was decisively beaten.[48] *

After the bill's defeat, the Equity convention rapidly developed into

* Just why Loftus did this has never been determined. Paul R. Fossum in his *Agrarian Movement in North Dakota,* a book which is not too reliable insofar as it deals with the League, argues that Loftus did not really want a state-owned elevator, preferring cooperative enterprise, and so deliberately attempted to kill the project (pp. 90–91). This hypothesis does not seem very probable in view of Loftus' long record as a crusader on the matter. He was an impulsive man with deeply held prejudices, and it seems likely that, considering the cause already lost for that session, he set about to whip up the farmers to press their demands more vigorously in the future, and perhaps to support the Equity more strongly.

a mass meeting of protest; angry farmers demanded hearings before legislators, which frequently turned into violent and bitter arguments. In the course of one of these a House member was reported to have told the farmers that the running of the state was none of their business and to have jocularly advised them to "go home and slop the hogs." This remark, attributed to Treadwell Twichell, was vigorously denied,* but, spreading like wildfire, it was destined to become a battle cry. Whether or not he said these particular words is today of little significance. What is important is that it served the purpose for many years to come of epitomizing the farmer's view of the way he had been treated by the "old gang" politicians. The Reverend S. R. Maxwell two years later aptly parodied the farmers' sentiments:

The politician is my shepherd, I shall not want;
Previous to election day he filleth my pocket with cigars and my
    present glory runneth over;
But although he causeth me to vote for him on election day, suddenly
    after election he knoweth me no more.
He eateth rich plums of political patronage behind closed doors, and
    me he cannot remember;
Surely the wool hath been pulled over my eyes all the days of my
    life,
And I shall dwell in political obscurity forever.[49]

Nearly two thirds of the population of the state, in any case, were readily convinced that they had been told in effect to mind their own business and let the politicians attend to the government. The farmers, however, had now seen the men they elected to office in action at close hand; they thought they had detected a certain political haughtiness and social discrimination. They had likewise seen the failure of lobbying even when backed by the great majority of the voters. The sense of injustice was acutely galling. North Dakota was ripe for revolt.

---

* L. L. Twichell, brother of Treadwell, years later explained that Treadwell had been talking rural problems with a group of farmers most of one night in a hotel room. Finally he pulled out his watch and remarked, "It is now 5 o'clock—time for us farmers to get out and slop the hogs." (*Bismarck Tribune*, Feb. 4, 1937.) Judge A. M. Christianson says that several years ago he was with a group which included D. C. Coates, an early League promoter, when Twichell entered the room. Coates jovially greeted him as "the man who started the Nonpartisan League for us." "But Coates," Twichell shouted, "I never made that statement." "I know you didn't," Coates laughed, "but we hung it on you and made it stick." (Interview, Sept. 1, 1948.) A. C. Townley admits that he never knew whether or not the story was true, but he recognized a good slogan when it came to hand. (Interview, Sept. 23, 1948.)

"Grass Roots" Operations

ONTO the stage thus set for a leader strode the magnetic figure of A. C. Townley. Frequently as important to the course of history as the familiar "man on horseback" is a young man with an idea, and Arthur Townley was possessed by an idea. The answer he saw for North Dakota was a nonpartisan political organization of farmers, not based on the halfhearted adherence to general principles which characterized the earlier political movements in the state, but with each member having a definite stake in success and pledged to support a concrete program of reform with his votes.* Townley was sufficiently astute in politics to know that elections are won in the precincts, and thus to be well aware of the essentiality of sound local organization. In the absence of such organization he saw one reason for the consistent failures of third parties in the history of America. This was one of two mistakes he was determined to avoid—the other was becoming a "third party" at all.

Townley, thirty-five years old in 1915, was born and raised on a farm near Brown's Valley in northwestern Minnesota, graduating from high school in Alexandria. After teaching school for two years, he went in 1904 to western North Dakota near the town of Beach, where he began farming with his brother, Covert. This "Golden Valley" section was just then being developed by the land speculators, and the Townley brothers contracted with many of them to plow, sow, and harvest their lands

---

* Credit for the original idea has sometimes been given to A. E. Bowen, a close associate of Townley's and one-time Socialist candidate for governor of North Dakota. Bowen had talked along these lines to many farmers at the time of the Equity convention, but did nothing more about it. It was Townley who developed a definite plan of action and ultimately put it into operation.

in order to improve them. After a year of this, followed by a year as an itinerant plasterer's helper, Arthur acquired with several others a tract of land near Cheyenne Wells, Colorado, and undertook large-scale wheat farming, which, however, proved unsuccessful.[1]

While there he married Margaret Rose Teenan, and soon took her back to Beach where his brother was still carrying on.[2] In 1907 the brothers commenced raising flax with considerable success, expanding their holdings each year until they became known as the largest flax growers in North Dakota. By 1912, Arthur Townley, now operating alone, was being pointed out by railroad land agents as the "flax king of the Northwest," a sterling example of what a man could do in a few years in this virgin country. That year he put 8000 acres into flax, and bought on credit ten traction engines and equal amounts of other farm machinery in order to plant and harvest the mammoth crop. The bankers, implement companies, and seed merchants were glad to take a chance with this man who was such a striking success.

Townley put everything he had and everything he could borrow into this project. Flax was selling at $3 a bushel, and he stood to make $100,000 on the crop. But in the year 1912 disaster struck the Northwest in the form of an early frost and an almost unprecedented snowstorm—only a fraction of the crop could be harvested. Even with this misfortune the young farmer figured that he could almost break even. He would get more credit and try again. But Arthur Townley had reckoned without the vagaries of the market on which he must depend. To his horror he discovered that wild speculations had forced the market down and he received less than $1 a bushel for his flax. The flax king of the Northwest was a bankrupt, $80,000 in debt.[3] A "plunger" by nature, A. C. Townley was accustomed to taking defeats with a smile, but this time, deeply embittered, he was determined some day to beat the powers which had broken him. He turned first to a political party.

The Socialist party was more strongly organized in North Dakota at this time than in any other agricultural state, having found fertile ground for complaint against the existing order. Its rather moderate platforms spoke in favor of state rural credit programs, state-owned mills and elevators, state insurance against diseases of plants and animals and against calamities, and unemployment insurance for labor.[4] The party had in certain areas managed to elect a number of important local officials and in some instances made respectable showings in legislative contests, but after six years of diligent campaigning on the same platform they were acutely aware of the fact that their program was in much greater favor than was the party. Unquestionably the great majority of the farmers heartily endorsed the proposals, but they were too much afraid of the name to go so far as to join the organization.

Accordingly the state committee of the Socialist party decided to experiment. They set up an "organization department" of the party, to which non-Socialists who favored the program could belong without having to sign the red card. Arthur Townley had read rather widely in earlier days in the fields of economics and politics, and in view of his recent experiences, it was quite natural that he should have gravitated toward the Socialists in his search for remedies for the social and economic ills he saw about him. In 1914 he was employed as an organizer for the new "department" to test empirically the difference in popularity of the party and the platform. Supplied by the state committee with a Ford and plenty of Socialist literature, he traveled about the state, holding meetings arranged by headquarters, selling literature, and taking pledges from the farmers as members of the "organization department." If the farmers were short of cash at the time, postdated checks, made payable at harvest time, were accepted.

To join, the farmer was required to sign a pledge to vote and work for candidates who favored the state program and to pay one dollar a month to support educational and campaign work. Success was instantaneous. In less than three months Townley had four organizers at work, and the response was excellent. Despite this superb progress, however, the January 1915 state convention voted to discontinue the program, feeling that it was in essence dishonest and, less altruistically, that the tail would soon be wagging the dog. The "department" already had almost as many members as the parent organization, and the doctrinaire Socialists who controlled the state organization were convinced that these new members were not adequately schooled in the principles of the movement.[5]

Townley, who had in the meantime been a candidate for the legislature from the 39th district in 1914 on the Socialist ticket, was miffed at the decision, and convinced that the Socialist party was as conservative in methods of operation and aversion to new techniques as the old parties, he broke with the Socialists and went to Bismarck at the time

24

of the 1915 Equity Society convention.[6] What he saw and heard there convinced him that the farmers were ready for organization—the job now was to sell them on a concrete program.

Townley mulled over for some time the idea of nonpartisan political action through control of the primaries. Meeting A. E. Bowen in Minot, he took him to a hotel room and set forth his proposals in detail. He had made up his mind, he said, and would go through with the plan alone if necessary, but he would like to have Bowen's help. One condition was laid down. There must be a clear understanding that Townley was to be the boss. Bowen thought the matter over, shook hands on it, and thenceforward unfalteringly lived up to the agreement. An extremely able speaker, he was for years a most trusted and faithful lieutenant.[7]

At the Bismarck convention Townley had renewed an acquaintance with a prominent Equity leader and successful farmer from Deering in the north-central part of the state, Fred B. Wood. To him he had expounded the core of his new idea, and had gained his tentative promise to help if Townley would come to see him in the spring after the snow had gone. Inactivity, however, was not in Townley's vocabulary, and he showed up at the Wood farm in late February, to receive a not too enthusiastic greeting. Mr. Wood and his two grown sons, Howard and Edwin, had heard many schemes of how to save the farmer, but their interest mounted as they listened to this intense young man who eagerly explained his plans until far into the night. F. B. Wood thought the whole proposition fantastic and unworkable, but Townley kept after him for three or four days, when at last youth, if not age, was won over. Late one evening, Howard Wood and Townley scribbled a brief "platform" on a scrap of paper by the light of a kerosene lamp in the kitchen of the Wood farm, and early the next morning they started out in a bobsled to talk to neighbors, Howard handling the introductions and Townley giving the sales talk.[8] The Farmers' Nonpartisan Political League of North Dakota was under way.

This later came to be a standard procedure in League organizing. Gaston describes the system in this way:

An early convert becomes a "booster" in his township. He is persuaded to accompany the organizer and break the ice with his neighbors. Sometimes organizers during the busy seasons of farm work have been known to hire a capable farm hand and take him along. The farm hand takes his place on the plow or the hay wagon so that the farmer may have time to hear the organizer talk. Sometimes the farm hand fills in while the farmer goes on a "boosting" excursion with the organizer.[9]

Arthur Townley did not make the mistake of going to the farmers to ask that they elect him to office; instead he proposed the grandiose scheme of capturing the entire state government—legislature, executive, and judiciary. The farmers constituted the great majority of the voters, but the grip of the professional politicians upon the state was based on the well-known maxim that farmers were never able to stick together. As long as they continued to vote blindly for the old parties for no better reason than that their fathers had, all was well with those who controlled the parties.

But Townley knew wheat farmers. A past master in the art of high-pressure salesmanship, he had a magnetic personality that warmed hearts and loosened purse strings; a phenomenal political experiment was in the making.

The pledge and platform which prospects were asked to sign was simple and direct, meeting the complaints of the farmers in a convincing way:

> State ownership of terminal elevators, flour mills, packing houses, and cold-storage plants
> State inspection of grain and grain dockage
> Exemption of farm improvements from taxation
> State hail insurance on the acreage tax basis
> Rural credit banks operated at cost [10]

The proposals were not new, but they had the advantage of having received general farmer approval for a number of years. The first, second, and fifth points were obvious demands. The proposal for tax exemption of farm improvements was designed to make the land speculator with thousands of idle acres pay a fair proportion of the tax, the experience in Manitoba, Saskatchewan, and Alberta having been noted with approval.[11] "They are going to bring Henry George to North Dakota," said the *New York Times* sourly.[12]

North Dakota actually had a State Hail Insurance Department, but its program was not compulsory and, though its premiums were lower than those of the old-line companies, it did not follow their practice of taking notes in payment. With the private company rate standing at 43 cents an acre and the existing state rate 30 cents, League organizers could well point significantly toward a neighbor on the north, Saskatch-ewan, whose acreage tax program cost 10 cents and paid a better rate on losses. Nor was the fact overlooked that in 1913 the private com-panies took in for North Dakota hail insurance a total of $1,079,813.62 and paid out in losses (a fairly bad year) only $500,109.10.[13]

The dues for the new organization were first set at $2.50 a year, to be collected by the organizer on the spot, but when it was seen how ex-pensive organizing and campaigning was going to be, they were raised to $6, within a year to $9, and after the first campaign were set at $16 for each two-year period corresponding with the term of state office holders.[14] Townley argued with considerable logic that if a farmer had put his money into a project, he would stick with it even if only to get a return on his investment. He put the matter with characteristic pro-fanity: "Make the rubes pay their God-damn money to join and they'll stick—stick till hell freezes over."[15]

The first day Townley and Wood were able to see nine men, and they returned home with the signatures of all of them. In fact, they signed up the first seventy-seven they talked to, and after that for some time the average ran well over 90 per cent. After a week F. B. Wood was convinced, and from that time on he devoted his life to the Non-partisan League. He was a highly respected man and with him in the car organizing was easy for miles around.[16] Since the first day they had been using the Woods' Ford for greater speed in seeing prospects but the gasoline soon ran out. Howard Wood and twelve neighbor mem-bers met the emergency by signing notes for funds to buy three Fords and a supply of gas, and the organization work sped on.[17]

Additional organizers were recruited from enthusiastic young farm-ers and "live-wires" among the Socialists, many of the latter group having been opposed to the abolition of the "organization department" of the party.[18] Each was carefully trained by having him observe an experienced organizer in action for several days, and dozens of Fords were soon canvassing the state. Memberships rolled in, but it is mute testimony to the financial condition of these farmers that the great ma-jority were unable to pay dues in cash.* They paid in a manner which, as we have seen, was not new, but for which the League was later to

* Organizers were at first paid $2.00 for each cash membership. Later they re-ceived $4.00 for cash memberships and $3.50 for those paid with postdated checks. "Still later even higher commissions were paid" (Bruce, p. 72n).

become famous—postdated checks payable in October when the harvest was in.[19]

At first the organizing was a relatively simple matter, the hymn of hate directed at the Chamber of Commerce being all that was necessary to establish interest, though it took clever salesmen to get many cautious farmers to part with their money to join another farmers' organization. Almost everyone had a grievance against some representative of "Big Biz," the grain buyer, cream buyer, banker, stock buyer. The organizer sought out this sore spot and then pressed on it until he got results. In a limited way the organizing for a time would almost take care of itself. In some instances, after working hard on a few prominent farmers in a particular area and selling them on the proposition, the organizers would leave, giving the situation time to ferment. The new members, "like the man who had just gotten religion . . . [and] wants everyone else to have it," spread the gospel to their friends and neighbors, and when the organizers returned the job was much easier.[20] If there was opposition in the towns, it was probably of assistance, providing a visible manifestation of how the "interests" were opposing the farmers.

Later, when the field of operations grew broader and the opposition stronger, highly trained organizers were essential, and a correspondence course was established to provide this training, though the observation technique was not abandoned.[21] Other courses were held at League headquarters. Although this particular program did not come for some time, its lessons are excellent indications of the general manner in which the organizers operated during the early period. It provided tips on salesmanship and applied psychology of which any modern personnel department might be justly proud. Sample subjects covered, for example, included the following: How a Salesman Puts Ideas Across; Motives by Which Men Act—how to analyze the individual and attack vulnerable points; How to Arouse and Hold Interest; Techniques of Persuasion; Difficulties Which Will Be Encountered, and How to Deal with Them (i.e., antagonism, indifference, interruptions, and the like); Typical Objections and How to Overcome Them.

The technique of the successful organizer is well illustrated by these instructions:

Arouse his interest with your very first statement. Your first statements are like the headlines of a newspaper. . . . Make this sentence fit the interests of the man to whom you are talking. . . . Then keep control of the interview. . . . Keep to the subject. Every farmer will agree to the fundamental principles of the League, a better marketing system, better prices for farm products, and more representation in the government. Discuss these things upon which we all agree and do not waste time arguing other questions and do not argue the details and methods by which all this must be worked out. We will solve these things as we come to them. The question now is to get organization and power in our hands to do the things we all agree must be done *now*. . . .

Remember that you cannot force him to join either by physical force or force of argument. You must persuade him as well as convince him. . . . It is not altogether a matter of satisfying his reason—it is a matter of appealing to his emotions as well. We do not always do the things we know should be done, we do the things which we feel we want to do. Remember that back of every act is both a thought *and* a feeling. You must make him think and you must make him feel; you must appeal to the emotions as well as to reason.[22]

One vital difference between the League program and that of previous movements advocating much the same thing was the continuous stress on the importance of "organization." Organizers constantly hammered home the idea that only through tight organization could the farmers ever achieve their objectives. Here was their chance to make the state government really serve the great majority of the population, but the powers they fought were closely organized. Everyone, they said, was organized except the farmers. League dues were always compared with the amounts paid in other groups: railway conductors $24 a year, firemen $18, shoe workers $1 a month.[23] Yet the League fee included a subscription to their own paper, to begin publication before the end of the year, and to *Pearson's Magazine* (one of the country's few remaining radical periodicals). Townley himself was a master at making this point effectively:

At one meeting Townley singled out the mayor of the town. "I don't know what business you are in, but I will bet you belong to some association and that you pay more a year than these farmers do," he challenged.

The mayor admitted that he was a doctor, that he did pay more than eight dollars a year to medical associations and considered it a good investment.

"There you are," said Townley, waving the question aside. The crowd waved it aside with him.[24]

League organizers were carefully trained in the best methods of bringing the argument to a climax, the psychological moment to hand the prospect a membership card and pen, and the way to get cash if possible, rather than a postdated check. A list of the signatures of neighboring farmers was always most effective. By way of a clincher for the "almost persuaded" the following was suggested:

"Here's the thing in a nutshell." Here he pulls a handful of change out of his pocket, two quarters, three dimes, three nickels, and five pennies—just a dollar in change.

"Now here is a dollar. For every dollar's worth of stuff you raise on this farm you get just 46 cents." Here he counts out and lays in one pile one quarter, two dimes, and a penny.

"This is what you get. But here," laying in another pile the other quarter, dime, three nickels, and four pennies—"here is what the other fellow gets—the fellow who didn't put in a day plowing and planting and harvesting. Now what you want is more of this pile. You want your share of that dollar the consumer pays for what you raise by back-breaking work. The other fellow gobbles this because he is organized. He controls the market—he makes the laws—he gets the money. Do you want more of this pile of money which belongs to you, Mr. Blank?"

Now he has the farmer where he has to answer "yes." He can't say he doesn't want that money for he does—any man does. And yet that "yes" carries with it the organization, too. It is rather a hard thing for a farmer to refuse to join after that "yes" . . . Any method which makes it harder for him to turn you down than to say yes and join, is a good method. Work out the one that fits your way of managing the solicitation.[25]

"Psychology" was a term which became virtually a watchword with League organizers. They heard it day in and day out. Townley's frequent meetings for organizers became refresher courses in salesmanship, of which he was an accomplished practitioner, and his concepts of applied psychology received constant stress. Crude though his instructional talks may have been, they were certainly not lacking in color and essential practicality. James Manahan recalled one forceful sendoff for new organizers: "Find out the damn fool's hobby and then talk it. If he likes religion, talk Jesus Christ; if he is against the government, damn the Democrats; if he is afraid of whisky, preach prohibition; if he wants to talk hogs, talk hogs—talk anything he'll listen to, but talk, talk, until you get his God-damn John Hancock to a check for six dollars." [26]

Townley is said to have once remarked that the Nonpartisan League was built on "an idea, a Ford, and sixteen dollars." It is no less true that a knowledge of wheat farmers blended with these principles of salesmanship literally sold the League to the farmers of North Dakota. The farmers did not organize the League—"they woke up one morning and found themselves organized." [27] From one point of view the League was less a movement *of* the people than *for* the people. It was a protest on their behalf. The farmers had long cursed their troubles but as a group had been inarticulate. Now the League was filling the need for a collective voice and the farmers embraced it eagerly.

It is not surprising that the overwhelming majority of the League's organizers throughout the years were Socialists. Most of the League's coterie of early leaders were Socialists or had some connections with the movement, and it was only natural that they picked men with whom they had been associated. Moreover, they found that men who had always been in the minority tended to be strong on argument and to know how to turn opponents into friends. They understood the underdog point of view, and in many cases had sharpened their speaking techniques in the rough and tumble of street corner oratory. A large number, in fact, were recruited by advertising in labor and Socialist publications. As one writer put it: ". . . the League copies the old parties, which never ask who a worker is, but what he can do. The purpose of the League, like the purpose of a political party, is to get members, votes, and money, and the soap-boxers, Socialists, IWW or other born radicals having been found best, the League uses them freely." [28]

Townley himself spoke almost constantly to groups and crowds wherever they could be gotten together, and his persuasive influence was electrifying. Nor was he at all averse to working on a single prospect. His effectiveness is well illustrated by the comments of one of his converts who later became an ardent League worker, Ray McKaig:

I first met A. C. Townley when I was Master of the North Dakota State Grange . . . As he indignantly told me how the food pirates had beaten down the price of grain just when he was ready to sell I became indignant too. He became bellicose as he told how they shoved the price up after cornering the market. I became bellicose too. Then came the appeal to "stick together." Would I stick? I was so "het up" by this time that I was looking around for a stick to hit a grainpit rattler . . . His promotive personality inspires confidence, and irresistibly makes one a crusader against economic wrongs.[29]

Townley was not a polished orator, but he had learned how to carry a crowd with him and he spoke the farmers' language. Friend and enemy alike testify to that talent. He also possessed a certain picturesque profanity which was both fluent and expressive, commanding immediate attention. Despite the usual affinity of political figures for publicity and photographs, he resolutely refused throughout most of his career to have his picture taken and consistently shunned newspaper writers insofar as possible. Almost the only existing pictures seem to be a few snapshots taken of him on a platform addressing crowds. McKaig described him as a speaker:

He is rather slow in action and exceedingly deliberate in the use of words. As he commences to talk he appears to be about "five foot ten"; when he finishes he seems to be about "ten foot five." Rather thin in appearance, he is yet strong in physical make-up. His eyes are set deep, but they match his sarcastic drawl. His hair is dark and his nose is rather prominent . . . He speaks slowly and enunciates clearly; his gestures go out after you, reaching out to tear down your refusals to agree with his ideals. His voice is expressive, strong, and resonant. As irony, sarcasm or sympathy is hurled at his crowd, his voice betrays his mood before his words articulate the thought. He is one of the great native orators of America.

As a stump speaker he knows his crowds, and entices interrupters. Woe unto him who tries the heckling game. He excels in dry humor, which punctuates every other paragraph. Ridicule is his favorite weapon. I think that Townley and ex-Governor Lind of Minnesota are the best two stump speakers of prominence in the Northwest. By that I mean men that can convince out-of-door crowds and change the heckler into a buffoon. He is a master of the art of singling out leaders of the opposition and putting the "monkey collar" on them.[30]

But what about this term "nonpartisan" which the organizers emphasized as the key to the nature of the new organization?

It would seem that an organization designed basically to benefit farmers was actually extremely partisan. As far as the League was concerned, however, "nonpartisan" indicated complete dissociation from the old party politics, an ignoring of party lines in order to promote the interests of this rural majority of the population. The only significant difference between the major parties, it was maintained, was in the realm of national politics.

Real issues had grown up in the state which were entirely distinct from the national ones, and the only purpose in injecting national parties into state affairs was "to obscure the real issues and divide the people." "It is time to get rid of this nonsense," said a League publication. "It is time to throw off the chains of party control and get down to business in state affairs." [31]

The League accepted members from all parties quite indiscriminately, being interested only in their willingness to vote for candidates favoring the League program. "Have the Socialists less right to take part in a good movement than Republicans or Democrats?" asked the *Searchlight*.[32] The farmers of the state have identical interests, argued League speakers; yet divided by party lines they get nowhere:

The mission of the League is to unite the farmers of this state—regardless of past party affiliations—into an organization that will stand apart from every political party, every political machine and free from every political boss and put men in office that will legislate in the interest of the members of that organization. Why should we exclude the members of one party any more than any other party? [33]

The Patrons of Husbandry (Grange) and the Farmers' Alliance had tried to operate primarily as pressure groups and on the balance of power principle of helping their friends and defeating their enemies. Finding success in this manner extremely limited, agrarian protest elements moved next to Populism, an attempt at political action through a third party, only to be swallowed by the Democratic party when all hopes were pinned in 1896 on the panacea of "free silver." The Equity Society and other cooperatives had endeavored to function outside the political arena and to seek salvation in control of specific economic enterprises that closely affected the members. The Nonpartisan League was a return to the belief in the necessity of political action if effective control of the economy was to be achieved, but it recognized both the inadequacy of balance of power tactics and the numerous failures of third parties. Cooperation, it felt, was useful but doomed to a minor role unless accompanied by political dominance.

The League was, therefore, a new departure in the techniques of agrarian protest movements. The direct primary had spread rapidly across the country; its supporters claimed it meant that control of political parties might be taken from cliques of professional politicians and placed in the hands of party voters. The League was one of the most striking attempts to actually so use the primary. It proposed to utilize that medium to gain control of the majority party of the state, make it truly express the will of the majority of the voters, and retain the benefits of its status arising from tradition and voter habit as well.

There were two important variations from the Socialist party tactics which help to explain in some degree the greater success of the League in North Dakota with an essentially similar program. The Socialists had preached the evils of the existing system, but they had also given the farmer some responsibility. He must, they said, plan intelligently, do his utmost to understand the business of farming and improve his methods, see that his children were educated, take advantage of every possibility of keeping out of the hands of the credit men, and work with other farmers in cooperative enterprises. All this meant more work for farmers already overburdened and fatigued. The League speakers told the same story up to the point of responsibility, and there they laid the blame for all the farmers' problems at the door of "Big Biz," which absolved the farmer from the necessity of feeling any personal sense of guilt.

Moreover, the League organizers convinced the farmers that there were too many of them to act efficiently as a group on important matters; that they were too busy and too widely scattered. The leaders must therefore be trusted to do the job, and be given full authority and adequate funds. The farmer need only pay his dues and vote—it would no longer be necessary for him to struggle personally with all the problems.[34]

For the first several months the organization of the Nonpartisan League was kept something of a "trade secret." Organizers and members were cautioned to keep the matter confidential—"to keep all knowledge of the movement from the leeches who sucked their blood." [35] Townley was well aware of the storm of opposition which would be loosed when word of the League reached the bankers and businessmen, and though this secrecy later furnished grounds for attack, it was unquestionably a major factor in the success of early organization efforts. J. W. Brinton relates an amusing incident concerning the reaction of the Fargo postmaster when Townley in the fall of 1915 requested mailing privileges for the *Leader*, which well illustrates the secrecy of the original organizing efforts:

"But," said the postmaster, "you must have a bona fide subscription list—with each subscriber signed up and the money paid. You say you printed 18,000 copies and want to mail them, but you cannot secure mailing rights until you have subscribers—paid subscribers."

"I have," replied Townley. "I have 18,000 paid subscribers scattered all over North Dakota."

"What," exclaimed the astonished postmaster. "You say you have 18,000 subscribers, and I never heard of your paper or your organization?"

"You're right," came back the wizard of farm organizers to the surprised postmaster. "I have been organizing farmers, not postmasters." [36]

The small-town weeklies were among the first to hear of the new organization, and they made haste to warn their readers that "slick operators" were trying to fleece them of their money. The *Steele County Ozone* commented:

Recently the *Ozone* referred to the presence in the state of a number of solicitors for membership in some kind of a party which was to be of special advantage to farmers, and who also offered a year's subscription to some paper or magazine as material inducement for joining. A fee of $6 was collected from each subscriber. . . . it is . . . evident that the farmers who took stock in the smooth strangers were too easy victims to a confidence game . . .

The *Ozone* believes . . . that this is only a game for fleecing the unwary . . . Our belief is that these are operating a questionable scheme, as there is no public knowledge of such a farmers' protective party as they effect to represent, and their avoidance of association or contact with townspeople, and advance dating of receipts are suspicious.[37]

It was in this manner that the term "six-dollar suckers" was coined, which was later to become virtually a League slogan, and by which many a farmer was to refer to himself with pride. The farmers were used to visitations from all sorts of smooth salesmen, and this was a vulnerable point of attack, but by this time the League had a good head start. Businessmen were inclined to smile tolerantly when they heard of the new farmers' organization. They had seen so many of these things before—a sudden flame which would as quickly flicker into oblivion. The farmers were urged "not to sign any papers or make pledges or promises until after they have consulted with their banker or with the editor of this paper." [38]

While most of the papers spoke disparagingly of the League, a few hailed its entrance upon the political scene with pleasure. "If the farmers get one-fourth value for the $6 they have put in the nonpartisan organization, it will be the most profitable $6 they ever invested," said the *Carrington Record*, while the *New Rockford Transcript* editorialized:

If the farmer wants to take a six-dollar flyer in politics, let him. It won't hurt him—and we believe it will improve politics . . . But the silence is getting on the nerves of some of our brethren, and they are waxing fretful. Our advice to our brothers is: Don't tear your Princess gowns in your great interest in the Non-Partisan League. Sit tight; don't rock the boat, and the result will redound to the glory and benefit of our great commonwealth.[39]

To the continual carping about the "robbing" of the poor farmers, the League had a ready answer:

A gang of politicians may steal $60,000 of the farmers' money, to be used to help more completely skin said farmers, and the dollarized press simply smiles a sweet smile and winks a sly wink. A farmer pays $6 to help perfect an organization for the purpose of protecting himself from sluggers and respectable highbinders, and the same dollarized press throws a series of conniption fits, turns in a double-alarm fire alarm, knocks the cat off the back fence and rips its low-necked nightie from hem to collar band.[40]

In laying the plans for the Nonpartisan League, the power of the press had not been overlooked, for Townley knew full well that the organization could be held together only if continuous information and stimulation reached the members through a publication devoted solely to that purpose. It had originally been planned to start the *Nonpartisan Leader* in December of 1915, and the members had been so informed. In August, however, it had become obvious that the opposition press was succeeding in causing doubts in the minds of many members; also it dawned on the leaders that most of the postdated checks were dated in October and that if the members heard no more of the organization before then, payment would be stopped on a great many. They therefore decided to start the paper as soon as possible.[41]

Joseph Gilbert, a successful Socialist organizer, at the time editing a Socialist paper in Seattle, was asked to serve as the first editor,[42] but when he replied that he would not be able to come for several months, H. E. Behrens was selected for the job. The services of Charles Edward

*A. C. Townley, organizer and
president of the Nonpartisan League
as he appeared about 1920*

*The president of the
League addressing an outdoor meeting
of farmers—one of the few pictures
of Townley in existence*

Russell, the well-known Socialist writer and lecturer, were enlisted, and publication was shortly begun in an abandoned church on a residential street in Fargo, the editors having to enter the building by a plank through a window.[43] Despite the mad scramble of the early days in acquiring pictures and sufficient good reading material, the *Leader* made its appearance on September 23, 1915, and rapidly became one of the most vital elements in League success.

The *Leader*, in general a moderately well edited paper with a breezy conversational style, served three principal purposes—it provided a channel of direct news and information, a means by which the leaders might guide the actions of the members, and a method of combating the tide of bitter opposition which almost instantly arose. Care was taken to answer regularly the charges of the opposition while still primarily devoting the publication to promoting the principles of the League. A typical early issue contained numerous editorials and articles on the evils which the League was fighting and the aims of the organization, several large cartoons, political news of the state and a column of Washington items, special articles on progress in other countries along the lines of the League program, information from the state Agricultural Experiment Station, pictures of League "boosters" on their farms, and an excessive quantity of "boiler plate" jokes, serial stories, and the like. The latter material and often many of the special features were crowded out as the political wars waxed hotter.

The initial editorial aptly illustrated the spirit of the new publication, as well as the type of approach:

Well, we're here! Your friends, the enemy, said we wouldn't get here but we did. What's more, we're here to stay. We're here with both feet and they're number twelves, too. Now watch the gang duck and dodge. Watch 'em hedge and flip-flop. They told you farmers that you would not get a paper; that it would be no good if you did, for, said they, "They haven't a newspaperman in the bunch."

Well, you should worry about that. Just plank the *Nonpartisan Leader* down along side any other paper in the state and see whether editors make any difference or not. The gang don't know, that's all. Besides it's none of their business. We don't have to ask them for editors nor papers either.

And while we are not screeching our horn from the windmill tower, we ask you to just sit right tight and watch our smoke. This is only a starter.

Nuff sed.[44]

The *Leader* showed constant improvement in both writing and appearance, but its vivacity never faltered. Forty years later, it is difficult for the reader not to be swept up in the spirit of crusading zeal, the stanch belief in the cause, and the faith in the future expressed in every line and drawing.

In common with most radical publications, it made telling use of numerous excellent cartoons, the work of John M. Baer being notable. In his drawings there was nothing subtle—all were direct and to the point. Baer's "Big Biz" and his caricature of the "old gang" politicians were to become the hated symbols of all the evil the farmers fought.

Fired!

John M. Baer's famous cartoon in the first issue of the *Nonpartisan Leader*, typifying the League's point of view.

In the first few issues a series of articles by Charles Edward Russell were featured. They dealt with the "power of tainted news," and warned the farmers of all the subterfuges which would be used to divide and confuse them. "You have launched in a just and honest way a just and honest cause," he said. "Do not believe anything you read about it unless you read it in your own journal or in journals that you know are absolutely with you." [45]

The advice was indeed pertinent, for almost at once the great majority of both city dailies and rural weeklies, led by the *Grand Forks Herald* and the *Fargo Courier-News*, commenced a campaign of violent opposition. It was based principally on the grounds that the League was promoting socialism and that the leaders were "carpetbaggers" bent on driving the state into financial ruin and filling their own pockets with the farmers' money.

The charge of unconstitutionality of state enterprises was made almost at once. It was met by the *Leader* in a straightforward fashion by proposing to amend the constitution, and in answer to the howls of protest it was pointed out that two of the most recently adopted state constitutions, those of Oklahoma and New Mexico, about which there had been no complaint, contained sections specifically permitting the state or any subdivision thereof to conduct any legal business and to use the public credit for the purpose.[46]

The theme of public ownership was continually played up by the *Leader*, especially as it related to the League program, and experience in other states and countries was given prominence, as for example the New Orleans terminal and the Seattle terminal warehouses. Farmers, it was suggested, ought to profit by Rockefeller's example—he was not satisfied merely to produce oil, but knew that money was to be made in control of the market. The basic dogma of farmer ownership was neatly presented in a Baer cartoon showing a massive monument surrounded by railroads, mills, and skyscrapers. On a pedestal decorated with the dollar sign stands the portly figure of "Big Biz," the pedestal being supported on the backs of farmers on their knees. The inscription reads: "Alex Bigbiz—He Doeth the Farmer 'Right'," and the accompanying text left nothing to the imagination:

North Dakota has erected a great monument.
This monument consists of gigantic railroad properties, huge milling industries, large terminal facilities, vast banking institutions and many allied and interlocking interests.
This monument is a necessity for it is useful.
North Dakota must use just such a monument.
But North Dakota should own it.
But instead North Dakota has built this monument and men who have in no way contributed to its construction own and control it. By virtue of such ownership this monument becomes a burden to the people who must use it. . .

39

And while they maintain and support it, its ponderous weight crushes them down, holds them down, squeezes the prosperity out of them, keeps them fighting the mortgage and keeps their children out of University and College.

In fighting to get out from under this burden the farmers of North Dakota are fighting for their dearest rights, for the future of their children, for industrial and social liberty.[47]

The *Leader* was accepted by the farmer members with unfeigned joy and pride in "our own paper," and for months columns of letters from jubilant supporters were printed in every issue. Not only was the new publication a huge success in the accomplishment of its original objectives, but by mid-winter, with a subscription list of nearly 30,000, it had the largest circulation of any paper in the state. The requests for a Scandinavian-language edition became so numerous that it was finally arranged in late February for *Fram*, a Fargo Scandinavian paper, to print important news and announcements of the League.[48]

Running weekly throughout the winter and less frequently during the rest of 1916 was a tremendously effective series of humorous articles by "N P Dictagraph" (later Dic T Graph) purporting to be accounts of meetings of "old gang" politicians in the office of boss Will B. Crafty. These cleverly handled columns, written by O. M. Thomason, former editor of the Socialist *Iconoclast* of Minot, hit the nail on the head by forecasting with considerable accuracy the next moves of the opposition. "Crafty" and his henchmen "Dodger" and "Slipry" very shortly became the standard farmer terms for the "gang," while Thomason's sly references to "Bigbismarck" or to "Dr. I. M. Guilty, editor of the Cargo Daily Distorted-Views" (Dr. L. T. Guild, a retired Methodist minister, who was publisher of the *Fargo Daily Courier-News* and one of the League's most vituperative enemies), practically convulsed his readers.

With its wide circulation and the strong influence which it had upon the farmers of the state, the *Leader* came rapidly to be recognized as a real power in state affairs. Moreover, it was able to hold something of a whip hand over small-town businessmen and rural papers. Despite the continuous attacks on "big business," the *Leader* disclaimed any desire for war on businessmen as such, holding that businessmen and farmers should cooperate to the utmost, but expressing regret that many of the former had aligned themselves with the "interests." The "qualifications" for farmer support were then set forth: "The *Leader* advises the farmers, all other things being equal, to stand by those business men who stand by the farmers, and the business man who really stands by the farmer also stands by the farmers' organization." [49]

When criticisms in some country papers became too extensive, a *Leader* editorial would quote pertinent passages, apply the terms used in describing the League leaders (such as "a lot of soreheads" or "belly-achers") to the members, and then ask them how they liked being called such names. After answering any charges which might have been made, the suggestion would be put forth that the Leaguers in that paper's area ought to remember these things when it came time to renew subscriptions.[50] Many an editor following the line of the city dailies had his ardor cooled considerably by a visit from a dozen irate farmer-subscribers and a rash of canceled subscriptions. The rural circulation of the city opposition papers took significant drops, with members frequently writing the *Leader* of mass cancellations in a particular area, while brief boycotts of towns which were centers of antagonism to the League were not unknown.

As has been noted previously, a vast number of farmers were dependent upon their local bankers, and many, especially the foreign-born, had customarily gone to them for advice as well as loans. The bankers consequently were quite in the habit of exercising considerable paternal responsibility, and this situation was one which the League found it necessary to break, inasmuch as the bankers almost universally opposed this new "radicalism." Opportunities were not lacking, for the banks were quite free with advice which was frequently easy to attack. In November, for example, the First National Bank at Stanley, in a letter refusing to get a farmer a Federal Reserve Fund Loan on the security of wheat in the bin, apparently because it was too much bother and not sufficiently profitable, concluded by advising the farmer not to try to hold his grain but to sell at once. "Holding grain for a higher price," they said, "is speculation, and speculation is not legitimate business."

To this the *Leader* commented acidly: "It is very illegitimate for farmers to hold their grain for higher prices. Farmers should be perfectly good and do nothing illegitimate. Therefore they should sell their wheat as quickly as they could and let the legitimate speculator speculate in it. That would legitimize the whole transaction, no doubt." [51]

The League was constantly cursed with the problem of bankers who would not cash checks for dues, at least "not without talking it over with the farmer." Checks were frequently sent back marked "no funds," although members later showed deposit slips proving that they had money in the bank at the time. One G. R. Meyers, cashier of the Farmers and Merchants Bank of Robinson, sent back all postdated checks sent to him for collection marked "bank won't pay on this paper." Later when a League representative presented one hundred such checks he was ordered out of the bank, but another visit made with a demand for the reason for nonpayment, and a reminder of the banker's duty under the law, finally brought about payment.[52] Later on organizers were instructed to have checks made out to a member of the crew and to try to get part of the payment in cash, so that amounts on the checks would vary, thus making it more difficult for bankers to detect checks for League dues.[53]

The impartial observer cannot fail to notice one very striking fact about the League opposition. They did not attempt for the most part to deny the existence of the evils which brought the League into being, nor did they appear to make any very serious efforts to remedy the situation. Had they been honestly intent on the welfare of the farmers as was claimed, and merely eager to save them from the hot-handed grasp of "anarchists and free-lovers," reform would seem to have been the most effective means of rendering the League impotent. Instead, however, they devoted themselves to vilifying the leaders and impugning the motives of the organization.

Although opposition to the League was continuous and vehement, support was forthcoming from many quarters. President Worst of the agricultural college, in his speech before the Tri-State Grain Growers Association convention in Fargo, January 20, 1916, took up the cudgel for the organization of farmers, though he did not mention the Nonpartisan League by name: "The remedy . . . is in your own hands. If the laws do not suit you; if the constitution stands in the way; if public officials are not sympathetic, (speaking for North Dakota), commanding 80% of the voting strength of the state, as they do, farmers need not be told where their remedy lies."[54]

The *Leader* consistently gave favorable publicity to activities of the Equity Society and its Cooperative Exchange, and, with many farmers belonging to both organizations, it was no surprise when in February the society resolved "that it unqualifiedly endorses the League program and its official organ the *Nonpartisan Leader*." [55] It was an occasion of perhaps greater significance, however, when the *Fargo Forum*, the evening paper of that city, which had for almost a year been attempting to stay on the fence, came out with qualified support. The *Forum* had decided that even if it did not know the League leaders, the organization must be all right since it was composed of the farmers of the state "almost to a man." Moreover, "today it is the dominant power in political affairs of the state." The *Forum* was not without other motives, however, for it had heard rumors of a forthcoming state convention and was seeking to make Fargo the convention city: "These men will not be radicals, or socialists or anarchists as some people seem to believe. They will be the farmers of the state in convention assembled . . . The *Forum* believes that great things may come out of this movement for the state of North Dakota." [56]

One of the most persistent charges leveled against the League was that it was undemocratic, and that Townley had never been elected president. The latter charge was, of course, true, although it might be pointed out that it was not the League membership which was worried about the situation. It is unquestionably a fact that throughout his career A. C. Townley desired to be the "boss," but more important at this period was the simple necessity of centralized control if any success whatsoever was to be achieved. The farmers were following a messiah—without a strong leader unified action of this nature would have been impossible. The spade work of organizing and campaigning is not carried on by means of debate, and Townley had every intention that a strong hand should be at the controls at least until his idea had been given a chance to reach maturity. The point was made clear by Townley himself in early 1916:

Suppose I should call an election now. What would be the result? Some opposing candidate for president would arise within the organization. Newspapers would advertise his candidacy. They would do their best to build up a faction supporting him. We should have politics within the League and the League's state campaign would be stopped before we could get to first base.[57]

It was also suggested that members who had signed up with an organization listing Townley as president had in effect endorsed him for that position.[58] At any rate it could scarcely be questioned even by

43

the opposition press that any League election at this time would have overwhelmingly acclaimed Arthur Townley as it head. As J. E. Buttree put it: "They believed that they were right; that theirs was a righteous cause; that another Saviour had come down to earth to save them, and, profiting by experience, they knew better than to crucify him." [59]

Another constant point of attack was the handling of League funds —it was intimated that they were being subverted to the personal aggrandizement of the leaders. This Townley answered repeatedly in stump speeches in this fashion:

Any member of the League, entitled to the information, can find out what is being done with the money. For their benefit I will say that there is a voucher on file for every penny that has been spent, and I will show them to any farmer member of this League who wants to see them, but we are not going to tell those who are our enemies what we are doing with our money, nor are we going to give them an opportunity to find out. [60]

For the first year no one but bona fide farmers were allowed to become members of the League, on the logical assumption that infiltration could easily prove disastrous. However, with the groundwork laid and the necessity for campaign funds looming large, it seemed wise to commence selling auxiliary memberships to persons from other occupations who asserted sympathy with the League program. Considerable numbers seem to have been sold, though such memberships apparently carried with them little in the way of "privileges." It was principally a matter of support and publicly aligning oneself "on the farmers' side."

The coming of winter had meant that the time was fast approaching when the groundwork for the 1916 elections must be laid—the first real test of whether or not the farmers could and would stick together. The first issue of the *Leader* had dwelt on the futility of electing to office men who were "friends of the farmer" only during the campaign. Nor would blind adherence to the old parties as such ever bring results; basically, it said, there was little choice between them. Farmers must be elected to represent farmers:

Instead of several hundred farmers spending time and money petitioning friends of the corporations after election to do something for them, it would be much more effective for all the farmers to spend a little time and money before election investigating the business connections and records of the men who want to be elected. They have determined to organize and make a united effort to find out who are their friends before they send them to Bismarck.[61]

Townley himself was not at all certain whether the farmers could be gotten together for local meetings, and as a consequence he scheduled a trial meeting in a small remote town where he hoped that a "flop," if it happened, would not receive too much publicity. One reason for the success of the secrecy program was that many farmers suspected that they had been "gypped" and that nothing would ever come of the organization. Often individuals who thought they were the only "suckers" in their community were amazed when they discovered that all their neighbors were members too. No one was in the room at the appointed hour though men kept looking in the door and leaving. Townley thereupon commenced talking to a few organizers seated near the front. Gradually farmers began to enter and sit down at the back, and then suddenly the room was filled to overflowing. The meeting was given a big spread in the *Leader*, and from that time on a hall could be filled almost anywhere in the state, even in the dead of winter.[62]

Beginning in December 1915, it was arranged for speakers from headquarters to hold dozens of meetings throughout the state, providing a chance for members and others to come and hear discussions of League principles and proposed political action. Several top-notch speakers were on the road, holding meetings daily in town halls, barns, or whatever other facilities could be provided. At some crossroads towns meetings were held for twenty to thirty people, while in other places attendance sometimes ran as high as seven or eight hundred. These meetings resulted in many new memberships from among the "doubters," but their real value lay in the renewed enthusiasm and confidence of members whose only contact with the organization for many months had been through the impersonal medium of the *Leader*. The analogy to old-fashioned revival meetings is not greatly strained, and it is certain that the movement was immeasurably strengthened by these hundreds of informal get-togethers. The zeal of men who would drive miles across the prairie in 40° below zero temperatures, often by bobsled, to listen to hours of speech-making is hardly to be doubted.

The effectiveness of these meetings cannot be better expressed than in the quite typical words of an Edmore farmer who wrote for the *Leader* an account of their local meeting:

Lord, what a meeting! Big opera house, lots of seats and yet 25 people stood up for 1 hour and 45 minutes. Local banker said that never in the history of Edmore had he seen as many rigs as were here today.

Even after the meeting the enthusiasm did not wane. Crowds met the speaker on the street and shook his hand and sent messages of good cheer to the boys at headquarters. "Tell them they're all right and playing a great game. This time we'll get something! If they need more money we've got that too."

It was reported on the streets that a prominent politician had said, "The League had the state all sewed up in a bag." The report spread like wildfire and everybody was happy.

At the meeting it was a continuous performance—short, hard jabs by the speaker and then wild cheering, clapping of hands and stamping of feet throughout the entire meeting. Never before has Edmore witnessed such a time.[63]

wwwwwwwwwwwwwwwwwwwwwwwwwwwwwwwww3

Up from the Sod House

AS THE long series of winter meetings wore on, and enthusiasm for the forthcoming campaign waxed high, slogans became inevitable. The most common, in recognition of the revolution against the maxim that farmers could not stick together, was simply "We'll Stick!" Before long buttons began to be seen in lapels and danglers on watch chains bearing the figure of a tired, abused, and rebellious goat. Beside it was the inscription, "The Goat That Can't Be Got," and this shortly became the unofficial emblem of the Nonpartisan League. The farmer was certain that he had been the goat for too long a time, and the League was his means of butting back. As one prominent Leaguer later jestingly explained: "A goat is an animal that works with his head when attacked." [1]

The *Leader* for January 27, 1916, had carried the first notice of precinct meetings of League members to be held on February 22 at the regular precinct voting places or other places decided upon by the local members. The purpose was to select delegates to district meetings at which would be chosen both legislative candidates and delegates to a state convention. In later issues the methods to be followed were developed more fully, and every member was also sent a personal notice of the meeting. The full responsibility was placed squarely upon the members—this was to be their first opportunity to exercise the privileges of membership, and it must be done with care. The men to be elected in the precinct caucuses would be the ones to judge the fitness of League candidates for office, and members were repeatedly warned against men who sought office of any sort. The keynote had earlier been given in a *Leader* editorial:

47

Farmers must keep in mind that they cannot expect right service and a square deal at the hands of a man who goes gum-shoeing for political preferment. Farmers do not need in office a man who seeks the glory of political prestige . . .

What the farmers want is a man who knows the farmers' needs, a man who is engaged in the same business as the regular farmer—not the farmer who farms farmers. Not only so but they want a man who is so adverse to political preferment that he must be "drafted" into service.[2]

In his "Call to Patriotic Action," published in the *Leader* on February 10, Townley continued to hammer at the theme of avoiding office-seekers and anyone who might be too friendly with bankers, middlemen, or big business:

. . . If you select for precinct delegates strong, level-headed men—men who seek nothing for themselves, but only the good that they may do for you—then will the men whom they indorse to make your laws be men upon whom you can depend, and when these men take up the affairs of this state they will have only one purpose—the greatest good for the greatest number.[3]

Unanimous attendance was constantly urged, for the League leaders well knew that this was to be the first real test of whether or not the farmers would "stick." Moreover, small attendance and manipulation by a few friends of particular politicians would obviously be disastrous. No official headquarters representatives were to be at the precinct caucuses—members were merely to elect a chairman and a secretary and then proceed to the business of selecting a delegate.

As Washington's birthday came and passed, Arthur Townley waited in nervous anticipation. The results were far from disappointing; they were, in fact, sensational. Dozens of precincts had 100 per cent attendance, and not one was below 90 per cent! [4] In many cases only impassable roads prevented every member from being present. The spirit of determination, loyalty, and unity evidenced in scrawled reports from the precincts was contagious, and the complete unselfishness in the selection of delegates nothing short of remarkable.[5] It was indeed a staggering show of political strength, when some 26,000 farmers met simultaneously in nearly every township in the state, and the old political powers were frankly worried. Hundreds of citizens for the first time experienced real personal participation in the democratic process.

Many farmers, having seen the strength of their organization, were eager for widespread political activity, but the leaders wisely made it clear that the League, at least for the present, had no intention of becoming involved in national politics, and that it would also steer clear of local matters: "In the matter of county and township elections the League will take no definite action. Most of such offices are of an administrative character and the officials are near neighbors and well-known to the men who elect them. The League will clean house at Bismarck—clean county politics will follow automatically." [6]

It had been clear from the first, although the opposition papers could not believe it for some time, that the League officials had no thought of seeking office. That would surely have been the road to shaken confidence and rapid disintegration, for it would have seemed at once that the organization had all the time been merely a personal machine. The *Leader* set the matter straight:

The men who started and built this organization are at work to place the government of North Dakota in the hands of the people of North Dakota—not to grab office for themselves.

The *Leader* is authorized by League officials to state in unmistakable terms that no one connected with the League in any official capacity or in any way connected with the *Leader* will be a candidate for any public office whatsoever. [7]

It must be borne in mind that the League had no intention of operating as a political party and nominating its own candidates. Instead, it proposed to enter the primaries of the existing parties and to nominate candidates favorable to the League program on those tickets. Once the candidates were nominated, it was expected that the members would vote for League men on both Republican and Democratic tickets with complete disregard of party lines in the final election. League caucuses and conventions prior to the primaries were thus not "subverting the primary law and nominating by convention," as was charged,[8] but were simply for the purpose of endorsing individuals to run in the primary of the party of their choice. Since North Dakota was normally Republican by about two to one, it was a foregone conclusion that the principal contest would be in the Republican primaries.

This situation, however, was not always crystal clear even to all the League membership, and the *Leader* received many inquiries as to how members should register for the primaries when the assessor came around. They were advised simply to register just as they had in the

past or as they wished to do, "and then prepare to vote for the candidates as *you endorse* them later." [9]

During the first three weeks in March delegate conventions were
held in all but a few of the state's forty-nine legislative districts. In
each, from one to four candidates for the lower house, depending on
the population, and one candidate for senator in the odd-numbered districts, were chosen. Since the senators served four-year terms, twenty-
four at the next session would be holdovers, making it necessary for the
League to elect nearly all its candidates and win over some of the holdovers to its program if it were to control the upper chamber. Once
again extreme care was utilized in the selections, and candidates were
picked with little regard for party affiliation, which, as the *Leader* remarked, was "as immaterial as the way he wears his whiskers." The
great majority, of course, were Republicans, but there were a fair number of Democrats, and two Socialists were included.[10]

The fact that the district conventions were not all held on the same
day provided grounds for further criticism. It was charged that League
officials traveled from one to another and handpicked the candidates.
But complaints were not forthcoming from the delegates, who were
admittedly novices in politics and welcomed the instructions and advice offered by Bowen and other lieutenants.[11] The actual influence
of these officials with respect to particular candidates is uncertain and,
since their acquaintanceship could hardly be very wide in every district, probably not extensive.

At any rate the candidates selected were certainly well chosen. As
one rural paper, formerly in opposition, commented on the candidates
from its area: "Their reputations are such that they could have been
elected any time they chose to seek the office, whether they were indorsed by any league or not." [12]

The plan suggested by League headquarters for the handling of the
endorsements for state offices provided that each district convention
should elect one delegate to attend a state convention, which in turn
would select the state candidates. In general the legislative candidate
who received the highest vote in the district convention became the
delegate,[13] which in effect established a nominating group composed
of men who were to work on the legislative aspects of the program in
cooperation with these state officials, if elected.

In the meantime an excellent object lesson in regard to office-seekers had presented itself. One George J. Smith, a newspaper publisher of Plaza, following time-honored practice, had on February 1 written to a farmer acquaintance near Minot stating that he was interested in obtaining the Republican nomination for governor and asking the farmer to attempt to round up some delegates to the Nonpartisan League state convention who would be favorable to his candidacy. The result was greater statewide publicity than Mr. Smith had anticipated in his wildest dreams—he got the entire front page of the February 10 *Leader*, where he was pointed out as the type of man to steer clear of.[14] Though he continued to campaign, he had become the laughingstock of the state, and his chances, if any, were completely ruined. His newspapers at once became violently anti-League, thus furnishing another object lesson.

Throughout the winter there was a constant stream of predictions in the daily and weekly papers of the state as to what candidates the League was going to support, as well as numerous "inside stories" on future League political actions. These became so persistent that it was necessary for the *Leader* to warn its readers repeatedly against these fabrications and to reiterate that what the League would do and whom it would support depended on the convention, news of which would be published exclusively in the *Leader*.[15]

The state convention was to be held in Fargo March 29 and 30, and for weeks the *Leader* gave a tremendous build-up to the two days of mass meetings which were to follow the delegate convention. Use of the municipal auditorium had been granted free of charge, merchants were to put on special displays, and the Fargo Commercial Club was to be the official host. There were to be parades and band contests, plus afternoon and evening meetings on each of the two days. Moreover, following the Fargo events, further mass meetings, with the candidates as speakers, were to be held in Grand Forks, Devils Lake, Williston, Minot, Valley City, Beach, and Bismarck.

On the evening of March 29 an earnest group of about forty-five farmer delegates assembled in Fargo, the seriousness of their responsibility showing plainly on their faces. After opening remarks by two or three League officials, the floor was thrown open, with every delegate free to suggest as many men for each office as he desired. As they were suggested, the names were written on a blackboard for everyone to see, and the discussion of each was frequently long and detailed.[16] The League speakers and organizers were called before the assemblage to give their views, since they were practically the only ones who had had the opportunity to size up men from all over the state as to what their neighbors thought of them and how they had appeared as boosters, as chairmen of meetings, and the like. The qualifications, record, experience, ability, and above all the loyalty to the cause of all those proposed were discussed for hours, and when everyone had had his say the delegates proceeded to a secret ballot.[17]

Selected to be the candidate for governor was a man previously unknown to public office, except as a township supervisor and local school board member, Lynn J. Frazier, a Pembina County farmer. Four of the men selected for other state offices were avowed candidates, who had, however, at various times expressed their agreement with the League program. These were Thomas Hall, then secretary of state, endorsed for the same position; William Langer, state's attorney of Morton County, for attorney general; Carl R. Kositzky, secretary of the State Tax Commission and a county commissioner of Burleigh County, for auditor; and Neil C. MacDonald, state supervisor of rural consolidated schools, for the position of state superintendent of public instruction.

The others, except for the Supreme Court candidates, were farmers, and included P. M. Casey, vice president of the North Dakota Union of the American Society of Equity, for treasurer; S. A. Olsness, who had been secretary of a cooperative fire insurance company, for commissioner of insurance; Albert Stenmo for lieutenant governor; John N. Hagan, a township supervisor of McHenry County, for commissioner of agriculture and labor; and M. P. Johnson, state president of the Equity, Charles Bleick, and Sam Aandahl, for railroad commissioners.[18] All except Casey were Republicans.

The Supreme Court candidates were Luther Birdzell, professor in the law school of the state university and a former member of the State Tax Commission, known to be a "single-taxer"; Richard H. Grace, a lawyer of Mohall having Socialist inclinations; * and James E. Robinson, Fargo law partner of William Lemke, a League attorney and one of the inner circle of League leaders. Robinson was an elderly gentle-

* He was later to become a stanch Harding man.

man with a flowing gray beard, known to be rather eccentric, though prominent as a crusader for judicial reforms. In 1908 he had campaigned for Congress with the unique tactics of ringing a cowbell through the streets in order to attract audiences, and in 1912 he had run for justice of the Supreme Court on a platform denouncing judges of the past as "tools of the big interests and servants of corruption." [19]

The mass meetings got under way with a whoop. The demonstration after ratification of the ticket was so big that it was difficult to quell in order to get on with the program. Fargo was jammed with more than 3000 visitors whose enthusiasm and confidence were infectious. The *Forum*, obviously impressed, described the opening session in the packed auditorium, giving the attendance at more than 2000:

The enthusiasm of the audience surpassed anything that had been witnessed in Fargo in many years and if this enthusiasm of the delegates present is to be taken as a criterion of the spirit of the other members of the organization, the Nonpartisan League is no small power in the state.[20]

The *Grand Forks Herald* did not, however, cease its campaign of derogation:

. . . the opening session yesterday was attended by as large a crowd as could be gathered by means of the escort of two bands. Including the local people and others who attended for the purpose of viewing the proceedings, the attendance numbered from 500 to 600 . . . The question is how far the candidates will go in accepting the endorsement of the league and approving the various isms contained in its platform.[21]

There were dozens of speeches, short and long; A. C. Townley, introduced as "the most maligned man in North Dakota," was twice received with deafening ovations.[22] The climax came with the Saturday evening parade—2000 farmers, four abreast, marching down Broadway, Fargo's principal business street, to the music of two bands and with the accompaniment of hundreds of dollars' worth of exploding fireworks. The *Leader* vividly described the scene:

Red fire lit up the street, the buildings, and the sky. The marchers carried banners with such wordings as "Privilege knows no party; why should the people be fooled?"; "Who are they who fear the people? Think it over. There's a reason"; "On to Bismarck 50,000 strong"; "It's do it ourselves or go broke"; "Let the grafters holler; the people have the votes"; "What have partisan politics done for you? Think it over"; "Everybody's organized; why not the farmer?"

Each marcher carried a torch and a sparkler and their cheering and singing as they marched made a deafening noise.[23]

Truly, another farmers' crusade was on its way.

Lynn Frazier, chosen to head the ticket, was forty-one years old, a graduate of the state university, and though widely respected in his own community was virtually unknown outside of it. Nor was the little town of Hoople, near which he lived, of wide renown. Though the Leaguers were overjoyed at the selection of a "real farmer," his candidacy was greeted with ridicule in many quarters. "Who is Frazier, and is Hoople a place or a disease?" asked the *Mandan Pioneer* sarcastically.[24] Or as another paper put it, even more forcefully, "Who in Hell is Frazier, and Where in Hell is Hoople?"[25]

Various stories have arisen as to how Frazier received the news of his selection—that a committee sent to notify him found him steering a load of fence posts across the bleak prairie,[26] that Mrs. Frazier had answered a telephone call from Fargo to say that her husband was out "slopping the hogs"[27]—but there seems no particularly good reason to question his own account as he told it to the convention on his arrival:

I drove into town with the girls Wednesday and they sent word to me that I was wanted on the telephone. When I got to the phone they told me it was League headquarters at Fargo talking and asked me to come up here right away. I told them I couldn't come that night, because I had my overalls on and no suitable clothing with me.

I went back to the farm and packed my grip and came up here and it was then I learned that they wanted me to run for governor and that the League delegates in their convention had nominated me.[28]

Here was a man, a lifelong Republican, to whom no stigma of socialism could be attached and against whose personal character there could be no reproach. As Townley introduced him to the convention, the stress was on the fact that here was one of the first cases since George Washington where the office had sought the man rather than the man seeking the office. Under the existing conditions he could hardly escape being immediately labeled "the modern Cincinnatus" who was "called from the plow to head his people and to govern a great commonwealth."[29]

Lynn J. Frazier was born in Rice County, Minnesota, on December 21, 1874, having come to North Dakota when his father homesteaded there in the spring of 1881.[30] He attended country schools, followed by high school at Grafton, from which he was graduated at the age of seventeen. For two years he taught in rural schools, saving his money in the hope of some day being able to study to be a doctor. After a year in the normal school at Mayville and two more years of teaching, he went in 1897 to the state university at Grand Forks, where among his classmates were William Lemke and Neil MacDonald—with both of whom he was now once again associated. A star football player and captain of his team for two years, he was graduated in 1901 with high academic honors as well. Unfortunately, at this time his brother, who had taken over the management of the family farm after the death of his father, died suddenly, and his mother, not wishing to lose the old homestead, asked him to come back. He gave up his long-dreamed-of career and became a farmer. Two years later he married Lottie Stafford, daughter of a neighboring farmer, who in subsequent years was to present him with three daughters and two sons.*

At forty-one Frazier was a physically rugged man, portly and quite bald—a family man who never smoked or drank or uttered an off-color word.[31] He had a dignified bearing and spoke distinctly and without flourishes in a deep bass voice. As they heard him speak, diffidently, but directly to the point and with firm conviction in the cause, the convention delegates were more than pleased with their choice. As one observer commented: "Frazier is a ruddy-cheeked, broad-shouldered, quiet, plain-spoken man . . . a purely American product who came up from the sod house and the pioneer's hardships, and you can tell by looking at him that he is as clean as a hound's tooth."[32]

Few of the opposition papers saw fit to attack the League candidates personally, though the *Mercer County Star*, apparently existing in an ivory-tower innocence of the political realities about it, remarked: ". . . a number of unknowns were indorsed and the League's candidates of this sort will get nowhere in this campaign. They will not even be considered a factor in the political scramble and the League will get but minor recognition from the powers in North Dakota politics."[33]

More astute newspapers, however, recognized the fact that different "political powers" were abroad than the *Star* remembered, and their attacks continued to be slanted toward the League leaders, with charges

---

* Frazier, a loyal alumnus of the state university, named his twin daughters Unie and Versie in its honor.

of subverted funds, "dictation" of the candidates selected, and controlling of candidates with "secret pledges." The hoary ogre of secret pledges was trotted out so frequently that the *Leader* finally attempted to dispose of the matter by printing a copy of the League pledge, which was stated to be neither secret nor compulsory, though virtually all the candidates had signed:

I hereby pledge myself to the following:
That I will allow my name to be placed on the _____ ticket to be voted on at the June primaries and, if nominated, will continue to act as the Farmers' Nonpartisan Political League candidate till after the polls close on Nov. 7, 1916; and if elected I will at all times vote and work for those measures and amendments that will assure justice to the farmers and all the people of the state, in accordance with the progressive and cardinal principles of the League and the wishes of my constituents.[34]

None of the candidates apparently ever indicated that the pledge was other than that printed, which would scarcely seem calculated to send chills down the spine of the most cautious individual. A year and a half later, William Langer spoke directly to this point:

In view of the fact that some of the newspapers of the Northwest have said that the men elected to state office in North Dakota were pledged to Mr. A. C. Townley, I want to say that not one of them was pledged to anything at the time he was endorsed by the Nonpartisan League of North Dakota. I want to say this to you, that immediately after I was endorsed for the position of Attorney General of North Dakota, I met Mr. A. C. Townley for the first time in my life. And I said to him: What do you want the Attorney General of North Dakota to do? And he said: I want a man in there who is going to enforce all the laws upon the statute books, and I want a man in there who is not going to put a man in jail because he steals a little flour for his starving family, and let a man who steals a lot of money from a bank go free. (Applause) He said: I want a man in there who is going to treat the rich man and the poor man alike. (Applause)[35]

Though handbills had been distributed in the streets of Fargo during the convention pointing out that 30,000 members at $6.00 each meant a total of $180,000, and asking what had become of the money, no mishandling was discovered, then or later. Just prior to the convention the Equitable Auditing Company of St. Paul audited the League's books and compiled statements for the convention, which named a committee to check the matter. It reported: ". . . we find that all funds of the League are properly accounted for, and we highly commend the leaders of the League for the economical and judicious manner in which they have administered the financial affairs of the League." [36]

The *Leader*, of course, did not miss the opportunity to reprint the opposition circular, directing these barbs at its anonymous authors: ". . . In the first place they afford some amusement that we are unwilling to miss. And in the next place, there may be some few of our members that do not know what an unscrupulous and dirty gang you are and if they will read your circulars they will learn that at first hand, which is always the best way." [37]

The charge that what the convention had really amounted to was a meeting of handpicked delegates to ratify a slate of candidates selected by the "big three" (Townley, Lemke, and F. B. Wood) was, however, the most persistent and the most bedeviling. To counteract it the *Leader* procured and published at frequent intervals statements from every one of the delegates as to whether or not they considered it a "bossed" convention.[38] The comments of Girdell Patterson of Donnybrook, delegate from the 43rd legislative district, were typical:

I did not realize that a state convention could be conducted so absolutely free of dictatorship, without prearrangement. Nothing was prearranged and nobody knew who the other fellow was going to put up. We were able to agree on candidates for all offices without friction of any kind. It was a marvel to me, explained only by the singleness of purpose and absolute lack of desire for personal honors by all present. The cause was the thing.

I want to say that those delegates present conducted that convention and nobody but them had anything to say about it.[39]

Though all of Mr. Patterson's colleagues were not as fluent as he, their opinions appear to have been virtually identical. The *Leader* went further than published statements; it invited its readers to write or call upon any of the delegates to ask them for the facts. It seems hardly open to question that in actuality the League leaders had settled in advance upon a number of possibilities for the state offices, though they were not so foolish as to attempt to ram their choices down the throats of the delegates. Several possible candidates were suggested for each office. It is likely that the information provided to the convention by the headquarters speakers was tremendously influential, and they indubitably made out good cases for the favored candidates.

Townley himself had naturally been actively interested, had instructed organizers to be on the lookout for likely prospects, and had interviewed a number of possibilities. His views when presented to the convention carried weight. In this sense it is no doubt true that to a considerable extent the League leaders were responsible for the slate selected.* On the other hand, the delegates obviously had no feeling of being dictated to, they were free to choose whomever they wished, and few people could quarrel extensively with the character of the candidates selected. Surely not all of the forty-five delegates would have quietly submitted to the barefaced "bossism" which the opposition claimed—as C. P. Peterson, the Towner County delegate, wrote: ". . . if it hadn't been [fair] you would have heard from me long before this." [40] Debate was not limited nor was coercion of any type employed. Under these conditions, if a prearranged slate of candidates was chosen, it should perhaps be considered a tribute to the wisdom of the selections and the convincingness of the arguments presented in their favor.

It happened that Albert Stenmo, originally endorsed for lieutenant governor, had also been selected in his home district to run for the Senate. Since he preferred the latter opportunity, it was necessary to choose a substitute, and a mail referendum of the delegates endorsed Anton T. Kraabel, a merchant of Clifford who was already a candidate for the office. Kraabel had been lieutenant governor from 1912 to 1914 and had served two terms in the legislature, and though the *Courier-News* sneered that he was a "McKenzie man," [41] the *Leader* stoutly defended his past record.†

* It has been commonly assumed that William Lemke was responsible for promoting Frazier, his university classmate, and Robinson, his law partner. Lemke himself asserts that "there was no control and the delegates were at liberty to nominate whomever they pleased." He adds that "I suggested Lynn Frazier's name, but the delegate from his county placed his name on the blackboard. If I was responsible for the selection of Lynn Frazier, then I am proud of it . . ." (Letter to the author, Aug. 27, 1947.) Townley had personally favored Frazier. Much of the debate centered around whether the League should endorse someone already a candidate who possessed a personal following or should draft a genuine farmer. The great majority wished to prove the strength of the organization by electing an "unknown" to the state's highest office. (Gaston, p. 103.)

† Lemke states that Kraabel's endorsement "was by no means unanimous . . . before he was endorsed he was finally asked whether he believed in the Nonpartisan League program, and would be fair, as Lieutenant Governor, to all factions. To this his answer was yes . . ." (Letter to the author, Aug. 27, 1947.)

A novel event in the history of American politics had taken place. A political convention had met, with an almost unprecedented singleness of purpose, to endorse candidates to run on the tickets of both major parties. While there was only one Democrat among the group running for state office, there was a better spread among legislative candidates: 98 Republicans, 21 Democrats, and 2 Socialists had been selected in the district conventions,[42] and it is interesting to note that while many districts were solidly Republican and a few had endorsed all Democrats, there were numerous cases of both Republicans and Democrats selected in the same districts, and one of the Socialist candidates had been put up in an otherwise all Republican district. Nonpartisanship was apparently working, though the idea was still too much for the *Herald* to grasp. Known Democrats at the Fargo convention had spoken publicly in favor of Republican candidates and vice versa! "Why," it asked plaintively, "is it the business of a Democrat to interest himself in the selection of Republican candidates?"[43]

First Blood

THE candidates had been chosen, and the long-awaited convention had come and gone, but the real battle lay ahead. With general farmer support, a largely Republican state ticket could hardly lose in North Dakota, and it was consequently no secret to the least politically minded that the actual fight for state control would come with the June primaries and not in November, unless something unforeseen developed. The League was more than used to the continuous barrage of slurs cast in its direction by the opposition press, and had for the most part turned them to good account, but League leaders were not wrong in forecasting at the conclusion of the convention a campaign of abuse and vilification that was previously unparalleled.

It was constantly insisted by the "antis" that the official platform of the League was merely window dressing, and that the organization was in reality working for international socialism. "State farms will follow state flour mills and creameries," [1] the farmers were repeatedly told; or, as it was put in the title of a pamphlet circulated later: *Are You Ready to Hand Over Your Farm to a Bunch of Socialist Adventurers? That Is What Townleyism Means, Mr. Farmer.*[2] The extravagance of such claims was pointed out in the League's simple reply, which merely asked, "Where would such a program ever get with the farmer?" Whatever might have been the ultimate desires of some of the League leaders, they were after all entirely dependent upon the votes of the farmers, whose socialistic interests for the most part went little further than control of their own marketing system.

The number of available allegations seemed endless. Not only was the League a "tool of the I.W.W."; it was even claimed that its real purpose was the return of the saloon to North Dakota, despite Frazier's being known in his home community as something of a "prohibition crank." But it remained for "Jerry" Bacon, archantagonist of the League, and his *Grand Forks Herald* to furnish even more refreshing logic:

. . . while it would be untrue to say that every socialist is a free lover, we know of no advocate of free love who is not an avowed socialist. Most of the men who are of the inner circle in the management of the Nonpartisan League are men who appear to have drifted into socialism through failure in every other line of activity . . . They are socialists not of the conservative, but of the destructive class . . . Among them are men who are advocates of almost every wild vagary ever put forth under the name of socialism.[3]

These attacks were cleverly handled by the *Leader*, which often reprinted choice quotations and turned the charges on the farmer members. It was "the farmers" who were being called anarchists and free lovers, "the farmers' candidate" (rather than the League's) was being attacked in the "gang press," and so on. In fact, the readers were so neatly identified with the slurs of the opposition upon the organization that, at this period at least, it is likely that the attacks served the League fully as much as they harmed it. Fume as they might at these tactics, the opposition papers were almost helpless against them.

Neither the *Herald*, the *Courier-News*, nor the *Bismarck Tribune* confined their editorializing to the editorial columns. The League was constantly attacked with great bitterness in "news stories," and the "slanting" of news items was rarely even subtle. To be sure, the *Leader* did likewise but it never laid claim to being a general newspaper or anything other than a "party organ." The insistence of the opposition press that they were not opposing the farmers' organization but merely its leaders was naturally taken with a grain of salt.

Hundreds of rural subscriptions were actually stopped, even before they had run their full time, but the influence of the city press was far from as negligible as the *Leader* would have liked to have had its readers believe. The League had its own problems with canceled memberships and subscriptions,[4] due principally to the opposition press and to town merchants, bankers, and the like, but out of the total membership the number was relatively insignificant. The confusion of many foreign-born farmers especially was at times almost pitiful. Penciled notes in

broken English tell of not knowing what to believe about the League—
it had sounded good when the organizer talked to them, but others on
whom they depended for advice had later talked it down. Many who
asked to be dropped from the organization changed their minds when
matters on which they had been misinformed were explained, particularly if a German- or Scandinavian-speaking organizer paid a call.

While the unity of League support behind the endorsed candidates
was amazing, it was naturally impossible for everyone to be completely
satisfied. A few had personal grudges against a particular man, one was
antagonized because Langer was a Catholic, and another complained
because a few of the candidates for state office were not farmers. All
this necessitated carefully phrased replies by Henry G. Teigan, executive secretary of the League, who pointed out that a few offices, such
as attorney general, superintendent of schools, and judges of the Supreme Court, required specialized training. Opposition to Lynn Frazier
seems to have been nonexistent among the membership.[5]

It should not be inferred that all the newspapers of the state were
opposed to the League, though a heavy majority were certainly in that
class. A number, in fact, usually in strong League areas, were stanch
partisans of the organization, even though they found the road strewn
with obstacles. A notable example was the *Devils Lake Journal*, a vigorous League supporter from the first, which in April of 1916 suddenly
found itself called upon by its major creditors to pay all its outstanding obligations in full at once, despite the fact that it had been making
a profit and steadily reducing its debt. The *Journal*, thus forced to the
wall, appealed to the League farmers for subscriptions, and with the
support of the *Leader* acquired a sufficient number to save its skin.[6]

One of the most successful hoaxes perpetrated upon the farmers developed with the publication in the *Herald* and the *Courier-News* in
early May of charges that it was the opinion of "able lawyers," none
of whom were named, that the League, since it was not incorporated,
constituted a partnership, and that therefore every member was individually liable for all the organization's debts. Townley's earlier financial failure was played to the skies as an example of what would soon
happen to the League.[7] Rural papers throughout the state picked up
the story, and it is not strange that such a threat struck fear into the
heart of many an impoverished farmer. Almost at once there was a
minor rash of canceled memberships, the reason being given that they

could not afford to risk liability, though the majority asked to have the *Leader* continued and promised to keep on "boosting" the League.[8] The postdated check system of course made stopping of payment an easy matter.

The *Leader* made haste to counteract this propaganda by securing statements from various lawyers of repute to the effect that such a charge was completely groundless [9] and then publicly offering the Reverend Mr. Guild, *Courier-News* editor, $1000 for proof of his statements. The offer was never accepted. The laws of North Dakota defined a partnership as "the association of two or more persons for the purpose of carrying on business together and dividing the profits between them," [10] and further provided that a partnership could not be formed without the consent of all parties, nor could new members be admitted "without the consent of every existing member thereof." [11] Arthur LeSueur, one of the League attorneys, in a memorandum on this matter further cited the case of *Clement v. Miller*, in the 13th North Dakota reports, in which Mr. Justice Morgan clearly stated that there was no individual liability of the members of a voluntary organization not organized for profit.[12]

Certainly the stipulations of the law did not include the League, and since apparently no one could be found to contend seriously that they did, the liability charges died a natural death. Subsequently, however, the *Leader* developed for the edification of its readers its own definition of "partnership": "Agreement between gang newspapers, corrupt politicians, and Big Business to break up the League if possible, for profit of Big Business. The members are individually responsible to every farmer in the state. There'll be an accounting June 28." [13]

The *Courier-News* then tried another tack by assuming in news stories that the Equity Society was supporting the candidacy for governor of Usher L. Burdick, endorsed by the Progressive Republican faction, and a statement from the directors of that society was necessary to brand the contention as false. The Equity, they said, was not in politics, but it did believe that the farmers should organize for political purposes.[14] One of the more humorous aspects of the campaign, indeed, was the change of heart toward the Equity evidenced by the anti-League press. Though many of them had fought it tooth and nail for some years, it now seemed mild by comparison and was suddenly represented as an "honest and sincere" farmers' reform movement.

The political situation looked distinctly ominous to those who had been in the habit of easily controlling such affairs in the state, and a conference had therefore been called for Minot on April 5 by N. C. Young, counsel for the Northern Pacific, and L. T. Guild, editor of the *Fargo Courier-News*. Leaders of both the Republican factions—Progressives and Stalwarts—were invited in the hope that some means could be found of uniting on one candidate rather than dividing their vote.[15] The Stalwarts were clearly in favor of Col. John H. Fraine, and though they considered Burdick as a compromise for a time, his relatively liberal record was eventually too much to swallow and the meeting adjourned without success. The *Leader*, in reporting this incident, did not fail to point out that while the League was meeting in convention to endorse candidates and was being charged with "secret manipulations," other small groups were meeting in hotel rooms to do the same thing, without so much as a mention in the press.[16]

The situation had become so serious by late April that for the first time in many months the portly figure of Alex McKenzie was seen on the streets of Bismarck. His efforts in the interests of unity, if such they were, proved fruitless, however, as neither Fraine nor Burdick had the slightest intention of withdrawing. Rumors were prevalent around Bismarck that the McKenzie forces were to copy the League methods by putting 50 to 100 cars in the field for personal calls on farmers in an attempt to undermine League strength,[17] but no such action developed.

The fact that neither the *Leader* nor the League itself ever made a distinction between the McKenzie ring and the Progressives, lumping them all in the term "old gang," was always a source of acute irritation to the Progressives, who felt that the League was stealing their proper credit for ending the McKenzie rule. The League assumed, rightly or wrongly, that there was little real difference on what it considered fundamentals.

One of the cleverest practices of the anti-League forces was the attempt to encourage respected farmers to run for the legislative nomination in rural areas, thus presumably dividing the farmer vote so that the town vote could carry in the conservative candidates. The success of this maneuver was limited due to a lack of willing farmers and to the fact that the *Leader* carefully and repeatedly warned against such proposals. It reminded its readers that even if a man was picked who was better than the League candidate, he was merely being used as a tool, and that success could only be achieved by sticking to the endorsed candidates.[18]

Organized labor in North Dakota was of extremely minor importance in the political affairs of the state, being limited for the most part to the three principal cities and the lignite mines, but small as it was its power was not to be discounted. The Trades and Labor Assembly of Fargo met on April 14, and after discussing common problems with League representatives for some four hours, passed resolutions of support and set up a conference committee. Their requests in the way of legislation were modest in the extreme: a labor lien law to protect workers against insolvent or dishonest employers, and a workmen's compensation act. A mass meeting of all organized labor in the city on April 30 went a step further and endorsed the League program and all its candidates.[19]

Grand Forks unions followed suit on April 30 by also endorsing the League program and candidates and setting up a campaign committee for the area. In both the 6th and 7th districts, each of which included a part of the city, the rural and city vote was about even, so that the labor vote might be of great importance. Since there was no League candidate in the 6th district, labor put up a man who subsequently received League endorsement.[20]

The board of directors of the North Dakota State Federation of Labor had sent a resolution along with a "fraternal delegate" to the Fargo convention of the League, urging the cooperation of workers and farmers, and asking the League to send a fraternal delegate to their forthcoming convention. When that group convened in Grand Forks on June 4, not only was a League delegate present, but Lynn Frazier was a guest of honor and featured speaker. The convention heartily endorsed the League program, plus one of its own on labor legislation, and pledged support of the candidates. Their desired legislation included a minimum wage law for women in industry, the prohibition of industrial child labor, a workmen's industrial insurance act, and the establishment of an efficient department of labor with powers of rigid inspection and control of industrial working conditions. All the resolutions were carefully drawn to apply to industrial labor, but not to farm hands. Also featured on the program was the reading of a letter from

65

Samuel Gompers lauding the cooperation of the two groups and point-ing to the success of such action elsewhere.[21] Of small significance though it may have been in North Dakota, the later to be famous farmer-labor alliance had had its beginnings.

The spring months are busy ones for farmers, and campaigning must simply wait its turn. It was therefore necessary to crowd the active part of the campaign into about three weeks of June, though previously Frazier had occasionally traveled about the state by auto speaking to various groups and seeking particularly to win the support of small-town businessmen. Aided by such able speakers as Bowen and Thoma-son, he and his theme of "what benefits the farmers benefits you" met with moderate success,[22] and there was no doubt considerable merit in giving the townspeople a chance to see that he was hardly a wild-eyed radical but quite a solid citizen.

With the coming of June there commenced a great demand upon League headquarters for speakers to come to picnics, and shortly an extensive series was arranged throughout the state, covering the period from June 7 to June 27. Candidates and the regular corps of speakers were parceled out in an attempt to answer all requests, and headquar-ters undertook to furnish advance advertising for all.

These all-day affairs became virtually the event of the year in many rural areas, with great crowds driving in from miles around, and many assumed almost the aspect of county fairs, complete with bands, soft drink vendors, baseball, and children's games. Time and again the big-gest collection of cars and rigs ever to be seen in a particular area was reported. Six thousand turned out at Maddock, half the population of an entire county, many coming almost fifty miles, while 5000 to 6000 were present at Bottineau.[23] In a territory where fifty people consti-tuted a crowd, such multitudes were unheard of. Cars filled with en-thusiastic farmers' families left those picnics covered with pictures of Frazier and League slogans, and thousands of campaign buttons sud-denly made their appearance.

Amazingly enough, however, despite the recreational features, the farmers came to these picnics to listen to hours of speech-making, and they listened with rapt attention and loud expressions of approval. In some areas there were talks in German and one or another of the Scan-dinavian languages as well as English. Tremendous enthusiasm and confidence were whipped up by these "revival meetings," and none greater than by the old master himself:

> If you can shut your eyes and imagine "Big Biz" wearing a red suit and a tail—which is easy to League members—it is no trouble to see Townley as Billy Sunday, calling on the crowd to rise up and smite a personal devil. . . .
>
> When he half squats in the posture which we used to call "sitting on nothing" in our school days, and puts his hands on his knees and talks to his crowd man to man, he carries them with him. It is not a great speech, but it has his personal magnetism and homely illustration behind it and it gets across.[24]

Nominating petitions were required in order to get the names of candidates on the ballot, but signers had certainly not been lacking. All records for signatures on such petitions were smashed, the state office candidates having from 15,000 to 24,000, while legislative candidates usually had at least ten times as many as were needed. Petitions flowed in to headquarters from every corner of the state for sorting, and when sent to the secretary of state, made a most imposing wagon load.* At last Arthur Townley could answer with pride the question, "Who named these candidates?": "The League candidates are now not only the candidates of the League. They are not only the candidates of the farmers. They are the candidates of the people of the whole state." [25]

On June 8, President Townley issued a call for precinct meetings to be held on June 21 at 2 P.M. in every precinct, for the purpose of laying plans to "canvass every nook and corner" and get out the vote. Thus, said Townley, the farmers can show the politicians that others can win at their game.[26] Writing to friends in town was also suggested, in order to "tell them the truth."

Meanwhile the opposition had not been dormant. Several business houses and banks sent out sheaves of letters to customers, agents, and associates telling of the "red menace" to the state,[27] while the newspaper barrage was unceasing. Of all the lengthy attacks on the "carpetbaggers," it was only natural that A. C. Townley should come in for the lion's share. Many of these were directed at his earlier failure at Beach, which was cited as an example of financial irresponsibility.

* The comparative party strengths were evident here, Frazier having approximately 20,000 signatures (only Republicans), Casey 3000 (only Democrats), and the Supreme Court candidates 24,000 (nonpartisan ballot).

The emphasis became so persistent that the *Leader* on June 22 printed a vigorous defense of Townley written by J. W. Brinton, mayor of Beach. Townley, he said, was not an issue in the campaign, but a man publicly called a crook and a deadbeat at least deserved a rebuttal in his behalf. After recounting the story of Townley's experiences in 1912, Brinton argued that the businessmen who gave Townley seed and machinery on credit were plungers just as much as he, gambling on his success. All of them lost together and only because of the weather and the market drop; the only crooked dealing was on the market. It was hardly a deadbeat trick, he asserted, to refuse to go through bankruptcy proceedings and give all one's property and possessions to his creditors. Thousands fail in business every year, including the *Bismarck Tribune* (a stanch opposition paper), yet they are not denounced as crooks for that reason. It was significant, he pointed out in conclusion, that although Townley had failed several years before, no one had called him a crook until he started the Nonpartisan League.[28]

The *Courier-News*, with a bit of the wind out of its sails, changed its course momentarily and took a swing at David Coates, then editing the *Leader*, instead:

But while jmbrinton was secured to emit a paid advertisement in the evening paper trying to rehabilitate Townley's reputation, nobody has been found nervey enough or rotten enough to apologize for Coatesy or to try to explain away his record . . . the job seemed too rank even for jmbrinton—and that is some putrid.[29]

Apparently not wanting in ideas, the anti-League forces in early June came up with a new wrinkle. "Leagues" having proven more than a little successful, there blossomed forth on June 5 the "North Dakota Good Government League," the purpose of which was announced to be the presenting to the people of the state "accurate information concerning the propaganda that is being fostered by the North Dakota Farmers' Nonpartisan Political League." The founders, it was said, were "substantial farmers and businessmen" who were not yet ready to turn the state over to the "carpetbaggers." [30]

Originating in Cass County (Fargo), efforts were made at once to spread units into towns throughout the state. Thousands of leaflets and full-page advertisements were utilized, while application blanks were mailed to businessmen and bankers in every city and village.[31]

Shaving the Farmer

A typical opposition view of the Nonpartisan League and the incomprehensible behavior of North Dakota's farmers (from the *Red Flame*).

Though the League valiantly strove to discover just who constituted the membership, the only names disclosed were those of Morton Page, a land speculator, mortgage dealer, and insurance broker, frequently called the richest man in North Dakota, as president, H. G. Carpenter, secretary of the Insurance Federation of North Dakota, as vice president, and Norman Black, former editor of the *Herald*, as executive secretary.[32] When the *Leader* stated the results of its investigation, the *Courier-News* replied huffily that though carpetbaggers could not be expected to understand, "to those who have been in the state long enough to know its people the names of Morton Page and Norman B. Black are guarantees sufficient of the stability and personnel behind." After a time, when better organized "the names of the members will be given to the public, and all the books and finances will be open to inspection."[33] What the objection was to doing so at the time remained a bit obscure; moreover, the promised publicity never appeared.

The copying of the Nonpartisan League tactics was so precise as to

69

be slightly humorous, despite its deadly earnestness. The organization was formed, said the publicity:

. . . not for the purpose of furthering the interests of any political party, but for the purpose of electing to office men who are known to stand for sound government principles, whether they be democrats, republicans, progressives, or what not . . .
The Good Government League should be just as nonpartisan as the so-called Non-Partisan League.[34]

Just who was included in the term "what not" was never elucidated.

The *Forum*, still striving manfully to stay on the fence, had commented naively that it understood the new organization was not going to mix actively in politics, but merely let the people know the "facts." As long as it continued on that basis it could perform a great service, but, the newspaper concluded sagely, it would fail "if it lowers itself to tactics of personal abuse and vilification."[35] The *Leader* dismissed the whole matter as just "a new mask for the old gang," and so the farmers considered it.

Beginning with June 1, the *Leader* carried a full front-page "pep-talk" by A. C. Townley each week, with the central theme of certain victory if every member worked his hardest and voted on primary day. There were also pages of reports from the field—dozens of letters from members oozing confidence in every line. Again and again the *Leader* emphasized the absolute necessity of nominating the legislative candidates; whatever else might be accomplished, there must be control of the legislature. For months, the names of former state legislators who had voted against the farmers' interests had been publicized, while in the weeks immediately preceding the primaries paragraph summaries of the records of legislators were furnished upon the request of members.

The *Leader* pointed out that election of all League senatorial candidates was a necessity if that body was to be controlled and warned that the "old gang" was concentrating its efforts on the Senate contests.[36] Nevertheless, in view of the extreme unlikelihood of a clean sweep it seems that the possibility of a Senate stumbling block should have been much more thoroughly impressed upon the minds of the members in order to forestall disappointment in the event all were not elected.

By mid-June even the *Fargo Forum*, the only city daily maintaining any show of impartiality, decided to string along with the "safe and sane" candidates and commenced promoting the Burdick group in both editorials and news stories. With the increasing seriousness of United States–Mexican relations and the consequent calling out of the national guard, the *Forum* as well as a number of other papers suddenly discovered what appeared to be a handy solution to the problem of unifying the League opposition on a single candidate. They professed to feel that Colonel Fraine, as head of the state militia, was "called to a higher duty" than a mere governorship, and should consequently withdraw.[37] According to the League, in the extensive newspaper support of Burdick the "old gang," knowing that Burdick was generally well liked in the rural areas, was merely attempting to split the farmer vote in the hope that Fraine, the Stalwart, could thus be nominated. A cartoon of a barber shop quartet, consisting of Big Biz and his satellites, rendering the "Song of the Kept Press" (to the tune of "You Wore a Tulip") drove home the point:

> You vote for Burdick,
> Your sweet Usher Burdick,
> And we'll vote for Colonel Fraine.
> Split up your ballots,
> Your own sacred ballots,
> And we'll be in power again.[38]

In actual fact, however, Fraine was so far out of the race by the primary time that his campaign committee found it necessary to publish an advertisement stating that the colonel was no quitter and that any rumor that he had withdrawn was completely unfounded.[39]

The *Leader* throughout the month of June was devoted almost solely to campaigning, both by providing detailed instructions and by whipping up the victory spirit. Whole pages of sample ballots were printed, and emphasis was placed on the fact that no national or local candidates had been endorsed. The rash of persons claiming League support for this or that position was almost too much to cope with. Provision was also made for obtaining quick returns from the rural areas by printing blanks for poll watchers to return.

One of the boldest strokes in campaign strategy was the Frazier "Victory Special," a train which from June 22 through June 27 carried the gubernatorial candidate over the entire Great Northern and Northern Pacific systems in North Dakota, making stops at virtually every crossroads town. Some were scheduled for only a few minutes, others for hours, but in every case there were speeches, and for overnight stops there were mammoth rallies. A special feature was the provision whereby any member could, by purchasing a regular ticket, travel on the train as far as he wished, usually to the nearest large town in order to participate in the longer meetings. Despite the chilly rain which fell during most of the trip, eager and enthusiastic crowds made it a huge success.[40] Its progress, however, was studiously ignored by the city press.

Lynn Frazier proved himself a magnificent farmers' candidate—he was so clearly one of them. "He was blessed by the substantial figure and confident pose of a statesman," said Jim Manahan. "He looked like a bishop . . ." The farmers drove for miles to hear him: "He stood before them sunburned and bald-headed. His voice was firm and persuasive. He spoke briefly and the tired farmers loved him." [41]

Burdick also made a speaking tour of the state, but, though he conducted an active campaign, in his heart he was not fundamentally opposed to the League or to the League program, and he frequently complimented the organization on its advocacy of exemption of farm improvements from taxation, as well as other items, taking issue only on state-owned mills and elevators.[42] While his associates attacked the League leaders and candidates, Burdick himself spoke highly of Frazier and did not stoop to tactics of personal abuse. Commenting on this election years later (1944), Usher L. Burdick stated his position of 1916 in this manner (speaking in the third person):

After campaigning for two weeks he dropped out of the race. It was evident that the League was stealing the show; moreover, being in full sympathy with the farmers in their uprising against the "interests" he had no heart for a fight against their new organization. Townley, recognizing him as a staunch friend of the farmers, had offered him the League's endorsement for the United States Senate, but his old Progressive Republican friends . . . would not consent to such a shift and he felt he had no choice but to stand by his friends and remain as candidate for Governor on the Progressive Republican ticket.[43] *

* In truth, he conducted an active though moderate campaign and in no sense "dropped out." Gaston says that Townley considered Burdick as a possibility for the League gubernatorial endorsement, but decided against him because he was unwilling to go all the way on the League program (*Nonpartisan League*, p. 103). Langer (*Nonpartisan League*, p. 23) insists it was because Burdick was unwilling to be bossed, leaving the reader to wonder if the implication is that Mr. Langer, in accepting endorsement for attorney general, *was* willing to be bossed. Townley says he felt endorsement of Burdick would have been equivalent to turning the

In the heat of the last days, the *Courier-News*, the *Herald*, and their satellites redoubled their activities, with charges that Frazier had promised appointments to various unsavory characters, that he was a direc-tor of a grain dealers' association which opposed cooperatives, and so on.[44] The *Courier-News*, in printing lists of candidates, established a dichotomy between those endorsed by the League, "so-called Republicans," and the "good men and true" who were not "suspected of being affiliated in any way with that organization," [45] meanwhile giving front-page prominence to a letter from one D. L. Campbell, publisher of the *Northwood Gleaner*:

With the help of the Nonpartisan Bleeder he [Czar Townley] has managed to hypnotize quite a few of them [farmers], who seem blind to the fact that the farmer, organized or unorganized, has always been the controlling factor in this, a purely agricultural state, and that our state legislatures have been largely composed of farmers, and that good, honest, old Roger Allin, of Grafton, North Dakota, left the plow to become governor of North Dakota, and gave the state a [sic] administration that was just passable—as good as could have been expected from a man untrained in business and intricate problems of statehood. Frazier, unpledged, and free, would probably do as well, but subject to Townley and his gang, his election would be the gravest menace that North Dakota has ever faced.[46]

Even the influence of the Catholic Church was thrown against the challengers. A letter in German signed by Vincent Wehrle, bishop of the Bismarck diocese, was sent to his people, and published in *Volksfreund*, the official organ of the North Dakota German Catholic Union. Bishop Wehrle condemned the organization as "the most partisan league imaginable, consisting of the most unprincipled office seekers." Townley, he said, was an insolvent debtor "highly esteemed only by those who know him from recent acquaintance," while J. Arthur Williams, a League organizer, was branded as "a free lover who believes that human beings should live together like animals." Following similar engaging sketches of various League officials, he strongly appealed to all Germans and especially to Catholics not to follow such leaders, who were "all Socialists and infidels." [47]

On June 25, the *Courier-News*, calling Burdick's campaign the great-

League over to him, since he already had a large following. As it was, many of his old supporters had now paid their money to see that someone else was elected. (Interview, Sept. 23, 1948.)

73

est and most effective in the past twenty years, quoted Torger Sinness, the Burdick campaign manager, to the effect that the "Nonpartisan tide" had been stemmed, which would result "in his actually beating Frazier outside the towns." [48] A news story on primary day let it be known that League strength had been greatly overestimated, and that "it is now believed" that many of their candidates would be defeated. Editorially, however, the paper was less sanguine, virtually conceding defeat in a "sour grapes" manner by advocating abolition of the primary system, and thus seemingly putting party tradition above the will of the voters:

Today will always be remembered as momentous in the history of North Dakota for it will determine whether or not it is possible for revolutionaries and unprincipled adventurers to seize the organization of an old, established political party, subvert its every principle and use it as a tool to accomplish its own designs . . .

There must and will be a revision of the laws guarding the sacredness of the ballot and of the method of nominations for office. Provision must be made for conventions which shall represent the voters who actually adhere to the principles of a political party . . .[49]

Exactly who constituted the Republican party of North Dakota if not the farmers of the state is an interesting question.

On the morning of primary day League headquarters was plunged in gloom. It was a day of violent storms—bridges were down, streams were swollen, communications were wrecked, and roads in the rural areas were deep with mud. It was in fact reported to be one of the worst downpours and electrical storms ever seen, and it was clear that the vote would be cut materially. Prospects looked far from bright, despite the fact that the *Leader*, apparently having had premonitions of disaster, had endeavored to prepare its readers for just such an eventuality:

The enemy is hoping it will rain . . . You can fool him. You can wade through mud. You can brave the thunder and lightning if it comes. Farmers are not fair weather fighters . . . Remember, everything has been preliminary to this one great day, Wednesday, June 28. That is the day for action. The rest has just been rehearsal.[50]

With wires down all over the state, the returns trickled in with maddening slowness. Burdick carried town after town, and Thursday morning the *Courier-News* cautiously headlined "Burdick Leading for Governor in Cities." [51] The course of the morning, however, told a different story as a deluge of rural votes swept Frazier overwhelmingly to the fore, and by nightfall it was clear that every League-endorsed man on the state ticket had been nominated and that most of the legislative candidates had been successful. Many a country precinct showed only one or two votes for Burdick and Fraine, while in a number there were actually clean sweeps for the League. Frequently there were cases of townships which voted almost solidly for the League surrounding villages which voted down the League candidates.[52] Stories were common of farmers who had tied their clothes on their backs to swim across flooded streams, while others had driven as far as twenty-four miles around impassable areas to get to the polling places.[53]

The final count showed Frazier with a clear majority over the combined votes of his three opponents and a plurality of 15,884 over Burdick. He carried forty-six out of fifty-three counties, Burdick getting Cass (Fargo), Richland (Wahpeton), Williams, and Sheridan, the latter by only fifty votes, and Fraine taking McIntosh, Sioux, and Stark. The vote was Lynn J. Frazier, 39,246; Usher L. Burdick, 23,362; John H. Fraine, 9,780; and George J. Smith, 2,981. The other state office candidates had majorities of approximately two to one, except Casey, who was unopposed but received 3000 more votes than any other unopposed Democratic candidate. Grace, who stood lowest of the three League candidates for the Supreme Court, was 4500 votes above the highest of the other four.[54] The League, having endorsed candidates in forty-four of the state's forty-nine legislative districts, had succeeded in nominating 17 out of 22 for the Senate and 87 out of 98 for the House.[55]

Sweet as was the victory, the *Devils Lake Journal* could not resist one final thrust:

LOST—A "Good Government League."

Description: Bears the earmarks of a jack-ass, run down at the heels, has crooked legs, a big paunch, a wobbly walk, distressed looking eyes and a tail worn hairless from switching Non-partisan stingers. Branded on the right shoulder L.B.H. and on the hip A.McK. When last seen it was in charge of Col. N. B. Black, from whom it escaped during the big stampede on June 28, 1916. Any information leading to recovery will be thankfully received by Morton Page or Parson Guild, Fargo, this state. Supposition is that it has wandered into the corral of the Insurance Grafters from which it is supposed to have been raised, although it may have fallen off the Red river bridge and drowned. While it looked like the devil, it was perfectly harmless.[56]

Daybreak on the Prairie

IT HAS often been stated that the Republican party of North Dakota was captured in 1916 by the Nonpartisan League. It would actually be fully as correct to say that the Republican party was captured
by the Republican voters of the state, who were using a political party
as it is theoretically supposed to be used—as a vehicle for carrying out
the will of the majority of its members. A. C. Townley and his circle
of close associates did not vote the candidates into office; that was done
by the farmers of North Dakota, and it is hardly open to question that
those farmers were thoroughly and enthusiastically in favor of the
League program.

With the overwhelming League victory in the primaries, the tactics
of the opposition were not slow in changing. Though there was little
letup on the leaders, the vicious attacks upon the organization were
largely replaced by calls for cooperation of all factions for the good
of North Dakota, and the farmer himself was no longer a "sucker." As
the *Leader* sarcastically put it: "Now he [the farmer] has become,
among some of these same Gang sheets, an "honest yeoman"; rather
stupid, it is true, and in need of fatherly advice (from the Old Gang)
but still a well-meaning sort of cuss." [1]

The *Fargo Forum*, as a loyal Republican paper not bothered by too
strong convictions on either side, concluded that since the League men
were now the Republican candidates * they were deserving of support,
but the other city dailies died hard. The *Courier-News* henceforth
devoted itself strictly to national affairs in the realm of politics, pro-

* Excepting Casey of course.

viding tremendous Hughes coverage, but no mention of the League for several months. In September, the Reverend Mr. Guild, apparently tiring of the battle and faced with a continuing loss of circulation, sold his paper to two young newspapermen from another state. In November, they, in turn, sold their controlling interest to the Nonpartisan Publishing Company, which represented the League in publishing the *Leader*, and the League's first daily began a long and important career.[2]

The *Herald* made no bones about the fact that it deeply regretted the outcome of the primaries, but it was not yet ready to endorse Democrats in opposition, and was hopeful that the League really did not intend to put its program into effect. Backing water a bit, it forgot about the "pledged" candidates long enough to remark that many were "estimable men" and that the character of the government depended upon them rather than upon the League leaders. Jerry Bacon, however, was no man to give up the fight. Apparently frustrated in hoping that the *Leader* would attack the calling out of the national guard for Mexican service, the editor of the *Grand Forks Herald* resorted to a "sin of omission":

There is not a syllable with reference to the calling out of the guard. There is no word of cheer and good will for the young men who have started on an expedition from which, it may be, some of them will not return; not a word of comfort for parents who have smiled bravely as they have bidden their sons goodbye . . . The *Leader* is pursuing its sinister policy of striving to create enmity and dissension.[3]

Many a small-business man had begun to see the light on June 28, and League supporters blossomed in a number of previously barren spots. Not a few, however, had divined the trend in advance. The business and professional men of New Rockford on June 26 had pledged their support and cooperation, while a similar spirit was shown in Bottineau, Valley City, Minot, and Jamestown.[4] In all those places there was a relatively favorable press.

Despite the *Devils Lake Journal*'s obituary, the Good Government League proved itself in subsequent months to be at least partially alive. After the primaries, however, it claimed not to be attacking the Nonpartisan League; it was simply an organization working for "sane" government on nonpartisan lines and against state ownership.

On August 8 Usher Burdick finally got around to cautiously congratulating Frazier on his victory and the fairness of his campaign, saying:

77

I differed with you on a question of principle only and now that you have won I hope your program will work to the benefit of the great majority of the people of the state.

Under the primary law you are entitled to the support of the party and if I can do you any good in the fall campaign I shall be glad to do what I can.[5]

A fairly large number of stand-pat Republicans, former Fraine and Burdick supporters, at various times wrote Frazier pledging their support as Republicans, but the *Grand Forks Herald* and its cohorts asked and gave no quarter:

The IWW is a menace to the country . . . because the spirit which inspires it is class antagonism. The Non-Partisan League is the creature of the same spirit. Without the appeal to class it could not have existed. And the appeal to class is as dangerous when it is made the basis of action by one class as when it actuates another.[6]

The farmers' picnics which had proved so successful before the primaries were not abandoned, but were scheduled throughout the summer, the brunt of the speaking being borne by Lynn Frazier, with considerable assistance from Jim Manahan, the crusading Minnesota attorney and former congressman, and of course the regular speaking staff. In town after town Frazier's obvious sincerity and strength of character made friends of many of those who had previously been uncertain. The *Bowman Citizen*, for example, commented editorially:

After listening to Mr. Frazier speak one cannot help but feel that, in choosing him to head the ticket, the farmers of this state must have been inspired, for it would have been impossible to have found another man, farmer or otherwise, with a combination of qualities that would have better fitted him for the leadership of a great agricultural state.[7]

It will be remembered that there were a few districts in which no candidates for the legislature had been endorsed by the League, owing to limited organizational work in certain counties up to that time, and that in some others one or more endorsed men had failed to be nominated. This deficiency was in large part made up during the course of the summer and fall by the process of holding district caucuses for the purpose of endorsing candidates in those districts to run as Independents or often as Democrats where there was no Democratic candidate.[8]

The outgoing administration, now in something of a "lame duck" position, showed at the end of August that it still had a few tricks up its sleeve. There was an anticipated state deficit for the year of $300,000, but the State Board of Equalization on August 31 calmly voted a flat reduction of 10 per cent in the assessed valuation of the state, amounting to about $30,000,000, though both the auditor and the treasurer opposed the action.[9] This was praised by the anti-League press as an economy made possible by efficient administration, but in reality it amounted to cutting revenue in the face of one of the state's biggest deficits, the apparent purpose being to saddle the next administration with an unusual financial burden and to place the onus of raising taxes on the Nonpartisan League administration.

After its initial success in the 1916 primaries, the League sent a few representatives into the three states bordering North Dakota—Minnesota, South Dakota, and Montana—to determine whether or not expansion seemed feasible. Much interest had been expressed in these and other states, but the League leadership was uncertain as to whether the local situations were such that the League might prosper. The reports were to the effect that the League was needed and could successfully organize in those states, but that it would meet a forewarned and much stronger resistance.[10] The seed was planted but there was little cultivation for the time being.

The Nonpartisan League moved into Canada in July of 1916 when one S. E. Haight returned to his Saskatchewan farm after working with the League in North Dakota for some months. He eagerly spread the League idea and a formal organization came into being the same month. In this area ideas and men crossed the international boundary with ease, and the grievances of the farmers in the Canadian prairie provinces were essentially similar to those of farmers on the northern prairies of the United States. In Saskatchewan and Alberta the farmers were eager for organization and the League spread rapidly, but it made little headway in Manitoba where the old parties were more firmly entrenched and the more conservative Grain Growers' Association was strong.

The League in the Canadian provinces kept closely in touch with the movement in the United States, and was in most ways virtually a carbon copy in terms of the techniques utilized. There was the same use of salesmanship methods, of postdated checks, and of Fords; the same slogans; and even the same kinds of charges by the opposition. The newspapers, the *Non-Partisan Leader* (Sask.) and the *Alberta*

Non-Partisan, were much like their North Dakota counterpart, and in fact regularly reprinted articles and cartoons, simply substituting the Canadian Pacific for the Great Northern, Canadian banking houses for Wall Street, and so on. The platforms of the Canadian Leagues proposed sweeping reforms, foreshadowing to a very real degree the Cooperative Commonwealth Federation and Social Credit movements of later years.[11]

An event of major importance in North Dakota in the early fall was the capture of the Republican State Central Committee by the League. The members of the committee under the primary law were chosen in the counties by county committees elected by the party voters. Though the League had made no fight whatsoever to obtain committeemen favorable to the program, the farmers in a majority of the counties had seen to it without instructions that the "right" men were elected. When the committee assembled in Bismarck on September 6 for the principal purpose of drawing up a platform, it was evident that Leaguers held a majority of a few votes, but as most of them were unused to political maneuvering, they allowed the former chairman to be made temporary chairman. The error was discovered when they found that this permitted him to name the platform committee, to which he appointed four "Stalwarts" and three Leaguers.

With the League members outvoted by this margin on every issue, the platform as proposed by the committee left out most of the League reforms, but the minority held up its presentation long enough to call in Lynn Frazier, who had already publicly stated his belief that the party should accept the "voice of the people." [12] Frazier told the committee flatly that regardless of what the committee or the meeting did, he stood squarely on the League platform, and recommended majority and minority reports, giving the whole meeting a chance to choose.

The platform committee finally compromised by including part of the League planks, but on the floor the Leaguers, under the leadership of Ray McKaig, fought for and got every League plank but one. The one omitted concerned a state rural credit law, and was passed over in order to give a new federal law of the same general nature a fair trial. On the election of permanent officers, the Leaguers also stuck together, electing William Lemke state chairman, Ray McKaig secretary, and Halvor P. Halvorson treasurer.[13] Thus, almost by chance, the actual machinery of the state's dominant political party had come into the hands of the farmers' organization.

The Democratic State Central Committee, meeting at almost the same time, was not to be outdone. Not mistaking the trend of the majority opinion, they agreed on a platform including state-owned terminal elevators, compulsory hail insurance, good roads legislation to cooperate with the new federal grant system, and a Torrens title registration system, despite accusations at the meeting that the party was deserting to the League.[14] This turn of affairs was the last straw, causing the *Courier-News* to throw up its hands and comment sarcastically: ". . . both candidates for United States Senator seem in love with the offspring of Townley's brain, and both parties are apparently under the control of that movement . . . Meanwhile the campaign rages— over what?"[15]

The ineffectiveness of the existing state hail insurance program and the need for a compulsory system were pointed up sharply in September with the announcement that only 40 cents on the dollar would be paid on losses. This was the lowest yet, the previous low having been 55 cents in 1912, when hail losses had been almost as heavy, and the *Leader* was thus provided with much ready-made ammunition.[16]

Fear suddenly stalked through the wheat fields of North Dakota with the issuance of a simple statement on August 7 by the Minneapolis Chamber of Commerce: "It is expected that the blight and black rust may make necessary some important revision of the grain grading standards."[17]

A short crop due to rust, floods, and generally adverse weather conditions would normally have brought the farmers higher prices, and it looked to the *Leader* as if the Chamber of Commerce was moving early to head off such an eventuality by getting the Minnesota State Board of Grain Appeals to raise the standards.

Although the Chamber was successful with most of its demands, it shortly took matters into its own hands and established four new "feed" grades not included in the Minnesota standard grades. The implication was that these grades were fit only for feed and not for milling, and they were consequently purchased at considerably lower prices. It was not long, however, before Dr. Ladd and his experimental mill were back in the limelight, for he proceeded to show that the so-called feed wheats could be blended in almost any quantity with other wheats and still produce good bread. And without any question, that was exactly what the mills were doing. As a matter of fact, the gluten content in these feed grades was found to be especially good, and Dr. Ladd contended that they were of equal value for flour products.[18]

Perhaps the most striking results of Dr. Ladd's investigations were his computations of comparative profits from the various grades, as shown below.[19] It was indeed not difficult to ascertain the reason for so

	Cost of Wheat	Receipts from Mill Products	Percentage of Gain
No. 1 Northern ..	$1.732	$2.1031	21.4
No. 4	1.45	2.0486	41.1
Feed B	1.14	2.0322	78.2
Feed D	.94	1.9914	111.9

much low grading. If the milling of No. 1 wheat was considered a profitable enterprise, what did the milling of Feed D constitute? It was natural that the League should make capital of these findings, pointing out for example that it was possible for a carload of "Feed D" purchased in Fargo for $653.01 to bring $2107.03 when its mill products were retailed in Fargo.[20] The 1915 crop had been unusually large, and even though prices had been low many farmers had money enough to join the League. The poor 1916 crop in a sense continued to play into the hands of the League, as the actions of the dealers provided a tremendous propaganda weapon and every farmer could readily feel the pinch.

In mid-September events occurred which were later to become widespread practice throughout the state. The League farmers of Stutsman County formed a stock company and took over the *Kensal Progress* and *Kensal Journal*, to be operated as one paper under the name of the *Progress*. This action was shortly followed by that of Bottineau County farmers, who formed a cooperative publishing company and bought the *Bottineau Courant*.[21] All three papers had been stanch League supporters from the first, so that the change of ownership was apparently simply in the nature of an investment by the farmers, plus insurance that pressure would not be brought to bear to force a change of policy in the future.

With Lynn Frazier and most of his associates on the state ticket looking more and more like "sure things" in November, the campaign during the fall months boiled down for the most part to a single issue. The Good Government League and the opposition press decided to concentrate their efforts on keeping control of the state Supreme Court, and the three League candidates were subjected to both abuse and ridicule. With the lines thus drawn, the *Leader* did not hesitate to pick up the gauntlet, and the real battle of the whole campaign was waged over those contests. Since the judges were elected on a separate nonpartisan judicial ballot, the chances were good that it would be neglected by many voters. The other three candidates for the positions on the five-man court were incumbents, and on the basis of past decisions the League was certain that they could be counted upon to join with their old colleagues to strike down any "radical" acts of a League legislature.[22]

Throughout the fall months almost the entire political emphasis of the *Leader* was upon the absolute necessity of electing the League judicial candidates if the work of the legislature was not to be thwarted. Members were told that they were the most important on the ballot and that they should be voted for *first*. The Good Government League, known more familiarly to Nonpartisan Leaguers as the "goos-goos" or "good-gougers," spoke in anguished tones of attempts to corrupt the courts and of trying to prevent the judges from the "fearless exercise of their duty," but the *Leader* countered with a number of stories on what it considered to be reactionary and biased recent decisions, designed to show that the court did not, in fact, consist of impartial arbiters above the smoke of political battle. Much criticism arose from a statement alleged to have been made by Townley at the Fargo convention in the spring, in which he was quoted as saying: "We've got to have a Supreme Court that will hold constitutional the laws we pass in the legislature." [23] While this was a thoroughly practical view, not at all uncommon in actual practice, its public proclamation was perhaps a bit impolitic.

An event of early fall contributed to the heat of the judicial campaign. Representatives from the city of New Rockford had been agitating for approximately a year for the removal of the state capital from Bismarck to that city, and since a constitutional amendment of 1914 made possible further amendments by popular initiative,[24] a petition for that purpose was presented to Secretary of State Hall in mid-summer. Everything appearing to be in order, Hall published the necessary notices to the effect that the proposed amendment would be submitted to the voters at the fall election. Immediately suit was brought by a group of Bismarck real estate owners to restrain the secretary of state from placing the proposal upon the ballot, and on September 11 a decision of far-reaching importance was handed down by the state Supreme Court. The court held that the words "at least 25% of the legal voters" meant any amount above 25 per cent which the legislature desired to fix, and further proclaimed that the amending procedure established by the 1914 amendment "is not, and was not intended to be, self-executing; but is only a mandate to succeeding legislatures to provide laws whereunder the Constitution may be amended by initiative petition." [25]

This decision not only shattered the hopes of the New Rockford Capital Removal Association, but it also dealt a body blow to League hopes for speedy constitutional amendments regarding public ownership after the fall elections. The *Leader* lashed repeatedly at what it termed fantastic logic and hairsplitting legalisms of the so-called "New Rockford case," [26] and the net result was probably at least a further stimulus to the campaign for the election of the League candidates for the court.

During the early fall months the three League candidates were given the opportunity in the *Leader* to air their views on the function of the judiciary, and the result was a highly unusual exposition of jurisprudential thinking for the times. Birdzell viewed the courts as political bodies which must of necessity keep pace with modern thought and human progress, Robinson discussed his favorite theme of preference for the substance of justice over legal technicalities, and Grace propounded a doctrine of the equality of the branches of government as opposed to a superiority of the courts. [27]

Following the previous practice, Townley issued a call for precinct meetings to be held on October 31 for the purpose of unifying the spirit of the members and in order to make plans and arrangements for the last week's drive in each locality. Meanwhile, the *Leader* was going all out in its efforts to get the voters to "Remember Casey." Every cartoon showing the candidates and virtually every political article and editorial carried the words "Remember Casey," while sample ballots always showed his picture with a large arrow in the Democratic column. In a full-page article on October 26, Townley stressed the point that the attitude of the Republican League members would be ". . . the test of *your fidelity* to the principles of the League . . . For you Mr. Casey represents the *Non-partisan idea*, the principle of choosing the *man fit for the job*, the man devoted to your interests, *without regard to old party lines.*" [28]

While the campaign for Casey was carried on in the *Leader*'s editorial pages, other pages carried political advertisements of the Republican State Central Committee, signed by William Lemke as state chairman, known to be a key figure in the League, which as usual pleaded for a straight ticket, including John Steen for treasurer.[29] Thus the capture of the State Central Committee turned out to have definite defects as well as merits, for many farmers were unquestionably confused despite the efforts of the *Leader* to make it clear that paid advertisements did not constitute official policy. Trying to pull both nonpartisan voters and the straight-ticket Republicans into the same fold provided its headaches.

Furthermore, with the Republican advertisements combining the names of the national candidates with the state ticket, it was constantly necessary to re-emphasize the fact that the League had endorsed no national candidates. The state Republican party, it was said, was now committed to the League program, but the League was committed to nothing Republican.[30] It was, moreover, no help to the appearance of impartiality for Frazier to come out publicly in support of Hughes, for Lemke and others to participate regularly in Hughes rallies, and for Jim Manahan to stump the state in behalf of Hughes. In the face of such seemingly inconsistent actions, the *Leader*'s constant warnings that the "old gang" was trying to divide the farmers by reviving the party spirit must have lost much of their effect. At least, however, the publication of the Republican state platform must have given something of a jolt to conservative party members in other states.

Henry Teigan, executive secretary of the League, lent a bit of variety to this picture. While the League's state candidates were stumping for Hughes, he was assiduously devoting such time as he could spare to the cause of Allan Benson, the Socialist nominee for President. A former state chairman of the Socialist party and once editor of the *Iconoclast*, he now acted as chairman of the Benson campaign committee for the state. His principal activity in this connection seems to have been the solicitation of funds from Socialist friends for the purpose of sending copies of a special edition of the *Appeal to Reason* to as many Leaguers as possible.[31]

During the last week before the election there was a constant flood of reports and claims that the League was supporting this or that national or local candidate, though all were steadfastly denied. The most persistent concerned the Republican candidate for the United States Senate, Porter J. McCumber, and though Theodore Saloutos has recently repeated the statement that the League "diverted sufficiently to support McCumber for re-election to the United States Senate," [32] there appears to be no evidence to substantiate such a claim.

It is stoutly maintained by some persons yet today that the League's 1916 campaign chest received a substantial contribution from the McKenzie forces in return for a pledge that the League would run no candidate against McCumber. Some attribute the deal to Townley and others to Lemke. Townley flatly denies that this ever occured, though he says he would have welcomed any good contributions by the time the campaign was shaping to a close.[33] The League never had any intention of entering national politics at this time, preferring to restrict itself to state activities, and it had publicly so proclaimed for months. It is conceivable, though impossible to prove, that in later years McKenzie did give some secret backing to the North Dakota League. If so, it was simply because of his undying hatred of the Progressives, since his economic interests were obviously quite contrary to League policy.*

The Republican city dailies found themselves in a most embarrassing position, not desiring to support either Democrats or League Republicans. While the *Courier-News* devoted itself solely to the national campaign, the *Forum* confined its treatment of state issues to straight reporting with no editorial comment. The *Herald* went so far as to print the entire Republican ticket at the head of its editorial columns throughout October, but it had little to say on the state candidates except to hope for the best.

A week before election day a virtual tempest arose over a one-column plate advertisement sent to weekly papers of the state by the

* Townley says he heard this rumor frequently but had no definite information on it. As to the attitude of the McKenzie ring, he comments, "Between two groups of S.O.B.'s they liked the Progressives least." (Interview, Sept. 23, 1948.)

"Independent Publicity Bureau" of Bismarck, praising Democratic candidates Wilson, Burke, and McArthur, and roasting Frazier at some length. John Burke, the former governor, for the past two years treasurer of the United States, and now candidate for United States senator, had been extremely careful not to make any attempt to discredit Frazier, especially since McArthur's campaign for governor was considered hopeless. Therefore, while Republicans called this simply Democratic dirt-slinging, the Democrats vigorously denounced it as a "dirty Republican trick" to make them lose farmer support for their national candidates.[34] Half-page advertisements on the subject from both sides filled the papers from then until election day, but no one seemed able to put his finger on the "Independent Publicity Bureau." It might be noted, however, that the technique of building up old-party antagonisms was well calculated to aid in splitting the solidarity of the farmers. The denial of responsibility by officials of both parties was more than likely completely honest.

By the close of the 1916 campaign the Nonpartisan League claimed a membership of approximately 40,000,[35] while its income had amounted to $270,000. Of this, some $50,000 had been spent for "Tin Henry's" for organizers, $40,000 for campaign literature, and most of the rest for various items ranging from salaries of speakers and organizers and office rent to campaign activities like the Frazier "Victory Special."[36] The battle, indeed, would not be lost from lack of effort.

On November 7 there were no storms to cut down the vote and the farmers marched to the polls to ring up once again a resounding victory. Lynn Frazier carried the state by better than four to one, winning every county, and receiving the greatest majority ever given a governor of North Dakota, while every state candidate except Casey, who lost by 200 votes, had overwhelming leads.* The League Supreme Court candidates ran well ahead of their opponents; Grace, having the lowest vote of the League candidates, was 13,000 votes ahead of the highest of the other three.[37]

Though nonpartisanship was notable in many areas, and especially as it concerned the legislative candidates, where in precinct after pre-

---

* The vote for governor was Frazier (R), 87,665; McArthur (D), 20,351; Johnson (S), 2615 (*1919 Legislative Manual, State of North Dakota*, p. 256). For treasurer, Steen (R), 51,349; Casey (D), 51,149 (*ibid.*, p. 258).

cinct there was an almost identical vote for two or more League candidates on opposing tickets, Casey's defeat would seem to indicate that the nonpartisan spirit had not yet completely triumphed over Republicanism. Actually he probably received most of the League votes and he carried a great many of the rural precincts, but of course did not get the "straight ticket" Republicans not affiliated with the League. It was also reported that many who otherwise voted a straight Democratic ticket scratched Casey, while a sizable number who voted for Republican national candidates voted for all the Democrats for state offices except Casey.[38] The fact that he was a Catholic may also have had some effect.*

A number of precincts went so solidly for the League as to be almost unbelievable, an example being the precinct of Sauter in Walsh County. According to the spring registration, there were only five qualified Republican voters in Sauter, yet Frazier received fifty votes to none for his Democratic opponent. The rest of the ticket was practically the same, with Casey winning over Steen by 48 to 2. The fact that this was normally a Democratic precinct was well illustrated by the vote on national candidates: Wilson, 44, Hughes, 6; Burke, 43, McCumber 6.[39]

It is also interesting to note that Frazier apparently received about three fifths of the state's normal Socialist vote, inasmuch as the Socialist gubernatorial candidate received approximately 2600 votes as compared with 5700 for the presidential candidate and 8500 for the candidate for the United States Senate.[40]

McCumber was easily re-elected to the Senate, yet despite the overwhelmingly solid Republican state and congressional victory, President Wilson carried the state by 1735 votes,[41] a result which scarcely the most sanguine Democrat had anticipated. "He kept us out of war" had a tremendously strong appeal in that part of the country, but it is also true that numerous acts of the Wilson administration as well as its general political philosophy found favor with many Leaguers. The secretary of the Republican State Central Committee, who before the election forecast that Hughes would carry the state by 10,000, commented

* Henry Teigan was convinced that Casey would have won had the count been contested, but said League officials did not wish to stir up more antagonism by so doing (Teigan to J. C. Hogan, Monroe, N.Y., Jan. 30, 1917, National Nonpartisan League Papers). Casey was later appointed sergeant-at-arms of the North Dakota House of Representatives.

a year and a half later: "I am convinced today that it would have been a national calamity if Hughes had been elected President. Mr. Wilson recognizes, more so, I believe, than Hughes could have ever done, that this war will be fought in vain unless industrial autocracy in this country is driven out." [42]

League successes at the polls extended to the legislature as well as to the state offices, but while in the lower house 81 Leaguers out of a total membership of 113 had been elected, four senatorial candidates failed to make the grade, which meant that control of that body was not achieved. The *Leader*, however, confidently predicted that the League would have the backing of at least seven holdover senators, thus assuring a majority. The make-up of the two houses was to be as follows: [43]

Senate		House	
Total membership	49	Total membership	113
Holdovers	24	Elected by League	81
Elected by League	18	League Republicans	68
League Republicans	14	League Democrats	13
League Democrats	4	League majority	24
Total Republicans	43	Total Republicans	97
Total Democrats	6	Total Democrats	16

The *Leader* quite naturally expressed its enthusiastic pride and happiness in the final outcome of the election, but its principal theme from that time forward was the big job remaining to be done. Readers were repeatedly warned that this was no time to rest on past laurels, but to bear in mind that the real test of the success of the organization would be whether the farmers could continue to stick together or whether they would gradually drift apart, as had been the case in the earlier movements. The long-heralded "new day" was arriving—would the clouds of strife obscure its glory?

A great victory had been won. The government of the state, said the *Leader*, was at last in the hands of the people. Optimism for the future characterized both League shepherds and the flock, but all was not sweetness and light in North Dakota. There were others who held out a different prospect for the state, their views being aptly expressed by a prominent businessman:

The Nonpartisan League is a band of Socialists, led by an anarchist, bent on the destruction of the country. It will set the state back twenty years, plunge it into an overwhelming debt, and make it the laughing stock of the nation. If it stays in power past the next election most of the businessmen will leave the state and let the damned anarchists run it to suit themselves.

But it won't last that long . . . When they do wake up . . . then they'll come back to us to borrow money to plant and harvest their crops, and when that time comes will be a good opportunity for us to talk to them earnestly about the fallacy of chasing after strange gods every time some soap box orator grafts his living off them by telling them they are being robbed by legitimate business.[44]

As the year 1916 came to a close North Dakota was providing a political phenomenon to make the nation sit up and take notice. Here was an organization, specifically formed for political action, dissociated in principle from any party or parties, yet formulating platforms, pledging support of candidates, campaigning, and then supporting those candidates with such impartiality that the controlling majority of a legislative house consisted of a mixture of Democrats and Republicans. The oft-repeated statement that the states in a federal system of government are valuable political laboratories for the nation was perhaps about to be illustrated.

Yet, despite an initial victory, the League was beset with a multitude of problems even aside from those involved in attempting to put across its legislative program and combating a continuously vigorous opposition. It must strive unendingly to keep united a membership to which the organization had literally been *sold*, and it must educate the farmers in the course of time to see further than just their own pocketbooks at the moment. It must figure out feasible means of coordinating the interests of farmers and laborers, for while organized labor in North Dakota was of insignificant strength, there was always the possibility of expansion. Finally, while rather autocratic control was perhaps necessary to get the organization on its feet, provision must somehow be made for increased democratic participation.

From the beginning the League had proclaimed two basic aims:

(1) To restore the government of the state of North Dakota to the people of the state;
(2) To use the power of the state government to aid in developing the state for the benefit of its citizens and to prevent its exploitation for the benefit of out-siders and to the injury of the people of the state.[45]

The first had presumably been accomplished; the second remained for the future.

In any case, the impossible had happened. The echoes of the 1916 election were heard and felt across half the nation, rocking the inner sanctums of "big business" with their lusty strength. "For the first time," cried the League, "the state capitol was moved from the Ryan Hotel in St. Paul to Bismarck." [46] The "new day in North Dakota," for better or for worse, was dawning. America's most novel political experiment was under way.

Farmers at the Helm

JANUARY 1917 brought bitter cold to Bismarck, but it also brought a new state administration. A farmer sat in the governor's office on capitol hill and farmer legislators, frequently looking a bit ill at ease, had come to "take over." There were some among Bismarck's residents who looked on with amused condescension, while the opposition newspapers indulged in thinly veiled sneers and considerable crude humor. For the most part, however, they carefully continued to direct their attacks at the League leadership rather than at the farmers of the state, and it remained for the editors of the *Saturday Night*, a St. Paul society and theatrical weekly, to express the extremes of class snobbery. It professed to regard with horror the election as governor of a man who kept hogs, one "untrained in the science of government." Slopping hogs, it said, was hardly proper training for a chief executive:

Even China is more careful in her selection of public officials than America. Only the most intelligent, the most carefully educated men in the country are entrusted there with high office, and the same custom holds in the several states of Europe. But in the United States, particularly in the unregenerate rural commonwealths, they elect rustics to the most exalted office in the gift of the state—and seem to be proud of it. That is, such calamities occur in states so fortunate as to be under the yoke of a Nonpartisan League. Unlucky North Dakota! She has our deepest sympathy.[1]

The sympathy was doubtless wasted, for at least the rural residents of this "unregenerate commonwealth" were looking forward eagerly to what "their" legislature might accomplish. The tone of the administration was set early when Governor Frazier promptly announced that the customary inaugural ball would be dispensed with. They were here, he said, for business, and there was no need for pomp and ceremony.* The same seriousness of purpose was expressed by Howard Wood on his election as speaker of the House, when, pledging absolute fairness to all, he urged upon the session its duty to carry out the will of the people, so clearly manifested in the overwhelming November victory.†

The enthusiasm of the Leaguers was sparkling and infectious. At last the chance had come to create a new order, and excited voices talked of a future bright for all mankind. There must be no turning back, no delay. Men must choose their sides; there was no time to "wait and see" —"you are either for us or against us." Nowhere was the unquenchable hope for a new day and the crusading zeal of the moment more strikingly set forth than in the pages of the *Leader*:

The United States is on the verge of one of those great political and economic revolutions that periodically shake nations to their foundations, revise old ways of thinking and doing things and make way for building anew on the ruins of outgrown ideals and institutions. This is to be a peaceful revolution by means of the ballot. It has found its place of incubation in the Northwest states . . . Through years of patient existence by the majority under political wrongs and economic abuses, the explosives that are to burst forth to light the progress of man to a better, broader life are accumulated . . . The fuel is there. The spark has been applied. The fire alarm has been sent in, but the conflagration cannot be stopped.

The tragedy of these movements is the fact that they sweep by so many so-called progressive and liberal-minded people, leaving them high and dry on deserts of doubt . . .

This is no time to be on the fence. The armies of progress are being organized. Their way is lighted by enthusiasm and loyalty to the cause. The bands are playing. The slogans of the people marching on to new and better things fill the air. This inspired army is passing your door. It is marching on to victory as certain as the rising of the sun tomorrow. You cannot wait. Soon its music and its shouting will be to you a faint sound in the distance, as the sound of battle at the front is wafted back to the slacker in the rear. Shall history put you down as a Tory of the new American revolution? We do not know anything of the hesitators and doubters and on-the-fencers of 1776. History has labeled

* Frazier had also been brought up in a strict Methodist faith which did not approve of dancing.
† The House also elected A. E. Bowen chief clerk and Edwin Wood assistant clerk.

every man of that period as a patriot or as a Tory. There was no middle of the road then. There is none now.[2]

Although newly elected officials had always taken office with the beginning of the new year following their election, the capital was stirred when on December 1, 1916, the three new justices of the Supreme Court appeared and demanded their seats. The three judges then sitting refused to vacate, and a stalemate ensued, with no one sure how the matter was to be resolved. Several important cases were to be decided during the month of December, and it was generally assumed that the League was eager to utilize its new majority, particularly in the rehearing of the so-called "Youmans bank case," which involved the closing by the State Banking Board of a Minot bank operated by a stanch League supporter, Grant Youmans.

The attorney general filed a petition in the Supreme Court to determine the date for taking office, but who was to constitute the court to decide the matter? The claimants could hardly sit on their own case, though Robinson contended that they could, and neither could the judges whose seats were being contested. The two holdover judges disqualified themselves on the grounds that the decision would affect them when their terms of office expired. A complete bench of district judges was therefore called, whereupon the claimants announced that they would not recognize the jurisdiction of such a court, and notified the district judges that they would incur their displeasure by sitting. The improvised court sat, nevertheless, ruling against the claimants, and the old court continued through the month of December, among other things denying the petition for rehearing in the Youmans case. There remained some question whether the new judges, when they took their seats, would recognize the actions of the court during December, but the decisions were allowed to stand, and the court subsequently denied two more petitions for rehearings in the Youmans case.[3]

The League, as we have seen, had complete control of the lower house, but control of the Senate depended upon how many holdover senators might be wooed into the League fold. The opposition papers assumed that the Senate would block radical League legislation, and the *Herald* praised the wise precaution of the framers of the constitution in providing for holdover senators "from the standpoint of safe conservatism."[4] The *Leader*, however, remained optimistic, pointing out that the great majority of the districts which the holdovers represented had gone overwhelmingly for the League, and insisting that they would feel compelled to follow the mandate. Moreover, most of them were Republicans, and the Republican state platform included the League proposals. Finally, the lieutenant governor, who appointed Senate committees, had been elected by the League.

The optimism faded perceptibly when the make-up of these committees was announced. Of forty Senate committees, Leaguers were given eight chairmanships, and they had a majority on only six. The committees given to the League were the relatively inconsequential ones customarily given to minorities, with the exception of the committee on warehouses and grain grading. Holdovers were in the majority on all important committees. Clearly the division was along League and anti-League lines rather than Republicans versus Democrats. In vain did the Leaguers argue a "mandate"—the fact remained that they lacked seven votes of a majority.

Lieutenant Governor Kraabel was savagely attacked as a "turncoat" who had accepted League support and then betrayed those who had elected him to office. Kraabel's reply to the charges of his having "sold out," though largely ignored, contained several reasonable arguments. He denied that the "old guard" had organized the Senate, and took full responsibility himself. He had been assisted, he said, by a committee consisting of two League and two non-League senators, and where there was disagreement he made the decision. It was the first time in the history of the state that the Senate was organized without a Republican caucus first. Forty committee assignments meant an average of eight and one-fifth per senator, yet League senators received an average of eight and two-fifths, even though in a minority. Party or factional affiliation was not considered, he claimed—the only factors were personal qualifications and regional spread. On every committee farmers were in a majority, and there was always a majority composed of Leaguers and Progressives. He could not, he insisted, conscientiously give the League a majority on committees when they numbered eighteen as against thirty-one, and any such action would have precipitated such bitter floor fights that no League legislation whatsoever could be passed.[5]

Governor Frazier's recommendations to the legislature were typically brief and to the point. Some of the more important things for which he asked were these: (1) enactment of the program of the Non-partisan League insofar as constitutionally possible and provision to change the constitution in order to make the rest possible, (2) reduction of the legal contract rate of interest from 10 per cent to 8 per cent, (3) a minimum wage law for women and children, (4) establishment of a labor bureau to assist on employment information and on all labor problems, (5) "at least a start" toward a state civil service merit system, (6) nonpartisan state and local primaries and elections, and (7) more state aid for rural schools and improved state supervision.[6]

The anti-League forces in the legislature, and particularly in the House, anticipated more success than their numbers would indicate because of the fact that most of the new League legislators knew nothing of legislative procedure and were painfully aware of their own ignorance of parliamentary law. But the opposition reckoned without A. C. Townley, who suffered no illusions about the political knowledge of the League legislators and had taken steps well in advance to handle the situation. The League had leased the Northwest Hotel for the entire session, and it was announced that a caucus of League legislators would consider all proposed legislation and determine League policy thereon. All members had pledged themselves to vote in the chambers in accordance with the majority vote of the caucus.

Meetings were held nightly in a large hall of the hotel, serving not only as a means of securing unified action, but also as an excellent school in legislative methods. D. C. Coates provided regular instruction in parliamentary procedure, and here inexperienced farmer-legislators, unused to public utterance, could speak their minds free of the restraint of the legislative chambers and the presence of opposition members. Townley subsequently made mention of this latter purpose in the course of platform humor in speeches in other states when he was telling the story of the North Dakota League. By way of "warming up" a crowd, he often described the early caucuses thus:

The new League legislators were good men, but they weren't used to speaking in public, while most of the opposition were able to talk indefinitely. Those fellows didn't feel at home in a legislative chamber, so we took the chairs and tables out of the hotel dining room, put in a few benches, and spread a little straw around. The falling plaster and hanging pieces of wallpaper were familiar too. They'd come down there and sit and they felt perfectly at ease. They began to talk to each

96

other and to argue, and before we knew it they were over in the legislature outtalking the best of them.[7]

Legislative caucuses were certainly no innovation, but the omnipresence and solidarity of this one and its publicly announced methods were indeed somewhat novel. Just as the League's endorsement procedure had operated outside the party system, so now the caucus virtually constituted the significant functioning of at least the lower house of the legislature. A howl of protest arose in the press when it was learned that the League had "legislative experts" at Bismarck to assist in the drafting of bills, and that Townley, Lemke, Bowen, Coates, and others were meeting regularly with the caucus. It was insisted that the caucus was nothing more than a device for forcing upon the League legislators the will of "Czar Townley," who completely dominated and controlled all meetings. The legislators, it was said, could not vote until they were told how to vote and then must vote as they were told.[8] The steering committee determined what was to come before the caucus, they charged, and the League leaders often took up the whole evening with speeches, ramming through resolutions with little or no debate when the hour grew late.

It was quite true that the Leaguers carefully followed their floor leaders, again in itself not a novel procedure for legislative bodies, but scarcely a one of these men ever deviated from the decisions of the caucus. If by chance they got tangled up on the floor, the House was recessed and the members came to the caucus room to get straightened out. The House opposition was furious but helpless in the face of this block voting. The story was widely and gleefully circulated that the League legislators had been instructed to vote "Aye" on bills which were read by the black-haired clerk and "No" on those read by the red-haired clerk,[9] a story which was of course purely a fairy tale. These men may have been inexperienced in legislative matters, but they were by no means fools. They learned quickly and it was not long before the caucuses could be devoted solely to discussions of pending legislation.

The opposition was likewise unhappy about the fact that the League legislators kept largely to themselves outside the chambers and were all segregated in one hotel. The secrecy of the League caucuses was the subject of frequent attacks, well exemplified by a *Herald* cartoon which depicted a large vault labeled "Secret Caucus Chamber," with

97

white-hooded guards dubbed "Socialism" and "Anarchy" on either side of the door. Over the door was inscribed "The Sky's the Limit," while a prominent sign gave the name of A. C. Townley as "President, Proprietor, Manager, Secretary, Treasurer, Dictator, and Janitor." [10] To be sure, only League legislators and League leaders participated in the caucus and others were usually barred, but guests, including even newspaper and magazine reporters, were not at all uncommon.

It is unquestionably true that the caucuses were carefully managed by the inner circle of League leaders, who usually, but not always, had their way. Townley almost invariably gave his views, and Lemke and the League lawyers who were engaged in drafting bills frequently discussed the measures proposed. It was natural that this group, at least some of whom had usually had an opportunity to become somewhat expert on particular propositions, should be extremely influential. It was the familiar problem of the technical expert versus the legislator who must be a generalist, but in this case the experts had the full confidence of the legislators.

Debate in the caucuses was not limited and there was opportunity for all to be heard. Many issues were threshed over until the entire assemblage was exhausted, and there were times when debates on one proposal ran for days. The steering committee always sought to achieve fairly general agreement, and no action was taken if there was a large minority in opposition—many changes were made in caucus and in some cases when agreement was never reached the matters were simply shelved.[11]

One may recognize the strong influence of the League leadership in the caucus without concluding that the kind of "bossism" claimed by the opposition press actually existed. It seems most unlikely that ninety-nine elected representatives would passively submit to such barefaced dictation day after day without someone balking. It was the League legislators, after all, who made the decisions, and they had to be convinced. If they voted for a measure it was because they were convinced, and they stayed together because they were agreed on the ends to be achieved and saw this procedure as the only means to success. The unit-rule policy of course made it possible to coerce to a limited degree those who might dissent on a specific issue but still were in agreement on basic principles. It also meant that, at times, only a minority of the House itself might favor legislation which passed because the League dissenters were bound by this rule. But the League organization had no hold upon these men other than through their commitment to the cause. There was little patronage at this time and few of them were interested in political careers—anyone could leave the caucus if he wished. They stayed because they were there for a purpose.

The informality of the new administration was well illustrated by the Monday noon "cabinet meetings" which soon developed into a routine practice. In order to talk over state problems and policy, state officers and occasionally guests convened weekly for lunch in the governor's office. A guest who had been invited to a luncheon with the governor was frequently somewhat taken aback to find upon entering the office that the group was gathered about two golden oak tables which had been shoved together and spread with newspapers. Upon joining the circle he was likely to be handed a bologna sandwich by the attorney general, a pickle passed by the commissioner of agriculture, and a mug of steaming coffee poured from a big tin pot by the genial governor himself. The session was then under way.[12]

The ultimate in "folksiness," however, was achieved by the bearded and venerable-looking Justice Robinson, who, much to the dismay of his judicial brethren, inaugurated the novel practice of publishing a weekly "Saturday Night Letter," in which he freely discussed the doings of the court in much the style of a "Personals" column of a country weekly. His comments upon the merits and demerits of his colleagues were often annoying, and his habit of publicly prejudging cases before the court resulted in numerous clashes, particularly with Judge Bruce. Robinson's rather queer and certainly unjudicial letters were not infrequently a source of some embarrassment to the League as well, but the old gentleman was not to be dissuaded from proving to the world that the state now had a truly democratic court in which pomp and ceremony had presumably given way to the substance of justice and a sort of neighborly informality.

The striking success of the League in the North Dakota election of 1916 quite naturally resulted in League headquarters being inundated with a flood of requests for information on the organization and its program from all parts of the country. There was understandably high interest on the part of farmers in adjoining states, and the limited organization work begun there earlier was now greatly expanded. The Farmers Nonpartisan Political League of North Dakota was raising its sights, and the name was soon officially changed to the National Nonpartisan League.

Shortly after the opening of the 1917 legislative session it was announced that the headquarters of the League would be moved from Fargo to St. Paul, the extension of organization work into other states necessitating a more central location. The *Leader* was to continue publication in Fargo, and in response to numerous requests was adding a four-page supplement weekly, containing the chief articles in German, free to any subscriber on request. That the guiding hand was to lose none of its strength seemed evident from the concluding statement of the announcement: "The different state branches, including the North Dakota branch, will be under the jurisdiction of the national organization and the activities of the different state branches and the organization work as a whole will be supervised and directed from St. Paul." [13]

The anti-League press lost no time in pointing out that it had taken an extremely short time for the North Dakota "throne room," so lately presumably restored to the state from the Twin Cities, to return to St. Paul. It was somewhat saddened, however, by the almost simultaneous announcement by Norman Black that the North Dakota Good Government League had been disbanded because of "lack of interest on the part of the members." [14]

There was no disputing the fact that some type of constitutional change was necessary before the League's program of state industries could be undertaken. The standard method of amendment, as we have seen, was painfully slow, and the decision of the Supreme Court in the New Rockford case had for the moment put a crimp in the initiative procedure. Even if the two houses could agree on provisions to make the section operative, which was doubtful, it could not go into effect until July 1. The possibility of calling a constitutional convention was at first seriously considered, but that was too time-consuming, expensive, unwieldy, and not at all certain to produce the desired result.[15] The farmers above all wanted action—more years of delay hardly seemed like the proper prescription for a long life for the League.

Taking all this into account, the League's legal advisers came up with a totally new proposal—simple and efficient, but lacking the halo of precedent. Basing their argument on the grounds that complete power resided in the people of the state, and contending that the constitution was silent on the procedure for establishing a totally new constitution, they proposed simply that the legislature frame a new constitution which should go into effect by a majority vote of the people. Screams of "anarchy" and "revolution" at once rent the air, but the Leaguers insisted that such a procedure was fully as democratic and no more "unconstitutional" than the accepted convention method, which was not mentioned in the document either. Writing a new constitution was, they said, always an "extra-legal" proceeding.

The proposed new constitution was shortly embodied in the famous House Bill 44, around which raged the central controversy of the entire session. To the Leaguers its enactment was basic to the achievement of the program to which they were committed—to the opposition it was the embodiment of all that was evil in this "un-American" movement which seemed bent on tearing at the very roots of constitutional government. The *Leader* pointed out that everyone knew that constitutional change was necessary if the program for which the people had overwhelmingly voted was to be put into effect, and that this was clearly the quickest and surest method.[16] Nevertheless, as so often happens, the actual provisions of the bill were soon lost in the welter of charges and countercharges which rapidly reached fantastic proportions.

House Bill 44, in the form of a concurrent resolution, proposed the following significant changes from the existing document:

Permitted the state or its political subdivisions to enter agricultural or manufacturing industries

Raised the state debt limit from $200,000 to $500,000 and permitted the state or its political subdivisions to issue or guarantee bonds in excess of the limit, provided the bonds were secured by first mortgages upon real estate or upon property of public utilities, enterprises, or industries

Made possible the exemption of farm improvements from taxation

Permitted taxation for state hail insurance

Provided for the election of state and county officers for four-year instead of two-year terms, with elections to be held between presidential elections in order to keep them as free as possible from national politics (no longer would there be holdover senators)

Liberalized the initiative and referendum provisions, providing for their operation upon the petition of 10 per cent rather than 25 per cent

of the voters in not less than half the counties, and specifying that laws
so adopted could not be declared unconstitutional by the courts

Made provision for the recall of state officials under the same terms
as the initiative and referendum

Provided that constitutional amendments might be adopted in the
same manner as initiated laws

Placed power in the legislature to apply the short-ballot principle to
state and county government

Specified that the Supreme Court could declare acts of the legislature
unconstitutional only by a four-fifths vote

Established the Torrens system of land title registration

Other changes were designed to cut out sections no longer meaningful
and to simplify language.[17]

These items today seem scarcely earth shaking in their revolutionary
character, but in the minds of the anti-League press the end of the
American way of life was clearly in sight. Jerry Bacon of the *Grand
Forks Herald* hastily issued a garish pamphlet entitled *A Socialist Constitution for North Dakota*, in which was presented a two-column comparison of the old and new constitutions accompanied by a commentary which stressed particularly sins of omission. Ferdinand Teigen, in
a typically flamboyant manner, later described the bill this way: "The
title of that bill in order to have expressed its real purpose should have
been: 'A BILL TO EXPUNGE from the CONSTITUTION and LAW of the STATE,
all GUARANTIES of PROPERTY RIGHTS, and to PREPARE the WAY for the
COMING of SOCIALISM'." [18]

Bacon's *Socialist Constitution* was distributed widely over the state
by public-spirited citizens who were willing to pay thirteen dollars a
thousand for them. A number were in fact sent out to constituents by
opposition legislators. Senator McGray was reported to have sent them
out with a note attached asking, "Shall I vote for this?" [19] At the same
time, of course, the *Leader* was ardently promoting the bill, devoting
whole pages to it in every issue, and members were repeatedly exhorted
to believe nothing they read in the "gang press" unless it was confirmed
in the *Leader*.

The debate in the legislature was likewise intemperate, but again,
interestingly enough, the most violent attacks were frequently made
less against the principal features of the bill than against various minor
items and what was proclaimed to be its "secret purpose." The climax

came on the floor of the House over the section relating to public education, when Representative A. G. Divet of Wahpeton sought to have reinserted the original wording. The provision of the old constitution read:

A high degree of intelligence, patriotism, integrity and morality on the part of every voter in a government by the people being necessary to insure the continuance of that government and the prosperity and happiness of the people, the legislative assembly shall make provision for the establishment and maintenance of a system of public schools which shall be open to all the people of North Dakota and free from sectarian control. This legislative requirement shall be irrevocable without the consent of the United States and the people of North Dakota.

As proposed in House Bill 44 the section read:

The legislative assembly shall make provision for the establishment and maintenance of a system of public schools which shall be open to all children of the state of North Dakota and free from sectarian control.

Now here, obviously, was a barefaced attempt to abolish intelligence, patriotism, integrity, and morality, and Mr. Divet demanded that the clause at once be restored to its pristine purity. When the author of the bill pointed out that the section retained the same legal effect, that a defense of education was hardly necessary in a constitution, and that the virtues here deleted were adequately covered by the words "public spirit" and "truthfulness" later used, Representative Divet poured forth his soul in a denunciation of this dastardly move to undermine the very foundations of society:

I say this change in this section was made designedly and I cannot pass it by without making the statement that to my mind those changes represent the malicious cut of a poisoned dagger of treason and licentiousness held in the secret hand of disloyalty and hate; that the hand that penned those lines and deliberately made that change would put poison in the wells in front of the country's armies, or would lead a little sister to the brothel.[20]

Seeking to build up a great wave of popular sentiment for the bill, the *Leader* printed a letter signed by all the League members of the legislature praising the proposals and asking for solid voter support.[21] For several issues it also printed petition blanks to be sent when completed primarily to holdover senators. Most important, however, was the scheduling of a series of mass meetings around the state, at which

Townley as the principal speaker explained to large and enthusiastic crowds the need for speedy constitutional revision. The situation was termed the greatest crisis yet faced by the League, one which demanded the utmost public pressure.

On January 26 the bill came up for final vote in the House, and a veritable field day of oratory ensued, with A. G. Divet and J. F. T. O'Connor, a Democrat from Grand Forks, leading the opposition. Various riders were unsuccessfully proposed but the attack was concentrated principally on the bonding provisions. With no limit, they said, the state would be plunged into a wild orgy of indebtedness from which it might never recover. A series of amendments was proposed in an effort "to find the top" which the League would accept—two million, five million, ten million—but all were beaten down. "In God's name," cried one member dramatically, "is there no limit?" "The sky's the limit!" shouted back a voice at the rear, and the opposition subsided in a roar of laughter. The League argued that the restrictions were quite adequate; there was no reason for not trusting the legislature and the people, and the referendum provisions under this new constitution would be greatly liberalized.[22]

On the final vote House Bill 44 passed the House by the lopsided majority of 81 to 28, six non-League representatives voting for the bill and five elected by the League voting against it. The *Leader* at once published the roll call under headings of "Your Friends" and "Your Enemies," with special venom reserved for those elected by the League who had "betrayed the farmers."[23] Three days later, to the surprise of no one, the bill was killed in the Senate 29 to 20, four non-League senators voting for it and one elected with League endorsement (Albert Stenmo) voting no.[24]

The *Leader*, of course, was bitter in its denunciation of this action, and from that time forward the holdover senators were the chief target of reproach for this "thwarting of the people's will." It did, however, magnanimously announce: "The people are not going to rise up in bloody revolution as they have done many, many times in the past under less provocation than the action of the Senate on Bill 44. They will try once more the ways of law and order."[25]

A League caucus subsequently determined to ask the people to initiate amendments accomplishing the desired purposes, hoping that petitions might be filed in time for the measures to be voted on at the general election in November of 1918. This would make it possible for the 1919 session of the legislature to carry out the League platform. It was agreed that legislation would be proposed to correct the defect in the amendment by initiative procedure found by the Supreme Court in the New Rockford case. If this too were blocked, it could only be hoped that the new court might overrule that decision.

Shortly after House Bill 44 was introduced, Senator McBride had endeavored to counteract it by bringing in a concurrent resolution providing for a referendum vote the following November on the question of calling a constitutional convention. If approved, delegates might be elected at the time of the June primaries in 1918, with the convention to meet July 12. The popular vote on ratification could then come in November.[26] Thus presumably the anti-League forces proved that they were willing to permit constitutional change as long as it was undertaken in the "proper" form. While the League condemned this as a delaying tactic, the *Grand Forks Herald* sourly questioned the need for it. A Supreme Court had been elected, it said, for the purpose of declaring all acts of the legislature valid—why bother with a constitutional convention?[27]

Within the next week several non-League senators introduced a variety of proposals for individual amendments to the constitution mostly designed to take the wind out of the sails of House Bill 44. Included were such things as state hail insurance, state rural credits, woman suffrage, ninety-day legislative sessions, and even a commission form of government for the state, modeled roughly on municipal commission government.

Of more significance was a bill introduced by Senator McGray after the defeat of House Bill 44 to permit the state to build elevators and turn them over to the Equity Society to be run as cooperatives. This, said the *Leader*, was a "repudiation of the principle of state ownership which the League stands for," and it branded the move as an insidious attempt to create ill-feeling between the League and the Equity Society and as fake legislation designed to cover up the perfidy of the Senate in killing the proposed new constitution.[28]

As the session progressed the League became more and more bitter over what it considered to be the deliberate delaying tactics of the opposition and the efforts in the Senate to pirate League legislation. It was charged that in the upper house there was a practice of bottling up bills introduced by League members that everyone agreed to be desirable while the opposition wrote similar bills for which they could then take credit. Senator Drown's bill for state grain grading was cited as an example. The bill had first been referred to the committee on agriculture, rather than warehouses and grain grading where the League had a majority, and it was then allowed to repose quietly for a week while the majority members of the committee wrote their own bill which was essentially the same. Whether the stealing of credit was the motive behind this action is debatable, but the Leaguers were convinced that such was the case.[29]

Despite all the bickering and mutual recriminations, the fifteenth legislative assembly ultimately produced a number of significant pieces of legislation, the most important being the following:

The establishment of a state grain grading system

The proposal of a constitutional amendment providing for the exemption of farm improvements from taxation

The proposal of an amendment for complete woman suffrage, and the granting of immediate suffrage on the election of presidential electors, county surveyors and constables, all officers of cities, villages, and towns except police magistrates and city justices of the peace, and on all questions or appropriations submitted to the voters by town officers

A state bank deposit guarantee law

A nine-hour-day law for women

A Torrens land title registration law

A moneys and credits tax

A reduced rate of assessment on farm machinery and improvements

Authorization of negotiable warehouse receipts with safeguards against fraud

The forbidding of discriminatory "long and short haul" rates by railroads

The forbidding of discrimination by railroads in furnishing cars or in permitting firms to construct elevators along rights of way

The establishment of a State Highway Commission and acceptance of the provisions of the federal highway grants

A virtual trebling of state aids for rural education while continuing the grants in support of higher education[30]

In addition to House Bill 44, the Senate had killed several other measures strongly backed by the League. These included a specification of the construction of Sec. 202 of the constitution relating to the initiation of constitutional amendments, the placing of state and local elections on a nonpartisan basis, a workmen's compensation act, a 28 per cent reduction of freight rates, and a minimum wage feature of the act prescribing maximum hours for women.[31] The House in return, as a matter of principle, killed a Senate bill to abolish the state streetcar line in Bismarck, which for fourteen years had operated a single car between the Northern Pacific depot and the capitol, and let a private corporation build a more comprehensive system.[32]

The *Herald* insisted that the session produced little if anything in the way of constructive results, but most observers of both political faiths felt the accomplishments to be reasonably good. All agreed on the serious nature of the session and the hard work put in by both sides. Lieutenant Governor Kraabel, who doubtless was glad to see the end arrive, praised the session and charitably concluded that although there had been differences of opinion all factions had been sincerely devoted to what they conceived to be the best interests of the people.[33]

The greatest excitement, however, came after the adjournment of the legislature with the veto by Governor Frazier of a terminal elevator bill passed in the rush of the last day of the session. The bill had been introduced by anti-League members in the Senate after the failure of League proposals on the subject. It provided for state erection of a single elevator and granted an appropriation of $300,000, $70,000 of which could come from the balance in the terminal elevator fund previously raised and the remainder from the general fund. League members in the House had been divided on the matter, but the majority felt that this would be at least a start and assumed that their constituents expected the session to produce some kind of a terminal elevator act after the preceding session had been so roundly condemned for failing to do so.

Frazier recognized the difficulty of explaining a veto of a measure of this sort, but after consultation with the League leadership he did so, giving as his reasons a belief that such enterprises should be financed by bond issues rather than taxation, returning earnings to pay for the investment; that a single small elevator could have little effect, especially unless reinforced by a state mill, and would simply give the opposition a chance to discredit state ownership; that the bill should provide that the elevator could be built only within the state; that the legislature had appropriated money for the project in excess of available funds; and, finally, that in two years it would be possible to get the mill and elevator system that the people really wanted, whereas this one would simply hamper true progress and retard the whole League program.[34]

The *Leader* of course gave a tremendous build-up to Frazier's "courageous and far-sighted" act, and insisted that this was no case of "play my way or not at all," but the anticipated attacks on the veto were not slow in coming. The charges by the opposition dailies were expected and could to some extent be parried in advance, but the action did have unpleasant consequences for the League in that it precipitated the first open rift in the ranks.

It hurt to have the state organ of the Equity Society editorially condemn the veto and for M. P. Johnson, state president of the Equity and a railroad commissioner elected with League endorsement, publicly to express his displeasure. The *Co-Operators' Herald*, however, continued to support the League on all other matters and Johnson received relatively little support for his position within his own organization. Doubts in the minds of the League membership were largely dispelled by the *Leader*'s emphatic editorials portraying the vetoed bill as simply another "old gang" trick to confuse and divide the farmers and by the vigorous action of the seemingly tireless Arthur Townley. He once again stumped the state explaining the governor's action and found few to dispute his arguments.[35]

Storm Warnings

SCARCELY a month after the adjournment of North Dakota's fifteenth legislative assembly the United States entered World War I, and for months the nation was in the grip of a kind of hysteria which it had rarely if ever before experienced. In scores of localities there erupted a fanatical brand of pseudo-patriotism, wherein certain self-righteous individuals took upon themselves the setting of standards as to what constituted "loyalty." Hundreds of innocent persons were injured in an orgy of name-calling and in the actual physical violence which soon followed. The attitude of the "super-patriots" was frequently childish in the extreme, yet having wrapped themselves in the flag in time of war they wielded tremendous influence and secured for themselves an almost unassailable position.

German music was considered in bad taste, German language instruction was dropped from school curriculums, German fried potatoes disappeared from menus, and persons of German descent, especially if they bore an obviously German name, were immediately suspect. Unfortunate as was such ignorance and petty action, however, the demand for absolute conformity, and the attempts to prohibit all criticism of things as they were, turned out to be far more serious. Anyone who took exception to the existing order could not escape the label of "pro-German" or "disloyalist," regardless of the terms or justice of his criticism. Clearly, here was a made-to-order method for "smearing" the Nonpartisan League, and the opposition was not slow to utilize it.

The people of the United States were by no means united in 1917 on the wisdom of participation in the European conflict, and the center of greatest opposition lay in the rural Midwest, particularly in the states of the so-called Northwest. Unquestionably there were some in this area whose sympathies lay with Germany before and perhaps in occasional cases even after our entry, but basically there was an antiwar rather than a pro-German attitude. The great majority had favored the Allies, but they nevertheless opposed United States involvement. If the League as an organization was antiwar before April 1917, it accurately reflected the sentiments of the bulk of its membership and of the people in the area in which it operated. League membership was not the determining factor. Those of the League leadership who had Socialist affiliations had also of course long been schooled in opposition to war as a matter of principle.

After the actual entry of the United States, the League formally backed the war effort, but its support for some time was not enthusiastic and it was highly critical of certain government policies at both the national and state levels. The war, to many of the leaders, seemed a matter of secondary importance and an annoying interruption of the progress of the League program. Later on, as the policies of the national administration came more and more into line with League thinking on the prosecution of the war, the organization became to a considerable degree the champion of the national government and President Wilson, while continuing its attacks on what it considered to be the shortsighted and oppressive actions of various state and local governments.

From the outset the *Leader* gave great emphasis to the necessity for a statement to the world of United States war aims and peace terms and the securing of agreement among the Allies upon such terms. The "crush Germany first" argument seemed to it to make no sense—America, it insisted, should hold its ideals before the world and demonstrate clearly that it had no ulterior motives. To the claims of the opposition press that it sought a "German peace," the League replied that it indeed desired peace at the earliest possible moment, but that its objective was a just peace which would in truth "make the world safe for democracy" rather than sowing the seeds of future conflicts.[1]

The most significant argument of the League, however, and the one which was the basis of the organization's war policy, was the demand for the conscription of wealth for financing the war. Conscription of men was clearly the most equitable method of raising an army, it said, and if that were just it seemed only logical that conscription of wealth was likewise the fairest means of financing. This theme had been started when the North Dakota House of Representatives adopted a resolution just before adjournment calling upon Congress in the event of war to make the first levy upon "swollen fortunes" from war profits,[2] and the League never ceased its advocacy. It vigorously insisted that no person should profit from war, and flayed unmercifully the "profiteers" who were coining millions "from the blood of America's youth." If profiteering were ended and wealth conscripted, it was repeatedly suggested, there might be considerably less incentive to prolong the war.

The *Leader* looked with approval upon Wilson's proposal in June that one half the cost of the war be borne by current taxes, although it felt that the President's recommendation did not go far enough. It insisted that bonds would in effect be paid off by those least able to do so, and moreover that much of the burden would subsequently fall upon the men in the armed forces who were already sacrificing far more than anyone at home. When the business and financial interests protested violently against the President's recommendations, the *Leader* was not slow to point out that these were the same elements which had but recently been sanctimoniously admonishing others to "stand by the President"—apparently they did not consider the advice applicable to themselves, at least in the event the President acted contrary to their interests. Everyone agrees, it remarked, that one who is drafted must serve. If he refuses he is branded as a traitor. One who opposes the draft is likewise labeled a traitor. Now when the government proposes a draft of wealth why are not those who fight that proposal also traitors? Yet by a strange twist of reasoning it was the advocates of wealth conscription whom the press was terming traitorous.[3]

Finally, the League contended, the national government had an obligation to secure the well-being of all its citizens by establishing food controls and price regulations, and by taking over and operating the basic elements of the national economy, particularly the railroads and communications systems, the major utilities, and the great natural resources like coal and oil.

Wilson's strictures on profiteering were given wide publicity by the *Leader*, which periodically questioned why the *Grand Forks Herald* did not charge the President with treason. Greatly applauded was the July speech in which the President sharply reminded the nation that it should not be necessary to "bribe" people to aid the war effort. "Let us never speak," he said, "of profits and patriotism in the same sentence." [4] Assistant Secretary of Agriculture Carl Vrooman, a favorite of the League's for his liberal philosophy, earned further plaudits when in a speech in Fargo on July 27 he hailed the patriotism of the nation's farmers and savagely attacked the "food pirates," proclaiming at one point: "We have the best blood of the nation; we must draft also the wealth of the nation." [5] The efforts of Senator LaFollette and a few others in the Congress to secure war revenue measures which would bear heavily on war profits were naturally given the stanchest support.

Each time the United States Department of Agriculture concluded that there was a further need for government action to control speculation and to narrow the gap between producer and consumer prices, the League was quick to point out the proposal as a vindication of its position. When Herbert Hoover told a congressional committee that the people of the United States were being robbed of $50,000,000 a month by profiteering on the item of flour alone, it was natural that the pro-League papers should chant a "we told you so" and ask what the total must be if all commodities were considered.[6] The taking over of all shipping in the fall by the national government was hailed as a step in the right direction. "Is this treason?" asked the *Leader*. "Why are marketing facilities so different?" [7]

While the League was in general gratified as various economic controls were gradually established, it was nevertheless deeply disturbed by the common assumption that government operation or government controls were for the duration of the war only. If they were desirable in time of war, why not in time of peace? The test of the worth of any machine, said the *Leader*, is its ability to work in emergencies: "The food marketing system of the United States—that costly, much-defended, widely-praised, economic machine provided for us by the geniuses of Big Business—cannot *meet the emergency of war times*." No longer is it necessary to prove that the system is "inefficient, unfair, and corrupt"; everyone admits that it cannot stand up under stress:

But what of all this talk about discarding this unfair, inefficient marketing system *for the duration of the war only*? If it's all wrong to trim the farmers and cheat the consumers in war times by the slick methods of the great middleman's system, why is it all right to do it in peace times? If government operation of elevators, warehouses, and railroads is "un-American," "Socialistic" and "visionary" in peace times, why it is "patriotic" and "efficient preparedness" in war times? [8]

The war hysteria was to have a more serious effect upon the League in other states than North Dakota, where it had majority support and controlled the state administration. Yet North Dakota was by early 1917 a state divided into two bitterly hostile factions. To conservatives and to the majority of the townspeople the League was a monstrous thing, an organization thriving on class hatred and seeking revolutionary changes in the "American system," led by fundamentally immoral anarchists and freebooters. To the Leaguer it seemed that the townspeople were blindly ignoring the justice of his reasonable and rather moderate demands, and were deliberately joining hands with the "Big Business" exploiters in an effort to keep him in a state of economic serfdom. The League was not reticent about its determination to win complete control of the state in 1918, and the business interests were equally determined that it should not.

The intensity of the feeling is incomprehensible to those who did not live through the period. Old friends ceased to speak to each other, families were split, churches and social organizations were divided, children barely able to talk knew where they stood, and in many a country school League and anti-League children did not play together.[9] Every town had its League merchants and its anti-League merchants, and brief boycotts of certain towns by farmers of the surrounding area were not unknown. In state capitol offices other officials appearing on business were treated differently depending on their political leanings, while the Supreme Court was almost rent asunder. Frequently Chief Justice Christianson was the only member on speaking terms with all the others, and he found it necessary to serve as a channel for communication in numerous instances.[10] "It is doubtful," says Lewis Crawford, "whether any society has experienced a more bitter partisan strife since the days of slavery than North Dakota passed through in the period of about ten years following the legislative session of 1917." [11]

Throughout the winter and spring of 1917 League meetings were held continuously all over the state, with enthusiastic turnouts everywhere. They served the dual purpose of maintaining interest and getting the farmers to sign up and pay dues for the next biennium. Picnics were held in every county during the summer, with speakers from headquarters present at each.

In the meantime, however, the opposition was not dormant. On April 11 what was proclaimed as an "anti-Socialist" convention met in Grand Forks for the purpose of organizing to combat the "red menace." There had been an effort, which had not met with a great deal of success, to make it appear that this was at least in part a farmers' movement; the effort had centered largely in seeking the attendance of disgruntled Leaguers wherever they might be found.

The *Minneapolis Tribune* professed to see this meeting as evidence that North Dakota at last recognized that she had been tricked and that the mass of the citizenry was now rising to overthrow the Socialists,[12] but even the promoters of the conference had no such delusions. Theirs must be, they agreed, primarily a publicity and "educational" enterprise at least for the present, so that the people of the state might be enabled to realize the folly of their ways.

Shortly thereafter it was announced that the *Fargo Forum*, the evening paper of that city, which had remained more or less neutral though not friendly to the League, had been sold to a group nominally headed by Norman B. Black, the former editor of the *Grand Forks Herald* and more recently the executive secretary of the North Dakota Good Government League.[13] The *Forum* at once launched into a policy of rabid opposition to the League and all its works which frequently rivaled the best efforts of the *Herald*.

Immediately after the success of the League in the 1916 elections, and particularly after the proposals advanced in the 1917 legislative session, Socialists and occasional other radicals all over the country, long starving for a place where they might see their theories actually put into practice, began to exhibit tremendous interest in the Nonpartisan League and North Dakota. The League's correspondence files are clogged with letters from such persons who had heard of this new movement "to throw the damned capitalists off our backs," and who eagerly sought further information, oftentimes offering their services.[14] Henry Teigan patiently assured them all that the League was on the right track and seemed bound to succeed.

Unfortunately for the League, however, it was also beseiged continually with dozens of "promoters"—some sincere, some outright "crooks," some cranks, but all anxious to utilize in some manner the name and prestige of the League. In its own best interest the organization should have stuck closely to the achievement of its basic program, and refrained from going afield, but the League name was potent and the temptation was almost too great to be resisted. As Bruce Nelson remarks: "The farmers had the bit in their teeth; they were ready to try anything." [15] In time the League did fall victim to a few of these schemes, but of vastly more importance were the various subsidiary enterprises either begun by the League leadership or fostered by persons connected with the League in one capacity or another.

One of the largest of these ventures was the Consumers' United Stores Company, incorporated in early 1917 by Howard Elliott, then state manager of the North Dakota League and former Socialist candidate for mayor of Minot, C. H. Heck, a former coal miner and Socialist lecturer, and Norbert O'Leary, secretary to A. C. Townley.[16] The moving force behind the stores project was, however, Job Wells Brinton, the former mayor of Beach who had from time to time held a variety of positions at League headquarters. The purpose of the Consumers' Stores was twofold. Primarily it was to distribute merchandise to farmer members at wholesale cost plus 10 per cent, the purchasing for stores throughout the state being done by a single agency buying directly from manufacturers. In the second place it was anticipated that the stores might well constitute retribution for village merchants who had proven themselves unfriendly to the League.

For some time a number of League members who were stanch advocates of cooperation had urged the use of the organization for cooperative buying, though it is doubtful if they envisaged the centralized type of setup which was devised. "Buyers' certificates," good for a ten-year period, were sold at $100 each, with most farmers giving notes for the amount. When a minimum of $10,000 had been subscribed in a community, a store was to be established and stock purchased with the proceeds. It was agreed that 90 per cent of the funds subscribed in any one place would be put into the local store, while the other 10 per cent might be utilized for general "promotional and educational" purposes at the discretion of the directors.

Three stores were quickly started at Kenmare, Minot, and Crosby, and others were opened from time to time until in 1919 about thirty were in existence. The company's general offices and warehouse were in Fargo, while distribution stations were set up in a few of the larger cities around the state. The Consumers' Stores handled principally "staple groceries, a limited variety of clothing, shoes, hardware, furniture and farm implements." [17] Memberships were sold in much the same manner as memberships in the League itself. Special organizers were given credentials carrying the Nonpartisan League letterhead, signed by A. C. Townley, and stating that the Stores project was "under the auspices of the National Nonpartisan League." [18] These organizers received a five-dollar commission on each membership sold. One who purchased a certificate gained thereby no voice whatsoever in the control of the enterprise—he purchased simply the right to buy at the store at, presumably, cost plus 10 per cent. Surely this was paternalism of a high degree.

The Consumers' United Stores Company was theoretically a separate organization from the League, but the close tie-in was quite generally recognized. All the subscribers were not aware for some time, however, that the 10 per cent earmarked for "educational" purposes was being utilized by Lemke and other League leaders for political activity and that they apparently did not restrict themselves to 10 per cent. In a number of communities far more than $10,000 was subscribed, yet in no store was even that much invested, and there were other places where stores never materialized, although limited amounts had been subscribed.[19] Money deposited to the Stores Company account was loosely handled and few if any records were maintained. Money was borrowed from Stores Company funds, perhaps with every intention of paying it back, and other money was borrowed from League banks on the credit of the company.

When these facts or rumors concerning them reached the ears of farmer investors, it was natural that the League as well as the Stores Company should suffer. As an economic weapon the venture met with mixed results. In some instances the threat of the competition brought about changes of attitude; in others it stimulated more vigorous opposition. Suppliers were frequently uncooperative, and the stores in most cases were not particularly successful in providing significant savings to patrons, owing in large measure to poor handling of funds. The fact is that the Stores Company was used more as a source of revenue than as a means of aiding the farmers. Properly managed along true cooperative lines it might well have been a valuable enterprise. In the fall of 1919 an attempt was made to reorganize on the patronage dividend plan, but the entire project eventually failed. It is indeed more than likely that farmers who lost investments became somewhat less ardent League supporters than they had been.[20]

Since such a large percentage of League membership fees were paid with postdated checks, the organization was faced from the beginning with the problem of securing cash for current operations on the strength of those checks. To handle this situation the League Exchange was early created with a capital stock of $100,000 subscribed by League members. It served as a sort of clearinghouse and rediscount agency for the League itself and various subsidiary enterprises such as the Consumers' United Stores Company.[21] It also for a time attempted to promote immigration to North Dakota by serving as an agency for bringing together persons desiring to sell land in the state and potential buyers. The service was free to homeseekers, and the commission charged the sellers was said to be nominal.[22]

Unfortunately the capital stock of the League Exchange was subscribed largely in farmers' notes, and in order to secure adequate loans on the notes and postdated checks it became necessary to acquire banks which would be friendly to the organization. The League first purchased the Scandinavian-American Bank of Fargo by the intriguing process of borrowing sufficient money to buy a controlling interest and giving as collateral for the loan stock in the institution which was purchased by means of the loan.[23] Under the guiding genius of John J. Hastings, former financial agent of the League and newly made vice president of the Scandinavian-American Bank, ably assisted by Porter Kimball and T. Allan Box, a number of banks were purchased or organized in various towns throughout the state. League members in the communities concerned subscribed the capital stock. Not only did these banks serve as a means of negotiating the farmers' paper held by the League and sundry enterprises, but like the Consumers' Stores they were a means of retribution for hostile local bankers.[24]

Jack Hastings was a financial promoter who would have fitted in well with Edward Harriman or Jay Gould, and some of his wildcat operations were later to bring grief to the League. He became a vice president and supervisor of virtually every League bank in the state, and he seems never to have failed to collect at least a 10 per cent commission for his services in purchasing or organizing the institutions for the farmer stockholders.

At one time Hastings is reported to have purchased a controlling interest in a bank at Wimbleton for $18,000, for which he gave a personal check on the Scandinavian-American Bank of Fargo, although he had no account there of any such size. Taking immediate possession of the Wimbleton bank, he made himself a loan of $20,000 which he deposited in the newly acquired bank and then drew a check on the purchased bank in favor of the Fargo bank in order to cover his worthless check given in the original transaction.[25]

Methods of acquisition and operation were in time to create serious problems in a few cases, but it must be admitted that most of the League chain of banks served both their patrons and the parent organization well, and control of financial institutions was undeniably essential to successful operation of the League under existing conditions.

The *Nonpartisan Leader*, as has been noted, was unquestionably one of the most vital factors in League success. From its beginning in September of 1915 it had been the most useful single medium of informing and unifying the scattered membership—its pages were avidly read, and, what is more significant, believed. The *Fargo Courier-News*, acquired in the fall of 1916, was filling the need for a city daily with a League point of view, but in many areas sentiment was growing for the establishment of country weeklies favorable to the cause. In a few instances groups of farmers had cooperatively purchased the controlling interests in rural papers, but vigorous promotion of this kind of action was not begun until shortly after the close of the 1917 legislative session with the organization of the Northwest Publishers' Service.

The Northwest Publishers' Service was expected to furnish syndicated material and League news and opinion to affiliated papers, but its primary function was the acquisition and control of the papers. The League had always had a healthy respect for the power of the press, and it desired to extend its coverage as widely as possible. The proposed chain of country weeklies was not expected to operate simply as a group of publicity organs on the order of the *Leader*, but to serve as regular newspapers, having the League viewpoint just as other papers might be Republican or Democratic. Ferdinand Teigen states that it was standard practice for a delegation of local farmers to call on an opposition editor to say that they couldn't continue to support a paper "whose editor sits up nights inventing left-handed compliments for the League." If the editor refused to mend his ways a representative of the Northwest Publishers' Service would drop into town and shortly a reorganized competitor or a new paper with League stockholders would be "filling a long-felt want." [26]

The Service carried on the acquisition of old papers or the establishment of new with commendable speed but rather remarkable open-handedness.[27] In a typical case 1010 shares of preferred stock were sold to farmers, while 450 shares of common stock, slightly less than half the total, went to the Northwest Publishers' Service "in payment for promotion and organizational work and for services rendered or to be rendered." Each holder of preferred stock had one vote regardless of the number of shares he owned, but in the case of the common stock, since the articles of incorporation did not fix the voting power, each share possessed a vote. For the Publishers' Service to lose control, therefore, the preferred stock would have to be sold to more than 450 stockholders, amongst whom complete agreement would have to be secured. Normally there were never more than 200 to 300 stockholders. The corporation charter provided that the corporation might buy out any stockholder bringing suit against the corporation or permitting his name to be used in such a suit by tendering him par plus a 10 per cent premium, the purpose of this clause being "to guard against litigation by entrenched wealth." The charter further made the preferred stock exempt from "all liability for corporate debts and obligations"; for the common stock it was also provided that there should be "no individual liability as to the holders thereof."

A dividend of seventy cents a share was to be paid annually on the preferred stock, and the remaining surplus then went to the common stock, up to a maximum of seventy cents a share. Any further surplus was to be divided equally between the two types. The preferred stock sold at ten dollars a share, while the common was listed at two dollars, yet both ordinarily received the same dividend. Vastly more important, however, the Northwest Publishers' Service without investing a dollar (though providing some services), had complete control of every newspaper so organized. In late 1918 the agency was reorganized as the Publishers' National Service Bureau in keeping with its expanded field of operations, and by the end of that year the League through the bureau controlled approximately forty-five country weeklies in North Dakota and some thirty in other states.

Among the appreciably less sound projects in which the League subsequently became indirectly involved were such things as the "Bering

Sea Fisheries Company" and the "United States Sisal Trust." The former was little more than a paper organization promoted by H. J. Hagen, president of the Scandinavian-American Bank of Fargo, and came to light principally because of a sizable loan made by that gentleman to himself in his Fisheries Company capacity on the security of uncaught salmon in the Bering Sea.[28] The League was implicated by the opposition because of its tie-in with the bank.

The sisal affair was somewhat more complicated. During the war years there was frequently a rather serious shortage of binder twine, a matter of no small concern to North Dakota farmers. Sisal, used for the best twine, came largely from Mexico, where conditions had been chaotic for some time, and there was a great desire for a dependable source of supply. One afternoon a young man from Florida appeared in Fargo and sought an interview with A. C. Townley. He proceeded to set forth a grandiose scheme for a tie-up between the state of North Dakota and a huge sisal plantation in Florida, whereby one would have a guaranteed supply and the other a guaranteed market. Townley says that he was not unfriendly to the idea, but that he did not consider it sufficiently feasible to bother with. Since the young man had spent all his money in getting to Fargo, Townley gave him enough to return.[29]

Brinton and Hastings soon got wind of the matter, however, and Brinton, always interested in moneymaking propositions, went to Florida on his own to investigate. Shortly thereafter the United States Sisal Trust was incorporated and theoretically capitalized at $1,000,000. Nominally headed by James Waters, it acquired some 22,000 acres of land in Dade County, Florida, and at once devoted itself to selling stock in the enterprise to farmers. The stock was advertised in glowing terms, but how much was actually sold is uncertain. The subsequent history of the Sisal Trust is shrouded in mystery, as is the role of A. C. Townley therein, but it is clear that nothing ever came of the project beyond convincing those who did invest that they had been most unwise.[30]

Again the League as an organization did not promote the venture, but it was obviously involved at least indirectly and such projects as these gave the anti-League press ample opportunity to hold up to ridicule what they termed harebrained schemes designed solely to part the farmer from his money.

In addition to this situation the League throughout its existence was cursed by a veritable rash of smooth salesmen who descended upon the

Some Leaks in the Pipe Line
An anti-League "dig" at the organization's subsidiary enterprises
(from the *Red Flame*).

farmers from time to time claiming to represent the League and endeavoring to sell fictitious stock in a St. Paul packing plant, a cooperative store, or any of a variety of other ventures. The *Leader* found it repeatedly necessary to warn its readers against such persons, pointing out that official representatives of the League always carried credentials which farmers should insist on seeing.

North Dakota, as has been noted, was rapidly "reorganized" during the winter and spring of 1917, most old members rejoining and many new ones being secured. The future of the organization looked bright, and hundreds of the previously doubtful were eager to get on the bandwagon. The initial work of organizing seemed also to be going well in a number of other states, with the greatest activity centered in Minnesota. Requests for the League to "come and help us" or at least to provide information and help in starting an organization, came thick and fast after the 1917 legislative session,[31] and gradually a program of expansion was undertaken.

Organizers had commenced operations in Montana in the fall of 1916 and an extensive series of meetings was held throughout the state during the winter months. In January at a convention in Billings the Montana Farmers' Federation, an association of various farmers' organizations and companies, endorsed the Nonpartisan League. The resolutions of the convention included many of the points of the League program, and it seemed evident that a sound groundwork was being laid.[32] The long domination of the state by the Anaconda Copper Company was a sore spot with many persons besides farmers.

In February a convention of the Idaho State Federation of Agriculture, strongest farmers' organization in the state, heard a speech by Ray McKaig and at once passed a unanimous resolution asking the Nonpartisan League "to extend their interstate organization to our state . . . and to begin such operations not later than May 1, 1917." [33] Conditions were especially favorable in that state because of the several years of agitation for marketing reform conducted by W. G. Scholtz, publisher of a weekly farmers' journal. Scholtz had been largely responsible for the creation of the office of state market commissioner and had been the first to hold that position. His dismissal by the governor at the end of Idaho's 1917 legislative session aroused a storm of protest which developed just as the League was about to commence operations in that state. Scholtz eagerly welcomed the League and shortly thereafter converted his magazine into the *Idaho Leader*.[34]

Miscellaneous groups of city radicals in the state of Washington expressed interest in the League and the support of some farm elements was also secured, but the organization did not make rapid strides "largely because of the very diverse character of agricultural production in the state and an overbalance of urban and industrial population." [35] Sometime later both the Grange and the Farmers' Union of Oregon endorsed the League and requested it to organize Oregon farmers for political action,[36] but no steps in that direction were taken for the time being.

Also in February a stockholders' meeting of the Farmers' Cooperative Packing Company of Wisconsin at Wausau passed resolutions condemning existing marketing conditions and issued a call for a farmers' convention at Marshfield on March 22 for the purpose of organizing a Nonpartisan League. When that meeting convened, F. B. Wood and Leon Durocher from League headquarters in St. Paul were present to advise, and plans were laid for the opening of a drive as soon as country roads were clear. The "drive" was slow, however, and divisions of opinion arose among Wisconsin farm groups as to whether or not the state League should be a part of the national organization. The Wisconsin Society of Equity led the move for independence, but after able peacemaking by Joe Gilbert and a statewide meeting of all elements at Milwaukee where the divergent views were aired, it was voted almost unanimously to affiliate.[37]

The Land League of Texas, an organization dedicated to the economic betterment of farmers and primarily concerned with the large landholdings and extensive farm tenantry in that state, sent Ernest Meitzen to North Dakota in April 1917 to investigate the Nonpartisan League and, if possible, enlist its support. Meitzen went into the field with organizers, attended numerous meetings, and conferred with many of the League leaders, rapidly becoming an ardent convert to the principle of nonpartisanship. "We in Texas are born Democrats," he said, "but we can still be Democrats and also be Nonpartisans."[38] The League did some token organizing in Texas and assisted in the establishment of a state organization, but it was too far from headquarters, too vast in area, and many of its most interested farmers were too impoverished to support the movement properly.

Organizing in Kansas began in the spring of 1917 in Ellsworth, Lincoln, and Rice counties, the movement receiving fairly strong Farmers' Union and cooperative backing.[39] The response for a time was enthusiastic, but the number of organizers was limited and national headquarters did not push large-scale operations. Much the same was true in Nebraska and Iowa. In Colorado better headway was made, largely because of more vigorous support by strong existing organizations in the state. On July 30 the State Federation of Farmers' Organizations, which included the Grange, the Farmers' Union, and several others, endorsed the Nonpartisan League and appointed a committee to confer with other interested organizations on beginning a state League. Three days later the State Federation of Women's Clubs also endorsed the League and appointed a committee, and the next week a convention of the State Federation of Labor followed suit.[40]

In most of these states the League national headquarters actively fostered the interest of farmer and liberal groups. One of the most ubiquitous and successful missionaries was Ray McKaig, master of the North Dakota state Grange and now a lecturer for the League, who once described himself as the "John the Baptist of the farmers' movement." McKaig's widespread Grange contacts were invaluable in securing him entree to meetings where the League idea might be put across and in selecting outstanding farmer leaders as key persons for new state organizations.[41]

The League had early assumed that success in South Dakota could be achieved almost as easily as had been the case in its sister state to the north. But the two states had then, as they have now, almost no contact with each other and relatively little in common. Moreover, the existing political situation in South Dakota was appreciably different.[42] South Dakota had experienced a greater degree of "insurgency and progressivism" than had North Dakota, discontent was far less prevalent, and in the governor's chair sat Peter Norbeck, who described himself as a "Theodore Roosevelt Republican." Norbeck was certainly not an extreme liberal, but he was a believer in the use of governmental powers to alleviate social and economic distress and was a sufficiently astute politician to listen carefully to farmer demands.

Norbeck first advocated a state rural credits system in 1912, and had made it a campaign plank in 1916. His recommendations to the 1917 South Dakota legislature had more than coincidental similarity to the League program: (1) direct state loans to farmers on real estate, (2) state acquisition, development, and operation of water power sites, (3) a study to determine the advisability of state hail insurance, (4) an investigation of the feasibility of the establishment and operation of a state coal mine, and (5) an investigation of the possibility of establishing terminal grain elevators within the state.

The legislature, apparently agreeing with Norbeck that the way to head off the League was to "steal its thunder," provided for the requested investigations, passed a rural credits law, established a workmen's compensation system, and created the office of state marketing commissioner to aid in the elimination of abuses. Subsequently a constitutional amendment was proposed to make possible bonding of the state for an estimated $50,000,000 to develop twelve dams on the Missouri River for the purpose of supplying power and water for irrigation. Although the *Leader* sourly insisted that these were merely "fake" measures designed to fool the people, it seemed probable that if the League program stirred enthusiasm in South Dakota it would be in spite of rather than because of the Norbeck administration.

The Nonpartisan League in the prairie provinces of Canada was still in the process of organizing when the 1917 provincial elections rolled around. Here it was necessary to operate as a third party, since there were no primaries at which an old party might be captured and the concept of nonpartisanship did not accord with a parliamentary system. The Saskatchewan League was cursed with inept leadership and consequently poor planning; its conventions were badly managed and torn by serious strife. Having nominated eight farmer candidates, it was successful in only one riding, and that was an instance in which the candidate had the nomination of all three parties, although he had been nominated first by the League. This failure was followed by bitter recriminations and ultimately the complete break-up of the organization. Never again was the League of real significance in that province.[43]

In Alberta there was better leadership, less friction, and a higher degree of success. Two of the League's four nominees were elected, and there was great optimism for the future. But in succeeding months the organization was subjected to a terrific assault, largely on the loyalty issue, because of its attacks on profiteering, its advocacy of conscription of wealth, and a fairly evident lack of enthusiasm for the war. In the federal elections of December 1917, none of the League candidates were successful, though considerable strength was shown in a number of areas. Failure here did not result in disintegration as in Saskatchewan; instead the League merged with the United Farmers of Alberta and ultimately forced it into politics.[44] Though never a huge success in Canada, the League promoted a class consciousness in the prairie provinces, united the farmers on a fairly definite program of action, gave them practical political experience for the future, and laid the groundwork for later agrarian and radical movements.

Once the organization seemed clearly on its way to success in North

Dakota, the greatest interest of the League leadership aside from the mother state centered in Minnesota. There the problems of the farmers were most nearly similar to North Dakota, and in the Twin Cities were located the headquarters of many of the great economic empires upon which the League had declared war. Farmers in the western counties of Minnesota had been interested in the League from the beginning and repeatedly sought the extension of its operations. Between eighty and ninety Fords, an equal number of trained organizers, and several experienced superintendents were transferred to Minnesota in the early fall of 1916, where they commenced an intensive farm-to-farm canvass, with the objective of capturing the state in 1918.[45] All activities were theoretically under the supervision of an executive committee of five Minnesota farmers, but the actual directing force lay with the National Executive Committee, consisting of A. C. Townley as president, William Lemke, and F. B. Wood.

The attendance at the spring mass meetings in North Dakota had been considered excellent, but when the speaking staff swung into Minnesota in June of 1917 it found an even greater response. Successive meetings in Montevideo, Glencoe, New Ulm, and Chatfield drew a total attendance of more than 10,000, with farmers frequently coming in from eight or nine surrounding counties. Businessmen's organizations in several instances provided facilities and furnished bands.[46] Enthusiasm ran high.

The highly successful all-day picnics made famous in North Dakota were transplanted to Minnesota with equal success. During the summer months picnics were held throughout that part of the state which had so far been organized, with the League's top speakers, A. E. Bowen, Joe Gilbert, N. S. Randall, O. M. Thomason, and others, making the rounds. Even Governor Frazier took time to attend a few such gatherings, and the farm families loved the easy informality of the farmer governor. All ages were present, from the old-timers to babes in arms. There were games, band music, singing, an abundance of speech-making, and plenty of good food when families gathered around cloths spread on the grass.

Even some who were inclined to be suspicious came away from such affairs filled with zeal for the cause. Commented the *Thief River Falls News-Press*:

Residents of Thief River Falls and Pennington County who attended

the Nonpartisan League picnic last Thursday expecting to hear out-
bursts against the government, tirades against the businessmen and attacks on the merchants were disappointed . . .

There was but little in any of the talks that the most patriotic citizen
could take offense at and there was much to be endorsed by the residents of any farming community . . .

Personally we must admit that this was the first opportunity we had
to hear the League principles advocated and explained. We had gained
the impression from the *Grand Forks Herald* and other radical newspapers that the organizers were anarchists, cut-throats, and thieves and
had been prepared for the worst. Instead the discussion was conducted
along generally approved lines, the truth of a majority of the assertions
was undeniable.[47]

The vastly greater urban population in Minnesota than in North
Dakota meant that if the League was ever to gain control of that state
it must somehow make an appeal to city dwellers as well as farmers; an
attempted alliance with organized labor was inevitable. Long experienced in the labor movement, Joe Gilbert took the lead in this work,
and for the first time in history the State Federation of Labor convention at Faribault had two representatives of a farmers' organization
seated as fraternal delegates. Gilbert conferred at length with officers
of the Federation, the railway brotherhoods, and other unions with
the result that working relations were shortly established.[48]

The obvious successes of League organizing in Minnesota during the
winter of 1916–17 stirred to action those who had cause to fear its program. This time, however, it was not just another anti-League association which emerged. Instead, in March 1917, the "Minnesota Nonpartisan League" was incorporated in St. Paul by a group nominally
headed by J. A. Stoneberg, a former Republican state central committeeman and close friend of "Boss" Ed Smith of Minneapolis, and a
Clarence F. Johnson. The same group also formed a "Nonpartisan Publishing Company" and announced that they expected to commence
soon the publication of a paper entitled the *Non-Partisan*. Headquarters
were located in a building adjoining League headquarters so that the
address might be essentially similar, the office utilized being that of
Stoneberg, who was a land agent and money lender.[49]

Johnson was quoted in the *St. Paul Daily News* as saying:

The purpose of our league is to work for women's rights, temper-
ance, eight hour day, government ownership, and exemptions for per-

sonal property of less than $200, and many other progressive measures. We shall charge members only $3 a year. We think we are better qualified to do this work than is the North Dakota organization, and as they charge $16 for two years membership, we can save the farmers of this state considerable money. There are many persons backing the new organization, but I can't give their names.[50]

The whole proposition was so transparent as to be ludicrous, but letters were immediately sent to thousands of Minnesota farmers, especially League members, making the "cut-rate" offer and subtly attacking the Nonpartisan League, largely on the grounds that it was an out-of-state organization. The letter indicated that officials of this league would not expect any salaries, leaving readers with any perspicacity to wonder just what was to be the source of livelihood for these selfless workers for the welfare of their fellow men.[51] The *Leader* gave wide publicity to the "fake league," warning its readers against it and pointing out that if it really sought the same objectives it would hardly have set up a parallel competing organization. The *St. Paul Daily News* concluded that it was "a despicable scheme, because it is trying to take from the real farmers' organization the name by which it has become famous throughout all rural America, and because obviously it is trying to disrupt and nullify a great popular and democratic movement." [52]

The *Non-Partisan* lasted almost five months, but in July the entire project, which had flopped miserably, quietly ceased to exist. Two years later, however, the League was delighted to learn that Clarence Johnson, the former secretary of the "fake league" and editor of the *Non-Partisan*, had filed suit for back pay, implicating in the previously hushed-up enterprise several prominent Twin Cities businessmen, bankers, and railroad officials. Striking "nonpartisanship" was evident, inasmuch as leaders of both the Republican and Democratic parties were involved, including Gust Lindquist, secretary to Governor Burnquist. Johnson played his role to the hilt, issuing a statement which concluded:

After 18 months of close association with the most bitter opponents of the Nonpartisan League, it is my opinion that a large part of that opposition is based on wholesale misrepresentation and half truths, given to the public as whole truths. The underlying and most bitter opposition to the farmers' program is based wholly upon the natural opposition of a group firmly entrenched in power and opposing any change from the existing order of affairs which would threaten their control.[53]

Ultimately more formidable than the "Minnesota Nonpartisan League" was the Minnesota Public Safety Commission. The commission, consisting of the governor, the attorney general, and five citizens appointed by the governor, was a wartime agency given broad police and regulatory powers subject to almost no restrictions. During the war its word was law in Minnesota, and its standards of "loyalty" the norm. From the first the League had feared this concentration of arbitrary power, and it always assumed that the commission's basic purpose was the destruction of the Nonpartisan League. Although such was not precisely the case, the commission frequently gave them ample grounds for the suspicion, and it is undeniably true that the existence of the League, as a suspect organization, was one important reason for its creation. County public safety commissions came into being after the establishment of the state body and many of them were even more arbitrary and antagonistic to the Nonpartisan League.

The first general ordinance or directive of the Public Safety Commission, designed to control more rigidly possible seditious utterances, did not allay the fears of the League's leaders. It was admittedly drawn to suppress "agitators of disloyalty" and "sentiments bordering on treason," although existing laws seemed quite adequate for necessary protection. The press reports announced that its purpose was "to prevent the agitators from seeking refuge under the free speech clause of the constitution," and the League was justifiably suspicious of "a law professedly drawn to repeal the constitution." [54] Shortly thereafter the commission, which had previously hired private detective agencies, established its own "Bureau of Intelligence," headed by T. G. Winter, a Minneapolis grain broker.[55] Its representatives were always present at League meetings, and the commission's news releases continually implied that the League was a disloyal organization. Clearly, there was trouble ahead in Minnesota.

The death of Congressman H. T. Helgeson of the first North Dakota district (the eastern counties of the state, including the cities of Grand Forks and Fargo) in the spring of 1917 forced upon the League a speedy decision on whether or not to enter the field of national politics. The organization had definitely established itself, the members had seen what it could do, and many were eager to expand in every direction. Townley was inclined, as he had been from the first, to favor restricting activities to the state level, but he was not antagonistic to the idea of attempting to elect congressmen and most of his lieutenants vigorously urged the step. Accordingly a convention of the 1916 delegates, for the most part the League members of the legislature, was called to meet in Fargo on June 1 to select a candidate.

Governor Frazier had called a special election for July 10, so quick action was essential. The convention followed the same procedure as had been utilized in 1916, with names proposed by the delegates and written on a blackboard. Fourteen possibilities were suggested and their qualifications were discussed for several hours. Agreement was finally reached on John M. Baer, a thirty-year-old engineer who had been the cartoonist for the *Leader* from its inception.[56] Baer, a Democrat and former postmaster at Beach, appointed by President Wilson, had lived in the first district only a relatively short time, but his name was known to every reader of the *Leader*, and he was a popular choice with the farmers. His telling cartoons they considered one of the best features of the magazine.

A question immediately arose as to the proper nominating procedure, inasmuch as the legislature had never provided how special congressional elections should be held. Since there was no provision for a primary and the convention nominating procedure had been repealed, Attorney General Langer ruled that nominations must be by petition and the governor so ordered. It was indicated that candidates might have any designation they desired on the ballot, and Baer's managers decided that his name should be followed by "Nonpartisan, indorsed by the Nonpartisan League."[57] Petitions were also filed for six other candidates, H. H. Aaker, "Nonpartisan Progressive Republican"; George A. Bangs, "Democrat"; Olger B. Burtness, "Republican"; F. T. Cuthbert, "Republican"; Charles W. Plain, "Republican"; and Henry G. Vick, "Republican."

Greatly disturbed by this multiplicity of Republicans, the anti-League forces called a "Republican convention" to meet at Grand Forks and decide upon a single candidate. It was agreed that the other four Republicans would withdraw in favor of the one chosen by the convention. Burtness was promptly selected, whereupon suit was brought in the Supreme Court in the name of the Grand Forks convention to prevent the election from being held in the manner laid down by Frazier and Langer. They demanded a party ballot with Burtness in the Republican column, and asked that the other Republicans be permitted to withdraw, despite the fact that ballots were already printed.[58]

Faced with this development, William Lemke, as Republican state chairman (and one of the chief backers of Baer), hastily called a meeting of the Executive Committee of the State Central Committee, which immediately voted eleven to one to endorse Baer. Armed with this action, Lemke departed at once for Bismarck to contest the suit pending before the Supreme Court, assuming that it would sustain Langer's view but now prepared to insist that if anyone were to gain the benefit of a Republican column it should be Baer.[59] The court unanimously ruled that all candidates were on the ballot by virtue of petitions rather than any convention endorsement, that the attorney general's opinion had been correct, and that no names could be removed from the ballots, since the law required the secretary of state to file certificates of nomination with the county auditors thirty days before an election and no changes could subsequently be made.[60]

Baer rapidly developed into a reasonably effective speaker, stumping the district as a "nonpartisan" who was not tied to any party and was therefore free to vote on every issue solely on its merits. The *Leader* did its utmost to make him appear to be a farmer, pointing out that he was the son of a farmer and that his wife had inherited a five-thousand-acre farm in western North Dakota which he had managed successfully for several years.[61] His candidacy was actively promoted by Townley, Frazier, and other top Leaguers at the mass meetings being held throughout the state during this period, while the *Leader*, maintaining that the opposition of the "gang press" and the "interests" proved Baer to be the right man, contended that he was truly nonpartisan because he was a Democrat before joining the League and was now endorsed by the Republican State Central Committee. Presumably, therefore, he should be supported by Democrats, Republicans, and Leaguers alike.

The *Fargo Forum* charged that Baer was one of the "organizers" of the League, and that his election would set a precedent for wholesale office seeking by League officers and organizers. To this the *Leader* replied that he was neither an officer nor an organizer; he had joined the League while farming at Beach and had subsequently been employed by the *Leader* as a cartoonist. Never one to lose sight of the "loyalty" issue, the *Grand Forks Herald* dwelt at length upon the seditious nature of a statement alleged to have been made by Baer in a speech at Cando that "Americanism is not an issue at this time." It was subsequently conceded that the full statement was "Americanism is no special issue at this time because we all are and must be Americans," but in the eyes of the *Herald* this was at best a "weak distinction." [62] Burtness said little about the League, leaving the attacks mostly to the *Herald* and *Forum*, and even made a mild bid for League support in advertisements which indicated that he was not really an enemy of the program.

As election day neared the *Herald* became steadily more and more optimistic, foreseeing an overwhelming victory for Burtness. The great majority of Republican precinct committeemen in the district favored Burtness, it said, and League members were flocking to him because they had no voice in the selection of Baer, usually referred to as "the socialist-democrat-picture-drawing candidate of A. C. Townley and William Lemke." [63] Only Baer, Bangs, and Burtness conducted serious campaigns. The last two, said the *Herald*, were loyal; Baer was merely a cartoonist and should stay in his place. Moreover, he had once cartooned for *Jim Jam Jems*, subsequently barred from the mails as obscene. The people, it claimed, resented this attempt of Lemke's to force upon them a renegade Democrat in the guise of a Republican.

The *Leader* made no secret of the importance of the election to the future of the League. Baer's defeat, it said, would set the farmers' movement back years. Townley's pre-election message dramatically emphasized that this was not simply a battle between Baer and Burtness, or even between opposing political forces in the district: "This battle is between big business in the United States and the farmers of the United States. The first congressional district of North Dakota is the place where this battle is raging." [64]

By the morning of July 11 it was clear that the League had won another striking victory, and this time in the very stronghold of the enemy. Baer had been elected with a clear majority over his two principal opponents, and had carried every county in the district except Grand Forks and Ramsey, the latter being lost by a margin of seven votes.* Amazingly enough, he carried both Fargo and Wahpeton. In Ransom County his majority was better than two to one over Burtness

* The vote was as follows: Baer, 13,126; Burtness, 8945; Bangs, 3301 (*Grand Forks Herald*, July 12, 1917, p. 3; see also *Leader*, July 19, 1917, p. 3).

and Bangs combined, while his majorities in Towner and Steele counties were almost as high.[65]

Baer was swamped with congratulations from all over the country. Among the most prized was a joint telegram from Senators LaFollette and Gronna which read: "As we are informed of the issues involved we regard your election as a triumph for self-government and we join in congratulations." [66]

The *Grand Forks Herald* was distraught with the fear that North Dakota would be placed in a false light before the nation, and to some extent its fears were justified, since the wire services tended to adopt a similar point of view. Although Baer had urged the prosecution of the war with all possible energy and had endorsed conscription (including conscription of wealth), astonishing distortions appeared in certain newspapers. The *Indianapolis Star* indicated that he ran on a platform calling for "immediate peace and repeal of the conscription law." The *New York Mail* reported that the League was opposing the sale of Liberty Bonds and Red Cross subscriptions, intimating that this was Baer's platform. It later corrected this version and apologized for taking the wire service report without question. The *Buffalo Express* commented that the election was "not creditable to North Dakota" because Baer was pro-German, while others stated that he was a Socialist and that the administration in Washington was alarmed because the election showed the inroads of pro-Germanism in the Midwest.[67]

Baer was well enough if indifferently received in Washington, but the anti-League propaganda had done its work in parts of the East. At the time he was sworn in the *Boston Transcript* self-righteously pointed to the fact that the 1910 census showed that North Dakota had a larger percentage of foreign-born population than any other state, and remarked that since the Swedes of the Northwest were imperfectly Americanized and were in sympathy with the Germans, the poison had undoubtedly entered the veins of the Nonpartisan League: "We must therefore regard the newly elected congressman from the first district of North Dakota, Mr. Baer, as the representative of a foreign influence in our Congress." Other sections of the country took a less serious view, the *Louisville Courier-Journal* commenting: "That North Dakota cartoonist elected to Congress can earn his stipend if he does no more than enliven the *Record*." [68]

Although Baer was classed as a Republican in the House, he at once appointed as his secretary D. H. McArthur, who had been the Democratic candidate for governor of North Dakota in 1916. This naturally led the opposition to charge that the League and the Democrats had been allied, and that McArthur had been promised that he would be "taken care of." [69]

Having leaped in, the League found the water fine, and from that time forward there was no doubt about its interest in national politics. Editorials and cartoons talked excitedly of electing the rest of the North Dakota delegation, to be followed by campaigns in other League states. They spoke in terms of fifty nonpartisans the next time, later a hundred, in time perhaps a majority of "farmer congressmen." [70]

Just as the League had initially proclaimed its intention of staying out of national politics, so had it also intended to steer clear of county politics. Officially, it maintained this position, but the same eagerness for expanded activity was prevalent here, and already by 1917 there were rumors of county tickets with League support and there were invariably dozens of candidates who claimed League backing. Although some of these were publicly disavowed by the state organization, they were too numerous to cope with and the battles had to be left for local settlement.[71] Townley claims that he always endeavored to keep the League free from county politics, but that "as time wore on there were too many people hungry for jobs and they went into county activity regardless of the League leadership." [72] Not until 1919 or 1920 did it become an extensive practice.

An adequate supply of labor during the harvest season was always a severe problem in North Dakota, and with the armed forces draining off manpower it promised to be even more serious in 1917. Disorders and disputes with the transient workers were frequently critical even in normal years. In order to meet this situation the state convention which met June 1 to select a congressional candidate authorized President Townley to appoint a committee of three to meet with representatives of the Agricultural Workers Union (I.W.W.) in an effort to reach an agreement on hours, wages, and conditions of work in return for a guaranteed labor supply. The Agricultural Workers Union had some 20,000 to 30,000 members and an organizer in most of the larger towns of the state who kept in touch with union headquarters in St. Paul. The hope was that the I.W.W. might ensure an adequate supply of workers and prevent disorders in return for satisfactory contract provisions.[73]

Townley accordingly appointed John N. Hagan, F. B. Wood, and N. E. Whipple of Eckelson, and after several conferences a tentative agreement was signed, subject to ratification by the League membership. It provided for a minimum wage of four dollars a day for a ten-hour day, with a sliding scale upward geared to the price of wheat. The I.W.W. would guarantee a harvest labor supply, make a no-strike pledge, and promise that the railroads would get fares instead of having rides stolen as in the past.[74] There are indications that closed-shop agreements may have been contemplated by both parties, as is evidenced by a letter written at this time by the secretary of the Minneapolis local of the I.W.W.: ". . . When a farmer comes to town after a man, the wobbly will ask him for his card in the farmers' organization. If he has none, the wobbly will tell him there is nothing doing. The members of the farmers' organization, on the other hand, will hire only I.W.W. men. The unorganized farmer and the unorganized worker will be out of luck." [75]

The *Herald* professed to be completely aghast at the strange bedfellows proposed for North Dakota farmers, and quoted a telling sentence from an I.W.W. pamphlet on tactics: "No terms made with an employer are final. All peace so long as the wage system lasts is but an armed truce." [76] To Judge Bruce the proposals seemed simply another indication of the "desire of the League's socialist hierarchy to bring about an era of sovietism and to obtain the votes and support of the radical laboring classes no matter what the consequences might be to orderly government." [77]

Townley presented these proposals to several meetings around the state seeking an expression of sentiment from the farmers. Shortly thereafter he notified the I.W.W. representatives that the wage scale which they demanded was too high to make agreement possible. Gaston says that a majority in all the meetings but one favored the proposition, but Townley turned it down because there was considerable opposition and "he did not want the responsibility of having urged it upon the farmers." [78] Governor Frazier then issued a directive to local law enforcement officials calling for strict enforcement of the laws against violence to employers or damage to crops or machinery, but coupled with it the insistence that peace officers not enforce their own ideas of what labor should or should not do. He pleaded for reason and fairness, asking that there be no suppression of peaceful assemblage or police action against workers seeking higher wages.[79] The harvest season in North Dakota, interestingly enough, saw much less disorder than existed in any of the surrounding states.

The continuous violent attacks upon the loyalty of the League drove its leaders to the conclusion that a comprehensive statement of the organization's position on the war was a necessity. A statement of principles was therefore drawn up by Joe Gilbert and adopted enthusiastically by the series of mass meetings held throughout the state in May and June 1917. This statement so aptly embodied the sentiments of the League that it was subsequently published in conjunction with a description of the origin and purposes of the League and widely distributed throughout the country. John M. Baer's initial public statement and press release after his election to Congress, also written by Gilbert, covered the same ground in similar fashion.[80] The war resolutions expressed a philosophy to which the League adhered, and their significance for the future of the organization was such as to make them of especial interest:

. . . Whatever ideas we as individuals may have had, as to the wisdom of our nation engaging in this war, we realize that a crisis now confronts us in which it becomes necessary that we all stand unreservedly pledged to safeguard, defend and preserve our country.

In making this declaration of our position we declare unequivocally that we stand for our country, right or wrong, as against foreign governments with whom we are actually engaged in war. Still we hold that when we believe our country wrong, we should endeavor to set her right.

The only justification for war is to establish and maintain human rights and interests the world over. For this reason we are opposed to waging war for annexation, either on our part or on that of our allies, or demanding indemnity as terms of peace. Bitter experience has proved that any exactions, whether of land or revenue, serve only to deepen resentments and hatreds which inevitably incite to future war.

We therefore urge that our government before proceeding further in support of our European allies, insist that they, in common with it, make immediate public declaration of terms of peace, without annexations of territory, indemnities, contributions, or interference with the right of any nation to live and manage its own internal affairs, thus being in harmony with and supporting the new democracy of Russia in her declaration of these fundamental principles.

. . . we demand the abolition of secret diplomacy . . . We demand that the guaranties of human conservation be recognized, and the standard of living be maintained. To this end we demand that gambling in the necessaries of life be made a felony, and that the federal government control the food supply of the nation, and establish prices for producer and consumer . . .

Patriotism demands service from all according to their capacity. To conscript men and exempt the bloodstained wealth coined from the sufferings of humanity is repugnant to the spirit of America and contrary to the ideals of democracy.

We declare freedom of speech to be the bulwark of human liberty, and we decry all attempts to muzzle the public press, upon any pretext whatsoever. A declaration of war does not repeal the Constitution of the United States, and the unwarranted interference of military and other authorities with the rights of individuals must cease.

The contributory causes of the present war are various; but above the horrible slaughter loom the ugly incitings of an economic system based upon exploitation. It is largely a convulsive effort on the part of the adroit rulers of warring nations for control of a constantly diminishing market . . .

A lasting peace is possible only on a new basis of human thought and relations. In waging this war it is well that we bear this in mind; otherwise we shall be fastening the shackles of new servitude, both mental and governmental, upon mankind.

At the close of this war sound international standards must be established on the basis of a true democracy. Private monopolies must be supplanted by public administration of credit, finance, and natural resources. The rule of jobbers and speculators must be overthrown if we are to produce a real democracy; otherwise this war will have been fought in vain.

Only in this spirit do we justify war, and only thus can lasting peace be established.[81]

Many a prominent nonconformist during World War I found occasion to repeat the words of Woodrow Wilson's great expression of liberal philosophy, *The New Freedom*. Just as Gene Debs was to read passages from this book to the jury in the final plea at his famous trial in 1919 on charges of discouraging enlistments, so now the League quoted the nation's President in support of its position. The *Leader* frequently printed paragraphs which might easily have come from one of their own editorials, League speakers quoted him constantly, and before long the organization commenced distributing the book at a special price to members, recommending it as a "textbook of League principles."

No person came in for more malicious vilification on the matter of attitude toward the war than did Arthur Townley. At his every speech the anti-League press screamed "treason," and suggestions that he be imprisoned or hanged were commonplace. His position was essentially that expressed in the war resolutions, and his public addresses were but expansions of the themes set forth. Nevertheless, his picturesque oratory and biting scarcasm made the issues stand out even more sharply than did the eloquent phrases of the resolutions. His venomous attacks on the "profiteers and food gamblers" had a sting which could not be ignored.

At the first three of the mass meetings in the spring of 1917, at Devils Lake, Williston, and Minot, there was no record of his speeches and the reports in the opposition press gave them a distinctly pro-German cast. For the next meeting at Valley City, Townley had a stenographic report made, and from that time on he made no public utterances without a League stenographer on hand. The Valley City speech was distorted by the *Forum* in much the same fashion as had been the previous ones, whereupon the *Courier-News* printed the full stenographic transcript and challenged the *Forum* to prove the accuracy of its quotations. There was no reply, but it was significant that he was not again misquoted in that paper.[82]

Townley's method of making a case for the League view can be well illustrated by excerpts from the transcript of his speech at Jamestown June 9, which was essentially the same speech delivered at all of this series of meetings:

They say I oppose the sale of bonds. I do not. If we can't find another and more efficient way to finance the war, then we will have to finance it by the sale of bonds. But if there is another and a better way, we have a right to propose that better way.

If a man can pay as he goes, that's good business and he ought to pay.

If a nation can pay, they ought to pay, today. There is a way to pay today . . .

I say to you that the first thing this government should do is to take the profits they [the trusts] are making today to pay the expense of the war.

Is this treason?

138

Is this anarchy?

More than that, if by the duration of this war, those profits are not enough to pay the cost of the war . . . there is still another reservoir: and that is the millions that they piled up before the war. We will take that, too!

And when the war is over we will not be in debt, and when those boys come back they may start life then anew, not to live for decades in the mire of national bondage . . .

You [who profit from war] must make this arrangement, that when we give our lives, all that we have, this nation will take first of your profits and then of the property you have got, if the profit is not enough; and after the war is over we will give back, as you give back of our lives, as much as is left, and no more . . .

It is absolute insanity for us to lead ourselves or anybody else to believe that this nation can succeed in war when hundreds of thousands of parasites, the gamblers in the necessities of life, use the war only for the purpose of exacting exorbitant profits. We are working, not to beat the enemy, but to make more multi-millionaires . . .

Now here is the seditious and treasonable and unpatriotic part of my discussion. We respectfully suggest, and then we demand, that this nation . . . take over the railroads and the distribution of foods and kick the gamblers into the sea or send them to war—so that when you gentlemen . . . shall produce an immense crop, you will be sure that crop will arrive at the camp where your boy is fighting for his country without your having to pay for it at that end four times what you received for it at this end . . .

Is this treason?

Demanding a measure that will enable us to succeed in the war cannot be treason, can it? [83]

One of the last of the mass meetings was scheduled for Fargo the night of June 16, and on June 9 the *Fargo Forum* printed an editorial that gave every appearance of a call to mob violence:

The *Forum* hopes that when Mr. Townley comes to Fargo, the members of the Home Defense league, 100 or 150 strong, will march into the hall, stand at attention during his address and give him a chance to repeat those remarks [speeches the previous week] or make others in the same vein.

If there isn't a public officer in the state with backbone enough to put the speaker behind the bars, there is enough spirit in the Home Defense league to prevent him from repeating the offense.[84]

Townley promptly accepted the challenge, promising to give the same speech, and the *Leader* used the incident as incentive for a large attendance. Farmers poured into Fargo on the afternoon of the 16th, and city residents were equally interested. Four thousand persons were packed in the hall and the "standing room only" sign was out long before time for the meeting to begin. Once again, in his inimitable fashion, Townley "poured it on," to the accompaniment of tremendous applause, whistling, and stamping of feet. There was no demonstration against him, and the meeting seemed a huge success. The tone of the *Forum* softened appreciably in reporting the meeting, apparently in the attempt to seem not to be fighting the farmers. It later claimed that Townley had "toned down" his remarks in Fargo, but the transcripts showed them to be almost identical with earlier speeches.[85]

Many of the subsequent attempts to prove that Townley had opposed the war effort, discouraged enlistments, and fostered pro-Germanism were based on remarks he was alleged to have made during a speech at Buffalo Lake, North Dakota, in July 1917. No transcript appears to have survived, while the widely circulated version publicized by the opposition, presumably attested by ten named witnesses, played an important role in derogation of the League. Townley denied its accuracy, and it does possess a flavor of interpolation. Nevertheless, it had somewhat the Townley touch, and the significant thing is that it was accepted in many quarters as valid and as convincing proof of the disloyalty of the speaker:

We have been dragged into this war by American autocracy, dragged into a war we did not want and we are told it is a war to liberate the people from the control of autocracy.

We are about to send millions of our young men over to Europe to fight the German autocracy, while the big bellied, red-necked American plutocrats, ten times worse than the German autocrats, coin the blood of our young men into profits for themselves.

You are about to have these young men drafted into the army, and they will be sent over to France to fight. They will have their legs shot off, their arms shot off, their chests ripped open, their eyes torn out, and as they lay there in No Man's Land at night, human reptiles will crawl over them, go through their pockets and steal their little trinkets and souvenirs. Their carcasses will become carrion for the vultures and the worms and the reptiles of the earth, while the human reptiles, the big bellied, red-necked American plutocrats continue to obtain their extortionate profits of $4,000,000,000 per year while loudly shouting that this is a war for liberty and democracy.

Who started this war? I will tell you who started this war. It was the big bellied, red-necked plutocrats. And I will tell you how to stop this war. Place these big bellied, red-necked plutocrats in the line of battle. Their big bellies will stop more bullets than the bodies of slim young men they are taking from your families. But this is not the reason why the war would stop. It is because they would not stand for being targets of German bullets. These big bellied, red-necked plutocrats would take care of their precious bodies by seeing that U.S. participation in this war were brought to a close.[86]

From the time of America's entry into the war, the *Leader* had consistently urged the highest possible farm production, in accordance with the requests of the national administration, but it never ceased to argue also that the government should control the marketing system and guarantee a price high enough to encourage heavy production. There was enthusiastic support for Food Administrator Herbert Hoover's action in August in appointing a commission to fix wheat prices, followed by dismay when the commission set a Chicago terminal price for No. 1 Northern and equivalent grades of $2.20. The price in Minneapolis and Duluth was three cents lower, and it was estimated that the price at a North Dakota country elevator would be about $2.03. It was another poor crop year with not much top-grade wheat available, and this fact, combined with the new federal grades, meant that little wheat was likely to be graded No. 1. The farmer would probably receive for No. 3 or No. 4, after transportation and storage charges were subtracted, approximately $1.85.[87]

In view of the fact that the cash price for No. 1 wheat on the day the order was issued was $3.06, it is not surprising that disappointment was widespread. It virtually amounted, said the *Leader*, to "commandeering the crop."[88] Nevertheless, the League, having so ardently demanded a guaranteed price, was in no position to protest too bitterly. After the initial shock it accepted the situation gracefully, though on the expressed assumption that other groups were to be treated similarly. Then, to their dismay, the food administrator announced that there was no intention to fix a price on flour; it was expected that the millers would reduce charges by "patriotic cooperation." At this the *Leader* hooted. Their kind of cooperation was evidenced by the recent 213 to 33 vote of the Minneapolis Chamber of Commerce doubling commission charges on grain handling.[89] Price fixing was proper, but it should apply to all. Why should the farmer be singled out for government coercion, while others were left to make all they could from the war boom?

Shortly after the issuance of the wheat price order the League began preparations for a huge "Producers and Consumers Convention" to meet in Fargo September 17 and in St. Paul the three succeeding days. A great variety of groups were invited, with especial emphasis on organized labor. Although it was immediately so publicized by the anti-League press, this was not designed to be a meeting of protest. Its aim, as clearly indicated by the advance publicity and the opening remarks of Governor Frazier and Mr. Townley, was to insist that price fixing be extended to all the necessities of life, and to advocate conscription of wealth, an end to profiteering, and government operation of basic industries. This conference was to provide a means of expression for the common people, so that the government might know the majority will and be assured that the producing classes stood shoulder to shoulder in support of whatever regulatory activities it decided to undertake.[90]

The Fargo gathering was to be addressed by Townley, Frazier, Baer, and Ladd, but this was merely a warm-up for the St. Paul meetings. Among the speakers scheduled for this affair was a rather striking array of prominent persons, including Senators Borah, Gronna, and LaFollette, Congressmen Baer and Young of North Dakota, Congresswoman Jeannette Rankin of Montana, Mayors Irvin of St. Paul and Van Lear of Minneapolis, representatives of the United States Department of Agriculture and the Federal Trade Commission, J. M. Anderson, president of the Equity Cooperative Exchange, Carl D. Thompson, secretary of the National Public Ownership League, leaders of organized labor, and various League and North Dakota state officials.[91]

The speakers unanimously proclaimed the support of the common man for the war effort and developed at length the general themes of the convention, with the keynote set in typical fashion by A. C. Townley:

While the farmers and other producers have been raising crops to feed the armies of liberty, making ships and munitions and implements of war, a lot of gentlemen have been spending their ample leisure in announcing their patriotism. When you work sixteen hours a day for liberty and democracy you haven't much time or will to wave the flag . . .

But now you have taken a day off to announce your patriotism. Yet you cannot do as much announcing as they do, those men who leave the production of all things to us. Those men whose hands are white and soft, and whose skins are round and smooth, have more time to wave the flag than we have.

If we were to put in as much time waving it as they do the whole world will starve to death. The profiteers and their kept press are very lavish of patriotism, but too much of it comes from money stolen from us . . .

We say to the profiteers: "Government price-fixing is all right. Come on in, the water is fine. We do not ask to fix the price of what you sell us according to the price we fix on what we sell you. We ask you to sell us according to the price you have fixed on what we sell to you." I believe there is enough patriotism in the country to see a square deal of this kind. I do not believe that America has been Prussianized yet.[92]

On the last day the convention passed a rather lengthy series of resolutions which pledged full support to the government and the effective prosecution of the war, urged the League's proposals on war finance and government controls, spoke in favor of close relations between organized farmers and organized workers and a number of economic and political reforms, and concluded, with more fervor than originality: "We pledge our lives, our fortunes, and our sacred honor to our country and our flag in this, OUR WAR." [93] The convention thereupon formally adjourned, but an important event was scheduled for that evening, the address of Senator Robert M. LaFollette, the most vigorous opponent in the Congress of United States entry into the war and since the entry the most able proponent of wartime policies similar to those advocated by the League.

The St. Paul auditorium was packed with more than 8000 persons, while almost as many more milled in the streets. It was four times the attendance at the regular sessions, a crowd which grew more and more impatient as preliminary events dragged on with no sign of LaFollette. The Twin Cities newspapers had played up the possibility of a "disloyal" speech, and the air was tense. LaFollette had submitted to the arrangements committee a prepared text, in which he dealt with constructive solutions to war problems and stressed the importance of free expression of opinion. Lemke and Manahan, influenced by the hysteria of the times, expressed the fear that it might put the League in an embarrassing position. He offered to withdraw but finally consented to speak extemporaneously, interspersing a discussion of war taxation with parts of his famous Chatauqua speech on "Representative Government."

LaFollette's entrance was greeted with a spontaneous demonstration, one of the greatest ovations he ever received, and his speech was received with the utmost enthusiasm. At one point he digressed briefly to mention why he had opposed a declaration of war. "Germany," he said, "had interfered with the right of American citizens to travel on the high seas"—here a dramatic pause—"on ships loaded with munitions for Great Britain . . . The comparatively small privilege of the right of an American citizen to ride on a munition-loaded ship, flying a foreign flag, is too small to involve this government in the loss of millions and millions of lives."

A man in the gallery shouted, "Yellow!"

"Any man who says that in an audience where he can conceal his identity is yellow himself," LaFollette roared.

There were cries in the gallery of "Throw him out!" and in a flash the entire audience was on its feet looking for the heckler. Panic threatened, but the crowd was quieted by LaFollette's firm voice. Angered, the senator launched into a defense of his war attitude, commenting, however: "I don't mean to say that we hadn't suffered grievances; we had—at the hands of Germany. Serious grievances!" [94]

Here was what the opposition press had been waiting for. All else about the convention was ignored, and news of LaFollette's "seditious" speech was trumpeted far and wide. At least, said the *Minneapolis Journal*, this has torn the mask from the Nonpartisan League and revealed what it really is.[95] The Associated Press sent out a report of his remarks which quoted him as saying: "I wasn't in favor of beginning the war. We had no grievance against Germany." Eight months later it admitted in a letter to a United States Senate committee that the inclusion of the word "no" had been an "unfortunate error." [96] Unfortunate was putting it mildly, for both LaFollette and the League were to suffer an unending torrent of abuse as the result of such reports and the fantastic interpretations of the speech by the press generally.

The Minnesota Public Safety Commission, through Senator Frank B. Kellogg, petitioned the Senate to expel LaFollette for disloyalty, and he was roundly denounced by "patriotic" organizations throughout the country. The *Minneapolis Journal* editorialized:

Robert M. LaFollette, fugleman of sedition, was permitted last night in St. Paul to make a speech more disloyal, more treasonable, than the utterances that have landed lesser pro-Germans in prison . . . He went to the extreme limit of anti-Americanism and pro-Germanism . . . He justified the sinking of the Lusitania . . . Has not the time come to put an end to this sort of thing? [97]

In vain did the League insist that the resolutions were the only act of the convention and that no one could take exception to their loyalty. It could not, it said, be held responsible for the views of any guest speakers. Few newspapers, however, printed detailed accounts of anything but the LaFollette speech, and it was necessary for the League to buy advertising space in the St. Paul papers in order to get the resolutions of the convention before the public. The flood of adverse criticism resulting from the LaFollette incident finally compelled even the *Leader* to disown the senator temporarily, apparently backing water a bit on its stanch advocacy of free speech:

The provocation was of course great, but in his heated defense of himself under the goading of the "hecklers," the senator said things he should not have said, no matter how honestly he holds these views—things for which those in charge of the program of the convention and the convention itself take no responsibility whatever.[98]

Townley, in the course of a grilling before the Public Safety Commission, was reported to have repudiated the speech and termed it seditious, though he later insisted that the commission had twisted his statements.

The *Leader* quickly recovered its composure and came to LaFollette's defense, especially when he was viciously attacked as a "neo-copperhead" and a "Hun within our gates" by former President Theodore Roosevelt, then on a speaking tour of the country. It referred to his speech in the Senate answering the charges of sedition as a "brilliant and telling" defense of free speech and the right of members of Congress to vote as they believe without having their motives questioned.[99] Fourteen months later, in December 1913, the Senate committee investigating the charges of the Minnesota Public Safety Commission against LaFollette reported that there were no grounds for action against the senator. The report was adopted by the Senate on January 16, 1919, and on August 24, 1921, that body directed that LaFollette be paid $5000 to reimburse him for the expense of "defense of his title to his seat."[100] The damage had long since been done both to Robert M. LaFollette and the Nonpartisan League.

The echoes of this convention, approached with such high hopes only to boomerang disastrously, had scarcely died away when the *Duluth News-Tribune*, no friend of the League's, broke a story concerning what had presumably been intended to be a secret conference. A meeting had been held in St. Paul, it said, of "business men, bankers, lawyers, manufacturers, newspaper representatives and publicists" to plan a huge "patriotic" convention to "counteract" the Producers and Consumers Convention. "The gathering," it continued, "was primarily for the purpose of opening a campaign to combat the traitorous and seditious influences in this state which have centered very largely in the Nonpartisan League." Apparently accepting the common but curious concept that the louder one shouts and the harder he waves the flag the more patriotic he is, the *News-Tribune* reported that:

The idea is to have the loyalty convention the most stupendous expression of loyalty possible; to arrange such a program that every loyal man and woman in Minnesota will want to attend the convention, and to make it so effective that it will stand as a final, crushing, cleansing answer to the polluting Nonpartisan league gathering in this city . . .[101]

The men at the meeting in St. Paul "compared notes," it was reported, and "discovered" the following:

That the League contains hundreds of members who openly insult the flag and get away with it.

That the League is so strong in some counties that those who are loyal have to take their loyalty and express under cover their belief in the United States government.

Speeches were made [by those at the meeting] which showed that sedition in some places was thriving and that to be known as loyal is almost as dangerous as it was for a man in the South to be known as Union after the ordinance of secession was adopted at Montgomery.

A number who spoke detailed personal experiences which showed whole communities to be almost solidly for the kaiser.[102]

That such fantastic tales could be believed by supposedly intelligent men is almost incredible, but is an accurate measure of the times. Plans went rapidly ahead for the mammoth "loyalty meeting," although considerable of the wind had been taken out of its sails by the premature disclosure of its true purpose and the League's promise to fight this attempt to "prostitute patriotism" by using such a meeting for "political skulduggery." Both President Wilson and Lord Northcliffe, the British special commissioner on the war, had been invited, but they declined, and the Committee on Public Information was asked to furnish speakers representing the national government.

The speakers selected constituted the final blow. George Creel, the chairman of the Committee on Public Information, either misunderstood the sponsorship of the meetings or proved himself possessed of a superb sense of humor. The speakers provided were Assistant Secretary of Agriculture Carl Vrooman, long a friend of the League, and Monteville Flower, a California farmer and member of the Committee on Public Information. Both delivered scathing attacks on profiteering and stressed the need for extending democracy at home as well as abroad. Both praised the patriotism and sterling work of the American farmers. Vrooman indicated that real conscription of wealth was on the way and concluded by saying: "The man who is a partisan is not loyal. We've got to sacrifice our own ambitions, we've got to sacrifice our prejudices and partisanship, in this great fight." Flower pointed out vigorously that if the government could control and direct the economy for the benefit of all in wartime, it could do likewise in peace: "We are at this moment in the process of the re-definition of government . . . We are surmounting political mountains that we thought we could never ascend." [103]

This brand of patriotism left an extremely bad taste in the mouths of the backers of the convention, and the Twin Cities newspapers, while largely ignoring the speeches of the United States representatives, went out of their way to condemn Creel for his choices. But the League was happy—at least it was clear that somebody else's convention could boomerang too.

The one tangible anti-League result which did emerge from the "loyalty convention" was the formation of the "America First Association." On the last day, without previous notice, the names of a representative committee consisting of one person from each county in the state were announced as a nucleus for this new organization to promote patriotism and loyalty.[104] The true purpose became clear when the Employers' Association of Washington notified its members on December 24 that steps were under way in the Pacific Coast states to organize a "Western Branch of the America First League in opposition to the Non-Partisan movement." [105] The various nationwide "antiradicalism" organizations which blossomed in this period, such as the "National Citizens Union" and the "National Security League," included the League in their attacks as a "self-evident menace."

A further incident of the war hysteria was the sentencing of Kate Richards O'Hare, a well-known Socialist speaker and earnest pacifist, to five years in the federal penitentiary. Judge Martin J. Wade of Iowa pronounced sentence in Bismarck on December 14, 1917, delivering himself at the time of a long and scathing condemnation of socialism and opposition to war. Mrs. O'Hare, a woman of deep convictions and much beloved by those who knew her, had been on a speaking tour of the country, repeating essentially a talk which had been heard by agents of the Department of Justice many times. One fall evening she spoke to a small gathering in Bowman, North Dakota, and during the course of her remarks she alluded to the currently prevalent talk that the German government was insisting that all physically able women become mothers in order to ensure the existence of another generation, saying vehemently: "American women will never permit themselves to be used as brood sows for future wars!" [106]

Following this speech charges were brought against her by certain local citizens, ultimately resulting in her conviction on what many considered to be "trumped up" charges and false testimony. It happened that during Mrs. O'Hare's stay in Bowman she was a guest of old friends, Mr. and Mrs. George A. Totten, known as prominent Leaguers. The anti-League press immediately heralded far and wide the story that this "seditious speaker," who had said that "Mothers of American soldier boys are no better than brood sows," had been sponsored by the Nonpartisan League.[107] Despite repeated denials of any connection, frequently coupled with insistence that Mrs. O'Hare had been grossly misquoted, North Dakotans were never given the opportunity to forget the charges.

Strong foundations of a farmer-labor alliance had been laid by the League in several states by mid-1917, and the fact that North Dakota labor was well satisfied with the results was evidenced by the enthusiastic endorsement and pledge of continued cooperation passed by the annual convention of the State Federation of Labor at Fargo June 3. A fraternal delegate from the League was present.[108] Of much greater significance was the inviting of A. C. Townley to speak at the national convention of the American Federation of Labor in Buffalo November 16, a meeting which was also addressed by President Wilson. Townley's theme of the need for a uniting of farmers and laborers against the exploiters was warmly received, and the convention engaged in serious discussions of the desirability of political action.[109]

While in the East, Townley was also invited to address a meeting at the famous Cooper Union, promoted largely by labor groups on the general theme of getting farmers and city workers together so that they might receive each other's production without extortionate profits being exacted en route. In addition, it was an opportunity to give the East his own version of the story of the Nonpartisan League, and to attempt to put an end to the idea that it was a seditious organization. Most eastern publicity on the League had come from the city dailies of the Northwest and was highly colored, but practically all the important eastern papers except the *New York Times* now gave both the Buffalo and New York speeches much space, fair treatment, and favorable comment.

Townley's sincerity and down-to-earth brand of oratory "caught on" well, and he studiously played the role of a simple son of the soil to good effect. Commented the *New York World*: "Townley won his audience heart and soul. His homely speech, his twinkling small brown eyes, his direct, logical argument and his habit of placing his right hand on his knee as he leaned forward to drive some point home, made his story as effective as it was picturesque." The remarks of the *New York Evening Mail* were quite similar: "There is something Lincolnesque about A. C. Townley, the North Dakota farmer who spoke before the meeting of the labor food conference in Cooper Union on Monday night. His homely, simple illustrations of his arguments went direct to the heart, as did his unaffected manner." [110]

Before returning home Townley made a brief visit to Washington, where George Creel, apparently hoping to sell him more thoroughly on the war, arranged interviews with both President Wilson and Food Administrator Hoover.[111] Townley managed to get across his plea for $50,000,000 in low-interest loans for farmers in drouth-stricken regions, but he was also favorably impressed with the sincerity of the national administration.

Shortly thereafter, those in the Northwest who were vigorously attacking the League at every turn were dismayed to learn that the Foreign Press Bureau of the Committee on Public Information was preparing releases on the Nonpartisan League for use in foreign newspapers, primarily Russian. The articles, which included photographs of Governor Frazier and excerpts from the *Leader*'s series on public ownership, were designed, it was said, to show how people under free political institutions could use their power to correct economic abuses and achieve progressive legislation.[112]

The Nonpartisan League, now organizing in thirteen states,* was beginning to find itself "spread thin" and more and more conscious of the wartime manpower shortage. Repeated requests for organization in other states were politely turned down. It advertised widely for personnel, largely in labor and radical publications and even in the *Leader* itself. "Managers, organizers, lecturers, and writers" were needed on a full- or part-time basis. Experience was not necessary, since the League training courses gave adequate preparation. The opportunity meant "good pay and . . . a big part in a big movement." [113]

Appealing to persons to work in the movement on the basis of the money that could be made clearly had its unfortunate aspects. To be sure, it was necessary for the workers to make a living while engaged in this activity, but the tone of some of the advertising and more particularly the letters of some League promoters gave the opposition frequent opportunity to make the organization appear to be simply a "fleecing" proposition rather than a movement truly for the benefit of the farmers. It is not surprising that many farmers were annoyed to see advertisements to the effect that "good money" could be made by easy work in organizing them. It was not difficult to get the impression that money was the chief objective of League employees, and in some cases, especially in connection with certain subsidiary enterprises, this probably was true. The fact was that few if any League organizers made much more than a bare living, and certainly none of the top officials were ever enriched by the organization. Yet the League itself continually needed large sums of money to operate on the scale which it did, and the opposition never departed from the theme that its principal function was to "clean up" the farmers.

* North Dakota, South Dakota, Minnesota, Montana, Idaho, Washington, Colorado, Nebraska, Kansas, Wisconsin, Iowa, Oklahoma, and Texas.

In December it was announced that with the new year the *Leader* would follow national headquarters to St. Paul, where it could secure more adequate facilities, be closer to the news from all states, secure supplies more cheaply and quickly, and provide faster mail distribution.[114] State *Leaders* were early established in Minnesota, North Dakota, Idaho, and South Dakota, and later in several other states, to handle in more detailed fashion news which was of more purely state interest. Less than one third of the total circulation of the *Leader* was now said to be in North Dakota, and its circulation figures provide one of the best clues to the rapidly expanding membership of the League in this period. The number was set at "more than 100,000" on September 20, 130,000 on October 25, and "over 150,000" by December 17.

The Reign of Terror

IN THE early days of League organizing in Minnesota its activities received relatively little attention, and in a number of instances there was interested cooperation by village and city commercial clubs in providing facilities for farmers' meetings. As the strength of the organization grew, however, so also did that of the opposition. The attack was led by the Twin Cities newspapers, whose views were frequently copied by many country weeklies, and the attitude of the Public Safety Commission was also extremely influential. Business interests throughout the state were given to understand that the Nonpartisan League was fundamentally disloyal and that any meetings it might sponsor could automatically be assumed to be seditious.

In vain did the League endeavor to concentrate on domestic issues, insisting that there was no dispute as to the need for effective and speedy prosecution of the war. Those issues the opposition resolutely ignored, other than by taking an occasional slap at "socialism," and the anti-League press hammered one theme to the exclusion of all else— this was a time for unity, and agitators who stirred up discontent or in any way challenged the status quo could be nothing else than traitorous. The loyalty issue was a handy and potent weapon against a political opponent who had the popular side of an argument, and the length to which this opposition and a fanatical brand of "patriotism" were carried constitutes a sordid chapter in the history of Minnesota.

The League had planned and announced a series of fall meetings at towns scattered over southern and central Minnesota, designed to secure new members and to serve as "pep rallies" for those already members. At the same time they were carefully made "loyalty meetings"—collections for the Red Cross were invariably taken, high production was urged, and the purchase of Liberty Bonds was advocated, though it was always emphasized how much more just conscription of wealth would be. By the time this series of mass meetings got under way, the lines were fairly clearly drawn and most townspeople had been conditioned against the League. A brief account of a few of these meetings gives some idea of the sharpness of the conflict, even in the initial stages, the kind of conditions under which it was necessary for the League to operate, and the major role played by misunderstanding and false publicity.

Trouble began with the first meeting, which had been scheduled for October 4 in Lake City (Wabasha County). The commercial club and various businessmen had put pressure on the mayor to prohibit the meeting, and the owner of the hall that had been rented was forced to refuse to open it. Some two hundred fifty farmers were soon milling in the street, and violence threatened when someone caused a fire hose to be laid out conspicuously along the sidewalk as an obvious threat. Townley, however, advised them not to insist on their right of assembly and announced that the meeting would be held that night at Dumfries, about twenty miles distant. Most of the farmers had to go home for evening chores, but by eight o'clock the Dumfries hall was packed, not with two hundred fifty, but with more than four hundred attentive listeners. Among those present were the sheriff and the county attorney of Wabasha County, both of whom stated publicly at the conclusion that it had clearly been a "patriotic" meeting and that the farmers were entitled to assemble freely wherever they wished. The president of the Farmers and Traders Bank of Wabasha then took it upon himself to invite the speakers to hold a meeting in that city on their first open date. Four days later Townley and former Congressman Charles A. Lindbergh addressed a crowded city auditorium there without incident.[1]

The commercial club of Litchfield had held a special session in advance of the League meeting scheduled for that village on October 9, and had petitioned Governor Burnquist to prevent the meeting. The Public Safety Commission, however, had had a stenographer at all League gatherings and was well aware that there were no grounds for such action. Despite the fact that a local paper reported the commercial club move in such a manner as to give the impression that the meeting would be prohibited, farmers flocked in to fill the opera house and listen to three hours of speeches. The sheriffs of Meeker and Kandiyohi counties were present and both agreed that nothing objectionable had been said. The Kandiyohi sheriff had come because a meeting was scheduled for Willmar on a later date, and he wished to determine his proper course of action. He asked Townley at the end of the meeting if he would make the same kind of speech in Willmar.

"Brother, I'll make just the same kind of speech that I made today, and that speech that I made today is just the kind of a speech that I've been making for the last six months," replied Townley.

"Well, that's all right," said the sheriff. "What you said there today is just what we all believe in." [2]

A meeting had been scheduled for the next day in Mankato, but two days before the date the owner of the hall returned the money to the farmers who had rented it, saying that businessmen and local politicians had threatened him with loss of business if he permitted the League to use the hall. The owner of the local opera house was approached and agreed to rent if the city authorities would approve. This they refused to do, Mayor Champlin reportedly commenting that the League was led by "a bunch of I.W.W.'s." The Mankato papers announced that the meeting would not be held and told the farmers that there was no point in coming to town. Nevertheless, early afternoon found more than five hundred farmers thronging the streets, especially in front of the city hall. Police officers tried to hustle them along, but met with strong resentment. Threats of no more trading in Mankato and "wait till the next election" were heard on all sides, but one farmer who had driven forty miles to attend perhaps best summed up the feelings of all when told that the meeting was not to be permitted. "Ain't farmers legal?" he asked. [3]

Meanwhile arrangements were being made to hold the meeting that night in Nicollet, some fifteen miles away. But word came that county authorities would not allow the meeting, so the farmers in charge stopped at St. Peter, the county seat, where the sheriff informed them that the safety commission had refused permission. It turned out that he referred to the county safety commission, headed by Herman Olson, a St. Peter banker. Olson admitted that he knew nothing personally of the League but that he had read in the Twin Cities papers that it was seditious. Farmers who knew him assured him that this was false and invited both Olson and the sheriff to attend. To this he finally agreed, and the meeting was approved.

There had been little opportunity for notice of the change of location, but the "grapevine" had been functioning and instead of the five hundred farmers who had come to Mankato more than a thousand swarmed into Nicollet. No hall in town could begin to accommodate a crowd of this size, and the meeting was consequently held outdoors. It was cold and the wind came in chilling blasts which cut through the warmest clothing, yet the grim-faced farmers stood in the open air for nearly three hours while Arthur Townley talked of the need to battle autocracy at home as well as abroad. Suddenly he brought forth his flair for the dramatic. He spoke emotionally of the tremendous difficulties the farmers were facing in building their organization, of how they were being driven from towns like cattle and falsely branded traitors to their country. The interests fighting the League were prepared to spend millions to beat it, he said, and they would feel that they had gotten off cheaply if they had a chance to buy off the members.

"We could get the money," cried Townley. "What if I could get you $1600 for each $16 membership—would you sell?"

"No! No! No!" shouted back the crowd. Then someone yelled "We'll stick!" and a thousand voices roared the old North Dakota battle cry into the icy wind.

Herman Olson was convinced. He thanked Townley and promised to tell the attorney general and the Public Safety Commission that it had been a loyal meeting. Furthermore, when the sheriff of Nobles County the next day threatened to prevent a meeting at Worthington, Olson on his own initiative called him by telephone to assure him that the League was "all right." [4]

Meanwhile, a meeting of county sheriffs was held in St. Paul, to which the governor sent a representative to answer questions on how to handle the League problem. They were told that "if a riot seemed imminent, the responsibility for the outcome of any meeting rested upon the sheriff, and that it would be for the sheriff to take action to prevent such riots." [5] Although there had been no instance in that state or any other of the farmers rioting, all mob action having come from the opposition, riots immediately became imminent in a number of counties whenever League meetings were to be held. In areas where the League was strongly organized, primarily the western part of the state, they were rarely molested.

On October 5, Townley received an interesting letter signed by Louis Keane, secretary of the Otter Tail County Public Safety Association, which read:

Information has reached this office to the effect that you contemplate speaking here in this county on Octo. 20.

I am instructed to notify you that this Association will not tolerate any kind of talk here except that which honors our flag and the country for which it stands.

So you will construe this notice as an invitation *not to come.*

If after the receipt of this notice you persist in trying to talk here we have made arrangements with our Mayor who has given orders to the police force not to interfere if small boys (and others) use ancient eggs and other missiles where with to punctuate your discourse.[6]

This open threat of mob violence made by officials pledged to preserve law and order Townley was eager to challenge. The mayor of Fergus Falls, where the meeting was to be held, decided, however, to forestall any incidents of this sort and forbade the holding of any meeting at which Townley was to speak. Since it was the policy of the League never to defy public authorities, arrangements were made for former Congressmen Lindbergh and Manahan to speak and they were not interfered with. The Fergus Falls opera house was filled to capacity, and there was but one dissenting vote on a resolution calling upon Governor Burnquist to remove the mayor for his illegal action.[7]

The following day, Sunday, October 21, when the farmers came to the city of Detroit they found the hall where the meeting was to be held locked and were informed that here too the mayor had forbidden Townley to speak within the city limits. Furious, they accepted the invitation of a Dr. Cowles to use his lawn, just outside the city, and for two hours hundreds of what one farmer termed "these free American citizens that the gates of Detroit were shut against" stood in a snowstorm to listen to the president of their League.[8] Surely this was more than common attentiveness to political oratory.

As a matter of fact, it seems likely that such tactics as these tended to gain converts for the League, which stoutly maintained from beginning to end that there was really no loyalty issue involved and that this was simply barefaced political persecution by officeholders who feared for their jobs in 1918. Certainly nothing was achieved by preventing meetings except the fostering of further ill-will and a deepening of the town versus country antagonism. The meetings were always held elsewhere, and who, after all, was being protected? If speakers actually did violate the laws they would then properly have been subject to arrest, but there were certainly no grounds for this censorship in advance by overly officious local authorities. There were many instances in which farmers refused to return to towns where their meetings had been banned, and merchants were forced to apologize and promise a changed policy in order to regain their lost trade. The entire situation was but a part of the almost insane hysteria of the times.

As fall progressed and winter came on, the breaking up of League meetings either by local officials or by mobs was almost standard practice, and violence became more and more common. League organizers and speakers in some counties were beaten, tarred and feathered, and threatened with lynching, which in several instances almost occurred. League members were subjected to personal assaults and destruction of property, and one farmer with a German name was "deported" from Rock County—taken across a state line clothed in hot tar and told never to return.

Merchants with League sympathies found their store fronts painted yellow and their windows smashed. Professors at the University of Minnesota suspected of pro-League attitudes found that their desks had been rifled at night, and it was later discovered that dictographs had been placed in certain classrooms. The editor of the *Park Region Echo*, who had reported favorably on a League meeting, came to his office in the morning to find the door open, his linotype smashed, his press damaged beyond repair, and his correspondence files stolen. Many a gathering of farmers was greeted with mud, rotten eggs, stones, buckets of yellow paint, or the blast of a fire hose, which in one case was said to have torn a six-month-old baby from its mother's arms. In more than one case Home Guards were utilized in breaking up these meetings. Local law enforcement officials in a number of instances openly threatened the use of force against League organizing or speaking, yet did nothing to restrain the lawless actions of self-styled "loyalists." [9]

This state of affairs, which George Creel later termed a "policy of brutal intolerance," seemingly had the tacit approval of the state officials, and the Public Safety Commission at one time went so far as to advocate mobbings. A publicity release of January 19, sent to editors of the state on official stationery, was headed "One Cure for Disloyalty —A Cure That Is Used in Many Cases with Good Effect." It told the unlikely story of a man in a small Minnesota town who allegedly tore a Red Cross button off another man's coat and threw it in a spittoon. In a moment he was set upon and "beaten to a pulp by a crowd of loyalists." When he recovered he was promptly fined $100 and jailed. The Public Safety Commission referred to the incident as follows:

This had a very salutary effect on the balance of the disloyal element and they began to seek information on the war and its causes in a conscientious manner. The time is coming when even a disloyal utterance or lukewarm attitude will be resented by the American people in every section. There is no "halfway" citizenship that can live in these times.[10]

There was a significant correlation county by county between the attitudes of local newspapers and the existence or nonexistence of mob violence. In places where such action occurred the papers were almost invariably in the habit of either actively encouraging it or excusing it as "natural" in wartime. The *Rush City Post*, for example, editorialized in March:

There is something refreshing in the [manner] in which direct punishment is being inflicted upon numerous disloyalists at street gatherings and public meetings throughout the country. Mob law is mighty effective when properly administered and usually carries justice in its right hand.

In a slightly more moderate vein the *Hinckley Enterprise* commented: "As much as we deprecate the violence of the acts that prevented a disloyal meeting, we had much rather be apologizing for the violence of loyalists than for the disloyal actions which cause them . . ."[11]

The standard argument of those seeking to prevent or break up League meetings was to the effect that this was "not the time to organize." The American people, they said, should now be concerned solely with the winning of the war; politics or economic problems should not be permitted to divert their attention. In response to the League's complaint that everyone else was already organized, they agreed that of course the farmers had a right to organize but "not at a time like this." Oddly enough there seemed to be no similar feeling in regard to the various organizations which were springing up in opposition to the League, nor could it be said that in North Dakota, where the shoe was on the other foot by virtue of a League-dominated state administration, there was any noticeable cessation of political activity designed to unseat incumbents.

By March of 1918 nineteen Minnesota counties had completely barred all meetings of the League, thus by local fiat suspending the right of free assemblage and in effect denying the right of political action to a large segment of the population. Up to that time no fewer than forty scheduled meetings had been prevented by local officials, and no one kept track of the number interfered with by self-appointed guardians of the public welfare.[12]

In view of the dangers they faced it is surprising that the League speakers and organizers were willing to continue their activity. A few did drop out, but to most this seemed a greater challenge, and they risked personal safety day after day to carry their message to the farmers of Minnesota. The crusading spirit was well illustrated by the case of Nels Hokstad, a Pine County farmer helping in local organization work, who was seized one evening by a masked gang as he was about to speak at the Turpville schoolhouse and treated to a dose of tar and feathers. In the midst of the pain as the hot tar was poured over him, Hokstad is reported to have shouted at the mob: "If you think this will stop my organizing, you'd better swing me, for a coat of tar and feathers won't do it." Two days later he was at another meeting where 750 farmers protested the outrage and swore that it would never be permitted to happen again in Pine County.[13]

In time a situation was reached in which League speakers expected to be arrested whenever they set foot in certain counties. Often the individual would be held just long enough to make the scheduled meeting impossible and then released, but in a few cases speakers were tried for alleged violations of some local ordinance. It was customary for a speaker who was informed by a sheriff that League meetings were not permitted to request the officer to put the order in writing. When this was done the meeting would not be held, but most refused to do so, and when not done, the League considered the order not binding. The arrests then usually followed immediately after the opening of the meeting, the grounds being such things as disturbing the peace or unlawful assemblage, although many papers regularly reported them as arrests for sedition.

In January 1918, League headquarters received a letter, addressed to

A. E. Bowen and signed by several officials of Jackson County, which directed the League to stay out of that county in the future. It intimated that the League might have German backing and that at any rate it was clearly disloyal, concluding:

You try to divert the attention of the American people from the great and only issue now before them . . . If there is anything wrong with our social or economic system, it can easily be deferred until peace. When the Nation is in a death grapple for existence, you and your organization are doing your worst to fetter and weaken it . . .

We do not want you here at all. Any attempt to hold further Nonpartisan League meetings in this County will be likely to result in serious disturbances. For that reason, we shall use every measure at our disposal to prevent you from speaking here, and to prevent your organization from holding any future meetings in this County.[14]

A meeting had been scheduled for Lakefield in Jackson County on January 23, and, deciding to put the matter to a test, Joe Gilbert, then organization manager for the League, departed at once for Lakefield to handle the meeting himself. He conferred first with a gathering of members of the county safety commission, consisting mostly of those who had signed the letter, but being treated in a peremptory fashion he finally took his following of farmers to a nearby livery stable yard and commenced to address them from a wagon. After listening for a short time, during which Gilbert called for conscription of wealth and commented that some county officials spelled their patriotism with a "P-A-Y," the sheriff stopped the meeting and placed Gilbert under arrest on a charge of "rioting," later changed to "unlawful assembly."

H. A. Paddock and former Congressman James Manahan came down to defend him, the latter promptly getting into trouble. When the court recessed the first evening, someone announced that a parrot would be auctioned off to the crowd of some two hundred fifty persons for the benefit of the Red Cross. Manahan finally bid it in at fifteen dollars and then leaped on a table to auction it again, badgering the prosecuting attorneys for their failure to bid. There were insulting remarks at the rear of the room, followed by a flurry of fists, and pandemonium broke loose. When this had been quieted, Manahan stepped outside only to face a mob which threatened him with tar and feathers and hanging if he did not leave town at once. Manahan appealed to the sheriff for protection, but got only a promise of "safe conduct" to the next village. Consequently this attorney, defending a client in a court of justice, was forced to beat an unexpectedly hasty retreat to St. Paul. In this atmosphere it is hardly surprising that the jury found Gilbert guilty. The case was promptly appealed, but it was never again called.[15]

Charges of malfeasance in office were subsequently preferred against Sheriff O. C. Lee and County Attorney E. H. Nicholas, but Governor Burnquist refused to take action.[16] At the time of Gilbert's conviction, several newspapers announced that a warrant had been issued for the arrest of A. C. Townley, as Gilbert's "employer," but the action did not then materialize. The League had up to that time done but little organizing in Jackson County, and with reference to the difference in attitude where the League was strongly organized, it is interesting to note that while the arrest of Townley was being considered here, he was attending a banquet tendered him by the businessmen and towns-people of Thief River Falls. He was holding in that area, unmolested, a series of rallies attended by thousands of farmers, at which, inciden-tally, he was urging the planting of the largest possible crops in order to help win the war.[17]

Incidents of mob violence at this period were occurring in various places throughout the country, all under the guise of patriotism, a situ-ation which the *Leader* expertly held up to ridicule in an editorial en-titled "A Lesson in Logic":

Come, let us reason together . . . Let us advance proof as to the truth of certain questions arising out of the war. We must see clearly in order to fight well.

First, we have only righteous motives in the war. Let us prove it to all the world by riding a woman on a rail.

Second, Germany has grossly mistreated Belgium, committing revolt-ing brutalities there. To prove this, let us put on masks, call ourselves "Knights of Liberty," capture a man with a German name and, after forcing him to kiss the flag, hang him on a tree till he is dead.

Third, everybody ought to buy Liberty bonds. Let us demonstrate the truth of that and prove to the German people that we have no base motives, by rounding up a few persons, stripping them, hanging them by their thumbs and flaying them with rawhides till they are almost dead.

Fourth, we are fighting for world democracy and justice. Let us prove that by treatment, milder but none the less convincing. Let us organize a posse of leading citizens, surround a defenseless man in the streets, knock him down and jump on his prostrate form . . . These things have all happened . . .

How much longer are we going to allow the degenerates among our citizenship to hurt our cause in the war and make us out a senseless, brutal people before the world? [18]

Throughout the winter months Governor Burnquist was besieged by a steady stream of resolutions from farmers' groups all over the state pleading for enforcement of the laws, demanding protection of peaceful assembly, and asking the removal of local officials who had prevented meetings or permitted mob violence.[19] On February 19 a delegation of League members, headed by Magnus Johnson of Kimball and A. C. Welch of Glencoe, both members of the Minnesota legislature, appeared at the governor's office and read a letter which set forth a long series of "outrages" and demanded action by the state's chief executive. It minced no words:

The rights of citizens to meet in peaceful assemblage, to discuss matters of public concern, to be immune from unlawful assaults, and to be secure in their liberties, have been flagrantly, repeatedly and notoriously violated . . .

Law abiding citizens . . . have been watched and followed from town to town by persons assuming authority to prevent such lawful pursuits; have been publicly and falsely vilified and accused of crime, and have been openly threatened with violence, torture, and death.

Public officials have joined in this carnival of intimidation and oppression . . .

Men have been coerced, assaulted, kidnapped; law has been denied; passion has supplanted reason; riot has been invited; the process of social order has been menaced by the approach of anarchy.

These things, Sir, have not happened in a corner nor in the dark. They are notorious. A period of nearly six months has not sufficed to exhaust the malignity of these assaults upon the peace and dignity of the State, and the scenes of their occurrence are widely scattered throughout its territory.

The circumstances point to the existence of a lawless propaganda instigated and sustained by persons higher up, working through the agency of the immediate actors . . . But whether or not there be a conspiracy against the public peace and order, it is clear and undenied that these things have occurred, and their continuing occurrence demands instant corrective action at your hands.[20]

On March 2 the attorney general ruled that the charges made by the delegation against the sheriff and county attorney of Jackson County, the sheriff of Rice County, and the acting sheriff of Ramsey County were insufficient to warrant their removal, and Governor Burnquist dismissed the whole matter as the work of "troublemakers." [21]

Judge McGee, the chairman of the Public Safety Commission, was reported as having later said to Magnus Johnson: "I came into the Governor's office when you were reading that, and if I had known what you were reading and had had a club, I would have knocked your brains out." [22]

On February 26 the state executive committee of the Minnesota League prepared a resolution concerning the "intolerable" conditions in the state which asked the aid and advice of the national officers. Townley forwarded this to Governor Burnquist, asking three questions:

FIRST: Are local officers in the municipalities of the State to be permitted to prevent meetings of the League?

SECOND: Are members of the League to be denied the protection of the laws?

THIRD: Is the National Nonpartisan League to be regarded by the executive and peace officers of the State as an outlaw?

Burnquist cautiously replied that no official had a right to prevent the holding of any legal and loyal meeting, that every citizen was entitled to the protection of the laws, and that insofar as the League complied with the laws of the state and nation it was not an outlaw. Incensed by what he termed these generalities and legal truisms, Townley restated the questions in more detail and requested a reply "specifically without any innuendo, implication, evasion, or equivocation," and a statement of the manner of noncompliance with the laws. There was no reply. [23]

Having apparently failed in their appeals to the state officials, the League next turned to the United States district attorney, and then in April the national and state executive committees published their *Memorial to the Congress of the United States Concerning Conditions in Minnesota, 1918.* This volume, and one to the President of the United States which was identical except for the introduction, claimed with extensive supporting evidence that citizens of the United States were being deprived of their constitutional rights and asked the protection of national officials since state officials refused to act. The national administration, however, had neither the time, the personnel, nor the inclination to attempt to intervene in this highly charged situation, which it considered to be primarily a local political battle.

In late March the National Committee on Public Information agreed at Townley's request to furnish "loyalty speakers" to deliver a series of patriotic addresses under League sponsorship, particularly in areas in which it was believed that support of the war might be lukewarm. Local officials in Cottonwood, Jackson, Martin, and Watonwan counties refused to permit such meetings as long as they were sponsored by the League, and in this they were backed up by the state administration.[24] In vain did Chairman Creel argue with the Public Safety Commission that if they were right as to the existence of disloyal elements it was to those localities that these speakers should go; there was nothing to be gained by preaching to those already converted. Permission was still refused.[25] Creel later summed up the situation in a letter to Charles Edward Russell:

. . . It was at Mr. Townley's request that I prepared to send speakers into the Northwest—men and women able to talk of the war as they had seen it, or else able to discuss America's aims from every point of view.

It was what we were doing in every state in the Union in our effort to remove misunderstanding, to promote unity, and to kindle enthusiasm.

It was such speakers that the state administration of Minnesota barred absolutely. It was not that they questioned the loyalty of the speakers; in fact, they asked for the use of them in their own campaigns. It was simply the case that they did not mean to let the Nonpartisan League hold meetings of any kind, even loyalty meetings. What stood clear in my mind then, as it stands clear today, is that Democrats and Republicans alike feared the political power of the Nonpartisan League and did not want it to be given any reputation for loyalty. In plain words, they preferred that the Nonpartisan League should be disloyal rather than loyal, in order that they might be provided with a campaign weapon.[26]

In mid-March the *Leader* uncovered a letter written by Governor Burnquist to a man in Nebraska in which he categorically stated that the League was "hindering the prosecution of the war." The *Leader* promptly boiled over. This, it said, was either a deliberate untruth or else the governor should be removed from office for failing to do his duty—there was ample power in the Public Safety Commission to abolish the League: "Why do you let an organization that is hindering the war continue, governor?" [27]

The League persistently contended that it was fully as essential to fight for democracy at home as in Germany; that it was completely inconsistent for the Public Safety Commission to spend huge sums of money to tell the people that this was a war for democracy and liberty while at the same time it ignored or actively encouraged the suppression of democracy in Minnesota. The commission's words would ring more true, it said, if accompanied by action against "autocracy and kaiserism in some of the small towns of Minnesota."

A bill by Senator Chamberlain of Oregon that provided for placing all cases involving the espionage act under the jurisdiction of military authorities came up for hearings in April, and Judge McGee, chairman of the Public Safety Commission and federal fuel administrator for Minnesota, went to Washington to testify. His remarks before the committee were startling almost beyond belief:

The United States Department of Justice in Minnesota has been a ghastly failure. The United States District Attorney in Minnesota is patriotic but he lacks a fighting stomach . . .

A Non-Partisan League lecturer is a traitor every time. In other words, no matter what he says or does, a League worker is a traitor . . .

Where we made a mistake was in not establishing a firing squad in the first days of the war. We should now get busy and have that firing squad working overtime. Wait until the long casualty lists begin to come in and the Minnesota woods will not be dense enough to hide the traitors who will meet punishment for their crimes. These men who are fighting our soldiers and stabbing them in the back are going to die.

The nation's life is at stake. The government has no more conception of the state of affairs in Minnesota than a child unborn. In these days the judges should not think in terms of peace. What we need is a military court. You can't fool the military court, but you can't depend on juries . . .

The disloyal element in Minnesota is largely among the German-Swedish people. The nation blundered at the start of the war in not dealing severely with these vipers.[28]

There was immediately a wave of protest in Minnesota at McGee's indictment of the Germans and Swedes and his statement that Minnesota was a hotbed of disloyalty. Newspapers which had at first played up his testimony found it necessary to say that his views were "in sharp contrast" to those of Governor Burnquist, who believed that "Minnesota is as loyal as any state in the union, people of Swedish extraction particularly." [29] On April 20 President Wilson sent a strongly worded message to the chairman of the Senate Judiciary Committee, which was influential in killing the "court martial bill":

I am wholly and unalterably opposed to such legislation . . . I think it not only unconstitutional, but that in character it would put us nearly on the level of the very people we are fighting and affecting to despise. It would be altogether inconsistent with the spirit and practice of America, and . . . I think it is unnecessary and uncalled for.

"Again," said the *Leader*, "the confidence of the American people in President Wilson has been proved well placed." [30]

The differences in attitude toward the Nonpartisan League on the part of the national government and the state of Minnesota were striking. The former at all times cooperated with the League, considering it an important spokesman for the northwest farmer, while the latter looked upon it as virtually an outlaw organization. Department of Justice agents frequented League meetings in all parts of the state, yet never made an arrest, while in some counties local officials were locking up their speakers on sight. Attempts to get the United States to prosecute League leaders repeatedly failed. League publications were granted second-class mailing privileges at a time when regulations provided that publications in this class must contain nothing in policy or in purpose which in any way might hinder the war effort. They were also allowed the one-cent rate to American forces in France, but at the same time arrests were being made in Minnesota on the grounds that League literature was seditious. It is scarcely open to question that the fact that 1918 was a state election year was a highly significant factor in this situation.

George Creel summarized accurately the attitude of the national government in a letter of May 13, 1918, to John A. Simpson, president of the Oklahoma Farmers' Union, who had written the National Committee on Public Information asking if there were any reason why a loyal farmer should not join the League:

It is not true that the federal government is pressing the Nonpartisan League in any manner, or that the federal government considers it an act of disloyalty to be a member of this League.

The federal government is not concerned with the political, economic, or industrial beliefs of any organization at a time like this, insisting only that every individual stand behind this war, believing absolutely in the justice of America's position.

The Nonpartisan League, by resolution and by organized effort, has given this pledge of loyalty. North Dakota, controlled by this organization politically, has as fine a record of war support as any other commonwealth in the Union. Mr. Baer, its representative in the lower house, has never even been criticized for a single utterance that might be termed disloyal.

Mr. Townley is under indictment in Minnesota, and there is a very bitter fight being made on the League in that state by certain groups. With this, the government has nothing to do, refusing absolutely to take part in these local differences.[31]

Sedition and discouraging enlistments were of course crimes under United States statutes, but Minnesota had passed similar laws supplementing those of the United States, and while the government against which the alleged crimes were perpetrated took no action, the state in a number of instances made arrests under its statute, especially in the months preceding the primaries.

In one of the first of these cases to come to trial, L. W. Martin, a League organizer, was indicted in Red Wing seven months after the speech on which the indictment was based. After three days of testimony and argument, Martin was acquitted on the first ballot, but the newspapers which had given the matter wide publicity, implying that his guilt was obvious, for the most part gave inconsequential notice to the acquittal. The prosecutor had made the mistake of asking Martin to repeat what he had said, and he thereupon launched into a full-fledged speech to the crowded courtroom. It was reported that after the acquittal a half-dozen farmers from the audience came up to Martin to ask for membership blanks.[32]

On February 28, 1918, County Attorney Albert R. Allen of Martin County, one of the counties which had consistently barred all League meetings, issued complaints against A. C. Townley and Joseph Gilbert, charging that they had discouraged enlistments in Minnesota by circulating a pamphlet entitled *The Nonpartisan League; Its Origin, Purposes, and Methods of Organization*. This was the pamphlet which contained the League war resolutions and Congressman Baer's public statement at the time of his election, although the great majority of its space was devoted to the League's economic and political program. It had been in circulation since the preceding June with no complaint from the national government, which had, in fact, granted mailing privileges for it. Moreover, much of its "war program" had by now become official United States policy. A later indictment also included the resolutions of the Producers and Consumers Convention.

County Attorney Allen was one of the state's most vehement "superpatriots," a young man with a reputation as a fiery orator and as an almost fanatical opponent of the Nonpartisan League and all it stood for. The depths of this antagonism are indicated by the fact that in the fall of 1917 he had gone so far as to demand of the state bar association that it investigate the possible necessity of disbarring and perhaps impeaching Governor Burnquist on the grounds that he was failing to suppress "rampant disloyalty and sedition" in the state.[33] Subsequently, in a speech before a county attorneys' convention in Minneapolis, he delivered himself of a tirade which was clearly the reasoned view of a dispassionate and unprejudiced law enforcement official:

God forbid that the prosecuting attorneys of America should slumber in the presence of this disloyalty. The League is the Kaiser's hope. Let us resolve that this criminal, disloyal political club that brazenly seeks to mislead thoughtless innocents, associate them with traitors and spies, corrupt our officials, capture our country and lead her blindfolded by the route of Russian bolshevikism to a condition of Prussianized slavery, shall not go slyly or successfully about its nefarious work.[34]

After issuing the complaints, Allen instructed Sheriff W. S. Carver to go to St. Paul, arrest Townley and Gilbert, and bring them back to Fairmont, the county seat of Martin County, to await trial. Carver proceeded to place them under arrest, whereupon they at once demanded to be taken before the district court of Ramsey County to apply for bail. Carver insisted that he had been ordered to take them to Fairmont, but after receiving legal advice as to the rights of his prisoners he took them to the court where bonds of $3000 each were furnished and they were released.

Returning to Fairmont empty-handed, the hapless sheriff met a thoroughly disgusted Allen, who insisted that the Ramsey County court had no jurisdiction and ordered Carver and Deputy Sheriff Roepke to go back to St. Paul and secure the prisoners. Townley in the meantime had left town on a speaking engagement but Gilbert was available and was again taken into custody. Carver decided to wait for a time in the hope that Townley might return, but in order to prevent Gilbert from taking any legal action to free himself again, he sent Roepke and Gilbert by automobile to Mendota, where after two or three hours' wait they caught the train to Fairmont. In the interim, League attorneys had heard of the events and had secured from the district court of Ramsey County a writ of habeas corpus, which was promptly served upon Sheriff Carver, ordering him to produce Gilbert in St. Paul at once.

Frightened by this time, Carver wired Roepke to return Gilbert to St. Paul, but the deputy, who received the telegram at Lake Crystal, suspected that it was a fake and continued to Fairmont.

Gilbert spent the night in jail, having refused to let Allen go his bail, and in the morning, to his great amusement, the sour-faced county attorney placed him on the train back to St. Paul. The following day, Sheriff Carver having at last produced Gilbert before the Ramsey County court, the court ordered him released on his original bond and he was directed to appear at Fairmont for trial the following Monday. Gilbert immediately filed suit against the Martin County officials on charges of kidnapping and false imprisonment, which was later settled out of court with a payment of $275.[35]

When the case came to trial, the attorneys for Townley and Gilbert at once entered demurrers to the charges, contending that they did not constitute a cause of action, that the resolutions and statements involved were so plainly patriotic that they could not be used as a basis for such charges, and that the resolutions and statements were almost in the same language used by President Wilson in his recent speeches and messages to Congress. Judge Tifft overruled the demurrers, but agreed, over the passionate protest of the county attorney, to certify two questions directly to the state Supreme Court:

(1) Is the section on which the indictments are based within the subject expressed in the title of the act?

(2) Do the facts constitute a violation of that section? [36]

While the case was pending before the Supreme Court, the indictments were used for all they were worth by the anti-League forces. News that Townley and Gilbert had been indicted for antiwar activity, with guilt customarily assumed, was given the widest publicity throughout the entire country, but especially in those states which the League was attempting to organize. The standard "proof" given of the disloyal nature of the League was that its leaders were under indictment for "sedition." The League's claim that this publicity cost it tens of thousands of votes in the 1918 primaries does not seem unduly far-fetched.

The case had been certified to the Supreme Court in March, but it was not until July 5, several days after the Minnesota primary election, that the court handed down its decision, written by Judge Quinn, whose home, appropriately enough, was in Fairmont. The court answered the first question in the affirmative without detailed discussion, and then, in consideration of the second, proceeded to sustain the demurrers filed by the League attorneys. Great emphasis had been placed by the prosecution upon one paragraph in particular from the resolutions of the Producers and Consumers Convention which read:

The moving cause of this world war was and is political autocracy used to perpetuate and extend industrial autocracy. It is the struggle of political overlords to extend and perpetuate their power to rob and exploit their fellowmen. Autocratic rulers who have robbed and exploited the fathers and mothers now slaughter the children for the single purpose of further intrenching themselves in their infamous position and securing and legalizing their possession of the fruits of others' toil and thrusting the world under the yoke of political autocracy, which is ever the shield and the mask of industrial autocracy.

The court decided to "play it straight," and accepted the contentions of the League attorneys that obviously this applied to the German-Austrian autocracy, since we had no autocracy in this country:

. . . the language, properly considered and taken in the light of the surrounding pertinent facts, cannot be held as tending to discourage enlistment in the army or otherwise to advocate that assistance should not be rendered the government in the prosecution of the war . . .

Judge Quinn remarked that since it is the federal government whose authority is challenged by seditious action, the rules as to what constitutes such action should properly be determined in the United States courts, and noted that "it is perhaps not out of place to say that the resolutions have not yet attracted the attention of the federal authorities." Regarding the League's war resolutions themselves, the court concluded:

The resolutions taken as a whole appear to be nothing more serious than a rhetorical, and somewhat flamboyant, platform upon which a certain class of citizens are solicited to join an organization whose avowed purpose is the amelioration of the alleged evils of present economic conditions, and to bring about a more equal distribution of the wealth of the world among all classes of mankind. The pursuit of this object does not violate the statute in question . . .

The court cannot inject by inference matter of substance between the lines of the resolutions, and predicate a conviction thereon, for the fact and not the prosecutor's inferences must be the basis of a conviction under the statute.[37]

The *Leader* hailed the decision as a sweeping and complete vindication of the League, which should put at rest for all time the false charges of disloyalty. It was overly sanguine. The day after the decision the *St. Paul Pioneer Press* gave front-page prominence to a statement of County Attorney Allen's to the effect that despite the decision the case had been a success, since it had convinced the people of the disloyalty of the League and had completely discredited both Townley and the organization.[38] Perhaps Albert Allen had achieved his purpose.

Less than a week after the indictments had been returned against Townley and Gilbert in the Martin County case, Gilbert was indicted at Red Wing for violation of the Minnesota sedition act on the basis of a speech made at Kenyon, Minnesota, a full nine months earlier. It was alleged that he had said, among other things, that the United States had been "stampeded into this war by newspaper rot to pull England's chestnuts out of the fire," and that the war would end in a hurry if wealth were conscripted the same as manpower.[39]

Gilbert and his witnesses had different versions, but the state's case was based largely on the testimony of seven witnesses, each of whom was able to repeat in identical order, word for word, the same ten sentences, admittedly not made originally in continuous fashion, from a speech delivered nine months before. Although the state's witnesses claimed not to have seen the indictment, all gave Gilbert's alleged words exactly as they were stated in that indictment. Despite this remarkable feat of memory, none of the witnesses was able to remember anything else Gilbert had said. One of these witnesses claimed to have written notes on the speech as it was being given. This was supposedly done in a notebook held on his knee and in a dimly lit hall, yet the notes were in ink and in small regular handwriting. In spite of the extremely unlikely validity of the testimony of what the *Leader* termed the "parrot chorus," it was accepted at face value.

Judge Albert Johnson had ruled at the opening of the trial that no member of the Nonpartisan League might sit on the jury, a move which the League claimed meant that only opponents would be permitted to serve, since neutrals at this time were few and far between. Later the judge had refused to permit the defense to attempt to show animus against the Nonpartisan League on the part of several of the state's witnesses, saying that "the League is not on trial." Yet when, after imposing the maximum sentence of a year in jail and a $500 fine, Judge Johnson was asked to grant the usual stay of sentence pending appeal, he proposed to make the stay conditional upon a promise that the League would refrain from all further activities in Goodhue County. This Gilbert refused to consider, and the stay was finally granted without the promise.[40]

In December of 1918 the state Supreme Court upheld the conviction, concerning itself for the most part with the alleged errors on the part of the lower court, and the League attorneys promptly appealed to the Supreme Court of the United States, claiming that the state statute was unconstitutional as a violation of the guarantee of free speech and as being legislation within the exclusive province of the Congress. Two years later, on December 13, 1920, the majority of the Court, speaking through Mr. Justice McKenna, held that the state statute involved merely cooperation with the United States and was not in conflict with the federal law. Moreover, it was a valid exercise of the state's police power which did not violate the Fourteenth Amendment in unduly abridging free speech. "The right of free speech," said McKenna, "does not cover false and malicious misrepresentation of the objects and motives of this country in entering upon a war . . ." [41]

Justice Holmes concurred in the result without subscribing to the majority opinion, while Chief Justice White dissented on the grounds that the subject matter was within the exclusive legislative power of the Congress, and the Congress having acted, the entire field was occupied. Mr. Justice Brandeis filed a powerful dissent, surpassing the majority opinion in both length and logic, in which he agreed with the chief justice but put his primary emphasis upon the free speech issue. The statute, he said, "aims to prevent not acts but beliefs." Free speech includes the right to teach a doctrine of pacifism and that the abolition of war is possible, "so long, at least, as Congress has not declared that the public safety demands its suppression." "I cannot believe," he concluded, "that the liberty guaranteed by the Fourteenth Amendment includes only liberty to acquire and enjoy property."

The Brandeis dissent, Chafee points out, was "the first time that any member of the Court, in any kind of published opinion, squarely maintained that freedom of speech is protected against State action by the United States Constitution." [42] The Minnesota statute, says Chafee, was the first attempt by a state to curb opposition to war since the early years of the American revolution:

It remained for our own day, when the doctrine of states' rights was supposed to be on its last legs, to establish by a Supreme Court decision . . . that the weapons which Massachusetts and Virginia used against the disloyal remain sharp and active in the hands of modern State governments and were not surrendered to the nation in 1789.[43]

Five years after the Gilbert decision, however, the Court in *Gitlow v. New York* was ready to agree unanimously with what was essentially the position on protection of free speech, through the Fourteenth Amendment, maintained in the Brandeis dissent.

While this variety of spectacular events had been occurring in Minnesota, all had not been precisely sweetness and light in the other League states, although nowhere did the situation reach the Minnesota proportions.

Local "loyalty leagues," "defense councils," or similar organizations occasionally attempted to bar a speaker or a meeting in certain North Dakota towns, and heckling or other disturbances were not uncommon, but with the League in control of the state administration and having such an extensive membership there were no official suppressions and no instances of serious violence. The battle was restricted to a much greater degree to the press and platform.

Throughout the fall and winter of 1917–18 hundreds of meetings were held in the state of Montana with no complaints of disloyalty, but by March the League was showing surprising strength and the publicity from Minnesota began to have its effect in the cities. At Columbus and Big Timber small crowds led by businessmen met organizer R. B. Martin and refused to let him get off the train. League officials promptly notified Attorney General S. C. Ford, who at once wired local peace officers to protect speakers. When Martin returned he found no mob but discovered that the use of all halls had been refused, and it was necessary for the farmers to content themselves with a brief outdoor meeting and demonstration parade.[44]

A few weeks later businessmen in Miles City and Terry refused to allow meetings and forced speakers to leave town, but at Billings, where Martin had been permitted to speak after considerable altercation, the businessmen who heard him congratulated him and invited him to return. Several days later he addressed a packed auditorium at a meeting sponsored jointly by the merchants and organized labor.[45] In general the state was for the present orderly. Attorney General Ford had issued a very sensible public statement on his position which the League termed "entirely satisfactory":

The legislature has provided us with the most stringent laws imaginable, and there is no excuse for the exercise of mob rule. Mobs establish dangerous precedents and it is far better that we follow the procedure established by law . . . the innocent often suffer under mob rule . . . If anyone makes any unpatriotic or disloyal utterance in any Montana county, I am more than confident that he will feel the strong arm of the law. But until he does so, it is utterly improper for citizens to adjudge him guilty in advance.[46]

In South Dakota Governor Norbeck advised the sheriff of Lake County, in answer to an inquiry as to whether he should prevent League meetings, that "no political organization should be interfered with. It has the right to hold public meetings. None should be prevented except such as are held for the purpose of embarrassing the government in the prosecution of the war." There were relatively few instances of prevention of meetings by public officials, and the League considered the governor's position to be satisfactory, assuming that this rule was to be applied on the basis of the actions of the League itself and not on "what the newspapers write about it."[47]

Nevertheless, there were numerous occasions on which meetings were stopped by local organizations or groups of citizens, one of the most notorious incidents occurring on March 13 at Gregory. League organizers and a number of members who had come into town for a scheduled meeting were cruelly beaten by a mob, the leaders of which then forced the Leaguers to walk several miles to the next town while they rode in autos, herding the farmers like cattle. At that town, the Leaguers were forced onto a train, guarded by part of the mob, and were compelled to go across the state line into Nebraska with instructions not to return.

Scores of affidavits concerning this outrage were filed with Governor Norbeck, who at once announced that there would be an investigation and that prosecutions would follow if the laws had been violated. The

Rosebud Investor, a country weekly in the area, promptly challenged the governor in a most insulting fashion:

> The governor's action in connection with the Nonpartisan League has of late been distasteful to loyal citizens. He has insisted on their rights to spread their unpatriotic propaganda, so long as they do not violate the letter of some motheaten law made for use in time of peace. His insistence makes no difference in Rosebud county, at least, for he may rest assured that regardless of his desires or commands, no unpatriotic move will be tolerated in this part of the state, and he isn't man enough, hasn't backing enough, nor influence enough, to compel it.[48]

After nothing happened for several weeks, the state headquarters of the League requested information, and Governor Norbeck wrote that he had evidence of the disloyalty of League organizers. The League immediately requested and then demanded that he make public or submit to the prosecuting authorities any such evidence, announcing that it would assist in the prosecution of any organizer or member shown to be disloyal and that it would cancel the membership certificate of anyone so proven. This the governor refused, and shortly thereafter he announced that the Gregory case was closed, following his removal of the head of the county council of defense and appointment of a new chairman. There were no punishments meted out to those involved in the mob action.[49]

In Colorado likewise, the state refused to outlaw the League, and repressive actions came entirely from certain local officials and groups. The State Council of Defense notified the Sedgwick County council in April that disloyal or seditious remarks were individual matters and that any person making such should be reported for investigation, but that "there is nothing inimical to the government in the League's constitution and by-laws. Therefore, there is no authority for interference with the League's operations so long as its conduct is within legal limits." [50] Nevertheless, Sedgwick County proceeded to prohibit League organizing. As the League grew stronger, banking and business interests financed a tour of the state by a Philip S. Bates of Portland, Oregon, whose purpose was to educate the public on the terrible menace of this un-American organization. Anti-League circulars were widely distributed, in part by merchants who wrapped them in packages for farmer customers.[51]

On April 19 a prominent Leaguer named C. T. Raywalt, a Colorado resident since 1886 and twice a member of the state legislature, was threatened by a crowd and ordered to leave Haxtun. His car was painted yellow and he was forced to leave town late at night in a fierce blizzard, although he was an elderly man and not accustomed to driving. He was permitted to hire a driver, but the car was soon stuck in the snow, and the two were forced to spend the night in a barn. The mob then tried to force Vance Monroe, editor of the *Haxtun Herald* and a League supporter, to denounce the League and ordered him to leave town if he did not. Monroe, however, was not one to give up easily. Barricading himself in his office with his two six-shooters and a shotgun, his wife and two-month-old baby by his side, he dared the crowd to come and get him. They did not. The League at once scheduled a mass meeting for Haxtun which overflowed the largest theater into the street, and there was no sign of mob action.[52]

The Nebraska office of the Nonpartisan League had early offered the State Council of Defense the services of its 10,000 members in any work which the council wished undertaken, such as the selling of bonds and Red Cross drives. The executive committee of the council immediately returned an insulting letter refusing the offer and charging that the purpose of the League was to undermine the American cause.[53] Subsequently the council attempted to enforce a decree to the effect that organizers and others employed by the League were engaged in "useless employments" and would have to either "work or fight." The League immediately entered a plea for an injunction against the enforcement of the decree.

The day before the hearing news of the decision of the Minnesota Supreme Court in the Martin County case was received, and the council representatives came to the hearing ready to compromise. They insisted upon only two things: that the League cease distributing the pamphlet on war aims and that it stop employing out-of-state organizers. The pamphlet had not actually been circulated recently, inasmuch as most of the demands had by this time been voiced by President Wilson and it was considered out of date. And since the League claimed that only three of the one hundred organizers in the state were non-residents, it was willing to comply with both demands. In return the Council of Defense agreed not to molest the organization further, and the suit was dropped. The Associated Press and many newspapers reported that the League had agreed to withdraw from Nebraska, but it continued its operations in that state under this agreement with relatively little interference.[54]

Some of the best organized opposition was found in Iowa, where League operations had been very limited. The "Greater Iowa Association" had been formed in 1914 by business and commercial interests of the state for the primary purpose of influencing the legislature to repay them what they had presumably voluntarily contributed as an addition to the state appropriation for an exhibit at the Panama Pacific Exposition. It was also to be a sort of "booster" association—the "bigger and better Iowa" type of thing common to many small-town commercial clubs. On January 22, 1918, a four-county meeting at Ottumwa set this association in motion as a force to combat the League, and it commenced to seek expanded membership, especially of farmers.[55]

The Greater Iowa Association distributed a continuous barrage of anti-League literature over the state, and employed speakers, headed by Woodworth Clum, to tour the state. These speakers made venomous attacks all too frequently based on complete falsehoods concerning acts of the League administration in North Dakota. Clum himself, a rabid "super-patriot," is reported to have once exclaimed in a fit of exasperation: "What Iowa needs most is 100,000 funerals in 100,000 Iowa farm homes."[56] Interestingly enough, although it always made a considerable fuss over the League's sixteen-dollar dues (for two years), the association asked farmers for ten dollars a year for a so-called "associate membership."[57]

One of the most amazing manifestations of the desire to wield power and to "be somebody" was the appearance in many small Iowa towns of self-appointed "secret police," often wearing badges of one sort or another and commonly carrying revolvers. Considering it their duty to protect their communities from all evil, these individuals were frequently leaders of mob violence.[58]

The League did not have a newspaper of its own in Iowa, but James M. Pierce, publisher of the *Iowa Homestead*, took up the battle against the Greater Iowa Association and practically devoted his magazine to that enterprise and to the promotion of the League.

In two other states where the League was poorly organized, Washington and Texas, extremes of violence flared. At 2:30 A.M. on the morning of April 26 Alfred Knutson, state manager of the Washington League, was dragged from a hotel in Winlock, completely stripped, covered with tar, and then, feathers being in short supply, rolled in cotton. Three nights later another mob took W. R. Edwards, a League organizer, from a farmhouse between Toledo and Winlock where he was spending the night, threatened him with hanging and drowning, and finally compromised on more tar and feathers. The same night another organizer, Joseph O. Golden, was given similar treatment near Sultan. In the first two cases particularly the men recognized several members of the mobs which assaulted them, but they sought action by law enforcement officers to no avail.[59]

On April 4 at the town of Mineola in east Texas three League organizers, A. A. Cother, H. F. Hoover, and H. L. Higdon, were taken from their hotel by local officers and jailed on a charge of vagrancy, although all possessed money and had driven into town in a car owned by one of the men. The succeeding nightmarish events can be no better related than in the sworn statement prepared by Hoover:

About 10:30 P.M. a crowd attacked the jail and broke off the outer door lock and entered the jail and tried to cut the lock off the cell with a cold chisel and hammer. They got tired of that and went out and got a heavy bar and smashed the lock . . . They took us out in the alley and loaded us into automobiles. They brandished guns, knives and I saw a rope in the alley nearby. I said to the man that had me: "What are you going to do with us?" He said: "We are going to hang you, you damn German spy."

They drove east of town, followed by several cars. After about two miles they unloaded us. One man stood in front of us with a pistol in his hand and raised it up and said: "Which one will I shoot first?" We did not say anything, but he did not shoot . . .

It was a crowd that seemed determined and well organized and was not noisy, but occasionally would call us names. In no case did any of them accuse us of disloyal remarks. The attack against us was solely because of our work in behalf of the Nonpartisan League.

They then made us lay on the ground on our stomachs and stripped the clothing from our backs and beat us with a blacksnake whip. I did not count the strokes but it must have been twenty-five or thirty each one. They did not cease beating us until some time after we began to cry out for assistance. Then they poured salt and water on the stripes.

Our bodies were badly bruised. After pouring the salt water on our bruised backs they cursed us and told us to "get up and go South."

We climbed through a barbed wire fence into a plowed field, and we were so exhausted that we fell several times while running. Then they shot at us, and in running through the woods to escape the bullets, we became separated.[60]

M. M. Offut, an elderly and prominent stock farmer and Methodist lay preacher, then acting as state manager for the League, was in town, and hearing of the mob action he rushed to telephone headquarters at Waco what was going on. He was seized, however, by a dozen men who dragged him to a secluded room and hacked off his long white hair and beard with sheep shears. This they packed in a box and sent to President Wilson, presumably as convincing proof of the loyalty of this community. After being kicked and dragged down the stairs, Offut was permitted to leave town on the train.[61]

The *Greenville* (Tex.) *Banner* treated this atrocity in a flippant manner as if it had been a good lark, referring to the action with hearty approval as "evidence that Americanism is not to be tampered with around Mineola." This strangely warped conception of Americanism appeared again in the conclusion of the paper's account of the beatings: "Their experience at Mineola, they said, converted them to Americanism. Both [Higdon and Cother] gave evidence of being so sore from their whipping they were hardly able to get about . . . we venture the prediction that they will not again undertake to work for the League in or near these parts." [62]

By mid-summer, after most of the primary elections, acts of terrorism became less common in most areas, though they did not entirely disappear. The *Leader* was ready to hope for a return of sanity after the "disloyalty craze" of the past months, and saw grounds for that hope especially in President Wilson's forthright proclamation of July 26 calling for an end to mob action and all violence, and exhorting governors and all law enforcement officials to end "this disgraceful evil":

I say plainly that every American who takes part in the action of a mob or gives it any sort of countenance is no true son of this great democracy, but its betrayer . . . How shall we commend democracy to the acceptance of other peoples, if we disgrace our own by proving that it is, after all, no protection to the weak? [63]

These months of terrorism in the League states constitute a period difficult to assess. The League always maintained that the reason for its persecution was purely political, engineered by those who either feared the end of their own political dominance or who feared the economic program to which the League was committed. It is scarcely deniable that this was a most important factor in the attitude of many high officials, persons in positions of economic power, and numerous newspapers, but it does not adequately explain the mob brutalities in hundreds of small towns. Nothing was more significant than the treatment of the League by the press, which largely determined the attitude of most persons who did not hear League speakers for themselves. Passions are easily inflamed in a war period when fear and hate are dominant. Many unthinking persons naively assumed that violence against those who, it claimed, were opposed to the war somehow demonstrated their own patriotism and superiority, and once a mob has been started on its way no one, of course, stops to reason. The possession of virtually unrestricted power by some local officials or citizens unused to such affluence often proved too great a temptation and led to abuse. Doubtless in some cases motives were mixed, but it was easy and socially acceptable to justify opposition to the League on patriotic grounds.

The desire to make a scapegoat of a minority probably also entered into the picture, a fact which is perhaps evidenced to some degree by the previously mentioned tendency for the greatest violence and bitterest opposition to appear in areas where the League was least strongly organized. The League was promoting a program which would normally have been popular with the classes they sought to interest, but its opponents were able to so emphasize the "loyalty" issue that all else was lost sight of by the average man. The popularity which it did achieve in the face of such tremendous opposition is in some ways little short of astonishing. It is worthy of note that there is scarcely a case on record of a League group reciprocating violence. It was well known what sort of publicity any such incident would receive, and the League desired always to be able to point to its membership as the peaceful and law-abiding element of society.

It is quite clear that a goodly number of League members were opposed to the war, certainly at least in the early days, and it is possible that there were some who entertained pro-German sentiments, though such a matter is difficult to prove. There may also have been members of the bankers' associations with similar feelings, but that fact alone could hardly condemn either organization. Judged on the basis of both the League's pronouncements and its actions, the charges of wartime disloyalty of the Nonpartisan League break down completely.

The war record of North Dakota, the only state with a League administration, was one of the best. Despite repeated poor crops the state oversubscribed all three Liberty Loans, the first by 140 per cent, the second by 70 per cent (the largest oversubscription of any state on this loan), and the third by 76 per cent. The record on volunteers for the armed services was excellent, while the cost per draftee in North Dakota was $1.83 as against an average of $4.23 for all other states. In the last Red Cross drive North Dakota more than doubled its allotment, and it subscribed $175,000 on an allotment for the YMCA of $100,000. In 1918 North Dakota increased its wheat acreage more than 630,000 acres at the request of the government. It was one of the first states to provide a moratorium protecting soldiers against foreclosures, and to decree that all persons between eighteen and fifty must be employed in essential occupations; it was the first to provide a soldiers' bonus.[64]

The postwar attitude of George Creel, the wartime chairman of the National Committee on Public Information, as to the loyalty of the Nonpartisan League was clearly expressed in response to an inquiry from Charles Edward Russell:

I am not at all unwilling to give you my opinion with respect to the war attitude of the Nonpartisan League. Never at any time did I consider it a disloyal organization. On the contrary, the war record of the state of North Dakota, controlled by the League, proved conclusively that the membership, taken as a whole, gave America faithful and ungrudging support in the hour of need.

There is no question, however, but that the Nonpartisan League in the beginning was poisoned by many misunderstandings. Particularly was this true in the matter of the lie that Wall Street was the cause of America's entrance, and that the war was nothing more nor less than the effort of rich men to increase and protect their profits. These beliefs, however, were not peculiar to the Nonpartisan League, but were held by great groups of workers and farmers of the Western States.

It was not a condition that should have caused any wonder. During the long period of America's neutrality, press and politicians alike were divided on the issues involved. . . .

I sent for the heads of various agricultural bodies and unions, and among those that came to Washington in response to the call was Mr. Townley . . . I found him, just as I found the others, full of distrusts and suspicions born of the many lies that he had read and heard. I took him, as I took others, to the President himself, and the interview removed every doubt as to the necessity of the war and the high purpose of America. And after that I took Mr. Townley to the office of Mr. Herbert Hoover, and for three hours the two men fought out disputed points. When Mr. Townley left Washington he had not only pledged the full support of his organization to the war, but he had struck hands with Mr. Hoover and promised every cooperative effort. These pledges were kept . . .

I am not familiar with the purposes or principles of the Nonpartisan League. For all I know they may be good or they may be bad, but what I do know is that the League itself had a better war record than that of many organizations operating in the name of a 100-per-cent patriotism . . .[65]

A New National Party?

POLITICAL apathy was no problem in the Midwest as the election year of 1918 rolled around. It was do or die for the League in North Dakota, where the organization had been looking toward this election since the day following the elections of 1916, when it had become obvious that control of the Senate could not be achieved. There was optimism among Minnesota farmers, where the real battle was likely to take place, and there was talk that there might be surprises even in the less completely organized states. Nor were the anti-League forces biding their time. North Dakota might be "lost," but if ever the Nonpartisan League were to be halted as a national organization, this was the year. There could be no action of any type on either side that did not have its political overtones in 1918.

Following a precinct caucus and district convention procedure identical with that used in 1916, the state convention of the North Dakota League met in Fargo on March 27. Re-endorsements for most state officers were foregone conclusions. Howard Wood replaced Kraabel as the candidate for lieutenant governor, and for the office of state treasurer, the only position lost in 1916, the League endorsed Obert A. Olson of Bowman County, a non-League member of the 1917 legislature who had consistently supported the League program. Harry A. Bronson of Grand Forks, an assistant attorney general, was endorsed for the Supreme Court, and Charles F. Dupuis of Temple, a League member of the House, and Frank Milhollan, backed by organized labor, for railroad commissioners, replacing M. P. Johnson and Charles Bleick. For the congressional seats incumbents John M. Baer and George M.

Young in the first and second districts were accepted, but there was considerable debate concerning the third district, where Congressman P. D. Norton had been assiduously attempting to stay on the fence. There was no violent dislike of Mr. Norton or his record, but his League sympathies were not completely trusted and as a consequence the convention endorsed James H. Sinclair of Kenmare, a League member of the legislature.[1]

The convention also approved seven new constitutional amendments to be initiated by petition and voted upon at the general election in November. Three others that had been started under the old procedure would also be coming to a vote. Designed in the main to make possible the enactment of the League program at the next session of the legislalature, they included the following provisions:

Authorized the state or its subdivisions to engage in industries, enterprises, or businesses

Removed the $200,000 state debt limit, but provided that all bonds in excess of two million dollars must be secured by first mortgages on real estate not to exceed half its value, or on real or personal property of state-owned utilities or enterprises not exceeding its value, and not over a total of ten million dollars on the latter

Contained two measures relating to the levying of an acreage tax for the purpose of state hail insurance

Permitted the legislature to exempt certain classes of personal property from taxation

Specified that no act of the legislature might be declared unconstitutional except by concurrence of four of the five justices of the Supreme Court

Provided that the legislature by a two-thirds vote of each house might declare an act to be an emergency measure, whereupon it would take effect ten days after the close of the session rather than the following July 1

Simplified the initiative and referendum procedure by (1) changing the requirement on signers for a petition from 10 per cent of the legal voters in a majority of the counties to 10,000 electors at large in the case of the initiative and 7000 electors at large in the case of the referendum, (2) providing that a referendum on emergency measures might be called not less than one hundred and not more than one hundred thirty days after the adjournment of the legislature on the petition of

30,000 electors at large or on order of the governor, and (3) providing for a publicity pamphlet to be issued by the secretary of state before all initiative and referendum elections

Provided that constitutional amendments might be submitted to the electors by a majority of both houses of the legislature, or by petition of 20,000 electors at large rather than 25 per cent of the voters in a majority of the counties, the amendments to take effect immediately after approval by the people

Allowed cooperative corporations to limit the voting powers of stockholders [2]

Thus it was proposed to achieve most of what had been attempted in the famous House Bill 44 of the 1917 legislature, aside from the short ballot and four-year term proposals, and the minor textual revisions. Henry Teigan seriously considered suggestions for a unicameral legislature, a preferential ballot, proportional representation, and a recall provision, but was inclined to feel that too much should not be attempted at one time.[3] Most of these "radical" proposed amendments the opposition at once violently attacked, with Judge Bruce expressing his fear of too much democracy in his comments upon the proposal to permit the initiation of constitutional amendments by "only 20,000 voters" one hundred twenty days before a general election:

This provision . . . is in direct accord with the League's whole policy which has been to stampede popular thought and to push through its program without thought and without deliberation and by the force of a class appeal and prejudice and passion. It must indeed be clear to all that four months is not a sufficient time for a law-ignorant, history-ignorant and often misinformed electorate to make radical changes in a constitution and in a system of law and of government and of civilization which has been the result of the experience of the ages and which it has taken centuries to formulate and to create.[4]

The League was supremely confident of success, the *Leader* claiming enthusiastically:

Never were men put forward for office more positive of overwhelming majorities . . . the state never had a governor and an administration more popular with the people. The League numbers over 50,000 active farmer members in the state today. At the election two years ago it numbered less than 100 over 40,000. The League opposition in North Dakota has dwindled away to a few sorehead politicians and a couple of discredited daily newspapers . . .[5]

It was doubtless true that the anti-League forces were none too hopeful of their chances, but they were not by any means ready to quit. A convention of so-called Lincoln Republican Leagues met in Minot May 1 to endorse a full slate of candidates for state office, headed by John Steen, the only anti-League winner in 1916, for governor, and Anton Kraabel, now rejected by the League, for lieutenant governor. These, presumably, were to be the "regular" Republican candidates at least by their own definition.

At this opportune time, and scarcely timed by accident, a creditor's suit was filed against A. C. Townley in the United States District Court at Fargo, growing out of his flax failure at Beach six years earlier. Townley entered a plea for bankruptcy, which was immediately contested, much of the effort being devoted to proving that the Nonpartisan League and all its enterprises were the personal property of A. C. Townley, or at least that he had enriched himself through the organization.[6] The hearings and investigation dragged on for a number of months, but in this pre-primary period the anti-League press made much of Townley's alleged diversion of League funds.

There was no contest in the Democratic primary and the Socialists did not enter a ticket in 1918, leaving the battle to rage entirely in the Republican primary. More and more the keynote of the opposition came to be the loyalty issue, although for the most part it fell rather flat in North Dakota. In several towns there was opposition to League meetings and there were frequently disturbances, but compared with most other states this remained at a minimum. Governor Norbeck of South Dakota contributed to the Steen campaign $200 and a letter insulting Frazier and denouncing his "pro-German" support. In the late days of the campaign Governor Burnquist of Minnesota made a brief speaking tour of the larger cities, exciting little enthusiasm and paving the way for more League charges of "Minnesota dictation."[7] The Twin Cities newspapers indicated that a Frazier victory would be a German victory, a view which was spread to the wire services, giving many persons throughout the country the impression that a League triumph would mean that a whole state had gone for the Kaiser.

The League had held many meetings during the early months of the year, but concentrated the bulk of its campaign in a ten-day period before the election. On Monday, June 17, A. C. Townley arrived in North Dakota to open a speaking tour carrying him to a series of all-day picnics and public meetings over the entire state. In addition to the candidates for office, the speaking staff from national headquarters was pressed into service. Townley's drawing power seemed undiminished; he spoke to some of the greatest crowds North Dakota had ever seen, and in nearly every audience were farmers who had come fifty to one hundred miles to hear him. At Lake Williams in the central part of the state, five thousand persons attended a three-day picnic.[8] Enthusiasm was at a peak. Victory was in the air.

The pre-election comments of the *Grand Forks Herald* were cautious. The election, it said, would not be a test of the loyalty of North Dakota, but whether or not the people of the state had reached a "sufficiently clear understanding of the facts." If they comprehended that the issue was between socialism and patriotism, Frazier would not receive enough votes to carry a small village precinct.[9] "Vote as You Would Shoot!" proclaimed the *Bismarck Tribune.* "There is only one issue in North Dakota. That issue is LOYALTY." [10] The *Tribune* was willing, however, to make limited concessions, although it was certain that extreme reforms should not be undertaken during the war: "The *Tribune* is unalterably opposed to the itinerant preachers of a destructive Socialism, and a damnable pacificism, but it believes the time has come in North Dakota for a complete readjustment of sentiment toward the economic demands of the farmers." [11]

The result was a complete and overwhelming victory for the League. Every state and congressional candidate was nominated, in most cases by vastly increased majorities over 1916. Frazier led Steen by nearly 17,000 votes and carried all but eight of the state's fifty-three counties.[12] Enough legislative candidates had been nominated to make possible control of both House and Senate by powerful majorities. The first test of the confidence of the people in a Nonpartisan League administration had been passed with flying colors.

The call for precinct caucuses in Minnesota had been issued for February 22, the same as North Dakota, and the familiar procedure was followed to the letter. The *Leader* carried detailed instructions, and special letters were sent to every League member in the state. To the 50,000 Leaguers in Minnesota the *Leader* flung this militant call to arms:

"Farmers of Minnesota! The hour has come to strike! . . . It is the opening gun of the campaign. It is the first step in redeeming Minnesota from the clutch of the politicians and the interests they serve."[13]

On Tuesday, March 19, a group of forty-eight farmers representing forty-eight of the state's sixty-seven senatorial districts met in an assembly room on the ninth floor of the Pioneer Building in St. Paul to select their state ticket. The nineteen districts not represented were located either in the large cities or in the iron range area where there was no substantial farm population. In those districts it was agreed that the League would back labor-endorsed congressional and legislative candidates. Republicans predominated among the delegates, but there were a strong minority of Democrats and a few Socialists and Prohibitionists. Several veterans of the Alliance and Populist movements were present.[14]

Laying aside their party affiliations, these men after long discussion selected a slate of candidates upon whom to pin their hopes for 1918. Endorsed to head the ticket as the candidate for governor was former Congressman Charles A. Lindbergh, a lawyer and operator of a small farm near Little Falls, a member of the House of Representatives for ten years, well-known writer and speaker, and father of the young aviator whose solo transoceanic flight nine years later was to make him a popular idol of the world. Endorsed with him were, for lieutenant governor, state representative R. E. Crane, a Mower County farmer; for attorney general, Victor Power, a lawyer and labor leader then serving as mayor of Hibbing; for auditor, S. O. Tjosvold, a pioneer farmer and former county auditor of Yellow Medicine County; for secretary of state, Henry Holmes of Big Lake, a state representative and former minister, now farming; for treasurer, Thomas Meighan, a banker from Preston, the only Democrat on the slate; and for railroad and warehouse commissioner, Fred E. Tillquist, a railroad engineer from St. Paul, endorsed by organized labor. Endorsements were not made until later for justice of the Supreme Court and clerk of the court; after much discussion a decision on whether or not to endorse a candidate for United States senator was indefinitely deferred.[15]

The two-day rally jointly sponsored by the League and organized labor which followed the official convention was attended by more than 7000 and was addressed by a battery of speakers which included William Kent, a former congressman from California and now a member of the Federal Tariff Commission, Gilbert Hyat of the United States Department of Labor, Judson King, secretary of the National

Popular Government League, Walter Thomas Mills, a well-known Socialist author and lecturer, Mayor Van Lear of Minneapolis, Townley, Frazier, and others.[16] Governor Burnquist, as chief executive of the state, had been invited to deliver the address of welcome, but, as anticipated, he refused, and in so doing wrote a scathing attack on the League and organized labor. The League, he indicated, constituted the pro-German element in the state, while the labor sponsors were mentioned simply as a "criminal element," apparently with particular reference to the current prolonged and much condemned strike of St. Paul street railway employees.[17]

After the governor's refusal to speak, the mayor of St. Paul also declined an invitation, and the words of welcome came finally from labor-backed City Commissioner Oscar Keller. For this action Keller was viciously condemned by the *St. Paul Dispatch* and *Pioneer Press*, but two days later he was renominated in the city primaries by the largest vote a commissioner had ever received in a primary election.[18] Messages were read from Carl Vrooman and George Creel. Vrooman was quoted as saying that "the National Nonpartisan League is the only movement which will save the United States from a revolution." Creel's letter stated: "Despite attacks, I believe intensely in the loyalty of the Nonpartisan League. I have done all in my power to defend it from unfair assaults." [19]

In his speech of acceptance Lindbergh spoke with deep sincerity of the seriousness of the world situation and the fact that success in the economic management of the nation was the most important single factor in the winning of the war as far as civilians were concerned. Those fostering distrust of fellow citizens and class prejudice by shouts of "pro-Germanism," he said, were seriously harming the nation's well-being. Few persons were really disloyal to the United States, but the most truly so were "the profiteers who subvert their loyalty to selfish action." Those "seeking to perpetuate themselves in special privilege and in office" fear the will of the majority and raise false issues of "loyalty," denying constitutional rights to honest and sincere citizens:

We must put into practice at home those principles for which we have sent our boys to fight abroad.

It will avail little to win a war for democracy abroad if in the prosecution of that war all the traditional rights and privileges of the people of this nation have been surrendered and abrogated.

189

This is the time to test our sincerity. We must guard against any acts in state or national life which would in any way place doubt upon our honesty or cast reflection upon our motives. The battles of industrial democracy are still to be fought at home . . .[20]

The resolutions passed by the convention were lengthy and far-reaching in their proposals. Pledging anew allegiance to the nation and support of the war effort, they condemned German autocracy and re-dedicated the group to the establishment of political and industrial democracy throughout the world. The platform viewed with concern the lawlessness tolerated or encouraged by public officials in Minnesota, yet persisted in the refusal to meet violence with violence. It is necessary, the platform said, to "maintain the dignity of good and peaceful American citizens," while at the same time standing firmly for principles of justice and against the suppression of democratic rights.

The platform incorporated the League economic program, adding to the list of projected state-owned enterprises warehouses, stockyards, packing houses, creameries, cold-storage plants, and pulp and paper mills. A tonnage tax on iron ore production was demanded, and the following labor program proposed: a state insurance system, state-operated free employment bureaus, state old age pensions, and a state eight-hour-day law, except in agricultural pursuits.

To further the national war effort it urged a series of measures: increased taxes on large incomes and excess profits, expanded presidential price-fixing power, a tax on unused land, permission for the national government to purchase and distribute "necessaries of life" through parcel post, government operation of munitions plants, government seizure and operation of all industries in which industrial disturbances occur which cannot be settled by federal mediation, assistance to and encouragement of agriculture, increased agricultural production, the extension of food market regulation after the war, and other measures.[21]

This platform the *Minneapolis Journal* denounced in no uncertain terms:

These are but the beginnings of a Socialist program such as has wrecked Russia. But the Bolshevists at least have been consistent . . . they have never attempted such a class combination as the Nonpartisan League is trying to put over in Minnesota—that of the capitalist farmer and the industrial worker . . . The plot will fail. The ears of the pro-German donkey stick out from the skin of the lion.[22]

However, William Kent, sent by Wilson to represent the national government and incidentally to determine whether or not the farmers of the Northwest were really disloyal, took a different view. His speech on the concluding day was a highlight:

Wilson knows what democracy means. He is not afraid of radical measures . . . We must go from profit to service. You are doing an everlastingly right thing . . . I shall go back to Washington carrying from you what I have seen and heard here—the message that you are loyal, and that you will stick.[23]

As proof of his faith, before leaving the state he sent Lindbergh his personal check for $1000 for use in his campaign.

At the crowded closing rally Arthur Townley in spectacular fashion called forth a mutual pledge. Pausing at a dramatic moment in his address, he said in a quiet but vibrant voice: "Farmers of Minnesota, is there any hatred in your hearts toward organized labor?" The building shook as the men from the country roared back "No!"

"Those of you who pledge your allegiance to the workers of the city will stand." Thousands of Minnesota farmers jumped to their feet and the applause was tumultuous.

"Workers of the city, if you likewise pledge your allegiance to the farmers of Minnesota, please stand." In an instant the rest of the packed auditorium was on its feet, while hats sailed in the air amid deafening cheers. Near the front of the hall, a few steps from the press tables, a man in the uniform of the St. Paul Street Railway Company, with a tiny baby in his arms, stood, his wife by his side. Tears rolled down the man's cheeks unheeded. The impossible in American politics, a farmer-labor alliance, was coming to pass.[24]

From the day of Lindbergh's endorsement it became customary to refer to him as the "farmer and labor" and soon as the "farmer-labor" candidate. *Leader* cartoons relating to Minnesota invariably pictured the farmer and the worker together, and there was unending emphasis on common objectives and the need for wholehearted cooperation. The pledge asked of legislative candidates was essentially that used in North Dakota except for the words "elected by the League *and organized labor*," and the reiteration of "farmers *and workers*." [25] At the opposition claims that the capitalist farmer and proletarian laborer could never successfully work together, the League jeered. Both were producers, it insisted, and both worked with their hands—their views of a just and equitable social and economic order were the same.

Charles A. Lindbergh was in many ways admirably suited for the League endorsement. All that he had stood for throughout his entire public career was in harmony with the program he was now pledged to support. Sincere, selfless, hard-working, quiet yet extremely forceful, he was respected by all who knew him and his integrity was beyond question. Nevertheless, he tended to be reserved and had few close friends. A fighter for principles in which he believed, Lindbergh was one who asked and gave no quarter. He had been sympathetic with the League from the beginning, writing a series of articles for the *Leader* as early as 1915, and assisting in the work of organizing Minnesota from the day he left the Congress in 1917.

Yet there was a sense in which Lindbergh was perhaps an unfortunate choice, for the reason that, rightly or wrongly, he was extremely vulnerable on the war issue. How important his background in this respect may have been no one, of course, can say. Anyone endorsed by the League would have automatically been vilified on this ground, and possibly it was best to take the bull by the horns. Although he supported the war effort consistently after United States entry, he had been strongly opposed to participation, arguing that "war will not get us any more rights than we can get without war. If we get in a war we will have to support it, but it is wrong and I don't want the country in." [26] Once the nation was involved, he greatly deplored the common attitude that the people should not question why the war was being fought; he was convinced that there should be public statements of objectives so that the people might know their goals.

To make clear his position on the war, Lindbergh personally published in July of 1917 a pocket-sized volume awkwardly entitled *Why Is Your Country at War, and What Happens to You after the War, and Related Subjects.*[27] This book was neither particularly well written nor in any sense seditious, but throughout the campaign it was misquoted, partially quoted, and quoted out of context the length and breadth of the state to "prove" its author's disloyalty. The day following his endorsement the *Minneapolis Journal* headlined "Nonparty Governor Candidate Author of Antiwar Book," [28] and from that day forward the opposition discussed no issues, but devoted itself to proclaiming that the League's candidate was opposed to the war, further evidencing the organization's disloyal nature.

The anti-League forces were well aware of the great importance of this primary campaign, and were prepared to spend almost any sum to defeat Lindbergh. As early as January it was rumored that there were moves under way to unite all "loyalists," both Republicans and Democrats, behind "loyalist candidates," the *Journal* commenting coyly:

It would be a handsome thing for the Democrats to come forward with organized support for the State Administration . . . And it would be a nice recognition of such service for the Republicans to suggest to the Democrats that they name a strong candidate for one of the state offices, the Republicans to give him support.[29]

Correspondence which later came into the possession of the *Leader* indicated that the opposition to the League was headed by a Twin Cities group whose executive committee consisted of an imposing array of prominent bankers and heads of commercial and industrial interests. The most active leaders and those known to the League from the beginning were F. H. Carpenter, a wealthy lumberman, Charles S. Patterson, a wholesale shoe dealer and municipal lighting contractor, and Rome G. Brown, attorney and lobbyist for several large corporations.[30]

Toward the end of 1917 representatives of this group dealt with a League organizer named Walter E. Quigley, offering to set him up in a law office and pay him $200 a month and expenses if he would announce that he had become disgusted with the pro-German leadership of the League and write a series of "inside story" pamphlets. Quigley led them on for some time, keeping the League informed of his activities, and finally on January 21, the *Leader* "broke" the story in great detail, citing it as proof that the opposition would stop at nothing.[31]

The anti-League forces, however, never ceased to seek an exposé and to hope that sometime internal dissension in the League might give them their golden opportunity. A few months later their efforts were crowned with partial success when they secured the services of Ferdinand A. Teigen, a former League organizer who had been discharged because of his habits of failing to turn in to headquarters the money collected from farmers and of telling foreign-born farmers that if they would join the League it could get the war stopped and have their sons brought home. Teigen was not particular for whom he worked as long as there was money in the proposition, and he shortly turned out a pamphlet entitled *The Nonpartisan League; Its Origin, Development and Secret Purposes*, which asserted: "The purpose [of the League] is to pull down the ideals of our fathers and to substitute in their stead other ideals that will compel the reconstruction of the entire industrial and social fabric of the nation on Socialist lines."[32] It was sold as widely as possible, primarily to small-town businessmen, and when it could not be sold was given away.

Beginning January 14, 1918, Minnesota subscribers received a Minnesota edition of the *Nonpartisan Leader*, but a month later this was discontinued and they began to receive both the *Nonpartisan Leader* and a new *Minnesota Leader*, the latter designed to be a newspaper rather than a magazine and so able to provide up-to-date local news.

To counteract the power of the League press, the opposition once again resorted to a news service for country weeklies. In early 1918 Tom Parker Junkin, former editor of the *Grand Forks Herald* and arch-enemy of the League, came to St. Paul to direct the "Reliance Publicity Service," designed to furnish free editorials and "news," this time coupled with the promise that lucrative advertising might be thrown in the direction of those papers that were on the "right" side. In May all rural editors were asked to return a questionnaire on League-endorsed legislative candidates, noting particularly anything of a pro-German nature that might be used against them.[33]

That same month Junkin was arrested for violation of the state corrupt practices act, when the Reliance Publicity Service issued 25,000 copies of a pamphlet scurrilously attacking Lindbergh. The statute required that political pamphlets carry the name of the publisher, the cost, a statement as to who had paid for it, and in whose interest it was circulated. The pamphlet had none of this information, and the prosecution claimed that it should state it was in the interest of Governor Burnquist, inasmuch as he was the only opponent of Lindbergh. Junkin promptly stated to the newspapers that this did not constitute a violation because it was a "loyalty pamphlet" rather than a political pamphlet.[34] Four months later he was acquitted after insisting that Lindbergh was disloyal and that the pamphlet was intended to serve the cause of the nation at war rather than of Governor Burnquist.[35]

Word of the huge "slush fund" built up to combat the League spread rapidly and just as a variety of "promoters" had descended on the

League when it first came into power, so now they hovered about the anti-League group in the Twin Cities, eager to have a hand in the till One of the first to be successful was H. M. Van Hoesen of Chicago who managed to sell the idea of publishing a large and attractive magazine giving the impression of being a general interest periodical but actually devoted to attacking the League. Elaborate advertising solicitations were gotten out and a staff of clerks was employed to make up a list of 200,000 Minnesota farmers from tax lists, rural telephone directories, lists of rural newspaper subscribers, and so on.[36]

On the Square—A Magazine for Farm and Home made its appearance in May, containing a few articles on farm problems and a fiction story, but confining itself for the most part to bitter denunciations of the League and discussions of the disloyalty of its leaders. Its purpose was clearly stated in a brief editorial: "In each issue of this magazine we are going to fight Socialism, half-baked Socialism, and the Socialism of the National Nonpartisan League—for all of them are the real enemies of the nation and its institutions." [37]

Since there was no paid subscription list the issue was of necessity mailed at regular rates, free to all 200,000, who also received a letter on fancily engraved stationery seeking subscriptions. The *Minnesota Leader* had obtained a copy of a confidential advance dummy for advertisers and exposed the whole scheme in advance, necessitating a fast change in layout before publication. *On the Square* did not receive the enthusiastic response which Van Hoesen had predicted; in fact it was a complete dud. The second issue was its last, and a *Minnesota Leader* reporter shortly had the pleasant task of watching the expensive office furnishings being moved out and sold to second-hand dealers.[38]

On the Square was later followed by two other short-lived magazine ventures of a very similar nature but with less camouflage, one having the imposing title of the *Pan-American Anti-Socialist* and the other a super-patriotic affair with a cover festooned with flags and goddesses of liberty entitled *America First*. The indefatigable backers, having lost heavily in this type of publishing business, turned again to the more feasible procedure of printing leaflets, and for some time *Minnesota Issues* was periodically distributed throughout the state.

In early June there occurred a minor revolt within the League ranks, when a "protest and recommendation" written by Joe Gilbert and

What Makes More Noise Than a
Pig under a Gate?

The *Nonpartisan Leader*'s method of dismissing opposition attacks.

signed by fifteen other "loyal workers in the League," was sent to A. C. Townley. From the beginning Townley's word had been law within the organization, and there were many, particularly the stanch Socialists, who chafed under this situation. They had been willing to agree that perhaps in the formative period one-man rule had been necessary, but they felt that the time had now come for greater democracy in operations of the League itself. That was the aim of this group, which included besides Gilbert such stalwart Leaguers as N. S. Randall, O. M. Thomason, Walter Liggett, Arthur Williams, David Paquin, William G. Roylance, and George Brewer.

In the best interests of the future of the League, they recommended among other things that the National Executive Committee be elected by the membership and be given broad policy powers and control of League administration, stating that they did not believe the organization could honestly lead in the fight for democracy when it itself was an autocracy. Townley promptly filed the document in the wastebasket and demoted most of the signers to less important jobs than they had held, but they were loyal to the cause, staying with the League, and little news of the disaffection got out. Although it failed at the time to produce any changes, it is likely that this movement had some effect on organizational changes undertaken by later national conventions.[39]

Lindbergh opened his campaign on April 25 at Willmar before a crowd so large that it had to be moved to the fair grounds in order to accommodate all those who wished to hear. He gave his views on the origin of the war and stated his conviction that America sincerely felt that she had entered to make democracy secure throughout the world. This aim, he felt, must be kept ever to the fore. His call for the fullest support of the war effort, the Liberty Loan, and the Red Cross was enthusiastically applauded by an audience which Haines says was "bespangled with Red Cross and Liberty Loan buttons." [40] Lindbergh concluded his discourse with a review of the League platform, which, he said, represented the surest way to secure democracy at home.

In some areas huge crowds turned out to hear the League candidate and he was greeted as a hero; in others he met violence such as few candidates in America have known. A feature of the last two weeks of the campaign was the mammoth parades of from 100 to 700 cars covered with flags and League banners which streamed through dozens of Minnesota counties. They were snowballing affairs, adding a car at every farm—one parade in Meeker County was claimed to be twelve miles long. The biggest meeting was at Wegdahl, where it was estimated that 14,000 persons attended an all-day picnic on June 14. Carloads of farm families came as far as seventy miles, and four mounted policemen were necessary to handle the traffic and parking.[41]

Yet there were Minnesota towns in which merchants closed every store on days when a League parade or rally was scheduled, and in some cases even the streets were barricaded. In the city of Red Wing the Home Guard was called out to disperse a League parade when city officials learned that it was nearing the city.[42] In some towns parades were met with fire hoses, ripe tomatoes, and yellow paint; cars were tipped over and side curtains slashed. It is a striking commentary on the times that a widely known and respected citizen who had served his state ten years in Congress should now be stoned, rotten-egged, hanged in effigy, and subjected to an unending torrent of abuse and vituperation. Towns and even whole counties were barred to this candidate for the Republican nomination for governor, and he was constantly followed by detectives. Lindbergh, however, was not one to flinch, as is well evidenced by an incident related by Lynn Haines:

He came out of a meeting and found the friend who had been driving him had been dragged from the car and was beaten nearly to unconsciousness. By sheer force of will and in a quiet penetrating voice, Lindbergh made the men listen to reason and they fell back. He helped his friend into the car and they went off. They had gone but a few rods when the mob began to shoot at them. Lindbergh turned to his friend and said, "We must not drive so fast." And with a rain of bullets hitting the car, continued, "They will think we are afraid of them if we do." [43]

In addition to the standard disloyalty charges, use was made against Lindbergh of a resolution he had introduced in Congress in July of 1916 asking for an investigation of the political activities of the Catholic Church and of those organizations which were accusing her of such activity. Though it was made to so appear, the resolution was not directed against the Catholic Church but was designed to clear the air of a welter of charges and countercharges prevalent at the time. The day before the primary, the *Catholic Bulletin*, official paper for the archdiocese of St. Paul, carried a two-column editorial disparaging his candidacy and making particular reference to the resolution, which was said to have been distributed widely throughout the state. Bishop Busch, closing his address at the commencement exercises of St. Benedict's Academy on June 7, was reported by the *St. Cloud Times* to have "begged the good Sisters of the Academy and all women to throw their whole souls into the prayer, 'Lindbergh shall not be Governor.' " [44]

Even one of the state's major cities, Duluth, went so far at one time as to lock the hall where the League candidate was scheduled to speak. The comment on this incident by the *Duluth News-Tribune* was a masterpiece of misrepresentation and a fair sample of his treatment by the daily press:

Lindbergh wanted to speak here. No one cared to hear him. The city objected to the disgrace. It has entertained too many returned soldiers, bearing the wounds of battle, to be willing to act as host to a friend of the Kaiser.

It had just gone away over on its Red Cross quota; it did not care to hear a man who objected to Red Cross contributions. It had just oversubscribed its quota of the third Liberty Loan. It did not want as guest a man who opposed these war loans.

Two thousand more of its sons are in France or on the seas or on the way. It did not care to listen to a man who had opposed enlistment and whose dirk has been aimed at the backs of these men.[45] *

Governor Burnquist and his supporting press announced that he was not campaigning this year because he "doesn't believe this is a time to go into politics" or to "advance his own candidacy." Devoting himself to being the hard-working wartime chief executive, he would not discuss issues or defend his administration, it was said, but he was "confident" that the "patriotic people" of the state would return him to office because he was "loyal." Yet beneath the surface a hard-fought campaign was being waged. Workers combed the state encouraging local groups to call "loyalty meetings" and invite the governor to make "loyalty speeches." In fact these engagements kept the governor busy every day for weeks prior to June 17, and oddly enough they had started just about when a governor making a campaign for re-election would have started. Burnquist's tactics, fumed the *Leader*, were simply a "dodge" to avoid having to discuss the real issues, and the "loyalty meeting" technique was nothing more than a method of campaigning at public expense, since the Public Safety Commission financed all such gatherings.[46]

* It is interesting that a man so reviled as a traitor and coward should be looked upon by a later generation in a much different light. Minnesota today has a state park named in his honor, and the only bust gracing the main hall of the Minnesota Historical Society library is one of Charles Augustus Lindbergh, Sr.

The *Leader* did not dare to seem too hopeful of success, and spoke cautiously on election eve of the youth of the organization in the state and the fact that the League had the support of no daily paper, yet it put strong emphasis on the significance of this election:

It can be truly said that the coming state-wide primary in Minnesota is one of the most important, if not *the* most important election that any state ever held. It will be the first test of the ability of farmers and city working people to cooperate and take over the functions of government for *producers*, who constitute two-thirds of the mass of the people, and who are consequently entitled to rule . . .

If organized farmers and organized labor can carry Minnesota, they can carry any state in the Union. Carried to its logical conclusion, this sort of cooperation will eventually mean the election of a president of the United States and of a majority in both branches of Congress.[47]

To the *Minneapolis Journal* it was clear that "the nomination of Lindbergh would be more than a disgrace—it would be a great misfortune." The emergency, it said, "calls for an omnipartisan counterattack to rout the Nonpartisan offensive." [48] Every action and utterance of Governor Burnquist's received extensive publicity, while Lindbergh's campaign was scarcely mentioned except in editorial attack. There was no doubt about the duty of every citizen, concluded the *Journal*:

The only way to be fair to your Country, State, and City in 1918 is overwhelmingly to vote down Socialism, wherever it shows its head . . .

The *Journal* believes Republicans and Democrats alike should vote in the primary for Burnquist in order that the stigma of disloyalty may not rest upon this state. In this way a loyal governor will be insured whether Burnquist or his Democratic opponent should win in November.[49]

"Patriots Battle at Primary to Rout Nonpartisans," read the election day headline of the *St. Paul Dispatch*.[50]

The League and its candidates had put up a valiant fight against tremendous difficulties, but the odds proved too great. Lindbergh was defeated by Burnquist for the nomination by a vote of 199,325 to 150,626,[51] yet in any ordinary year he would have had a decisive victory. Never before had the total vote in a Republican primary reached 200,000 (168,308 in 1916), but here was a total of nearly 350,000. Many prominent Democrats had joined their voices to the persistent appeals of the Twin Cities dailies for Democrats to vote in the Republican primaries for Burnquist, Minnesota being an open primary state, and the pleas had obviously had their effect. The Democrats had polled 93,112 votes in 1916, but dropped to 32,649 in 1918.[52] Lindbergh carried thirty of the eighty-six counties, lost six others by fewer than 100 votes, and ten others by fewer than 300.[53] In nineteen counties the League had been forbidden to hold meetings.

The only League-endorsed candidate to win nomination was the candidate for clerk of the Supreme Court, Herman Mueller, who emerged with a plurality of 3000 in a three-way race.[54] Approximately three fourths of the League's candidates for the legislature were successful, assuring, thought the *Leader*, "at least . . . a strong minority that will be the balance of power." [55] The *Journal* saw the results as heart-warming proof "that the vast majority of the people of Minnesota . . . are true-blue loyalists." [56]

But the *Leader*, for its part, was not in the least downcast. With a membership of 50,000 the League had polled 150,000 votes, and in each of the counties in which it was at least 50 per cent organized its candidates had received overwhelming majorities—often two or three to one. Labor wards in the cities had likewise returned large majorities. Both farmers and workers had "stuck," it said, and the results were in fact an amazing victory, considering the odds faced, the shortness of time for organization, the character of the opposition campaign, and the fact that this was the first attempt at farmer-labor cooperation. If such inroads could be made in two years, what could be accomplished in four or six? Surely the outcome of this election ensured "the permanency, growth and final complete triumph of the people's cause in this state." [57]

Organization in the other states in which the League was operating had moved much more slowly for a variety of reasons. As has been previously indicated the national organization had spread itself a bit too thin to function at top effectiveness in thirteen states, and it had tended to concentrate its activities in North Dakota and Minnesota for the present. Experienced and trusted lieutenants were sent to take charge of the work as new states entered the fold, but it took time to train organizers and a headquarters staff. In many of the other states the grievances of the farmers were less pronounced than in North Dakota, or at least attention could not be so easily concentrated on a single source of evil. In some there had been a fairly high degree of "progressivism" in state politics, and there was consequently less dissatisfaction with those holding state office. In North Dakota the League was launched at the proper psychological moment to catch fire almost immediately. In most other states a longer period of "education" was necessary to convince farmers of the merits of a program which had seemed a panacea in North Dakota. Finally, in North Dakota the League had taken the state by surprise, but in the others the opposition was forewarned and forearmed.

In most of the states other than North Dakota and Minnesota there was somewhat less emphasis upon the man-to-man contacts which proved so successful in the initial drives, with more reliance placed upon meetings and speeches. Fewer organizers meant a natural tendency to try to reach more persons at a time in a formal meeting. Perhaps in retrospect the success in North Dakota seemed so easy that some persons at first expected full-fledged organizations to blossom forth with only light cultivation. In a few instances the League was slow to adapt its program to the varying needs of the different states, though in most cases this was gradually remedied.

The League had always emphasized the importance of newspaper coverage and had conclusively proved the value of having its own press, yet outside of North Dakota and Minnesota its press coverage was woefully weak. In no others did it have more than one or two weekly papers and in several there were none at all. The *Nonpartisan Leader*, though presumably a national organ, always devoted most of its attention to the two states where there was most activity. Setting up a newspaper was an expensive proposition, and since a state with low membership could not support it, such a paper if established there meant a drain on the national treasury.

In Texas and Oklahoma special problems were faced in that most of the small farmers, while happy to give the organization their blessing, were too impoverished to be able to support it, and both states were never more than a burden on the national League. In a few states, notably Iowa, the competition of a relatively new farmers' organization, the Farm Bureau, became a significant factor. In the spring of 1918 the Iowa Farm Bureau was no more than a skeleton organization, set up in a few counties, with plans for a program of gradual expansion. At that time, however, Governor Harding warned its directors that the Nonpartisan League was planning an organization drive, that Iowa farmers were ripe for organization, and that the League would be successful unless the Farm Bureau got there first. Investigation showed that the League was marshaling its forces to begin in the northern counties, and the Farm Bureau at once decided on a whirlwind campaign. Starting in the northern tier of counties and working south ahead of the League organizers, they were highly successful, and the League never got a good head start.[58] The League always insisted that the Farm Bureau was a creature of Wall Street, designed to divert the farmers from an organization which could really be of help to them, and while this was not true, it seems clear that the growth of the more conservative Farm Bureau effectively stalled the Nonpartisan League in a number of areas.

Primaries in all League states other than North Dakota, Minnesota, and South Dakota came in September rather than June, and consequently state conventions were not scheduled until mid-summer. A statewide conference in South Dakota during March had concluded that the organization was not yet strong enough to enter the primaries against Governor Norbeck, but determined to make a fight in the November election.[59] A meeting of top Republicans in late 1917 had already decided the strategy for the Norbeck campaign, settling upon three general lines of procedure: contrasting Norbeck's record of achievement with the failure of the League to get its program enacted in North Dakota in 1917; supporting constitutional amendments permitting additional state enterprises; and attacking the League leaders as radical Socialists, disloyal to the United States.[60]

An April 30 League meeting at Madison quickly agreed that Wisconsin was not sufficiently well organized to place a ticket in the field in 1918, after Walter Thomas Mills, O. M. Thomason, and Beecher Moore from League headquarters had argued that a serious failure might be a blow to the whole movement. Many, however, were eager for action and ready to ignore the necessity for sound organization. Equity leaders called a meeting for the next day to set up a separate "farmers' ticket," and the League agreed not to oppose such action, although it could hardly be expected that the public would readily dissociate the two.[61]

The Idaho League held its state convention in Boise on July 2, 3, and 4, selecting a complete ticket, agreeing upon a platform, and deciding to enter its candidates mainly in the Democratic primary. Following the selection procedure developed in the other states, the convention first offered the gubernatorial endorsement to state manager W. G. Scholz, who wisely declined, in keeping with League policy. They then turned to Henry Floyd Samuels, a prominent and wealthy lawyer and retired mine operator, now clearing and farming a 10,000-acre ranch. Samuels, a former chairman of the Bonner County Republican Central Committee, had been interested in the League since its inception and had stumped the state in its behalf at his own expense. He was well known and widely respected.

Farmers were endorsed for lieutenant governor, auditor, and first district congressman, the incumbents (Republicans) for treasurer and superintendent of public instruction, a railroad conductor for secretary of state, a miner for inspector of mines, and a friendly newspaper editor for second district congressman. Republican Senator Borah and Democratic Senator John F. Nugent, appointed by the governor to fill an unexpired term, were both given backing. The platform pledged full support to the war effort and called for state-owned flour mills, terminal elevators, packing plants, sugar factories, warehouses and storage plants for farm produce, state ownership and distribution of water power, rural credit banks, "equitable" taxation, the initiative, referendum, and recall, and several items of labor legislation.[62]

Shortly before the primary Townley came to Idaho for a brief speaking tour, which was largely without incident except for the concluding speech at Boise. The Ada County council of defense forbade him to speak in the city and the hall was locked. However, after the pro-League county sheriff deputized most of the crowd, Townley spoke from the steps of the state capitol, and a mob which endeavored to break up the meeting met ignominious defeat at the hands of the newly made deputies. Its leaders thereupon were subjected to a heavy treatment of the famous Townley ridicule.[63]

On primary day the Idaho League scored a clean sweep. H. F. Samuels received more votes than his two opponents combined and even carried Ada County. League Democratic and Republican endorsees alike were nominated, and enough precinct committeemen were elected to give the League control of the Democratic party organization. Legislative candidates were successful in nearly every county where entered. Idaho, having scored the first complete victory outside North

Dakota, was therefore, concluded the *Leader*, henceforth entitled to be known as "the second League state." [64]

In Montana only the House and half the Senate were to be elected, since state officers served four-year terms. The League, concentrating its attention upon the well-organized counties, succeeded in nominating fourteen out of twenty-three Senate candidates and forty (slightly more than half) for the House. In many counties party organizations were taken over, and slates for county offices were nominated in a number of instances. [65]

In both Colorado and Nebraska it was decided that the organization was not yet strong enough to enter the state race, and emphasis was placed on electing legislative candidates in the counties which were sufficiently well organized. In Colorado the seventeen such candidates endorsed were all nominated, [66] and a subsequent state convention gave general endorsement to most of the Democratic ticket and to a number of other legislative candidates on the basis of their replies to questionnaires. [67] Likewise in Nebraska the legislative candidates were successful in almost all of the relatively few districts where endorsed. [68]

The opposition was especially active against the League in Nebraska, where League organizing was specifically forbidden in a number of areas. In July of 1919 the *Leader* began publication of a series of articles by Ralph A. Moore, a former operative for the Thiel Detective Agency who had secured employment as a League organizer in Nebraska in 1918 for the purpose of obtaining information with which to fight the organization. The agency had been hired in April 1918 by a group of Omaha business interests to prove that the League was disloyal and pro-German, but it was unsuccessful, and Moore himself shortly became enthusiastic about the movement. [69] One of the most active centers of anti-League sentiment seemed to be located in Wahoo, Nebraska, where in August the Saunders County council of defense attempted a neat but largely unsuccessful maneuver. Letters were sent to each League member in the county, which read:

The Saunders County Council of Defense desires to give every loyal citizen an opportunity to withdraw from the Nonpartisan League.

You will find enclosed herein a withdrawal blank and also an assignment of your receipt which you received from the organizer.

Action will be brought against the League (without expense to you) to recover the $16 paid by you, and whatever may be recovered to be donated to the Red Cross.

You will therefore sign the withdrawal blank and the assignment and return the same with your receipt from the organizer, in the enclosed envelope.[70]

In Washington there was no prospect of entering the race in 1918, but even the slight progress the League had made was bitterly contested in every possible manner. The extremes of this antagonism were evidenced at the annual convention of the state Grange in Walla Walla June 6. William Bouck, the state master, in his annual address endorsed the League strongly and spoke approvingly of its progress. Immediately there came a barrage from the newspapers and commercial interests, and demands were made that the Grange repudiate Bouck; the answer was his re-election by a large majority. Local newspapers fanned the excitement in the city, and the school board hastily met to order the convention out of the high school auditorium. All other halls were also closed to them. The situation was tense but orderly as the delegates marched out of the auditorium singing "America."

The local council of defense ordered the group out of the city, but they went instead to a church where they had previously been invited to attend a prayer meeting. They were refused admittance, and when permission was asked to hold a prayer meeting on the steps the church representative replied: "We cannot permit you to contaminate either our church or our church grounds. You are all disloyal and pro-Germans in sympathy." Mrs. Bouck thereupon led an open-air prayer meeting some blocks away, concluding, in a voice throbbing with emotion, "Father, forgive them, for they know not what they do." [71]

In the first six months of 1918 the circulation of the *Leader* jumped another 50,000, and the utmost emphasis was being laid on the solidarity of all producers. Before this time, it was said, the broomcorn grower in Colorado had no interest in the activities of the Wisconsin dairy farmer, but now all were watching with interest the successes or failures in other states and all looked to North Dakota as the guiding example. Meanwhile the opposition did not slacken its pace. Private detectives infiltrated League headquarters, and continuous attempts were made to bribe League officials into breaking with the organization and writing another exposé.

In July and August these latter efforts met with limited success when a series of ten articles, directed more against Townley than the League itself, appeared in the *St. Paul Dispatch*, written by the Rev. S. R. Maxwell. Maxwell had started as an organizer in Colorado and had later been made one of the lecturers on the national staff. He had once attempted to get the job of the Colorado state manager, and had later aspired to a congressional endorsement, meeting with failure both times. After an abortive attempt to separate the Colorado League from the national organization, he came to St. Paul to plead forgiveness and was given another chance. Since there were at the time no big meetings which required the services of a lecturer, he was asked to go out for a time as an organizer, but considering this a demotion, he quit and the newspaper articles soon began to appear.[72] The series, for which Maxwell was reported to have received $10,000, was largely a discussion of the "autocracy" of the League organization, but while it doubtless confirmed the views of those already enemies of the League, it probably did not make any serious impression on the membership.[73]

In Minnesota the efforts to elect a state administration were not abandoned with the defeat of Lindbergh. Delegate conventions of the League and of organized labor assembled separately in St. Paul on August 25, and endorsed David H. Evans of Tracy, a well-to-do hardware merchant and owner of a small farm, for governor, and Tom Davis of Marshall, a lawyer and member of the preceding legislature, for attorney general. Evans, well along in years at this time, was not a well-known political figure, but had been a stanch Populist and now classed himself as a Democrat. It was the first time in the history of the state that labor had called a political convention. Though they met separately, the two conventions worked closely together, and the *Leader* recognized that they had deviated from previous principles and had "virtually formed a new party, and are contesting with nominees of both old parties."[74] The petitions were originally filed for the candidates to run as independents, but because of a ruling of the attorney general that names could be printed on the ballot only as the candidates of some party, the name "Farmer-Labor party" was adopted.[75]

The Minnesota campaign continued to be conducted along essentially the lines laid down before the primary, though there was far less excitement on both sides. No wave of enthusiasm had been generated by the Evans candidacy, and the opposition clearly felt him to be a much easier candidate to beat than Lindbergh. The Public Safety Commission's publicity department, maintained for the purpose of circulating "loyalty literature" throughout the state, continued to be of tremendous help to the campaign which Governor Burnquist was or was not waging, depending upon how one looked on his activities. It distributed endless attacks upon the League, and much of its literature contained fulsome praise of the governor and all his works.

In North Dakota it was the League which carried the attack. The picnics, the oratory, the hurling of imprecations at "Big Biz," at Wall Street, and frequently at townspeople in general, were but little changed. Arthur Townley was still the unquestioned star performer, and he played his role to the hilt. Sensing in the huge and enthusiastic crowds the imminence of an overwhelming victory, he exhorted and cajoled, pleaded and thundered. As he lashed at the minions of corporate wealth with his inimitable sarcasm and irony, the sea of sunburned faces responded with roars of vengeance and pledges to "stick" through thick or thin. His contempt for the "hired servants of the exploiters" was stinging and infectious. "If you put a lawyer, a banker and an industrialist in a barrel and roll it down hill," he gibed, "there'll always be a son-of-a-bitch on top!"—and the crowds rocked with laughter.* North Dakota was indeed in the hands of a new messiah.

The anti-League forces in North Dakota, meanwhile, had taken a leaf from the League's book, and were in the process of developing the Independent Voters' Association, generally known simply as the I.V.A., presumably to be based on strong local organization and paid memberships. Originally set up to combat the proposed constitutional amendments in 1918, it quickly became the core of the opposition to the League, thus further obliterating the already badly faded party lines in North Dakota. There were local and county units in addition to the state organization. Regular memberships sold for $10 and included a two-year subscription to the *Independent*, to be published weekly, and later on also a copy of a pamphlet entitled *Townleyism's Future in*

* Bruce Nelson records a conversation with Townley in 1946 in which he asked about the authenticity of this remark. After thinking it over Townley replied that it was difficult to remember what one had said thirty years ago, but then with a smile he added: "But put it in your book anyway; if I didn't say it, I wish I had!" (Nelson, p. 269.)

North Dakota. "Development memberships" were sold at $25. Twenty per cent of all membership fees reverted to the county organization for campaign use as soon as county and local committees were organized. Another 10 per cent was to be used to pay the expenses of delegates from local units to the state conventions. The fees from development memberships were dedicated to a fund to provide speakers, advertising, and other publicity.[76] The I.V.A.'s chief strength was always in the cities and villages, and it never had complete coverage of the state, but it steadily grew and for several years was one party in what came to be essentially a new two-party alignment.

By mid-1918 the pamphlet war which had begun almost with the birth of the League had reached a peak. Leaflets and booklets of one sort or another appeared almost weekly, the great bulk of them anonymous. The League itself published a number of items from time to time, but it did not begin to match the literary output of its opponents, which must indeed have been a boon to the printing trade. In the three months preceding the Minnesota primary no fewer than twenty-one anonymous pamphlets made their appearance in that state, and by the first of September League headquarters claimed to have secured and catalogued 550 different anonymous pamphlets published in the various League states during its three years of existence. In addition there were a goodly number for which credit had been taken.[77]

The League, however, continued to have more of a preoccupation with newspaper publishing, and the last week of September a new League daily, the *Grand Forks American*, commenced publication. Designed to combat and counteract the effect of the League's arch-enemy, the *Grand Forks Herald*, it had capital stock subscribed by 1000 Red River Valley farmers, while the Publishers' National Service Bureau secured a major voice in its control through the procedure described in connection with its acquisition of rural weeklies. It was housed in a new building constructed for the purpose and had available the most modern equipment. Operating in the center of anti-League territory and under the handicap of competing with a long-established paper which had for many years been the only daily in the area, the *American* was never by any means as valuable as the *Fargo Courier-News* and was never a financial success, but it nevertheless played a moderately effective role for a considerable period of time.

As the League had expected when it filed the initiative petitions for the constitutional amendments, the I.V.A. promptly brought suit for an injunction to restrain the secretary of state from publishing the proposed amendments or submitting them to the voters, on the grounds that the amendment permitting the initiation of constitutional amendments had never been legally adopted and was not self-executing. However, the League's confidence that the present Supreme Court would overturn the ruling of the New Rockford case was not misplaced, and the court, over the dissent of the chief justice, held that the proposed amendments might be properly submitted.[78]

As the North Dakota campaign reached a climax, the League-controlled Republican State Central Committee published *The Truth about the Constitutional Amendments*, the committee stating that it "guarantees the entire accuracy of and assumes full responsibility for each and every statement herein contained." The amendments were described as means of making the government responsible to the people and ending "the domination of the state by Big Business monopolists." Voters were warned that since a majority of all votes cast in the election was required for passage, one who did not vote on the amendments in effect voted against them. "The ten Constitutional Amendments are the foundation which will make North Dakota the most progressive and most prosperous state in the Union," it concluded.[79]

The *Grand Forks Herald*, on the other hand, was not only fighting all ten of the amendments but was vigorously supporting the Democratic candidates, now backed by a so-called Joint Campaign Committee of anti-League Republicans and Democrats. Its marked sample ballots were labeled "How to Vote against Socialism," and its pre-election editorial asked somewhat plaintively:

Don't you think it is time for us to quit placing power and confidence in the hands of revolutionists?

Don't you believe it is time for us here in North Dakota to realize that we have made some mistakes and are on the wrong track?

Don't you believe that for the good of yourself and the state, your family should be surrounded with an environment of decency?

Don't you think it's time to urge your neighbors to vote for safety and against Red Socialism all along the line on November 5?[80]

To the *Minneapolis Journal* the Minnesota situation was equally clear:

The issue on election day is precisely the same as it was on primary day. The name of the Townley tool then was Lindbergh; now it is Evans. But the plot of Townley and his Socialist cabal to add the State of Minnesota to his political realm . . . has not changed . . .

Under their red flag, they have gathered the forces of discontent and radicalism, the pro-Germans, the pacifists, the visionaries—and the demagogues who farm the farmer and work the workingman . . .

There is really but one great issue in the state campaign—the issue is loyalty. The Townley machine is essentially seditious and disloyal . . .[81]

In Minnesota Governor Burnquist once again emerged victorious, this time by a vote of 165,611 to 111,966 for Evans, although he lacked a clear majority. The only successful League candidate for state office was the clerk of the Supreme Court, who, it will be remembered, had the Republican nomination.[82] Seven League senators and twenty-five representatives were elected, while Minneapolis and St. Paul labor contributed five senators and nine representatives.[83]

North Dakota, however, continued to lead the way, the League securing virtually a clean sweep of all three branches of the state government. Frazier led Doyle by nearly 18,000 votes, and the rest of the state officials were swept in by similar majorities, with the exception of the superintendent of public instruction. For this office, for which women had the vote, Minnie J. Nielson of Valley City unseated Neil MacDonald by a little over 5000 votes.* Bronson was elected to the Supreme Court, giving the League four of the five members of that body. All three congressmen were elected, and both houses of the legislature were now completely dominated, the League having thirty-six senators and seventy-nine representatives.[84]

Fully as important was the passage of all ten of the constitutional amendments, by majorities ranging from 12,000 to 24,000. Despite these majorities, however, five of the amendments lacked a majority of all votes cast in the election. Although the League had repeatedly warned its members during the campaign that this was necessary, Attorney General Langer now decided that all that was required was a majority of the votes cast on the amendment. The state canvassing board, by a three to two vote, thereupon declared all amendments passed.[85]

The I.V.A. immediately appealed this decision to the Supreme Court,

---

* Frazier, 54,517; Doyle, 36,733 (Doyle's vote in the Democratic primary had been 7280). Nielson, 58,324; MacDonald, 52,777 (MacDonald had led in the primary 64,339 to 60,320). *1919 Legislative Manual, State of North Dakota*, pp. 282, 284.

which on January 31 ruled four to one that the amendments had all passed. The provision in question read that an amendment must secure a "majority of all legal votes cast at such general election," and the court held that a person who did not vote on a measure had not cast a legal ballot at the election so far as that measure was concerned.[86]

The League was now free to enter upon its economic program, and the opposition could hardly have been more bitter if it had seized power by force, yet the League itself had provided some of the most liberal initiative and referendum measures in existence. It was a foregone conclusion that the anti-League forces would challenge all important legislation; thus it would not take effect until approved by the voters.

The South Dakota League had selected its slate of independent candidates at a convention held at Mitchell on July 23 and 24. For the nomination for governor they chose Mark Pomeroy "Roy" Bates, a prominent and highly respected stock breeder from Letcher. A labor candidate from Aberdeen was selected for treasurer, a League attorney for attorney general, the city assessor of Mitchell, a former state auditor, for auditor, and the rest were all farmers. The Democratic nominees for senator and first district congressman were also endorsed.[87]

Bates' reputation was such that it could not easily be attacked, and Governor Norbeck therefore found it necessary to hammer at the "Socialist leaders" of the League and the "loyalty" issue. He argued in general that his record of steady progress should not be exchanged for the mere promises of the League, contending that South Dakota already had more progressive legislation than North Dakota and more was yet to come. He strongly supported the proposed constitutional amendments to be voted on in November, which would permit a number of state enterprises, but he was careful not to promise these things—merely that they would be investigated. Oddly enough, he was bitterly attacking the Leaguers as "Socialist agitators" for proposing much the same things as he recommended, but he stoutly insisted that he was not a Socialist and that his program did not entail Socialism; it was just sensible cooperation. While he was unwilling to go quite as far as the League, he was quite ready to undertake "practical" measures of state ownership.[88] To the question of how to beat the Nonpartisan League Peter Norbeck had a ready answer: "When the water gets too high, let a little of it over the dam." [89]

There was continued violence against the League during the South

Dakota campaign, especially while Townley was accompanying Bates, and the latter grew extremely bitter about the matter, commenting at one time that he was being "hunted down by Norbeck's henchmen." Norbeck, caught between his desire not to seem to be responsible for persecution of his opponent and his campaign tactic of insisting that the League was disloyal, finally endeavored to guarantee protection to Bates, once even going to Bonesteel to see personally that no violence came about. He would not, however, make the same guarantee for Townley, and the two were frequently on the same platform.[90]

Finally the governor wrote a letter to the chairmen of the county councils of defense ordering them to prevent meetings where Townley was to speak, but the next day the order was rescinded. Providence, in the form of a "flu" epidemic, had intervened, and health officials banned all public meetings after October 17.[91] Until that time, however, the encounters had grown more and more bitter, Norbeck charging that Bates had "no issues except that of being mobbed" and was simply trying to gain sympathy. Bates finally exploded and accused Norbeck of stealing his program, to which the governor replied: "If Norbeck stole your thunder as you claim . . . it was done before the League was born."[92] Whether or not Norbeck actually "stole" the League program, it is probable that the League threat considerably expanded his "progressivism," and it is certainly true that he based his campaign on the policy of going far enough along the League road to satisfy many people and cause the League demands to lose their potency.

At any rate the governor's formula proved successful, and his slate won all the state offices. All constitutional amendments were passed, and the League managed to elect only five senators and thirteen representatives.[93] Not long thereafter Norbeck told Governor Allen of Kansas: "I believe the best way to meet the League proposition is to give the farmers every reasonable thing they ask for and refuse to go with them on the impractical."[94] In the same vein he wrote R. A. Nestos of Minot an analysis of his success which was strikingly different from the I.V.A. policy of fighting anything proposed by the League:

First, we supported every good suggestion the farmers made. Second, we did not even oppose their going into new experiments of uncertain value, providing the risk connected with the venture was only nominal, for the farmers themselves were the main taxpayers, so why should they not be permitted to have some experiments if they honestly and sincerely asked for it [sic] in the belief that it would better their conditions.[95]

In Idaho, for which high hopes had been held after the primary victory, the results were disheartening. Senators Borah and Nugent were both re-elected as were the incumbent Republican state treasurer and superintendent of public instruction, who had received League endorsement. H. F. Samuels and the rest of the slate, however, went down to defeat, owing in part, no doubt, to the general trend toward Republicanism in the western states. Eight senators and fourteen representatives were elected, giving that state the third largest League representation in a state legislature.[96] The new Montana legislature was to contain three League senators and eighteen League representatives, while in Nebraska it was one senator and seven representatives, and in Colorado two of each.[97]

The *Leader* was clearly disappointed with the results outside of North Dakota, but it recognized the tremendous odds faced in the wartime shortage of organizers, the disloyalty smears, the forcible restraint of activities in some areas, the almost universal press opposition, and the like. Nevertheless, great gains had unquestionably been made and there seemed no reason why the membership should not continue to expand, especially now that the war was over. Why not 400,000 to 600,000 members by 1920? Already in Minnesota and South Dakota the League had replaced the Democrats as one of the two major parties. "Defeat," it said, "is impossible!" [98]

At the time of the 1918 elections the total paid-up League membership amounted to 188,365, of which 131,443 were located in the four states of Minnesota, North Dakota, South Dakota, and Montana.[99] Actually the League never really dropped members who had once joined, and it considered the total to be something over 200,000. This would theoretically have meant an annual revenue of $1,600,000, but it was never anywhere near that figure, owing to defaults on postdated checks and on partially paid memberships, especially in poor crop years. By mid-1918 the League's field staff of speakers and organizers consisted of more than 500 men, and its headquarters staff occupied an entire floor of one of the largest office buildings in St. Paul. Meeting such a payroll, plus the support of twelve additional state offices, campaign expenses, and publications, required no small income.[100]

The League organizational structure centered around the National

Executive Committee of Townley, Lemke, and Wood, with Townley actually having the controlling voice. There was a state committee of farmers in each state, but they did not in reality control their own state organization to any extent. The state managers were appointed by the National Executive Committee, and they in turn selected their field foremen, whose job it was to select, train, and supervise the organizers. These foremen received $150 per month plus expenses and the use of a Ford. The corps of national speakers was likewise selected by the National Executive Committee, and each received $200 per month, expenses, and the use of a Ford. These speakers were picked on the basis of past performance and were an extremely able group, but the criterion of a good speech as far as the League was concerned was whether it brought in members. Townley's instructions were concise: "Cut out all this fine stuff and get down in the manure pile with the farmer and get the money." [101]

The editors of the state *Leaders*, the national organ, and the North Dakota dailies were also chosen by the National Executive Committee and were responsible to them. At the bottom of the hierarchy were the organizers, who at this time received 25 per cent commissions (20 per cent when payment was by postdated check), and were bonded for $1000. A Ford was sold to each organizer, which he paid for at the rate of $50 per month out of his commissions. All money went to the national headquarters, which then supported all the state headquarters and newspapers as well as its own activities.[102]

The first national delegate convention of the National Nonpartisan League was called for the week of December 3 in St. Paul, in accordance with the Articles of Association, which provided for periodic conventions of this sort. North Dakota had had such business sessions before, but many of the state organizations were only approximately a year old, and this was the first opportunity for a national gathering. Each state which had been sufficiently organized to participate in the 1918 state campaign was to be represented by its entire state committee of five members, while the other six states were to send one member of their state committee. Business to be considered included the revision and adoption of the Articles of Association, an investigation of League business and accounts, the adoption of resolutions dealing with the League position on postwar reconstruction, and the filling of the vacancy on the National Executive Committee caused by the expiration of the two-year term of office of A. C. Townley.[103]

The convention met as scheduled and in the course of a week accomplished all its objectives. A committee consisting of one delegate from each state went through the customary procedure of checking the League books and reported complete satisfaction on all counts, commenting with especial favor on the regular audits and the bonding of all persons handling money. A special investigation was made of the salary and expense accounts of A. C. Townley, and finding them to be moderate, the convention unanimously voted to raise his salary from $3600 to $5000 per year.[104]

A postwar program was agreed upon with little dispute. After a preamble calling for complete political and industrial democracy, the resolutions pledged the support of the League to the following measures:

The creation of democratic world government, a "United States of the world," to end all future war

A reconstruction program ending monopoly, providing full employment, and reducing the cost of living while at the same time maintaining the income of producers

National ownership of all means of public transportation and communication and "all other undertakings which in their nature must be either great private monopolies or public enterprises"

The relief of unemployment through public works, coupled with free schools for vocational training

The complete enfranchisement of women, equal opportunities with men, and equal pay for equal services

National government loans to the states on state bonds to make possible state loans to farmers at cost

Reduced passenger and freight rates, especially on food and fuel

An immediate end to all interference with the political rights of employees in the public service and to all post office censorship

Liquidation of the national debt through steeply graduated income and inheritance taxes

The restoration of the "rights of labor surrendered for patriotic reasons," and the repeal of laws limiting civil rights as war measures

National legislation to the effect that "the use of the mails, telegraphs, telephones, express companies and banks shall be denied for making sales of goods, properties, investments or securities, except for the direct delivery by the owner or his authorized agent, and then of the specific goods, properties, investments or securities involved, in order to eliminate gambling and speculation in necessities of life" [105]

The formal Articles of Association adopted by the national convention were designed, claimed the *Leader*, to "provide the most democratic form of organization possible consistent with protection to the membership of the League against seizure of power or influence in the organization by outside hostile influences or forces." [106] The old fear of infiltration by opponents or factional strife which might bring to power someone who would "betray the cause" was still dominant. In essence the articles left the selection of political candidates, determination of platforms and legislation, and the election of the state and national committees to the democratic process, but retained control of the League organization itself in the hands of a virtually self-perpetuating National Executive Committee.[107]

The management of League affairs in each state was nominally vested in a three- or five-member state committee of resident farmer members, elected by an annual state convention. Delegates to the state conventions were to be chosen as usual through precinct and district caucuses. Each state committee then was to select a chairman, who automatically became a member of the national committee. The national committee therefore had as many members as there were states in which the League was organized, plus the members of the National Executive Committee. Thus in order for a man to become a member of the national committee he must first be chosen in his precinct as a delegate to the district convention, then chosen as a delegate to the state convention, there chosen a member of the state committee, and finally chosen chairman of that committee. Presumably in this process all self-seekers were to be weeded out and it could be assumed that anyone surviving this elimination would be in full accord with the program and purposes of the organization. Though the state was to elect its own committee, the state manager was still to be an appointee of the National Executive Committee, and it was specifically provided that "he shall be subject to directions, instructions and removal by the National Executive Committee."

The national committee was to meet on the first Tuesday of each December and at such other times as called by the chairman of the National Executive Committee or two members of that committee. A majority of the national committee was to have the power to remove any League officer or member of any committee and at any time to amend the Articles of Association. But the real operating power remained in the National Executive Committee, which was to be "the executive and managing board of the association and, except as limited by these articles, shall have full and complete power and authority to fix, collect and disburse the membership fees and other funds of the association; to control and supervise, generally and specifically, the organization work in the several states; to prepare rules and regulations for the affiliation of other political and industrial organizations; and shall have power and authority to do any and all acts that a private individual may lawfully do." It could not, however, bind the members for financial obligations in excess of the dues paid or agreed to be paid.

Moreover, anything which might have been overlooked in the foregoing statement was included in a "catch-all" article: "All other matters, facts, things, powers and duties, proper and necessary to exercise in carrying out the functions and purposes of this association, not herein expressly provided for, are hereby expressly delegated to the jurisdiction of the National Executive Committee."

The true locus of power in that three-man executive committee was indicated by Section 12, which specified that the chairman was "the chief executive officer" of the association, and that he was empowered, except as limited by the articles or by a motion or resolution of the national committee, "to do, perform, and carry out, all and singular, the matters, facts and things authorized to be done by the articles in carrying out the purposes of this association."

The touchiest point, and the one which the League felt compelled to explain and defend at length both in the *Leader* and by pamphlet, was the manner of selecting the members of the National Executive Committee. The first executive committee had been specified in the original articles to consist of A. C. Townley for a two-year term, William Lemke for a four-year term, and F. B. Wood for a six-year term, beginning January 1, 1917. The articles now provided that at the end of each two-year period a candidate to succeed the member whose term expired should be nominated by the National Executive Committee itself, and his election should then be by the national committee. Vacancies were to be filled by the executive committee.

League leaders defended this scheme by insisting that the utmost harmony was essential on this powerful committee. The members must be able to work together and present a united front; no internal friction which would help the enemy could be allowed. It was also feared that unless done this way there might be a multitude of candidates, "resulting in electioneering, pulling and hauling and the creation of factions . . . [that] might leave an open sore dangerous to the solidarity of the organization." [108] The philosophy was clearly stated by Walter Thomas Mills:

Is the Nonpartisan League now a democratic organization in the sense that in the selection of its officers, in the writing of its program, and in the carrying on of its work, it is now governed by its own membership after the same manner in which it proposes that the state and nation shall be governed by its citizens after the state and national programs of the League shall have been adopted?

The answer is that it is not. The battle is on now, and the war for democracy is at its worst. There must be a commander now. When the war is over and the democracy for which the League is fighting has been established, neither a League nor a commander will then be necessary.

Let it be plainly said. It is impossible to fight the political machines built, financed, and managed by the great private monopolists, except by the building of a machine with which to fight them. The League came into existence to fight a battle, and battles can be fought only with some one in command. [109]

Mills was not unfamiliar with Karl Marx.

The national committee promptly proceeded to re-elect A. C. Townley, coupling the action with an adulatory resolution of appreciation and praise:

Recognizing the great service that he is doing for the people of the United States, and for humanity at large, it is our deliberate opinion that he is the greatest leader of the common people who has arisen in this nation since the day of Abraham Lincoln; and we pledge to him our undivided and unfaltering support in the great task that still lies before us. [110]

Immediately after his re-election, Townley announced that he would accept only if the action of the national committee were approved by a referendum of the membership. Townley, all of whose waking hours were devoted to the League, knew of course that there was really no question about the matter, but he took this means of trying to quiet the charges that he was a self-appointed dictator and giving the membership the feeling that they had had some direct voice. His sentiments were hardly as disinterested as the *Leader* would have had its readers believe: "Mr. Townley has no personal feeling in the matter. He frankly is willing to devote his genius for organization to the great cause, but not unless he has the confidence of the membership." [111]

This was not presumed to be an election; that had already occurred. It was merely a question of approval of the action of the national committee. For three weeks the *Leader* printed ballots, which read: "Shall the action of the national committee of the League electing A. C. Townley to another term as president of the organization be approved or disapproved?" Members were instructed to mark the ballots "For A. C. Townley for president of the League" or "Against A. C. Townley for president of the League," and the generous rule was announced that all members could vote even if in arrears in dues, or whether or not enrolled for the new membership period. The national committee appointed a canvassing board consisting of the 1918 gubernatorial candidates: Frazier, Lindbergh, Evans, Samuels, and Bates. On January 27, the board announced that the vote had favored Townley by slightly better than a hundred to one, the actual figures being 98,391 to 978.[112] Many farmers enclosed personal letters to Townley, expressing their faith in him, and a sizable number included checks for renewal of membership.

From the beginning the opposition press had evinced an almost tearful concern over farmers spending their hard-earned money to join the League, and rumors were endlessly repeated as to how the League leaders were diverting organization funds to their own pockets and living in luxury on the contributions of nearly impoverished members. The investigating committees at every League convention had always been satisfied from their examinations of the records that such was not the case, but the most convincing proof grew out of the Townley bankruptcy case, which had started as a result of the creditor's suit before the 1918 primaries and came to a head in January 1919.

The case had been dragged out primarily because of the demand of the attorneys for the creditor, interestingly enough some of the most prominent I.V.A. lawyers in the state, to see all the books of the League. The attorneys claimed that they could then prove that there had been vast diversions of funds which Townley must have hidden away. Yet a most searching probe by the keenest legal brains the opposition could engage, backed by almost unlimited time and plenty of money, failed to unearth anything against the honesty of Townley or any mismanagement of League finances. The statement of Federal District Judge Charles F. Amidon in granting Townley's petition for discharge in bankruptcy put the matter succinctly:

> The trustee [representing the creditors in the proceedings] has been permitted to go through the record of all these concerns [the League and its affiliated enterprises] as with a lighted candle. He has found no trace of any grant of any of the funds or property of the Nonpartisan League or its subordinate agencies to Mr. Townley, except a salary of $300 per month . . . On the contrary, the record shows clearly and affirmatively that the Nonpartisan League and its subordinate agencies have never granted to Mr. Townley any part of their funds or property as his personal estate . . . and that he has never used them for any purpose except that of a political leader, devoting them honestly to the achievement of the objects of his party. The record is full and has been honestly kept, and it shows an honest purpose to give an account of an honest stewardship.

But Judge Amidon did not stop with this. He was perfectly aware of the thousands of dollars that had been spent by someone to hire lawyers, detectives, and accountants to investigate for months for what was on the surface a $900 creditor's suit. He knew that the case had been utilized to the utmost in anti-League propaganda, and he minced no words in setting forth the real purpose of the suit as he saw it:

> At the time the petition in bankruptcy was filed A. C. Townley had been for three years the leader of the Nonpartisan League. His examinations before the referee and later before the court have had to do, not with his private estate, but with the funds of the League and the agencies which it has created to carry out its program . . .
> The search [for hidden funds] has been pursued not only with the zeal of creditors intent on collecting their debts, but that of political adversaries seeking to discredit a party believed to be dangerous. Detectives were hired to ingratiate themselves with the wife of the bankrupt . . . As the result of months of following up these clues by the trustee, the creditors and their detectives, counsel for the trustee state frankly on the argument at the recent hearing that no secret deposit or specific property held upon trust has been found. The conclusion is justified, and the court so finds the fact to be, that the reason why this hidden treasure has not been found is that it does not exist.[113]

"The New Day in North Dakota"

THE sixteenth session of the North Dakota legislature convened in January of 1919 amid an air of eager expectation such as seldom if ever has surrounded the opening of such an assembly. This was the culmination of more than three years' work and struggle; this was the legislature that was to enact the program which would bring about the long-awaited "new day in North Dakota." Arthur Townley spoke to the opening legislative caucus, keynoting the session with one of his most earnest, idealistic, and moving addresses. Gone was the "rabble-rouser" technique—the day of opportunity was at hand:

What does the North Dakota legislature mean to you? This is what it means to me:

For the first time in the history of the United States the lawmaking power of a sovereign state has been taken away from the exploiters and devourers, the beasts that prey, and has been placed in the hands of white men—men who have a noble purpose, who are raised from out themselves.

We can depend upon the collective judgement of this group of men. Do not rely on my judgement, for I make mistakes. Every man makes mistakes.

My only fear is that we may become entangled in the jealousies and prejudices that have kept the people apart for centuries, that we may let little personal desires intrude and so forget the big things.

Let us guard this magnificent instrument which is ours to employ for the betterment of humanity. Let us make it an organization to serve the people, for everything in the League belongs to the people and it will survive only so long as it dedicates itself to unselfish service.

We have arrived at the place and the time to either accomplish the

League program or quit coming to Bismarck. Much depends upon our action—not only the prosperity, safety and happiness of the people of North Dakota, but the fate of the toilers all over the United States.

The special interests are not saying much just now, but this is only the lull before the storm. In a few days the most vindictive, vituperative, vile, dishonest flood of criticism in the history of the United States will be let loose. We will be abused as few men have ever been abused because we have the courage to stand for a new order.

But if you can really succeed in carrying out the League program you will have done more toward the common good than any group of men in the world before you . . .[1]

The *Grand Forks Herald* remained a prophet of doom, foreseeing nought but disaster from this rule by the "Socialist carpetbaggers." The League's wild program would cost the state an extra $70,000,000 the first biennium, plus millions of dollars in bond issues, it said. A 600 per cent increase in the tax rate would be necessary, and endless new taxes were inevitable.[2] Yet worse by far was the ending of all that had been cherished in the American way of life:

When the legislature ratifies that amendment [on the method of making amendments] constitutional government in North Dakota, to all intents and purposes, will have been wiped out . . . the Declaration of Rights will have no greater dignity or permanence than the statute prescribing the length of hotel bed linen.[3]

After contests over four seats had been decided in favor of two League candidates and two I.V.A. candidates, leaving the League with a three-fourths majority in the Senate and a 70 per cent majority in the House, the caucus settled down to the problem of the House speakership, the speaker for the last session, Howard Wood, now being lieutenant governor. The caucus was divided between Walter Maddock of Mountrail and L. L. Stair of Bottineau, but after long discussion by both sides, Stair won out by the narrow margin of one vote. The opposition press gave wide publicity to the "split" in the League caucus, charging that Stair was the "machine candidate," dictated by Townley. But the caucus gave convincing evidence of its solidarity. Although the I.V.A. caucus offered Maddock its entire vote in the hope of promoting disharmony, Stair was nominated the next day by Maddock and received every League vote.[4]

The League caucus, with the bit in its teeth, could not have been held back; it needed only to be shown the way. The old five-point pro-

At the Parting of the Ways

The *Nonpartisan Leader* looks to the future.

gram was yet to be accomplished, but that now seemed a mere minimum platform—new and bigger things were also possible. This was the
great chance to lay the foundation through state action for a new society. After a professedly careful study of public enterprise in the
United States and abroad, recommendations, savoring in several respects of the then fairly new arguments for council-manager city government and further evidencing the close tie of the League to the
various contemporary reform movements, were made to the sixteenth
legislature:

1. That North Dakota required a thoroughgoing system of state
ownership, not merely a corporate or cooperative organization, working under state regulation.

2. That the system of state industry so established should be financed
by the credit of the state and repaid by the profits of the industries.

3. That the authority to establish and to operate the state industries,
with commensurate responsibility, should be definitely and certainly
placed.

4. That such authority and responsibility should be reposed in a small
board directly elected by the people.

5. That this board should have absolute authority to appoint and to
dismiss the manager or directors of each industry or enterprise, and
that the latter should have like power to appoint or dismiss and should

be responsible for all experts and employees within each industry or enterprise.

6. That the state industries should be operated for service and not for profit, but that charges for services should be ample to cover all costs and for the building up of reserves.

7. That the state should establish and operate its own bank, for the financing of all state departments, industries and enterprises, for the handling of all public funds and for the making of farm loans and the stabilizing of credit in all industries carried on in the state.

8. That the recall of elective state officers would be necessary in order to enable the people to exercise an effective control over those responsible for the management of the state industries.

Thus the chain of responsibility is complete and unbroken, from the people to every officer and employee in their service. Indirection and complication are eliminated; the shifting of responsibility is impossible; the entire organization stands out in the open, subject to the scrutiny and criticism of every citizen honestly interested in the securing of an honest and efficient public service.[5]

Although Minnie J. Nielson had received a majority of some 5500 votes for the office of superintendent of public instruction, when she appeared on January 1 Neil MacDonald refused to surrender the office on the grounds that Miss Nielson lacked the necessary qualifications. She at once appealed to Attorney General Langer, who, despite the fact that Frazier, Townley, and Lemke were reported to be backing MacDonald, secured on January 10 a writ of mandamus from the Supreme Court compelling him to turn over the office.[6] MacDonald thereupon instituted quo warranto proceedings in the District Court of Burleigh County, claiming that Miss Nielson was not a "holder of a teacher's certificate of the highest grade issued in this state," as required for a state superintendent by a statute of 1911. Her certificate had been issued in 1902 and was the highest given at that time, but the 1911 act had changed the classes of certificates and she did not now qualify for the top grade. The District Court held in favor of Miss Nielson, and the next fall a unanimous Supreme Court did likewise, saying that there was clearly no intent to make the statute retroactive and that her certificate was the highest issued in the state within the meaning of the act.[7]

Stories that a "bolshevistic" political organization had seized control of the state of North Dakota were spread so widely that when the legislature convened in January a number of correspondents from the

East were on hand to report the complete collapse of democratic government which would follow as a matter of course. Many of them wrote back rather surprised reports of what they had seen, one commenting that the legislators, the administrative officers, and the Supreme Court appeared to be "neither visionary theorists nor wild-eyed radicals . . . I have seldom observed a State legislature whose controlling majority was so obviously sensible, moderate and intelligent. The extremist of every type, the voluble expounder of radical notions, or the reformer with his one all-sufficient remedy for social ills, was conspicuously absent." [8]

Much of the real lawmaking activity took place in Patterson's Hall, adjoining the McKenzie Hotel, League headquarters for this session, where the nightly caucus was held. The caucus operated in essentially the same fashion as it had in 1917, considering every important measure to come before the legislature, with each member bound to vote in accordance with the majority vote of the caucus. Since no attorneys were officially provided to handle the drafting of legislation, the League supplied its own, including James Manahan, H. A. Paddock, and Vince A. Day. Townley, Lemke, F. B. Wood, Walter Thomas Mills, and occasionally others constantly advised with the caucus—or dictated to it, depending on one's point of view. W. G. Roylance, formerly a professor of economics at the University of Idaho, served as tax consultant and economic adviser.

Actually, discussion of measures in the caucus was quite free and open, but it is true that the caucus activities were closely directed by the steering committee. Such a body was of course essential for so large a group which must consider a vast number of proposals in a relatively short period of time, and it is not surprising that the committee should tend to follow the lead of the so-called "inner circle" of advisers who were devoting full time to the proposed legislation and who were the trusted leaders of the movement. The steering committee could kill proposals simply by holding them indefinitely, and its favorable recommendation was of the greatest importance in securing acceptance. Having been over the matter before, the members of the committee and others whom they might call in usually had the best of the floor debate. Nevertheless frequent changes were made in the caucus and it not uncommonly turned down proposals completely.

Townley always expressed himself on important measures before the caucus, and was naturally extremely influential. His "applied psychology" was in evidence. At times he gave the impression of wishing to be cautious—perhaps it would be best not to go too far or too fast—letting the pressure build up from the group until he finally "yielded." Some charged that it was standard practice for many evenings to be taken up with long speeches by Mills or various guests, while reports of the steering committee were rammed through when it had grown late and everyone was tired.[9] Yet though some might chafe occasionally at being bound by the majority of the caucus, the legislators themselves did not seem to have the feeling that the procedure was unfair.

After approval by the caucus, action by the legislative committees and by the chambers themselves was largely a formality. In the event that changes should be made in committee, however, the caucus rules provided that all changes must come before the steering committee and all important changes before the caucus as well.[10]

The secrecy of the League caucus was always one of the chief points of attack, although visitors were permitted on Wednesday and Saturday nights and by special dispensation at other times. Caucuses, of course, are not generally public affairs, and the real purpose of this provision was to make possible smooth and uninterrupted operation. What happened in those meetings was for the most part a matter of public knowledge in any case.

Many visitors who anticipated witnessing a cut-and-dried affair were surprised at the animation and vehemence exhibited. One eastern correspondent commented: "If this was fair sample of the League's caucus —and what I saw that evening and the next would lead one to think it was—it appeared, taken by itself, to be a pretty fair replica of the old-fashioned New England town meeting." [11]

The seriousness with which the work of this session was taken and the extent to which members were impressed with the need for solidarity are well evidenced by the words of the *Capital Daily Press*, a daily paper published in Bismarck by the League during the legislative session:

The time has come to act. The farmers of North Dakota expect the legislature to act. And farmers and workers all over the United States are looking toward this state in the hope that its law-makers will write a new Declaration of Independence which will free the producers of America from the oppressive shackles of monopolistic exploiters . . .

If any League legislator is planning to doublecross his fellow legislators and his constituents—let us give him one piece of advice in advance. Let him prepare to leave North Dakota. Let him lay his plans to move into some remote territory. North Dakota will be too hot for him. He will be remembered forever as the Judas of the farmers' movement.

And if he has children, let him reflect that he will betray them, too— that his treachery will mean their name is forever disgraced.[12]

Despite such admonitions there were two or three defections during the course of the session, without quite the dire consequences predicted. Almost at the outset, Representative Pleasance of Pembina was disciplined for voting contrary to the caucus decision regarding acceptance of the constitutional amendments, and he withdrew from the caucus to forestall ejection.[13] At a later time Senator F. W. Mees of Morton County fought for hours in the caucus a bill setting the legal rate of interest. As the night wore on, with everyone in essential agreement except Mees, who obviously could not be won over, Townley lost his temper and when Mees finally asked, "But what am I going to tell my people if I vote for this bill?" he replied, "Oh hell, Mees, go home and lie like a damned horse thief!" The guffaws following this sally broke up the argument, the caucus voted favorably, and Mees walked out.[14]

The sequel to this event proved even better. Mees, who had been vigorously stumping his district against the League during a subsequent campaign, attended a big rally held in a New Salem lumber yard which was addressed by Townley. At one point Mees heckled the speaker, shouting: "Mr. Townley, didn't you tell me in a legislative caucus to go home and lie like a horse thief?" "Yes, Fred," shot back Townley, "and you've sure been doing it, haven't you?" Then with a wink to the crowd: "Mees always does what I tell him!" [15]

The work of the session progressed rapidly. By mid-January the constitutional amendments had all been ratified, a good portion of the major League bills had been introduced, and a few significant measures had already been passed. Little bitterness was in evidence on the floor of either house. The minority opposed the League measures as a matter of principle, but knowing that they were certain to pass did not except in a few cases press that opposition in any extreme fashion. "On the whole," said the *Grand Forks Herald*, "the procedure is being taken on both sides as a matter of course, and the opposition is more formal than fiery." There was usually considerable good humor on both sides, with the Leaguers "standing pat" and "enjoying the experience of being in the seat instead of under the wheels of a 1919 model steam roller . . ." [16] Moreover, the *Herald*, after watching the session for a time, was willing to concede that the League leaders seemed to realize the magnitude of the undertakings and the committees were proceeding with careful deliberation on the "radical" measures.

The legislature disposed of several I.V.A. bills early in the session, notably two which had been introduced at least in part for purposes of anti-League propaganda. The first, the defeat of which was to become something of a *cause célèbre*, proposed to prohibit the display or carrying in a parade of any flag other than that of the United States or its allies, and especially red or black flags. When challenged in other states about the defeat of the "anti-red-flag law," Townley replied that they were not afraid of the red flag in North Dakota; in that state the lot of the common people was to be made such that there would be no possibility of bolshevism taking root. This, as might be expected, hardly satisfied the anti-League press, and the defeat of this bill was used in every state to prove that the League was really the "American International." [17]

The caucus likewise killed a bill, similar to those being enacted in many states during this period, which would have made it a crime to advocate "criminal syndicalism." This was intended to be a not too subtle slap at the League, and the caucus further considered it unwarranted in the light of existing legislation. Its defeat caused the *Grand Forks Herald* to exclaim that the state legislature had thereby "endorsed sabotage and the list of vile crimes of like character." [18]

The principal League measures before the legislature included proposals for the creation of an Industrial Commission to manage state enterprises, the establishment of a state bank, the creation of a Mill and Elevator Association to develop a state system of flour mills and terminal elevators, the making of the state hail insurance system compulsory, the establishment of a state-backed Home Building Association, the exemption of farm improvements from taxation, the authorization of bond issues for state enterprises, the levying of income and inheritance taxes, the creation of a Board of Administration to exercise supervision over the educational system and public institutions, and the selection of official newspapers in each county to handle legal printing. All these measures were attacked, but with varying degrees of enthusiasm, and on only a few were there really violent controversies.

As a matter of fact the bill for an Industrial Commission developed almost more dissension within the League ranks than on the floor. Arthur LeSueur, then serving as a legal adviser, held out emphatically for a commission composed of directors elected specifically for that purpose, while Townley was convinced that a three-man board of state officials would be most desirable. Each had his backers and each insisted that his method would provide the best popular control. The decision as to which to recommend was finally left to John Hagan, who chose the latter system, whereupon LeSueur promptly resigned.[19]

As finally written the statute provided for an Industrial Commission to consist of the governor, the attorney general, and the secretary of agriculture and labor, whose function was to be nothing less than "to manage, operate, control and govern all utilities, industries, enterprises and business projects, now or hereafter established, owned, undertaken, administered or operated by the State of North Dakota," except educational, penal, and charitable institutions. They were, of course, to constitute the over-all policy and directing body; to handle the actual management they would hire experts who would be responsible to the commission.

In addition to the power to appoint and remove managers and other officials and employees, the commission was empowered to determine locations, acquire and maintain property, fix the prices of things bought and sold (making provision in the process for paying back the original legislative appropriations and amortization of the bond issues), make rules, regulations, orders, and bylaws for the businesses, negotiate bonds as provided by law, and conduct investigations of any matters bearing on the enterprises. Unusual authority was vested in the governor—it was provided that no action of the commission could become effective without the approval of the governor, as chairman.[20]

Considered by many to be the most important single state enterprise, basic to the others, the Bank of North Dakota was created for the primary purposes of providing low-cost rural credits, financing state departments and enterprises, and serving as a clearinghouse and rediscount agency for banks throughout the state. On the theory that public funds should not enter the channels of trade and commerce to be utilized for private profit, but should be used wholly for the benefit of the state and its subdivisions, it was required that all state and local government funds be deposited in the Bank of North Dakota. The Bank might receive the deposits of any government, individual, or corporation, which would be guaranteed by the state and exempt from any state, county, or municipal taxes.

In order to stabilize and equalize credit conditions throughout the state, the Bank was empowered to redeposit funds in any bank on terms and conditions set by the Industrial Commission. It might transfer funds to other departments, institutions, or enterprises of the state, to be returned with interest. It might make loans to political subdivisions or to state or national banks. Loans to individuals, associations, or corporations were possible when secured by first mortgages on real estate or by warehouse receipts. The state examiner was required to examine the Bank at least twice a year and to report to both the Industrial Commission and the legislature. One hundred thousand dollars was appropriated to establish the Bank, to be repaid from earnings, and it was to commence operations as soon as it received the two million dollars from the sale of bonds authorized for capital.[21]

". . . for the purpose of encouraging and promoting agriculture, commerce, and industry, the State of North Dakota shall engage in the business of manufacturing and marketing farm products and for that purpose shall establish a system of warehouses, elevators, flour mills, factories, plants, machinery and equipments, owned, controlled and operated by it under the name of the North Dakota Mill and Elevator Association . . ."[22] This was a comprehensive authorization, leaving the types of industries to be established, the number, size, and location to the discretion of the Industrial Commission. Obviously it was never expected that a single mill and elevator would be able to influence the market sufficiently to correct the evils claimed by the farmers, but that an extensive state system would ultimately be established which could be a determining factor in the total marketing structure.

The Home Building Association was intended to be essentially a state-controlled building and loan association, differing from others primarily in that the state was to undertake to build the houses, thereby presuming to save the profits of both the contractors and the retail building material dealers. The objective was the promotion of economic security by assisting persons in the low- and middle-income groups to become owners of their own homes.

Individuals desiring to benefit from this service were to form a Home Buyers' League of ten or more depositors in the association. When a member had deposited 20 per cent of the cost of a house, the association was to build and convey title to the house to him, amortizing the rest of the cost over a ten- to twenty-year period, to be paid in monthly installments. The revenue of the association, beyond the deposits of members, was to come from the sale of state bonds secured by first mortgages on the property. Each member was to be liable for all contracts, debts, and obligations due the association from his Home Buyers' League to the extent of 15 per cent of the price at which his home was sold to him. To join a Home Buyers' League a person had to secure the written consent of all existing members. No home in an urban community was to be built at a selling price of more than $5000 and no farm home at more than $10,000, including barns and other farm buildings. The association was empowered to acquire land by purchase, lease, or eminent domain, and was authorized to build parks, sidewalks, and other improvements on tracts obtained for housing developments.[23]

The state hail insurance statute was extensively amended to put the system on an acreage tax basis. All growing crops were to be insured unless specifically withdrawn. The act levied a flat tax of three cents per year on every acre of tillable land in the state, excepting that within the corporate limits of cities, towns, or villages, public roads, rights of way of common carriers, and land used for mining or manufacturing. The commissioner of insurance was then to determine annually the amount in addition to the flat tax which would be needed to cover the losses for that year and to maintain the department, this indemnity tax to be levied on all land actively cultivated and cropped, except hay and meadow land, provided that the total amount should never exceed fifty cents per acre. The owner who withdrew his land, which must be done by affidavit before June 15 of each year, thereby escaped the indemnity tax, although not the flat tax.

Local assessors were required to report annually data on tillable and cropped land, supported by affidavits of the owners regarding the cropped land, to the county auditors, who in turn were to report consolidated data to the state office. The maximum indemnity was set at seven dollars per acre, with no indemnity paid for a loss of less than 10 per cent and a loss of 85 per cent or more being deemed total. The risk would be spread over the entire state, since the state would have a virtual monopoly. Inasmuch as the premiums were to be a lien on the land and could be sold in the same manner as delinquent tax warrants, the state would not be subject to the loss of premiums, always a factor in the rates of private companies.[24]

Dr. Ladd, who had been appointed state grain inspector in 1917, estimated that the 1918 crop in North Dakota sold at an average of five cents a bushel higher than it would otherwise have sold because of the authority given the state by the 1917 legislature to check grading. At his suggestion the law was considerably strengthened in 1919, by requiring that buyers must pay the market value for dockage, granting to the state inspector rate-fixing powers, placing the inspection of elevator scales in the hands of the grain inspection department instead of the Railroad Commission, and requiring the filing of the records of elevator purchases and sales in order to make it possible to see that they did not sell more high grades than they purchased. The state inspector was empowered to establish uniform grades and weights, and to issue comprehensive regulations on grading, weighing, handling, storing, inspecting, and so on.

The state inspector was also to license all persons or firms engaged in buying, weighing, inspecting, and grading grain, after they passed a prescribed examination as to competency, whereupon they were to be designated "Deputy Inspectors of Grades, Weights and Measures." The license was to be renewed each year and was subject to revocation for cause. These "deputy inspectors" were to issue to farmers a certificate giving the grade, test weight, and reasons for all grades below No. 1. They were also required to preserve a sample, which was to be forwarded to the state inspector upon request. Any producer was entitled to appeal grades to the state inspector. A person or firm had to be licensed to buy or grade grain, and the condition of the license was compliance with the statute and regulations of the state inspector. Penalties were prescribed for violations.[25]

All improvements on farm lands were exempted from taxation. Exemptions of $1000 were granted on urban homes used as residences by the owners, and there were additional small exemptions for certain classes of personal property such as tools and implements.[26] The legislature also enacted an inheritance tax, and a personal income tax which was scaled from ¼ of 1 per cent on $1000 to a maximum of 10 per cent on all in excess of $40,000 for earned income and from ½ of 1 per cent on $1000 to 10 per cent on all in excess of $30,000 for unearned income. The exemptions were essentially the same as under the United States income tax statute. Corporations were to be taxed 3 per cent of their income plus fifty cents per thousand dollars' value in excess of $10,000. The three-man State Tax Commission was replaced by a single tax commissioner, and counties were given the option of replacing township assessors with a county assessor appointed by the state tax commissioner. Finally, the classification system for property taxation was changed, appreciably raising the assessed valuation of the state.[27]

The most acrimonious battles in both chambers came not over these far-reaching measures but on two proposals sponsored by the League which were not truly "program bills." Governor Frazier had recommended to the legislature that it simplify the control of the educational system by creating a new board for over-all supervision and abolishing the State Board of Education and the Board of Regents. At once the opposition charged that this was a sinister plot to take away the powers of the state superintendent of public instruction, the only I.V.A. state official, and certain proposed provisions lent credibility to the argument. It was also insisted that the League sought to secure control of the school and university lands in order to "squander" the income.

League speakers publicly defended the proposals, maintaining stoutly that neither of the charges was true, and that the state superintendent would probably in fact have more powers than before. This, they said, was simply an efficiency and economy move—a matter of sensible administrative organization. Under the law finally enacted, the public school system, all state educational institutions and all state charitable and penal institutions were placed under a Board of Administration, to be composed of three appointive members and two ex-officio members, the state superintendent of public instruction and the commissioner of agriculture and labor. It superseded the State Board of Education, the Board of Regents, and the Board of Control of Charitable and Penal Institutions.[28]

Even the previously solid League caucus was rent asunder by the two bills for the designation of official newspapers in each county, fostered by J. W. Brinton, then acting as head of the Publishers' National Service Bureau. Senate Bill 158 provided that beginning with the next general election a single official paper in each county would be selected by the voters, and that it would thenceforth publish all state, county, and municipal legal notices. At the time three official papers to handle legal printing were being selected by each county board of commissioners. Senate Bill 157 proposed to establish a State Printing Commission to coordinate and supervise all state printing, and it would have authority to designate official papers for each county until the next general election. It was this last clause of Senate Bill 157 which brought about the oratorical fireworks.

The League vigorously insisted that the important thing was the election of papers by the people; appointment by the State Printing Commission was merely a stopgap measure. This would mean the development of a truly free press, according to the League spokesman, since the papers desiring this lucrative legal printing would have to devote themselves to serving the best interests of the people rather than advertisers. Not only would they be more responsive to the popular will, but they would no longer need to curry favor with the county commissioners, and this important source of patronage would be removed. Taxpayers should be saved an appreciable sum of money each year since fees for legal printing would be paid by all units of government to only one paper instead of from three to five. A citizen need subscribe to only one paper to be certain of getting all necessary information and fully protecting himself. Farmer-owned papers, they said, were frequently discriminated against by county commissioners, whereas all should have equal opportunity. Finally, if there were actually some rural weeklies which were able to exist only because of support from legal printing, their continuance was not justified.

The I.V.A., on the other hand, contended with at least equal vehemence that the real purpose of the measures was to subsidize the League press by creating a monopoly on legal printing; that favorable papers would be rewarded and unfavorable punished, thus directly threatening the freedom of the press and the free expression of opinion. This would destroy, they said, dozens of small weeklies which relied on this source of revenue to keep operating at a slight profit instead of at a loss. While governmental costs might be reduced somewhat, the people would not actually be saved money because they would be forced to buy papers to which they might otherwise not subscribe, perhaps published at some distance from their own communities. Lastly, vesting such power in a state commission would remove from the county commissioners a part of their constitutional power to manage county affairs, and at any rate local officials were in a much better position to select the papers than would be a state body unfamiliar with local situations.[29] In the end, however, both bills passed, though with a few defections from the League ranks.

On virtually all the major bills of the session the League was able to secure in each house the two-thirds vote needed to declare them emergency measures and thus have them become operative shortly after the close of the session instead of the following July 1. Moreover, 30,000 signatures were required for a petition for referendum on emergency measures rather than the normal 7000.

The emergency clause was defeated in connection with the newspaper bills, whereupon all possible pressure was brought to bear to influence votes in the legislature. The delegation from Stark County was reportedly threatened with a cut in the appropriation for the Dickinson Normal School, causing Representative Roquette to announce the next day when voting on a reconsideration: "I vote 'aye' not because this measure has more merit than it had yesterday, but because I deem it good policy." When two reconsiderations failed to produce the necessary two-thirds vote, the matter was finally dropped.[30]

In order to ensure the two-thirds vote in the Senate on some of the principal measures, since some League legislators considered the requirement of 30,000 signatures for a referendum too high, Governor Frazier went before that body and pledged himself to call a referendum if petitions signed by 15,000 voters were filed. He felt that the cost of an election was too high to take the action for 7000, but he desired to be fair to everyone and assumed that if objections to some measures were widespread 15,000 signatures could be secured without difficulty.[31]

In addition to the major acts of the sixteenth legislative assembly, there were a number of other progressive measures of considerable significance.[32] The office of commissioner of immigration was created and given a $200,000 appropriation for the purpose of publicizing the state and its advantages in order to secure desirable settlers. It was heatedly charged by the opposition that the real purpose was to disseminate League propaganda throughout other states by means of public funds, and doubtless the motives of the bill's supporters were mixed. In many cases it would be difficult to decide which was being done; the two could hardly be kept separate, and certainly the commissioner did not attempt to do so, although he did concern himself honestly with promotion of the state.

The Minnesota system of distance tariffs for railroads, already upheld by the United States Supreme Court, was put into effect, designed to end the long-standing discriminations in freight rates against North Dakota. A constitutional amendment providing a system of recall of public officers was proposed to the voters, a state fire and tornado insurance system for public property was established, a one-half-mill tax was levied on all property in the state to provide a soldiers' bonus fund, a state experimental creamery was authorized, and a fairly extensive amount of labor legislation was enacted, including a workmen's compensation law (exempting agricultural labor and domestics), an eight-hour day and minimum wage law for women, a limitation on the use of injunctions in labor disputes, and the establishment of safety regulations for coal mines and provision for state mine inspection. The labor measures were enacted in all sincerity, but it is quite true that there was present something of a double motive, since they provided excellent propaganda for securing labor cooperation in other states.

The 1919 session closed with less good humor than it started. During the last days fifteen members of the House minority signed a widely circulated letter issued by Theodore G. Nelson, secretary of the I.V.A., which called upon the people of the state to unite to defeat these "monstrous" League measures in a referendum. The letter claimed among other things that the state was to be plunged into tremendous debt, that its credit would be ruined, that the immigration bill was designed to furnish funds to import I.W.W.'s, and that the purpose of the Board of Administration act was to pollute the public schools with socialism. In the closing hours the state affairs committee of the House brought in a concurrent resolution censuring the minority members for their action, claiming that they had signed statements they knew to be false and were consequently unfit to hold public office. The resolution passed the House 86 to 21, but after limited debate in the Senate, whose members had not been involved, the resolution was tabled, a number of Leaguers speaking against it.[33]

The session adjourned six days ahead of schedule, whereas turning the clock back had perviously been considered standard practice, and it cost the taxpayers less than any preceding session. Despite the bitterness at the end—as the *Herald* put it, "no good natured throwing of ink wells and paper"—it had probably also accomplished more than had any preceding session. Even the *Herald* had apparently become interested:

The session was the most important in the history of the state, and it accomplished the most far reaching legislation yet enacted. The state is now the socialistic laboratory of the country, and unless the people veto the administration measures the experiment soon will begin . . . The most interesting experiment in the history of the country will be carried out in this state during the next two years.[34]

After looking at the situation a bit longer it was willing to concede further: "There is nothing Bolshevist, so far . . . It is straightaway Socialism of the old fashioned kind, whatever the leaders of the Nonpartisan League may have in the back of their minds." [35]

Leaguers hailed the results of the session with tremendous enthusiasm. Every plank of the League platform had been carried out and more; all would be well in North Dakota. Hastily the League published the major laws of the session in a pamphlet entitled *The New Day in North Dakota*, and commenced its distribution throughout the other League states, meanwhile plunging with zealous fervor into the task of putting the program into operation.

The joy of the *Bismarck Tribune* was, however, somewhat more restrained: "With each day bringing forth more radical and more vicious class legislation, everyone in North Dakota who loves fair play and ordinary honesty must rejoice upon learning that the 16th general assembly finally adjourned at one o'clock Sunday morning." [36]

Schisms and Prosecutions

IN NO state other than North Dakota did the League have sufficient representation to be a really significant factor in a state legislature, yet fear of the League as a future political force was everywhere evident. As a rule, League proposals were unceremoniously beaten down, although in Montana an opposition-sponsored bill for a state-owned terminal elevator at Great Falls was passed. The "anti-red-flag" and "criminal syndicalism" bills so widely adopted at this time were proposed in a number of states with one eye on the League, but most significant were the attempts to abolish the direct primary and return to the convention system, in the expectation that the League might then be unable to take over existing parties. In Montana, Idaho, Nebraska, and Kansas the primaries were actually abolished, if only temporarily in some cases, but similar bills were narrowly defeated in Minnesota and Colorado. In South Dakota the primary system was amended to make "infiltration" virtually impossible.

Other unsuccessful proposals in Minnesota indicative of the apprehension of the anti-League elements included bills establishing a motor corps Home Guard designed largely to control mass meetings and demonstrations, forbidding display at meetings, parades, or otherwise of signs or banners inscribed with criticisms of the state government, and prohibiting labor unions or farmers' organizations from spending more than $10,000 in a political campaign.[1]

In North Dakota the I.V.A. was energetically circulating petitions, but they had shrewdly determined to utilize the initiative as well as the referendum. Not only were they requesting a referendum on several of the League measures, but they sought to initiate laws on a state mill and elevator, home building, and rural credits, which if adopted would supersede the acts of the legislature. The acts to be referred included those creating the Industrial Commission, establishing the Bank of North Dakota, providing for official newspaper selection by a State Printing Commission, creating the Board of Administration, providing for a commissioner of immigration, replacing the Tax Commission with a single commissioner, and redistricting the state for judicial organization.

The I.V.A. was outmaneuvered, however, by the League board of strategy when Governor Frazier, without waiting for the filing of petitions, called a referendum for June 26 on the seven League statutes listed on the I.V.A. petitions. Since it was required that initiative petitions be filed ninety days before an election, this made impossible a vote on both types of measures at the same time. Contending that the I.V.A. action was intended simply to confuse the issues and that the voters could not be expected to vote accurately for and against a variety of similar sounding measures on the ballot by title only, Frazier was frank in stating his reasons for calling the election when he did rather than on the July 8 date that the I.V.A. had been preparing to demand. He said:

I have decided on a date for the referendum . . . early enough to invalidate the initiative petitions and to prevent a hopeless confusion on the part of the voters. The referendum petitions place before the people for a vote seven measures adopted by the legislature and the issues should, and must, remain clear, so that a verdict of the people can be obtained.[2]

In order to overlook no possibilities, in April suit was filed in the United States District Court in Fargo in the name of one taxpayer from each of forty-two counties in the state to have the League acts declared unconstitutional. It was alleged that they involved taxation for other than a public purpose and that they thus constituted a deprivation of property without due process of law. Although the action was presumably started by the taxpayers' group, the array of legal talent appearing for the plaintiffs made this seem highly improbable. Years later a prominent Minneapolis attorney frankly admitted that the "42 taxpayers' suit" was prepared in his Minneapolis law office and was backed by large banking and business interests.[3]

Scarcely had the 1919 legislature succeeded in enacting the League program into law when there occurred a disastrous split in the ranks of the League-elected state officials. The three "non-farmers," who had been candidates for their offices before acceptance by the League convention in 1916—Attorney General William Langer, Secretary of State Tom Hall, and State Auditor Carl Kositzky—turned from League supporters into rabid opponents, precipitating a series of violent political struggles which were to leave the state in turmoil for years to come.

This was the break for which the opposition had been working and waiting, and the I.V.A. leaped to their support. Hall had never been a really ardent League backer, but he had sought the League's support in 1916 when it became clear which way the wind was blowing. The others had actively campaigned for the organization, had supported virtually its every action, and had frequently been lauded in the League press for the work of their departments. But Langer and Kositzky were ambitious men, never content for long to play second fiddle, and friction between them and the League leadership had been growing for some time. They professed to continue to support the League program, but to be disgusted with the current leaders and many of their actions.

William Langer had first taken issue with the League hierarchy at the time of the controversy over the office of state superintendent of public instruction, and they crossed swords again in February. Langer heard that J. J. Hastings and T. Allen Box were purchasing for a group of farmers the American National Bank of Valley City, and he decided, as a member of the State Banking Board, to investigate the transaction before approving the transfer. The investigation disclosed that Hastings and Box, operating as the "Federal Development Company," had secured $200,000 from farmer stockholders for the purchase of the bank and had charged a commission of 10 per cent, or $20,000, for their organizational work. This they had a legal right to do, but it also appeared that they had actually purchased the bank for $15,000 less than had been represented to the stockholders. Langer and Hall, as the majority of the Banking Board, of which the governor was the other member, forced the repayment of this amount and the securing of notes of Hastings and Box before approving the change of ownership, while the League leaders and their newspapers made the mistake of trying to defend the actions of the "Federal Development Company." [4]

241

During the legislative session Townley became incensed at certain alleged lobbying activities of Kositzky and the two clashed repeatedly, whereupon Kositzky commenced devoting his time to digging up and publishing information on what he considered to be "padded" expense accounts of League leaders and state officials. When Townley told him to quit worrying about trifles and to go after the big things, he joined with Langer in expressing opposition to the Board of Administration and official newspaper bills.[5] While the plaudits of the anti-League press were still ringing in Kositzky's ears, the *Leader* thoughtfully published excerpts from one of his speeches made at Dawson, North Dakota, during the 1918 primary campaign: "As long as the *Grand Forks Herald*, the *Fargo Forum*, the *Bismarck Tribune*, and the *St. Paul Dispatch* roast me it is prima facie evidence that I am remaining true to the farmers. But if those papers ever start to praise me it is a sign that I need watching."[6]

When Langer issued a statement denouncing certain League measures before the legislature, Townley countered with a public announcement that Langer had turned "traitor" and had for some time been working against the farmers' cause. The press on both sides immediately took up the battle, and Langer shortly issued a vitriolic challenge in the form of a public letter to Townley:

You and your hirelings have lied to and are deceiving the farmers of North Dakota. You who had the greatest opportunity ever given to any man in North Dakota, were not big enough for the job. You hold your personal interests above the interests of the farmers who trusted you. Greedy for power, hungry for money, self-indulgent in your whims and with a mighty hate for all honest men who dare to counsel moderation, you betray the farmers of North Dakota.

You, who hold nothing sacred; if the educational system lies in your path you ruin it; if the independent press dares tell the truth, you wreck it. If an honest man exercises his American privilege of opposing certain bills, he is a crook, a coward, a dub and a fool.

You imported into North Dakota radicals by the score. . . . These men . . . have no interests in North Dakota. To them North Dakota is nothing but an interesting experiment . . .

You and your hirelings have said that I am a crook, a traitor, and that I have sold out and betrayed the farmers of North Dakota. . . .

Prove it and I will resign the office to which I was elected. . . . Prove that I have done one crooked act as Attorney General of the State of North Dakota. Prove that out of nearly a thousand opinions given by me as Attorney General, I have given one that wrongfully favored "big business." Prove that I have betrayed the farmers of North Dakota and the resignation will follow. And if you with your horde of detectives, organizers, spies and associates can't prove it, then stand convicted before the farmers of the State of North Dakota, the men who trusted you. Stand convicted as a self-confessed liar and an assassinator of character, a man more despicable than the ghoul that sneaks out under cover of darkness into "No Man's Land" and robs the dead.[7]

The challenge was not accepted nor did Townley, apparently, stand convicted before the farmers. The League press in North Dakota continued to flay the rebels with every printable bad name at its command, while the national *Leader* summarily dismissed them as "deserters and political hacks, paid by Minnesota business . . . who proved untrue to the men who elected them."[8] Langer and Kositzky in particular were in positions where they could do tremendous damage to the League, and they henceforth devoted both their personal abilities and energy and their offices to discrediting the organization and especially its leadership. Lionized by the opposition, they shortly became influential figures in the I.V.A.

On June 14 Judge Amidon in the federal District Court at Fargo dismissed the "42 taxpayers' suit" for want of jurisdiction. In the first place, he held, none of the plaintiffs had shown injury to the extent of $3000, and secondly no controversy arose under the Fourteenth Amendment to the United States Constitution because the taxation involved was clearly for a public purpose. The discussion of the second point was detailed and included a review of the history of the demands for the League legislation in North Dakota. Judge Amidon's comments in that connection on the proper spheres for the exercise of state power savor more nearly of a post-1937 than a 1919 court:

What may be done by the state to protect its people and promote their welfare, can not be declared by a prior reasoning . . . The state must be as free to change its remedies as the evils that cause human suffering are to change their forms . . .

It is hopeless to expect a population consisting of farmers scattered over a vast territory, as the people of this state are, to create any private business system that will change the system now existing. The only means through which the people of the state have had any experience in joint action is their state government. If they may not use that as the common agency through which to combine their capital and carry on

243

such basic industries as elevators, mills and packing houses and so fit their products for market and market the same they must continue to deal as individuals with the vast combinations of those terminal cities and suffer the injustices that always exist where economic units so different in power have to deal the one with the other.[9]

Meanwhile an intensive campaign on the referendum was being waged by both the League and the I.V.A. League mass meetings were again much in evidence, with A. C. Townley engaged in one of the most concentrated periods of speaking in his career. Thousands of Fords throughout the state bore stickers reading "Vote Yes 7 Times." The State Federation of Labor circulated to its members a pamphlet pointing out what the farmer legislature had done for labor. The League press talked of little else but the need for an overwhelming victory.[10]

In general the I.V.A. campaign was along the standard lines of "saving the state from socialism," but zealots in some areas went to extremes. In a number of localities, particularly where many farmers spoke or read little English, rumors were circulated too late for the League to counteract to the effect that farms were to be seized by the state if the measures were approved. Fraudulent notices made up to look like court documents were used to convince the doubtful. In heavily Catholic communities many persons were told that approval meant that parochial schools would be taken over and no more religious teaching allowed. In Stutsman County several hundred copies of a so-called "free love bill," introduced as a joke at the last session of the legislature by an I.V.A. member, were printed and circulated with the implication that it was a League measure. It was reported that a group of frantic mothers started for Bismarck to ask Governor Frazier if there were really a law compelling women to submit to the attentions of any returned soldier who approached them. They were headed off and assured that the law had not been enacted, but the story was widespread.[11]

The I.V.A. optimistically predicted in full-page advertisements that a big surprise was in store for Townley, while the *Grand Forks Herald* editorialized: "Those who are familiar with the high standard of intelligence among the state's voters are calmly anticipating the result that the answer will be No, and that it will be given with such enthusiastic emphasis that no one can misunderstand the real meaning of it."[12]

On election day the *Herald*'s editorial lead proclaimed: "Today North Dakota will stand up and declare in a ringing voice that Socialism shall not triumph," [13] but it was doomed to disappointment. If the *Herald* had properly assessed the intelligence of the voters, it was clearly out of step with the times, for all seven measures carried decisively, with majorities ranging from 13,256 on the Bank of North Dakota to 6914 on the official newspaper and Printing Commission act.[14]

The voice of the people having been heard, the administration was now free to put the measures into effect. The *Bismarck Tribune* was despondent: "There is nothing to do now, but to hope that the venture into state socialism will be as painless as possible and that the tax bills will prove the best antidote by the time the next election rolls around." [15]

Inasmuch as the law provided that the Bank of North Dakota must be open and doing business within ninety days after the adjournment of the legislature, organizational activities had proceeded without waiting for the referendum. The Industrial Commission had organized immediately after the adjournment of the session, and it shortly appointed, over the protest and negative vote of Attorney General Langer, James R. Waters as manager of the Bank. Waters had served three years as state bank examiner, and claimed twenty years' previous banking experience, though the claims were perhaps more than a trifle tenuous. In addition to his official capacity as bank examiner he had been involved in several of the League's subsidiary enterprises.

Waters soon appointed as director-general of the Bank F. W. Cathro, cashier of the First National Bank of Bottineau for twenty-six years and at the time its president. Well known in banking circles, Cathro had served as the first president of the North Dakota Bankers Association. The Industrial Commission leased for the Bank a new brick building in Bismarck, equipment was purchased, personnel hired, and by mid-June it was announced that the Bank would be ready to commence operations as soon as the capital stock bonds had been issued and deposited.[16]

Whether or not any private bank cooperated with the Bank of North Dakota was theoretically a voluntary matter, though refusal to join the "system" meant that it would not be used as a depository bank, and most small banks counted heavily on deposits of public funds. Moreover, any depository bank that did not carry part of its reserve funds with the Bank of North Dakota was not permitted to rediscount. The

Bank "strongly recommended," though it did not require, that persons seeking real estate loans appoint a local bank as agent in securing the loan and thus maintain friendly relations with the banker, who might sometime be useful.[17]

While all public funds were required to be deposited in the Bank of North Dakota, it decided at the outset not to accept private deposits from within the state, in order not to injure local banks. On the public funds the Bank paid 2 per cent interest, while banks in which they were redeposited paid 4 per cent. The explanation of this differential was that local banks were thus assured a steadier level of public deposits than formerly, and that they received other services from the Bank which justified the higher rate. The basic functions of the Bank of North Dakota were summarized by Alvin S. Tostlebe as follows:

. . . the Bank's relation to the existing credit structure was to be similar to that of a federal reserve bank to the member banks in its district. It was to do a very limited business aside from that conducted with banks; the reserves of the state were to be concentrated in it; it was to be the center of a par clearing and collecting system; it was to furnish its credit to the public primarily through the medium of the local banks which would rediscount with the Central Bank; it was to be intimately connected with the fiscal operations of the state, for it would have charge of the sale of state securities and would be the sole legal depository of all public funds. In one respect it was to go further, "It was to meet the needs for and perform the functions of a joint stock land bank." [18]

The providing of relatively inexpensive rural credits was, of course, presumably the fundamental reason for the establishment of a state bank, and the Bank launched into that activity immediately after it opened for business on July 28. At first only farm land was eligible, and city real estate and ranch land were not considered. Loans were made for thirty years, with the borrower paying 7 per cent of the original loan annually, which amount included the 6 per cent interest and the amortization of the loan. The average interest rate for farm loans in the state at the time was estimated by the United States Department of Agriculture to be 8.7 per cent. Improved lands were favored, especially if the owner lived on the land and engaged in reasonably diversified farming. The Bank demanded the best security the borrower had to offer, and the amount of the loan could in no case exceed 50 per cent of the value of the property mortgaged.[19]

Inevitably there were claims by the anti-League forces that the Bank favored League banks and often endeavored to break unfriendly banks by its handling of redeposits of public funds. Moreover, they insisted, it was standard practice for lands belonging to League members to be appraised liberally, while most nonmembers had their applications rejected, and also excess loans were made to some Leaguers on lands held for speculative purposes.[20] There is limited evidence that things of this sort did occur upon occasion, but discrimination and favoritism did not appear to be a calculated policy and were not widespread. Anyone whose application was refused was quite likely to assume that he was somehow the victim of shady tactics. By the end of 1919 farm loans by the bank stood at more than $1,000,000, with applications for twice that amount pending, and the farmers who received these loans were saving on the average almost 3 per cent interest.[21]

The League was well aware that the planning and construction of a large-scale mill and elevator establishment would take at best a considerable period of time, yet it was eager to prove its case with respect to the milling industry and felt that it could not brook longer delay. Consequently the Industrial Commission authorized the manager of the Mill and Elevator Association to purchase or lease one or two small mills to be run on a sort of experimental basis to demonstrate what could be done. In early August a small mill was purchased at Drake, the citizens of that community having subscribed the necessary bonds. It was too small to be a good investment, having a daily capacity of only one hundred twenty-five barrels, and its equipment was seriously out of date.[22] Opened with much fanfare at the end of the month, it resolutely but somewhat unwisely commenced buying wheat at an average of twelve cents a bushel more than competitors, if grades and freight rates are taken into account, and selling flour at an average of fifty cents a barrel lower and feed at $7.50 less per ton than others.[23] It did not actually keep this up, although it claimed to be doing so.

Meanwhile plans for the major state mill and elevator were being drawn, and the manager of the association was directed to investigate and report on sites. At once he was flooded with letters, petitions, and offers of aid from practically every city in the state with even the vaguest hope of being chosen. Suddenly the cities, and especially their businessmen, became less antagonistic toward this "socialistic" project and began to think in terms of the business it would bring to their communities. Unused to being courted by such groups, and anticipating the possibility of further mellowing with the passage of time, the Industrial Commission decided not to rush a decision.

Dr. Ladd, as state grain inspector, went methodically about the work of putting into operation the authorizations of the 1919 legislature, having particular success in compelling payment for dockage. He appointed D. J. McGrath, a scales expert from Minneapolis, as inspector of scales and weights, and in the first few days of operation the latter condemned a wagon load of false or inaccurate scales and parts. In one instance he was able to make up a bill of nearly $3400 against one elevator for wheat fraudulently secured, and his first report on October 25 was an amazing record of commercial malpractices.[24]

As in the case of the mill, those in charge of the Home Building Association were eager to create a favorable impression and have useful propaganda for other states, and they plunged into a building program with astonishing disregard for the express provisions of the statute. In the space of a few months fifty-seven houses were started, fifty-one of them simply on the basis of oral contracts and with only a very few having made a 20 per cent down payment or ever having joined a Home Buyers' League. Vast amounts of materials were purchased and stocked at various places around the state, little attention apparently having been paid to either price or utility.[25]

The hail insurance system was not held up by the referendum and, with its background of experience, seemed to be functioning with reasonable smoothness. It was not without its opponents, however, notably the insurance companies whose business was to suffer. There were some newspapers that specifically urged farmers to withdraw from state coverage, and the League claimed that certain local assessors and county auditors were falsifying the anticipated cost of state insurance and telling farmers that only total losses would be reimbursable. Representatives of several insurance companies were reported to be distributing forged official withdrawal blanks. In mid-June the *Leader* secured an affidavit of a man who had been recently offered a position with the Insurance Economics Society of America, organized to combat legislation contrary to the interests of insurance companies. He had been told, he said, that seven large companies, greatly disturbed about North Dakota's hail insurance and workmen's compensation systems, had established a fund of $1,000,000 to beat the National Nonpartisan League.[26]

The statute creating the State Fire and Tornado Fund required that all public property within the corporate limits of cities and villages be insured by the state against destruction by fire or tornado. Public property of other units might be insured at the discretion of the appropriate governing bodies. The Insurance Department charged the same rates as private companies until the size of the fund warranted reduction, when considerable savings were effected, and it insured property up to 80 per cent of its value. The state did not force cancellation of existing contracts, but assumed the risk when they expired. The department claimed an overhead expense of only $3.07 out of every $100 in premiums, as compared with $35 for private companies.[27]

One other state insurance system was in operation for which the League frequently took credit, especially in publicity designed for other states, although it had actually been started before the League administration. Rather minor amendments in 1919 constituted the League's only claim, but since it was a successful public enterprise the League naturally was anxious to provide publicity on it. All public officials whose duties required bonding were bonded by the state at remarkable savings over private rates. A sizable group was involved, including many state, county, city, village, and township officers, and the treasurers of more than 2000 school districts. Out of every $100 received in premiums, the net loss because of defalcations was only $4.15, while the overhead amounted to $5.74. Thus in a relatively short space of time a large fund was built up, making possible appreciable rate reductions from the standard rate level at which operations had been commenced.[28] In 1948 the status of the fund was such that no premiums at all were being required until the balance was lowered enough to make them again necessary.[29]

The Workmen's Compensation Bureau had been promptly organized, but its operations were impeded for several months by a variety of litigation and by the tactics of State Auditor Kositzky, who held up numerous warrants for "investigation" for such lengths of time as to virtually paralyze action and who brought suit to compel the bureau to submit to his audit before it had been in operation two months. Ultimately the obstacles were cleared away, the state Supreme Court upheld the constitutionality of the law,[30] and the bureau went on to provide a valuable service.

In choosing the top personnel for the management of the various state enterprises, the League had insisted that merit was to be the sole basis. The Industrial Commission was to seek the best; it was to "prove the falsity of the argument that you can't get a man who can make money for himself to work on a salary for the state."[31] Frazier and Hagan, who were the controlling members of the commission, were sincere and honest men but both lacked business experience. With Townley in St. Paul and concerned largely with other matters, they came to rely to a great degree on the the the advice of William Lemke, nicknamed the "Bishop" of the Nonpartisan League by Justice Robinson in one of his "Saturday Night Letters." Lemke became more and more the directing genius of the North Dakota League. He, too, was personally honest, but unfortunately he was often a poor judge of men and was too willing to continue to back those he considered his friends even after it should have been clear that they were no longer deserving. Some of the selections of the Industrial Commission were good; others definitely were not.

Picked to head the Mill and Elevator Association was J. J. McGovern, who for two years had served as chief deputy grain inspector for the state. Before that he had been an inspector at the Equity terminal elevator in St. Paul, to which he had come from a background as a country grain buyer in South Dakota.[32] The qualifications of Manager Waters and Director-General Cathro of the Bank of North Dakota have previously been mentioned. Robert Blakemore of Fargo was appointed manager of the Home Building Association. A member of the state legislature in 1913, he had been in the real estate and loan business in Fargo since 1888, and was presumed to have a wide knowledge of home construction and valuation of real estate. For six years before his appointment he had served as commissioner of water works for the city of Fargo.[33] John H. Worst, former president of the North Dakota Agricultural College, was named commissioner of immigration.

The Workmen's Compensation Bureau came under the general jurisdiction of the commissioner of agriculture and labor rather than the Industrial Commission, while the state insurance systems were under the commissioner of insurance. Appointed by Governor Frazier as chairman of the Workmen's Compensation Board was S. S. McDonald, the president of the State Federation of Labor. To handle the legal aspects of administering accident insurance an attorney named L. J. Wehe was selected, while for the important task of setting rates the services of Emile E. Watson of Ohio were secured. Watson was one of the first men in the United States to specialize in the technical phases of workmen's compensation, and had done similar work for the states of Ohio, Maryland, and Idaho. During the war he had served as an actuary for the national government in establishing its wartime insurance program.[34]

In August the Industrial Commission appointed as its secretary and attorney for the Bank of North Dakota William A. Anderson, a Minneapolis lawyer with considerable experience in the grain trade. Anderson was expected to be something of an adviser as well as secretary, and only a few weeks after his arrival in North Dakota Commissioner Hagan requested his opinion of the managers of the various enterprises. After a brief investigation he rendered a confidential report stating that Cathro was very capable and that the insurance programs appeared to be well handled, but strongly recommending that the commission get rid of Blakemore at once. The man, he said, was a gross incompetent, and the subordinates whom he had appointed were equally poor. Lemke, however, insisted that Blakemore be given a "fair trial," citing his excellent record with the Fargo water works, and the commission took no action.

Anderson also stated that in his opinion both Waters and his assistant, Roy Halliday, were unsatisfactory, and recommended that either McGovern be dismissed as manager of the Mill and Elevator Association or at least that an immediate audit be made of his activities. He prepared to send auditors to Drake, but at the last minute Lemke talked the commission out of the idea on the grounds that it would merely be an unnecessary expense. Later events showed that Anderson's suspicions that the reports from Drake were falsified were all too correct. McGovern had purchased far too much grain without hedging, and when the market took a severe drop the Drake mill found itself in a precarious position. Nevertheless, McGovern kept on buying when he should have been selling, and by the time League auditors discovered the true state of affairs at Drake the damage had been done.[35]

The State Printing Commission, consisting of Hagan, Hall, and Railroad Commissioner Sam Aandahl, met on August 9 to choose the newspapers to receive the "official" designation until the general election of 1920. They selected, in most cases by a two to one vote, all League papers except where there were none in a county, though in three counties, including Grand Forks, they made no selection for the time being because the League papers in those counties could not yet meet the statutory requirement of having been published for a year in their present locations.[36]

The convention of the North Dakota Press Association in Mandan that summer devoted itself almost entirely to bitter attacks on the newspaper laws, the League, and the "subsidized press." The chairman at first refused to permit League editors to be seated, and by the time the ruling was changed they had all departed and were happily writing editorials on their exclusion from the meeting of the "gang press." The League newspapermen proceeded to strengthen the "People's Press Association," which had been started the preceding winter, and the North Dakota Press Association agreed to unite for a finish fight. It established a Bismarck bureau to coordinate the battle and to act as a clearinghouse for members, while for the next three years the *N.D.P.A. Bulletin* carried a boldface subtitle, "Official Organ of the Unkept Press." [37]

Not only did the official legal printing go to the official papers, but in practice most of the private legal advertising did likewise. Many persons feared that items would have no legal effect if published elsewhere, a misconception which the official papers were happy to foster. Documents that went through the hands of any state agency were automatically routed to the official papers. In 1919 a total of sixty-one weekly papers went out of business, nearly twice as many as the year before when the greatest previous number was recorded. Many others which did not fail, including some large papers, suffered severely.[38]

To the Board of Administration, set up to exercise general control over the educational system and state institutions, Governor Frazier appointed as public members George A. Totten of Bowman, a former minister and long-time radical whom the opposition quoted as having said that he "had grown beyond Socialism and believed in the teachings of Emma Goldman," [39] P. M. Casey, the 1916 League candidate for state treasurer, and Robert Muir, a brother-in-law of William Lemke's. Totten was named chairman and was always the dominating force on the board, frequently running its affairs in an extremely arbitrary fashion.

Despite the fact that League speakers and the League press had categorically maintained during the debates in the legislature and the referendum campaign that the act would in no way result in taking powers away from the state superintendent of public instruction, one of the first acts of the board was to create the post of "educational adviser to the board and general school inspector," and to name to that position at the same salary as the state superintendent none other than Neil C. MacDonald. His wife was also put back on the payroll. The board then created an "Educational Commission" of five members to undertake a revision of the public school curriculum, presumably a function of the state superintendent. Miss Nielson was made chairman, but the other four members were reportedly chosen by MacDonald.

Finally, the board created the position of secretary to the Educational Commission and supervisor of teacher certification, to which was appointed one E. P. Crain. Crain was at the time secretary of the state Motor Vehicle Registration Department, a post which he did not relinquish, and his new duties were in fact exercised by Kathleen MacDonald. Subsequently Mr. Crain, who should by this time have been an extremely busy individual, was also made state high school examiner, replacing the president of the University of North Dakota, and was given the task of preparing the state eighth-grade and high school examinations. With Miss Nielson vainly protesting that most of these things were her "constitutional duties," the board had nine cartloads of records and other materials relating to certification removed from her office.[40]

To add insult to injury, the board in its first annual report recommended that the office of state superintendent be either abolished or made appointive by the board.[41] Though Miss Nielson was a member of the Board of Administration, the other members frequently held meetings without notifying her and studiously ignored her requests for copies of the minutes of meetings. Although she was a strongly opinionated and vocal young woman who unquestionably was most annoying to Mr. Totten, that was hardly grounds for such treatment, and she naturally made the most of her "martyrdom." Miss Nielson's comments on the situation in her warning to the women of Minnesota to avoid the fate of North Dakota were melodramatic: "The fight is not a political fight; it is a fight between civilization and Christianity on the one hand, and Socialism and atheism, masquerading under the guise of a 'farmers' program,' on the other." [42]

After the board had taken from the state superintendent the power to prescribe and control courses of study, Attorney General Langer brought suit in her behalf, alleging that this constituted a removal from a constitutional officer of a power inherent in the office. The court, over the dissent of the chief justice, held, however, that the power actually inhered in the legislature, which could confer the power as it wished.[43] In effect it ruled that the act did precisely what the League had contended at the time of its passage it would not do.

In the early summer a Dr. Charles E. Stangeland of New York was hired by the Board of Administration to make a survey of the facilities and collections of the Public Library Commission, which was primarily concerned with traveling libraries. Stangeland was said to be a "liberal intellectual" who had spent a number of years in Germany attending the University of Berlin and editing a periodical, and had traveled widely in other parts of Europe. He had been a member of the United States consular service in South America and in England, resigning about a year after the war started.[44]

Dr. Stangeland's recommendations as to periodicals which the library should have available seem scarcely hair-raising in their subversive character, yet the anti-League press screamed at once that it was the beginning of an attempt to indoctrinate the state with socialism. The list included the *Political Science Quarterly*, the *Quarterly Journal of Economics*, the *Journal of Sociology*, the *Preussische Jahrbucher*, the *Fabian Socialist Publications*, the *Nation*, the *New Republic*, *LaFollette's*, *Capper's*, the *Atlantic Monthly*, the *Literary Digest*, the *Public*, the *Survey*, the *Science Monthly*, and a dozen or so other flaming radical publications of which the *Wall Street Journal*, the *Manchester Guardian*, and the *National Geographic* were outstanding examples. Charles Selden, writing in the *New York Times*, commented superciliously that while this list might not have occasioned a second glance in the more sophisticated New York, it was "strong radical meat for North Dakota." [45]

That Stangeland was brought to North Dakota for the primary purpose of "liberalizing" the state library is hardly open to question, but in the mind of George Totten this was merely a matter of bringing it up to date. The manner in which Stangeland got the job is an interesting illustration of the undercurrent of Socialist activity on the part of many League officials which ran parallel to their work for the League. Though the League was an end in itself for Townley, who had no particular use for the Socialist party, to Henry Teigan and several others socialism was the ultimate objective and the League simply a means to that end.

On February 6, 1919, Teigan wrote to M. A. Stanley, whom he had earlier helped to secure a position as assistant secretary of the Senate by recommending him to Axel Strom, then state manager for the League, as a "good Red," that a Mrs. Signe Lund, a "famous Norwegian musician," was to arrive soon in Bismarck and should be given every assistance. He was secretive about her mission, saying only that she was "not on a musical errand." [46] Some time later Stanley notified Teigan that she had left, saying that he understood that "the man in whose interest she was working secured a position with the League," [47] and Teigan replied, "Yes, Mrs. Lund was very successful in her errand on behalf of Dr. Stangeland." [48] Signe Lund, who besides being a musician was an ardent Socialist, was shortly thereafter hired as an instructor in music at the Mayville State Normal School, where she remained until too great a furor arose over the fact that she was energetically circulating petitions for the release from prison of Kate Richards O'Hare.[49]

Even though the war had ended months before, throughout 1919 and occasionally even later there were from time to time further incidents of mob violence against the Nonpartisan League. They occurred spasmodically in a number of localities in several states, but most notably in Kansas, where soon after its organization the American Legion commenced to play a leading role in this type of "purification" of the state. As a rule these were not the relatively spontaneous large mobs that sometimes appeared during the war days, but small organized groups bent on ridding their communities of "agitators" by means of threats or by violence if necessary.

Although this sort of thing had largely disappeared in Minnesota, the enemies of the League were not yet through with the disloyalty issue. Ironically, at almost the same time that the *Nonpartisan Leader* was receiving an award from the National Committee on Public Information "in recognition of patriotic services" during the war,[50] A. C. Townley and Joseph Gilbert were once again going on trial. After County Attorney Allen of Martin County failed in his attempt to "get Townley," Allen's close friend E. H. Nicholas, county attorney for the adjoining county of Jackson, undertook the task. This time, however, the indictment was not based on a charge of discouraging enlistments but of conspiracy to do so.

The charge was based primarily on an alleged conspiracy to distribute the pamphlet containing the League war aims and to send an organizer named Irving Friday (referred to in the indictment as Irwin Freitag) into Jackson County, where it was claimed that he made disloyal statements in the course of his organizing. This organizer, whom neither Townley nor Gilbert had ever met, was a young ministerial student and Socialist who had taken a job as an organizer during the summer of 1918 on the recommendation of Nelson Mason, secretary to Governor Frazier and an old friend of his family.[51] Although limited organizing work had been done in Jackson County, all League meetings had been prohibited and no League lecturer had ever spoken there with the exception of the few remarks by Joe Gilbert at Lakefield for which he had been arrested a year before.

Despite the fact that the atmosphere in the county was highly charged with antagonism to the League, Judge E. C. Dean did not consider a change of venue. Neither would he disqualify himself, despite the fact that some months earlier he had publicly expressed his bitter opposition to the League in a newspaper interview and was said to have declared in conversation that he was convinced that the League was financed by German money.[52] In view of the fact that the leading League candidate had come within thirty-one votes of carrying the county in the last election, it was astonishing to find that there was not one member or friend of the organization in the entire venire of 144 men drawn for possible jury duty.[53] Moreover, the judge refused to have the jurors segregated, and they spent their time when not on duty in the anti-League atmosphere of the village and reading the local and Twin Cities papers, which always assumed the guilt of the defendants.[54]

The prosecution, in which the county attorney was aided by state Assistant Attorney General James E. Markham, introduced excerpts from various speeches of Townley and Gilbert designed to show their antiwar attitude.[55] They produced two witnesses who swore that Friday had made seditious statements, one of whom was flatly contradicted by a farmer who had been present at the conversation. The other claimed that the remarks had been made to him in private conversation, and there was thus no direct way of refuting his testimony. However, the defense produced a dozen farmers who had been organized by Friday or who had traveled with him as "boosters," all of whom testified that he had never made disloyal remarks and that he did not discuss the war in his organizing.

The direct evidence of conspiracy was based almost entirely on the testimony of Ferdinand Teigen, the former League organizer who had been dismissed for dishonesty and had subsequently authored an anti-League pamphlet. Teigen, whom the prosecuting attorney called his star witness, had just gotten out of jail in Manitowoc, Wisconsin, where he had been on a forgery charge, whereupon County Attorney Nicholas sent him fifty dollars to get to Jackson. He was a happy-go-lucky sort of young man, not bothered by any particular scruples and known to handle the truth rather carelessly, yet his was the most important testimony of the trial. Teigen claimed that Townley had made statements such as the following to him while he was a League employee: "We are against this God-damned war, but we can't afford to advertise it." "Don't write or say or do anything that they can get you for, that is, any open opposition to the war. It is far better to let your position be known and understood by indirect methods." ". . . I am going out, I have got to go out. I am compelled to, and make patriotic speeches, and I have ordered all of the other men . . . to do the same thing, because if we don't they are going to get us." [56] The prosecution devoted itself largely to attempting to prove that the speeches of Townley and Gilbert bore out this testimony.

The court refused to permit the testimony of Teigen's associates in Wisconsin, where he had recently again been doing a bit of League organizing prior to having signed the chief organizer's name to a check. They had damaging evidence as to his veracity, and were to have told how he had informed them on his release from jail that he could get money from Jackson County to get back to Minnesota. After receiving the fifty dollars from Nicholas, he stopped off at a meeting near Fond du Lac with another organizer and delivered a "rattling good" League speech before catching a train to go to testify against Townley! [57]

With reference to the pamphlet on League war aims, the defense endeavored to introduce Wilson's "Fourteen Points" in order to show their close similarity, but the court ruled that they were not pertinent.[58] In vain did attorneys Hoke, Lemke, Paddock, and Sullivan insist that the state Supreme Court had already ruled that the pamphlet was not disloyal and that the federal government had in effect approved it in several ways.

The defense then set out with vigor to prove beyond question that Townley and Gilbert were not only loyal to the United States, but had actively and effectively promoted the war effort. The town was crowded with returned soldiers, fathers with sons in Europe, farmers, and war workers, all eager to testify as to how Townley's speeches had inspired them to help in the winning of the war, how he had encouraged enlistments, urged the sale of bonds, and fostered the planting of larger crops. There was a letter from President Wilson thanking Townley personally for his patriotic cooperation. There were similar letters from George Creel and other nationally known figures. Joseph Joyce of the United States Department of Justice and the sheriff and prosecuting attorney of Isanti County were present to testify as to the loyalty of certain speeches. There were transcripts of more than 190 Townley speeches, and a mass of letters, editorials, cartoons, and the like, urging support of the war.

Yet scarcely a shred of this testimony was ever presented to the jury, Judge Dean ruling that the task of the defense was not to prove that Townley and Gilbert were loyal, but to prove that they were *not disloyal*. The testimony of one witness after another was ruled out as the objections of the prosecuting attorney were regularly sustained. The prosecution was permitted to roam far beyond the bounds of the indictment, while the defense was rigidly limited to replying to specific accusations. Though the prosecution introduced excerpts from one speech made after the indictment was returned, the judge allowed it because it "showed the defendant's state of mind." At the same time he was refusing to permit the introduction of material from any of the scores of Townley speeches other than those which had been placed in evidence by the prosecutor. The state's witnesses were allowed to tell the effects of the defendants' speeches upon them, but the defense witnesses were not permitted to tell of speeches which had had an opposite effect on them. The judge not only allowed Nicholas and Markham to make long "patriotic" speeches at frequent intervals, generally prejudicial to the defendants, but often endorsed the sentiments expressed and implied that he considered the defendants guilty.

The efforts of the defense attorneys to show that there was a political motive behind the trial were likewise foiled. They endeavored to prove that this was but a part of a political conspiracy to render the League impotent, and moreover that the prosecuting attorney was a party to it. County Attorney Nicholas testified that he had never helped Teigen in disposing of his anti-League pamphlet, and the court refused as irrelevant an attempt by the defense attorneys to show that the statement was false.* Testimony of five witnesses as to financial interests backing the fight against the League was ruled not pertinent.

When the evidence was closed, County Attorney Nicholas delivered a four-hour harangue to the jury laden with appeals to "patriotism" and prejudice. Then came a dramatic moment. It was Saturday night and the packed courtroom was extremely hot. Counsel for the defendants announced that they were withdrawing from the case and terminating their employment as attorneys for Mr. Townley, and then asked if one of them might address the jury solely as attorney for Mr. Gilbert. The court ruled that only one concluding argument could be permitted for each side. Townley then rose in his shirt sleeves, saying: "I am advised that . . . I may dispense with the services of my attorneys and handle my own case. I have done that and I now ask the permission of the court to address the jury in my own behalf, not in any measure representing Mr. Gilbert."

The prosecuting attorney was on his feet protesting. "Mr. Gilbert waives the right to an address to the jury in his behalf," said one of his attorneys, thus clearing the way for but one defense argument. Judge Dean delayed, toying with a pencil. Townley reminded him that Debs, Nearing, Eastman, and even the I.W.W.'s at Chicago had not been denied this "immemorial privilege" of a final personal statement to the jury. The judge remarked that he had been ably represented by four attorneys, to which he replied: "This involves my life work. I have

* Photo copies of letters from Nicholas to Teigen dated March 27, 1918, and June 13, 1918, concerning his efforts to distribute the pamphlets to businessmen in the area may be found in the National Nonpartisan League Papers.

spent years on this; my attorneys have spent a few weeks. I feel that I can present my case better to these plain men. Two hundred fifty thousand farmers in my organization are interested here also."

The request was denied, the court ruling that since Townley had not testified in his own behalf he should not now be permitted to make an unsworn statement to the jury on which he would not be subject to cross-examination. An attorney for Gilbert then said: "Mr. Gilbert forbids me to argue the case under the circumstances for him," and the case went to the jury without argument on behalf of the defendants. The surprising thing was not that the jury returned in less than two hours with the foregone conclusion, but that on the first ballot three jurors, including the foreman, voted for acquittal.[59]

Needless to say, news of the conviction was given tremendous publicity in the anti-League press for months to come and it was effectively used against League organizing activities. Yet it was also easy for Townley to appear to be a martyr, and it seems fairly clear that in many areas the trial served to increase League strength. Though such newspapers as the *Minneapolis Journal* concluded that the verdict "confirms public opinion,"[60] there was sufficient criticism so that when Townley and Gilbert appeared in mid-September for sentencing and to plead for a new trial, County Attorney Nicholas was allowed to deliver a half-hour speech to endeavor to clear himself on the matter of his earlier relations with Ferdinand Teigen and once again to attack the League vigorously.

The judge himself read a ten-page statement defending his conduct of the trial and replying to published attacks upon it, stating among other things that the interview in the *St. James Plaindealer*, wherein his opposition to the League had been stated, had been published without authorization and was "garbled." He had never before repudiated it or sought retraction, and he did not now deny his personal prejudice.[61] The maximum sentence for a misdemeanor of ninety days in jail was imposed on both defendants, and appeals were promptly filed.

The *Jackson Republic* dismissed the attempts of the defense to prove the loyalty of Townley and Gilbert with the remark that "because a man steals a horse on Monday and does not on Tuesday is no sign that he is innocent of horse stealing,"[62] but for weeks after the trial the *Leader* carried in large type on its front page the statement of Townley after the verdict had been reached: "Judges and lawyers may quibble, but in the court of public opinion the common sense of the people will never approve a ruling that says a man may merely deny he is disloyal and is forbidden by constructive testimony to prove that he is loyal."

The comments on the conduct of the trial by even the Twin Cities dailies were strangely reserved,[63] and many persons who were far from being friends of the League spoke of the affair in most uncomplimentary terms. Concluded the relatively neutral *St. Paul Daily News*:

The outstanding feature of the Townley-Gilbert trial at Jackson was not the verdict of the jury convicting the defendants of conspiracy to teach disloyalty . . . It was the regilting of the somewhat tarnished halo of martyrdom gratuitously presented to Mr. Townley and the League last year by Governor Burnquist, Judge McGee, and Ambrose Tighe . . .

There has been left in the minds of a very large number of people an impression of a bitterly prejudiced court and a wide feeling that this trial—staged in an obscure and almost inaccessible spot, a year or more after the events concerned, before a judge who had previously admitted prejudice in declining to preside over a similar trial—savored more of persecution than of prosecution.[64]

Revenge Politics

THE thirty-seventh annual convention of the Minnesota Federation of Labor, held at New Ulm on July 20, 1919, took action that was to have far-reaching consequences. It endorsed unanimously the recommendation of a labor political conference, which had preceded the regular convention, to form a Working People's Nonpartisan League, designed to be the political arm of the labor movement and to work closely with the farmers' Nonpartisan League. The decision to take this step followed an address by S. S. McDonald, president of the North Dakota Federation of Labor and newly appointed chairman of the state's Workmen's Compensation Board, in which he described the benefits to North Dakota labor from cooperation with the League:

They exacted no pledges or promises from us. All they did was to inquire what laws organized labor in North Dakota wanted passed. We submitted eight measures. Every one is now on the statute books of the state, and it cost organized labor just $110 . . . There is no state now in which the labor men wouldn't give $100,000 to get the laws labor got in North Dakota for $100.[1]

William Mahoney, president of the St. Paul Trades and Labor Assembly, was named head of the new league, and Thomas Van Lear, the former Socialist mayor of Minneapolis, was elected secretary-treasurer. Its program, which did not vary greatly from various earlier pronouncements of joint farmer-labor conferences, called for the following:

Recognition of an unqualified right to organize and bargain collectively

An eight-hour day and forty-four-hour week

262

A state workmen's compensation system

Public works during depressions to prevent unemployment

Government regulation of the system of distribution of goods and the fostering of cooperation to reduce the cost of living

"Public ownership and operation of railways, steamships, banking businesses, stockyards, packing plants, grain elevators, terminal markets, telegraphs, telephones and all other public utilities; and the nationalization and development of basic natural resources . . ."

Securing of government revenues primarily from income and inheritance taxation and a system of "land value taxation, which will stimulate rather than retard production"

Continuation of soldiers' life insurance and the extension of government insurance of almost all types to all men and women

The complete equality of men and women in government and industry

"The autocratic domination of the forces of wealth production and distribution . . . shall be gradually superseded by a process of government supervision . . . for the benefit of all the people"

Equality of educational opportunity throughout the nation through the cooperation of the national government

The immediate and complete restoration of freedom of speech, press, and assembly [2]

The annual convention of the North Dakota Federation of Labor at Minot on June 1, 2, and 3 had unanimously voted to call a later convention for the purpose of forming a political organization to cooperate with the Nonpartisan League. Meeting in Fargo on August 31 the delegates organized the North Dakota Workers' Nonpartisan Political Alliance, and pledged the organization to support the Nonpartisan League and to recommend to the new national Labor party that it nominate Lynn Frazier for President.[3] Its program was almost identical with that of the Minnesota "labor party." A month later South Dakota's organized labor followed suit, establishing its own Working People's Nonpartisan League at a meeting at Aberdeen.[4]

Meanwhile, when Attorney General Langer of North Dakota discovered that the League Exchange was securing control of 51 per cent of the stock of banks that it organized without putting any money into them, he brought a resolution before the State Banking Board instruct-

263

ing him to warn the farmers of the state against the scheme. The resolution passed by the usual vote of Langer and Hall against Frazier, and on October 1 Langer issued his warning, which put a definite damper on bank organizing activities.[5]

The Scandinavian-American Bank of Fargo, which, as we have seen, was taken over by the League for the primary purpose of securing operating cash on the strength of farmers' notes and postdated checks, was not in good condition when purchased and did not improve greatly. In April 1919 it was examined by Deputy State Examiner P. E. Halldorson, who warned that its condition was serious. Near the end of September the State Banking Board sent the state examiner, O. E. Lofthus, to Florida to investigate a sisal company seeking to sell securities in the state, and a few days later Halldorson and Assistant Attorney General Albert E. Sheets appeared at the Scandinavian-American Bank to make another investigation. On October 1 they reported excessive loans of $734,000, generally of an unsatisfactory character. A number of other loans were also considered to be bad. As a result of their report, a hastily called meeting of the State Banking Board declared the bank insolvent and appointed Halldorson receiver. News of the event was of course trumpeted far and wide, and in many states the impression was widespread that the Bank of North Dakota had failed.

The bank's capital and surplus amounted to $60,000, which meant that under North Dakota law it would be permitted to loan not more than $9000 to any individual, firm, or corporation. Halldorson's report showed eleven loans in excess of this amount; the largest, $170,000, had been made to the Consumers' United Stores Company. Others to which some of the larger excess loans were made included the National Nonpartisan League, the League Exchange, the Publishers' National Service Bureau, and the United States Sisal Trust. On the face of things there were no loans of more than $9000, but in each case a series of individual notes were in actuality one line of credit and and the bank so considered them. All were secured largely by farmers' notes and postdated checks, which the examiners contended were of "no substantial value" as collateral. This paper was handled almost entirely by one woman who maintained most inadequate records, and at the time of examination it was discovered that much of this collateral was not in the bank at all but was in the hands of the League, the Stores Company, or some other agency, for collection.

Immediately after the bank was closed, the Banking Board ordered that from then on no bank might carry postdated checks as collateral, though most of them, League and non-League alike, had been doing so for years. Obviously this would force banks to demand other security from the League at once, putting it in a most difficult position.

Meanwhile the directors of the bank had succeeded in locating Lofthus in Florida, and he returned posthaste to apply to the Supreme Court to be placed in charge of the bank. This being the proper function of the state examiner, the request was granted, and the court at the same time issued a temporary injunction against enforcement of the order forbidding the handling of postdated checks.

For the next six days Lofthus and M. W. Thatcher of the Equitable Audit Company, which handled all League auditing, made their own examination of the bank, coming out, to no one's surprise, with almost completely opposite conclusions. Lofthus agreed that there were some excessive loans and ordered them reduced at once, but he insisted that the bank was sound and that there had been no grounds whatsoever for declaring it insolvent. The difference in the reports, of course, aside from disagreements over whether or not certain loans were collectible, turned largely upon differing conceptions of the value of postdated checks.

The state examiner having declared the bank solvent, the Supreme Court on October 24 granted his petition for the reopening of the bank, ignoring Attorney General Langer's petition for modification of the earlier order, in which he claimed that he would soon be able to present evidence that would lead to the conviction of officers of the bank and perhaps others.[6]

As soon as it became clear that everything was to work out satisfactorily, the North Dakota League state committee called a mass meeting for October 21 in Fargo. The purpose, it said, was to show the "bank-wreckers" that farmers "stand back of their collateral." The bank affair was pictured as simply another attempt by the hirelings of "big business" to ruin the farmers' organization, and the meeting was to be another testimonial of faith.

Several thousand farmers appeared to listen to Townley, Frazier, and others, and to march behind a band. A number brought their savings to deposit in the bank, and the meeting voted to increase the capital and surplus of the bank to ten times the previous figure, making it the largest private bank in North Dakota. Selling stock, however, proved to be a totally different matter from securing deposits, and in that enterprise the "shake-down session," as the *Grand Forks Herald* termed the meeting, had extremely limited success. Subsequently stock salesmen were sent around the state, but the returns were meager.[7]

With the acquisition of power had come, of course, a multitude of problems, in the solution of which the League leaders too often attempted to assume a mantle of infallibility. By 1919 there was an increasing tendency for the League to pillory not only the opposition but also anyone on their side who was unwary enough to offer public criticism of League policy or leadership, however honest and constructive it might be. Such a person was immediately condemned as a "traitor to the farmers," a "tool of Big Business," and was rarely if ever given a hearing. Doubtless there were some who more or less deserved the appellations, but others were motivated simply by a sincere difference of opinion.

This extreme intolerance of any deviation, defended on the grounds of a need for unity, was uncalled for and most unfortunate. It resulted in the ignoring of sometimes useful criticism and in the needless loss to the League of a number of valuable supporters who were committed to League principles but differed occasionally on methods. Criticism and suggestions within the organization were not completely stifled, though they were not always too welcome, but letting them get to the public was considered prima-facie evidence of having "sold out." In time the League discovered, as have others, that forbidding dissent frequently results in the loss of the unity that such action had been intended to achieve. The League leaders, of course, were convinced at the time that the forces of organized wealth could be defeated only by an organization possessing absolute solidarity.

In November the state was suddenly blanketed with copies of one of the most lurid political periodicals ever published, entitled *The Red Flame* (That Is Burning the Heart Out of North Dakota). Started by Langer and Kositzky, with the latter subsequently taking most of the credit, it was nominally published by the "Citizens' Economy League," said to exist solely "to fill a vital need in this state for educational enlightenment . . . [on] the frightful situation with which our state is confronted." Its initial blast set the tone for all future issues:

The Red Flame is SOCIALISM!

Blind, unreasoning, radical SOCIALISM that has stolen into North Dakota under the guise of a 'Farmers' Movement' . . . Political power and . . . millions of dollars . . . are being misused and squandered by a small coterie of red-tide fanatics who are not farmers, not workers, not property-holders, not tax-payers, not home owners, not producers in any sense,—*in a number of instances not even American citizens*, and who are not Socialists of any philosophical or constructive type, but who are AGITATORS, bent upon RENDING, DESTROYING, and TEARING DOWN . . .

Inaugurated as a farmers' movement, the National Nonpartisan league has degenerated into pure Bolshevism . . .

It is dominated wholly by Mr. A. C. Townley and a group of radical, international socialists, who have nothing in common with and no real sympathy for the farmer.

They are, a majority of them, men who have never done an honest day's work; men who despise work, and have nothing but contempt for the worker.

They are PARLOR SOCIALISTS, men who live by their wits, and who eat bread produced by the honest toil of others.[8]

This publication, in magazine form and usually comprising at least thirty to forty pages, was published monthly and was devoted entirely to attacks upon the League and the state administration and to promoting I.V.A. candidates. Approximately half its space was taken up by cartoons, many of them modifications of cartoons which had originally appeared in the *Leader*, now turned about on the League and the state administration. The covers, invariably in red, portrayed such themes as Liberty burning at the stake, while sensational themes of "free love," "anarchism," "I.W.W.'ism," and "bolshevism" were the chief stock-in-trade. League leaders and state officials were customarily referred to as "Comrade" Townley, "Comrade" Frazier, and so on, and the virulence of the attacks was almost inconceivable.

The *Red Flame* claimed to exist entirely on contributions and sales, though in practice it was distributed free. It was, moreover, an expensive type of publication and was printed in considerable quantity, which, combined with the fact that various issues were shipped by the thousands to other states in which the League was operating, lent more than a little credibility to the assumption that most of the "contributions" came from moneyed interests with a stake in the defeat of the League. The state enterprises and their management were one of the central

A typical cover of the anti-League *Red Flame*

objects of attack, the high salaries ($5000 per year) of the managers being hammered at repeatedly.

All the opposition press made much of Lynn Frazier's Labor Day speech in 1919 as definite proof of the revolutionary character of the League movement, quoting him rather loosely as saying: "If we can't have what we demand through the peaceful ballot, then revolution must come." [9] Frazier was actually emphasizing a familiar League argument to the effect that if the type of reforms which it advocated were not permitted to come about, some persons might seek to bring about change by violent methods. The League prided itself on a belief in change by the ballot, insisting that it was the type of movement that could forestall revolution. The presumably more accurate version of his remarks, however, was also looked upon by many as a barefaced call for the overthrow of the American system, if a minority could not prevail over the majority:

Our forefathers in 1776 had no voice in the taxes they had to pay, so they organized the revolution and broke away from tyranny. It was a just revolution. I hope to God we can change things here by the use of the ballot. I think we can. But if we can't it may be necessary to have another just revolution.[10]

Though the League may have been "socialism" to the Minneapolis Chamber of Commerce, most of the bona fide Socialists did not so regard it. It is interesting that along with the continuous attacks from the right there were not uncommonly attacks from the left as well. The Socialist party convention at St. Louis in 1917 had condemned the organization and forbidden Socialists to join. Victor Berger was understandably bitter when Baer and Sinclair astonishingly voted against seating him in the Congress, and the *Socialist Year Book* for 1919 referred to the League as a bourgeois rather than a true proletarian movement.[11] There were many of the old-line Socialists in North Dakota who were never won over, even though the great majority worked with the League. To this sort of opposition the *Leader* was always happy to give publicity, since it strengthened the claim that the League was really a moderate reform movement, existing as a workable alternative to revolution.

The leading contenders as sites for the state mill and elevator, owing to their locations, population, and railroad connections, were naturally Fargo and Grand Forks, with the former in a somewhat more advantageous position. The competition of the two anti-League cities for the state utility was rather amusing in these days of strife, and the League made it clear that one of the bases for choice would be the willingness of local business interests to purchase large amounts of mill and elevator bonds. The final decision was based on a variety of factors, not the least of which was a desire to punish Fargo. The selection of Grand

Forks was announced by Townley at the Fargo mass meeting at the time of the Scandinavian-American Bank affair; it was claimed that Fargo businessmen and banks had helped to embarrass the Scandinavian-American by withdrawing funds when secretly informed that it was to be examined. It was indicated that when Fargo realized the error of her ways she might be considered for one of the smaller units.[12]

Grand Forks businessmen had agreed to furnish a site and to purchase a million dollars' worth of the bonds, and the League was not unhappy at the prospect of winning a degree of support from this long-time center of antagonism. The Commercial Club suddenly became eager to cooperate, and even the *Grand Forks Herald* conceded that the project would be "a big thing for the city."[13] The Commercial Club and the Labor Assembly cooperated in selling the bond issue locally, and though Jerry Bacon did not cease his opposition to the League, there was a noticeably changed attitude in the city at large. Later it even went so far as to ask for the 1920 state convention of the League.[14] This "revolution" in Grand Forks was well evidenced at the annual meeting of the stockholders of the *Grand Forks American* on January 13, 1920. After listening to two or three Commercial Club speakers praise the mill and elevator project and discuss their bond-selling campaign, Arthur Townley rose to give the main address:

It all seems a good deal like a dream to me. Will some of you please tell me whether you hear the same things I hear? I feel as if my work was nearly done. This is a great day for me, one of the greatest in my life. It is worth many years of effort to see this spirit of cooperation between business men and farmers in bringing about the realization of the farmers' program.[15]

It had been decided during the regular session of the sixteenth legislature to hold a special session some months later to review the newly established industrial program and make any corrections shown necessary by practice. Enough money had been saved on the regular session, it was maintained, to pay the cost of the special session, which was expected to run only about a week. Governor Frazier issued a call for the session to convene on November 25, asking for the following actions:

Ratification of the national women suffrage amendment

Extension of the time for meeting county seed and feed liens, and a provision that only one half of real estate taxes should become delin-

quent March 1 and the other half November 15, these measures to re-
lieve farmers who had had another year of poor crops

Authorization of a bond issue, secured by first mortgages on real
estate, to provide funds for initial operation of the Home Building
Association

Creation of a special joint committee of the House and Senate to
investigate attempts to destroy the credit of the state by misrepresenta-
tions, election frauds, and the illegal acts of public officials and illegal
expenditures of public funds

Creation of the office of state sheriff

A resolution requesting the United States Supreme Court to advance
the "42 taxpayers' suit" on its calendar in order that the state industrial
program might not be held up longer

Repeal of the money and credits tax because of "general dissatisfaction" and "to prevent needed money being withdrawn from the state"

An increased levy for the soldiers' bonus

Making of the Railroad Commission also a State Trade Commission
to cooperate with the Federal Trade Commission "to investigate and
place the responsibility of profiteering" [16]

Frazier later asked a special investigation of the "traitor" state officials. There had been talk for some time of the possibility of impeaching Langer, Hall, and Kositzky, but it was doubtful if the necessary
vote could have been obtained, and there were other ways of hamper-
ing their activities pending the primaries which were only seven months
away. It was no secret that the rebels were to be "taken care of."

The session had scarcely gotten under way when Representative
Burtness made a "sensational" discovery. While browsing through the
state library he noticed a stack of books on top of a box used to circu-
late books to the public schools. Among them were Ellen Key's *Love
and Ethics*, Upton Sinclair's *Profits of Religion*, Gustavus Myers' *History of the Supreme Court*, a number of books on socialist topics by
well-known writers, and Charles A. Beard's *American Government
and Politics*. That evening Burtness did a bit of reading and the next
day he appeared on the floor of the House to deliver a tirade on the
attempted corruption of the school children of the state by forcing
them to read books promoting socialism, advocating free love, and
attacking organized religion. He quoted choice paragraphs from Ellen
Key, Sinclair, and Myers, and vigorously attacked Dr. Stangeland and

Anna Peterson, the new librarian, both of whom had been brought from New York on the recommendation of Dr. Charles A. Beard of the Rand School.[17] Immediately a tremendous hue and cry was raised in the opposition press.

Following Burtness' charges in the House League members at once moved that an investigating committee be appointed. A five-man committee, consisting of three Leaguers and two I.V.A.'s, investigated the situation for a week and presented a unanimous report to the House. None of the books in question had ever been sent to schools, it said, and there was clearly no intent to do so. The box on which they happened to be stacked at the time of the discovery by Burtness was merely being used as a shelf. Books were sent out to schools only upon the request of teachers, who were solely responsible for the selections. Most of the books were standard works which might be found in any city library, and the volume by Ellen Key was the last of a series of five, the first four having been purchased before the League administration. The committee refrained from evaluating any of the subject matter, saying that it did not consider itself qualified to do so and had no desire to attempt censorship.[18]

Nevertheless, Representative Burtness, not to be cheated of his glory, continued to quote selections from time to time, and the anti-League press never permitted the "scandal" to die. It was contended that even if the schools were not involved, there was a sinister motive behind even the purchase of such books. Ultimately it was Dr. Stangeland who was sacrificed to the wolves. A resolution of the Board of Administration spoke of the "vicious assault" made upon him by the I.V.A., and requested his resignation to prevent diversion of attention "from the industrial program to other issues." Stangeland felt that he had been victimized, but complied in a letter to Chairman Totten in which he stated: "I believe the time will come when a clearer vision will make the controversy which has centered around me and my efforts in a different light, and that light will reveal the truth which the passions and fears of the day are making obscure." [19]

One of the central points of the I.V.A. attack was the increased taxes in 1919, admittedly 118 per cent over the 1918 levy for state purposes. Actually little could be found to criticize about the actual expenditures. Over 40 per cent was for state educational institutions, more than half of the amount being for long-needed new buildings, while 22 per cent was for the other state institutions. Hail insurance and the soldiers' bonus accounted for sizable amounts, although they were not included in the computations made by the League. Only 6 per cent went into the new state industries, and this was expected to be returned.[20] The tax commissioner pointed out that Minnesota taxes were up 133 per cent and Wisconsin's 124 per cent, but such comparisons do not salve the wounded pocketbook. The special session concluded that some appropriations had been overly generous and that others would not be needed for the time being, and ordered a rebate of 25 per cent in general state taxes.[21]

The legislature granted most of the requests of Governor Frazier, and in some respects went beyond them. Both houses adopted a resolution calling upon Attorney General Langer to resign, charging that he had endeavored to wreck the Scandinavian-American Bank by false charges and that he had failed to protect properly the state's interests in connection with suits involving the industrial program. The appropriation for his office was cut from $99,000 to $30,000, leaving only $5000 for operation until July 1, 1921. The number of his assistants was reduced from five to two, the right to appoint special assistants was removed, and the governor was given power to employ such special counsel as might be needed. The appropriation for the state auditor was cut from $71,000 to $33,000, leaving $8000 until the end of the biennium. Kositzky was then removed from the State Auditing Board, the State Board of Equalization, and the Emergency Fund Commission. Secretary of State Hall also suffered a budget cut and was removed from the State Auditing Board.[22]

Inasmuch as these actions could not immediately go into effect, Langer and Kositzky drew upon their original appropriations to supply their offices with sufficient mileage allowances to carry them a year. Langer then had warrants drawn in favor of two of his assistants, paying them salaries one year in advance on the basis of a contract dated December 17, despite the fact that statutes forbade paying anyone for services not performed. The State Auditing Board, consisting of Langer, Hall, and Kositzky, promptly approved these maneuvers.[23]

As the end of the session approached Carl Kositzky had his day. He refused to pay the members of the legislature their per diem and mileage allowances, contending that there was not enough money in the general fund. The Senate then passed a resolution ordering payment and sent a committee to demand that Kositzky issue the warrants. Kositzky resisted service of the resolution, engaging in a fist fight in a corridor with Senator A. A. Liederbach, and finally locked himself in his office. He was then ordered to appear before the Senate, and upon doing so was asked why the warrants had not been issued. He stated that there was other important work to be done and his office staff was forbidden by law to work more than eight hours a day. After further questioning he agreed to issue as many warrants as there were funds available to pay.

Kositzky then issued warrants to I.V.A. members, admitting that he had paid his "friends" and claiming that this was justified on the grounds that they had applied first. He was quoted as saying, however: "They tried to get me. Why shouldn't I try to get back at them?" [24] Senator Cahill, as majority leader of the Senate, brought suit against Kositzky for payment, but the matter was shortly settled without intervention by the courts, and stranded legislators got away from Bismarck.

The four acts of the 1919 special session which aroused the greatest storm of opposition were the absent voters law, the "anti-liars law," and the statutes creating an investigation committee and the office of state sheriff.

The first provided that any woman voter residing one-half mile or more from a polling place and any voter expecting to be absent on election day might within thirty days before an election mark a ballot in the presence of a notary and send it to the county auditor. The League was understandably worried about the feminine vote, having learned by experience that it tended to be heavy in the cities and woefully light in the rural areas. On the surface this statute did not appear to be anything tremendously unusual, but the I.V.A. at once proclaimed that it did away with the Australian ballot and opened the door to corruption. "A more villainous bill was never enacted," said the *Grand Forks Herald*,[25] and Jerry Bacon professed to foresee a veritable scourge of League notaries making the rounds for a month before each election, armed with bribes and threats: "The Townley Socialist administration in North Dakota has utterly destroyed the secret ballot . . . undoing work of 25 years to protect sacredness of . . . [the] ballot." [26]

The state sheriff was to be appointed by the governor, and all sher-

iffs and deputies in the state were to be made members of a state con-
stabulary subject to the direction of the state sheriff. Although this
was essentially similar to the provisions in a number of states, the opposition saw in it a personal police force for Frazier and Townley and
assumed that it would be utilized to guard corrupt officials while they
gleefully stuffed the ballot boxes. Since the state sheriff was empowered, with the consent of the governor, to appoint all the deputies he
might need at the rate of five dollars a day and expenses, the *Red
Flame* envisaged a force of ten or fifteen thousand, overawing local officials, dominating elections, and liquidating anti-Leaguers. They would
doubtless, it said, "import their deputies from the four corners of the
earth, all red socialists, with no regard for law or order, human life,
morals or anything else." [27] Remarked J. E. Buttree: "Most extraordi-
nary power is conferred upon the State Sheriff; power slightly limited
as compared with Trotzky's. It is so arranged that we can have our
red army, not quite so red as Lenine's but one whose hue may become
more and more sanguine." [28]

The "investigation committee," popularly known as the "smelling
committee," consisted of two senators and three representatives, and
was given wide powers to examine or investigate, upon the written
complaint of any person or upon its own initiative, "any department
or public office of this state, and all acts, efforts, attempts, transactions,
proceedings and conspiracies to destroy or injure, or which are designed
or intended to injure or destroy the property, reputation, freedom,
right or business of any person, group, association, company or group
of persons in the state of North Dakota, or any of the industries, enterprises or utilities owned by the state of North Dakota or the credit
of the state of North Dakota." It might also investigate any attempt at
violence or corruption in connection with any election. Any member
of the committee as well as the committee itself was empowered to
issue subpoenas and search warrants and to compel attendance, testimony, and production of documentary evidence.[29] Twenty-five thousand dollars was appropriated and deposited in the Bank of North
Dakota to the credit of Senator J. I. Cahill, as chairman, subject to no
check as to its expenditure. The American revolution, said the *Red
Flame*, was fought "on less provocation than is contained in House
Bill 48." [30]

The "anti-liars law" made it a felony for any state official to "wilfully publish any false statement in regard to any of the state departments, institutions or industries which . . . shall tend to deceive the public and create a distrust of the state officials or employees in charge of such departments, institutions or industries, or which tends to obstruct, hinder and delay the various departments, institutions and industries of the state." [31]

If confined to its absentee voter provisions, at least, there could be little serious objection to the absent voters law, but the other three were unworthy of the high ideals of liberalism to which the League professed to subscribe. It was obvious that the League had in some degree been driven to the defensive, and it moved to protect its program through repressive measures which it would have denounced in no uncertain terms had they been enacted by elements opposed to the League in any state. Although there was certainly no intent to carry them to the fantastic lengths claimed by the opposition, it is just as well that they never went into effect.

None of the acts of the special session was declared to be an emergency measure, but the legislature did enact what was termed by some a "general emergency law." House Bill 60 stated that since the constitution did not specify when the acts of a special session were to go into effect, they should become effective ten days after the adjournment of such a special session. Referendum petitions were promptly filed to suspend the operation of the absent voters, state sheriff, and investigation committee laws, while the "anti-liars law" was challenged and never enforced, but on December 22 the battle over whether or not the other measures were in effect began. New members endeavored to sit on various boards and commissions, the governor refused to recognize certain actions of the attorney general, and so on. Confusion reigned until on January 16 the Supreme Court ruled House Bill 60 unconstitutional, saying, despite the protests of Justice Robinson that eleven months might intervene with the hands of the legislature and executive tied, that the constitutional provision that all acts become effective on the following July 1 applied to special as well as to regular legislative sessions. [32]

By the end of 1919 the pressure for greater freedom of state Leagues from the national organization and for more democratic internal organization was reaching significant proportions. League membership remained over the 200,000 mark,* and the state organizations were now old enough to have experienced the emergence of leaders who were eager for more power for themselves. Some were able and sincere men; a few were concerned primarily with personal prestige. In many respects in most states the League had become another political party rather than being nonpartisan. It developed its own groups of professional politicians, and the faithful were defended against "outsiders" regardless of their merit.

The national committee of the League met in St. Paul on December 10, with all members of state committees invited to attend. There was the usual audit approval, followed by a discussion of a nationwide organization of League women and selection of a committee to bring it into being. The convention reaffirmed its confidence in A. C. Townley and commended the National Executive Committee for its management of League affairs. Its formal resolutions dealt with the continued devotion of the organization to reform through the ballot box and to majority rule, the need for improved protection of free speech and assembly, the essentiality of close farmer-labor cooperation, demands for nationalization of the coal mines and for government ownership and operation of the railroads, suggestion of a national soldiers' bonus to be paid from a tax on war profits, opposition to the proposed national alien and sedition laws, opposition to militarism and especially compulsory military training, a demand that United States troops leave Russia, and a call for the cessation of jingoism regarding Mexico.[33]

Townley again suggested the possibility of his stepping down from the presidency and becoming an "organizer at large," with an actual farmer holding the top office, but it was generally felt that too much depended upon him for this to be done.[34] The really significant action

---

* Henry Teigan gave the following approximations of paid-up memberships by states in a letter to Herbert Iverson, New York City, December 8, 1919 (National Nonpartisan League Papers):

North Dakota	40,000	Idaho	12,000
Minnesota	50,000	Washington	10,000
South Dakota	25,000	Iowa, Kansas, Texas,	
Montana	20,000	and Oklahoma	11,300
Wisconsin	15,000		
Nebraska	13,500	Total	208,800
Colorado	12,000		

If one were to include those who had not renewed their memberships but who still received the *Leader* and counted themselves Leaguers, the figure was presumably in the neighborhood of 250,000.

of the convention was the establishment of a new plan of county organization. Counties which considered their membership sufficiently well organized were authorized to elect a county committee of one member from each voting precinct at the time of the regular precinct caucuses. The committee then would assume full responsibility for maintaining the membership, for further organizing, and for local political activity. They would employ a county organization manager, who would work under the general direction of the state manager. Where county organizations were not developed the state organization would carry on as before.

The county organizations were henceforth to receive seven dollars of the biennial dues paid within the county, now raised to a total of eighteen dollars because of "increased costs," the state four dollars, and the national seven dollars. The seven dollars to the national League was to cover two-year subscriptions to the national and state *Leaders* and maintenance of the national headquarters. County organizations were to be given a relatively free hand on local activities as long as they did not conflict with general policy, and they might at their discretion enter local politics, thus departing from the old rule of state politics only.[35] These changes were widely hailed as a distinct forward step which would strengthen the organization and rejuvenate the clearly flagging interest and activity of the membership.

Year of Crisis

NINETEEN TWENTY was recognized by the League as a decisive year—the year which would determine whether the organization was to march forward as a national power or lapse slowly into obscurity. With the opposition already massing for an "all-out" drive, the League called its precinct caucuses for the end of January, a month earlier than usual. In many areas, of course, county organizations would be formed at this time, and it was hoped that a bit of additional time before the state conventions would give them a chance to get more solidly on their feet. For the first time, officially at least, candidates were being endorsed for local offices in those counties.

The state conventions of the Minnesota Nonpartisan League and the Working People's Nonpartisan League met March 24 and 25 in separate halls, keeping in touch with each other through the medium of a conference committee consisting of one member from each congressional district in each body. In both cases the usual blackboard nominating procedure was followed, and after a full afternoon of debate on a candidate for governor the committees from the two Leagues carried the predominant sentiments of their groups to a conference. The principal possibilities considered by the farmers' League were Henrik Shipstead, a young dentist and member of the state legislature from Glenwood, former Congressman James Manahan, Thomas Van Lear, former mayor of Minneapolis, and Willis M. West, former chairman of the department of history of the University of Minnesota, then farming near Grand Rapids.[1] In addition to these men, the labor League also considered Charles A. Lindbergh, the 1918 candidate, Victor Power, 1918 candidate for attorney general, and Carl A. Ingerson.[2]

The committee from the labor League was split as was the convention, but in conference the groups from both organizations agreed that the sentiment was strongest for Shipstead. He was called before the conference committee and questioned for nearly two hours, whereupon he was reported upon favorably to both conventions, which promptly endorsed him. The other endorsees were as follows: for lieutenant governor, George H. Mallon, a labor leader and former army captain, holder of a Congressional Medal of Honor and one of Pershing's "100 war heroes"; for attorney general, Thomas V. Sullivan, a League attorney; for secretary of state, Thomas Vollom, a farmer and manager of a cooperative; for treasurer, Lily Anderson, manager of a farm and active in the Equity Society; for railroad and warehouse commissioner, Paul I. D. Ostby, a farmer; and for justice of the Supreme Court, George Siegel of St. Paul, a leader of progressive forces in the state legislature.[3] It later developed that Miss Anderson could not file because only thirty-five states had ratified the suffrage amendment, and she was replaced by Charles Lund of Vining, a League farmer and banker.[4]

For the congressional seats labor candidates were endorsed in the city districts, including the incumbents W. L. Carss from the iron range area and Oscar Keller, elected in a sensational upset as an independent labor-backed candidate in a special election in St. Paul the preceding year. District conventions in the other districts endorsed H. A. Fuller of Mankato, a stanch League and Equity farmer, in the second, Frank E. Little, mayor of Brainerd, in the sixth, the Reverend O. J. Kvale of Benson, a Lutheran pastor, in the seventh, and N. E. Thormodson of Dalton, a farmer, in the ninth.[5]

There had been talk for many months of starting a League daily newspaper in Minnesota in time for it to play a role in the 1920 campaign, and a considerable amount of stock had been sold in the enterprise. In February of 1919 articles of incorporation of the *Minnesota Daily Star* had been filed and a building was subsequently purchased in Minneapolis.[6] This was to be a separate concern, not subsidized by the League organization and not under the control of the Publishers' National Service Bureau. Stock sales were slow, however, and were made for the most part to persons who had but little to invest. Since the promoters did not wish to make a start until adequate capital had been obtained ($750,000), the first issue was long conspicuous by its absence, not appearing until the middle of August.

Beginning with the February 9 issue, however, the *Nonpartisan Leader* and the *Minnesota Leader* were printed on their own presses in the *Star* building. By mid-March the *Minneapolis Labor Review* and the headquarters of the national League, the Minnesota League, the Working People's Nonpartisan League, and the Women's Nonpartisan Clubs were all housed in the building.[7]

Meanwhile the Minnesota Sound Government Association, backed by a huge campaign fund and designed to coordinate the opposition to the League, had established headquarters in the Exchange Bank Building in St. Paul. The association, which freely admitted that the League would win the state unless a Republican-Democrat alliance were achieved, sent copies of *Minnesota Issues* free to every farmer in the state, and, taking a leaf from the League's book, carefully trained speakers for the campaign in the attempt to achieve some uniformity of arguments.[8]

Nor had those who were intent upon tapping the resources of the anti-League forces disappeared. In 1919 one Jack Bryant and several associates had formed the "Northwest Warriors' Americanization Committee" to fight "anarchy" and "bolshevism," meaning apparently the Nonpartisan League and organized labor. They were successful in collecting considerable sums of money from Twin City businessmen, and briefly published the *Northwest Warriors' Magazine*. In order to stimulate contributions, they managed to bring former President Taft to St. Paul and Minneapolis for a series of "Americanism" lectures. Having fairly well drained the Twin City sources, Bryant and his companions expanded their operations into other states, meeting with particular success in Omaha. After collecting all the cash possible, but with little accomplished in the way of combating anarchy, the Bryant group sold a sizable number of one-dollar tickets to what the backers had understood was to be a free lecture in Omaha, then hastily departed for Canada, leaving the *Leader* to chortle: "Who are the suckers now?"[9]

Governor Burnquist did not seek renomination, and as a consequence there was a rash of candidates, three of whom, Frankson, Schmahl, and Preus, held state offices. Republican leaders, recognizing that under such conditions Shipstead was certain to secure the Republican nomination, decided to hold an "elimination convention" on May 8 to settle on a "pure" candidate upon whom the anti-League forces might concentrate their votes. This the *Leader* termed defiance of the primary law, and several of the eight or nine prospective candidates threatened not to abide by the decision, Tom Frankson and Julius Schmahl being particularly displeased. It was widely charged that the convention was "rigged" for the selection of State Auditor Jacob A. O. Preus.[10]

The convention, as expected, endorsed Preus, and ultimately most of the other strong vote-getters withdrew, Schmahl doing so with ill grace on June 7 "for the sake of the party," after considerable pressure had been put upon him. The race then settled down into what was primarily a battle between Preus and Shipstead.

Henrik Shipstead opened his speaking campaign on April 20, commencing a steady tour of the state which continued uninterrupted until primary day. Demands for "Townley meetings" poured in from nearly every Minnesota county, and Townley was being sought at the same time for speeches in other states. Since speed was essential, a small airplane was secured, and henceforth the president of the League, "disregarding all personal risks," campaigned by air, virtually living in the plane for long stretches of time.[11] Flying between picnics, he addressed, it was claimed, as high as 15,000 persons a day during the peak period. Although they were not always particularly welcome, League speakers were not barred from towns as they had frequently been two years before, and it was interesting that some communities which had barred Townley in 1918, such as Fergus Falls and St. Cloud, now formally expressed their pleasure at his visits, the latter city even declaring a "Townley day" in early June.

Preus delivered his opening speech at Mankato, devoting it largely to an attack on socialism, complete with random irrelevant quotations from Marx, Engels, Liebknecht, and the *Appeal to Reason*. Basing his entire campaign on an identification of the League and international socialism, he reached the climax in a peroration:

This is not my fight for office, nor of any Republican candidate. It is the fight of the honest God-fearing electorate of Minnesota to prevent the government and resources of this state from being exploited by professional Socialist agitators.

You pay too much for your pottage when you trade your birthright of private property, religious freedom and sacred ties of home for the impracticable visions of Socialist adventurers. Let us not despoil ourselves ot our heritage; let us cherish the institutions of our fathers; let us preserve the Republican form of government instituted by our fore-bears and perfected by ourselves. Let us still believe in our American institutions, our families and our homes.[12]

A movement was at one time started to charge that Shipstead and his running mates were not in fact Republicans and could not run in the party primary, but it was shortly dropped. During the last week farmers were warned by many rural papers that if they had voted for Farmer-Labor candidates in 1918 they would be violating the law by attempting now to vote in the Republican primary, but the *Leader* quickly told them that they need only swear that they had "supported the party generally" in the last election, and warned them not to be "bulldozed" by officials attempting to refuse them Republican ballots.[13]

For two weeks before the election, the Twin Cities newspapers ran daily editorials pleading for a heavy Republican vote (including Demo-crats), savagely attacking the "Socialist" leadership of the League, and assailing the League administration in North Dakota. Concluded the *Minneapolis Journal*:

. . . the people of Minnesota are confronted with a plain, simple is-sue . . . Do the voters of Minnesota who purpose entering the Repub-lican primary want to turn the Party and along with it the State Government over to the Nonpartisan League, to the Socialist schemers who dominate it, to the projects of exploitation and heavy taxation with which they have loaded North Dakota?

Or do the voters elect to save our great commonwealth from such a fate, to conserve and develop its resources, to keep to the path of conservative, safe and sane progress? . . .

We have not a word to say against Dr. Shipstead personally. But he was chosen by a secret meeting of handpicked delegates on the orders of the Nonpartisan League boss and assistant bosses. He represents a vicious and dangerous scheme of government.[14]

On June 21 only 27,000 Democrats failed to heed the call to save the state, and Preus defeated Shipstead 133,832 to 125,861.[15] Despite the defeat, the League was able to claim a considerable advance, since Ship-stead lost by fewer than 8000 votes compared with the 50,000 deficit in 1918. Moreover, he carried fifty-four of the state's eighty-six coun-ties, adding twenty-four to the thirty carried by Lindbergh. Interest-ingly enough, Shipstead narrowly missed carrying Jackson County, scene of the famous Townley-Gilbert trial, and Tom Sullivan, the candidate for attorney general, who had been one of the attorneys for Townley and Gilbert, did carry it.[16]

Sullivan, as a matter of fact, proved to be the closest contender, running ahead of the incumbent Attorney General Hilton consistently enough that the newspapers conceded his nomination in their afternoon editions the day following the primary. The next morning, however, it was announced that a "mistake" of 4000 votes had been discovered in St. Louis County (Duluth and the iron range), giving the nomination to Hilton by a narrow margin.[17] The only successful League state candidate was Siegel on the nonpartisan ballot for Supreme Court justice. Carss and Keller were renominated in the eighth and fourth congressional districts, one on the Democratic and the other on the Republican ticket. Fuller in the second and Thormodson in the ninth lost in extremely close races, while in the seventh Reverend Kvale edged out Andrew J. Volstead of Prohibition fame, only to be later disqualified in a court suit for having charged during the campaign that his opponent was an atheist.[18]

Before the end of 1919 I.V.A. "fighting squads" were touring the state of North Dakota, speaking and laying the groundwork for the 1920 campaign. An I.V.A. convention was held in Grand Forks on February 5 in the attempt to unify all "anti-Townley" forces and to lay comprehensive plans for campaign organization and financing. In addition it was decided to initiate an "anti-red-flag" law, a bill for which had again been killed in the special session.[19]

Confusion was the keynote of the efforts to endorse candidates for delegates to the Republican national convention, presidential electors, and national committeeman. Ultimately there were three separate conventions—of the McKenzie-McCumber element, the Progressives, and the Leaguers—for that purpose. The Progressive conference declared all party offices held by Leaguers vacant, and instructed the remainder of the State Central Committee to fill the vacancies,[20] this only two weeks after the "old guard" conference had refused to seat certain Progressives on the grounds that they were "Bull Moosers" and not Republicans! Following the League Republican convention, however, William Lemke as state chairman called a meeting of the State Central Committee to endorse the League slate. But after all this maneuvering the secretary

284

of state refused to accept list filing, contending that it must be done individually, and in this he was upheld by the Supreme Court.[21]

A raging blizzard swept the state on March 16, the day of the presidential primary, and the vote was extremely light. In some areas the precinct polling places were never opened, one third of the total in Walsh and Pembina counties, for example. Hiram Johnson, whom the League convention had endorsed for the Republican presidential nomination, won easily over Leonard Wood and Frank Lowden, and a mixture of delegates, largely anti-League, were elected. Of probably greater importance, however, was the carrying of four League-sponsored constitutional amendments, the most significant one being that which established a procedure for the recall of elective officials.[22]

Scarcely had the battle between the state auditor and the legislature at the end of the special session died down, when Kositzky and several assistants appeared one morning at the Bank of North Dakota to demand the privilege of conducting an audit. This was obviously a political move, and Director-General Cathro at once telephoned William Anderson, the attorney for the Bank, to ask what he should do. Anderson advised him to refuse them admittance, since the bank was not a state department subject to the general powers of the state auditor and the statute creating the bank specifically provided that it be periodically audited by the state bank examiner. This position was upheld by both Judge Neussle in the District Court and the Supreme Court, but the state auditor went through the same procedure with the Drake mill and the Workmen's Compensation Bureau.[23]

Kositzky of course knew perfectly well the provisions of law on this matter, but he knew also that he could make the League look bad whatever it did. If an audit were conducted it was likely that some sort of attack could be built up as a result, while a refusal naturally gave the impression that something was being hidden. Kositzky was admittedly on a "torpedoing" mission, but it seems probable that even though legally correct the refusal to allow an audit was a political mistake, as any charges which might have arisen out of an audit could probably have been more easily combated than could this apparent secrecy. The I.V.A. made real political capital out of the refusal to "let the people see what is going on," nor did they overlook the fact that O. E. Lofthus, the state bank examiner, who was the only one authorized to audit these enterprises, was an appointee of the governor and had been the candidate for state treasurer on the Socialist ticket in 1916.[24]

By mid-April the state administration had dispensed with the services of several persons whom it apparently considered liabilities, including Dr. Stangeland, Signe Lund, Neil MacDonald, L. J. Wehe of the Workmen's Compensation Bureau, James Waters, manager of the Bank of North Dakota, and his assistant Roy Halliday. George Totten was rumored to be next, but he remained in office for some time.[25] F. W. Cathro from the time of Waters' departure served as both manager and director-general of the Bank, incidentally drawing both salaries.

At the same time that these various officials were being dropped, a process which unfortunately did not go far enough, the League set about to "shake down" the faithful. In January all state employees received letters from Joseph Coghlan, Supreme Court reporter and law librarian, requesting campaign contributions. He pointed out that donations from office holders were customary and that 10 per cent had been expected under previous regimes, concluding with a suggested amount from the individual concerned. All money raised, he said, would be used for legitimate purposes, and postdated checks dated April 1 or sooner would be acceptable.[26]

The I.V.A. state convention, called by a committee consisting of both Republicans and Democrats, was held in Minot on May 12 and 13. William Langer and Rangvold A. Nestos, a Minot attorney prominent in I.V.A. affairs, had previously announced that they desired the endorsement for governor, and it was rumored that Langer might not abide by the action of the convention because he was dissatisfied with the manner of selecting delegates. Further dissension appeared when Sveinbjorn Johnson, chairman of the Democratic State Central Committee, announced that the Democrats would not affiliate with the Republicans, but would hold their own convention in Fargo on May 19. The I.V.A. convention, however, proceeded harmoniously and after considering Langer, Nestos, and John Steen, endorsed Langer by a three to one vote. Hall, Kositzky, Steen, and Minnie Nielson were then foregone conclusions for secretary of state, auditor, treasurer, and superintendent of public instruction.[27] District conventions subsequently endorsed legislative candidates.

The convention prepared a "redemption" platform which asserted feelingly that League policies and actions were both "un-American" and "un-Republican." It emphasized the "sacred" character of private enterprise and denounced most of the League measures, though it did not recommend abolition of the mill and elevator program, hail insurance, or the workmen's compensation system. There was the usual commentary on bolshevism and free love, the I.V.A. insisting that "the real issue in the campaign in this state is between Americanism and socialism." [28]

The Democratic convention the following week endorsed a full slate of candidates headed by J. F. T. O'Connor for governor and including Minnie Nielson for superintendent of public instruction. Prominent I.V.A.'s were in control of the convention, and it seemed fairly clear that this Democratic slate was a form of insurance to hedge against the possibility that the League candidates might be successful in the Republican primary. At the time of the Democratic convention it was announced in Fargo that a "joint campaign committee" of three Republicans, three Democrats, and three I.V.A.'s had been formed to engineer the fight against Townleyism, in particular the financing of the fight. Speakers used by the I.V.A. throughout the state were to perform a neat trick. They would, it was said, "discuss general issues and . . . back both the anti-Townley Republican and anti-Townley Democratic tickets in the June primary." [29]

The League convention at Fargo on May 14 re-endorsed Frazier by acclamation. Hagan as commissioner of agriculture and labor, Wood as lieutenant governor, Milhollan and Dupuis as railroad commissioners, Olsness as insurance commissioner, and Baer and Sinclair in the first and third congressional districts were likewise re-endorsed. For the other offices the following were selected: for attorney general, William Lemke; for auditor, D. C. Poindexter, a labor-backed candidate; for secretary of state, state Senator J. I. Cahill; for treasurer, state Representative R. H. Walker; for superintendent of public instruction, Ruth M. Johnson, superintendent of schools at Tioga and daughter of a League farmer; for the third railroad commissioner, C. W. McDonnell, a League legislator; for justice of the Supreme Court, Seth Richardson, one of the special counsel appointed by Governor Frazier; for United States senator, Dr. Edwin F. Ladd, now president of the agricultural college as well as state grain inspector; and for second district congressman, state Senator Thomas Pendray.[30]

The endorsement of Lemke for attorney general was the first departure from the long-standing rule that no League officer might run for public office, and, though the I.V.A. claimed that this was a move by Townley to save himself from prosecution, it was in fact evidence of the extent to which the North Dakota organization had gotten out of his hands. He did nothing to stop the endorsement at the time, but he later had occasion to wish that he had gone before the delegates to tell them that it was perfectly all right to endorse Lemke, but that if done he would no longer hold any League office or have any connection with League newspapers.[31]

On the continued devotion of the League to Lynn Frazier the *Red Flame* produced a parody entitled the "North Dakota Coronation Hymn":

> All hail the power of Frazier's name
> Let the Leaguers prostrate fall.
> Bring forth the loyal band of Reds
> And crown him King of all.
>
> Ye needy farmers slop your hogs
> But heed ye Townley's call;
> "Give me your dough, but vote for Lynn,
> And crown him King of all."
> . . . .
>
> Let Ellen Key with all her tribe
> Dance at our new King's ball;
> What happens then we'll not describe,
> For Lynn is King of all.[32]

The *Dayton* (Wash.) *Press* had its own interpretation of why the League had been so much more successful in North Dakota than in other states: "No wonder that the Nonpartisan bunk became so popular in North Dakota. The census taker found only five bathtubs in four counties. Uncleanliness and ignorance are ever companions, instance the Bolsheviki in Russia and the Bolsheviki hoboes of the I.W.W. and other unclean classes in the United States."[33]

The anti-League forces within North Dakota, however, were not so foolish as to indulge in such inanities. In large measure they devoted themselves, aside from the charges of "socialism," to the issue of increased taxes. Literally reams of statistics were published by both sides in an effort to prove their respective cases, until anyone seeking a simple set of facts must have been hopelessly bewildered. It was quite true that taxes had gone up, just as they had in all states, and it was also true that state taxes comprised but a relatively small portion of the total increase. Only three fifths of a cent out of the state and local tax dollar went into the state industries.

Yet it was not particularly fruitful for the League to point to the higher taxes in other states, to the higher local government taxes, to the meritorious uses to which the money was being put, and to the fact that North Dakota had the lowest per capita tax of any state in the Northwest at the end of the preceding fiscal year. The fact remained that taxes were higher, and for that the administration in power must always bear the consequences. The farmer could not forget that from the beginning the opposition had dinned in his ears that the League program was going to increase taxes, and to many the tax statement seemed somehow more concrete than the claims of the League press that League actions such as enforcing honest weights and grades, compelling payment for dockage, providing cheaper rates on hail insurance and lower interest rates on loans had already saved the farmers of the state collectively nearly $18,000,000.[34]

The air was likewise clouded with conflicting charges and counter-charges concerning the operation to date of the various state enterprises. While the League insisted that the Bank of North Dakota had shown a profit, had materially reduced the average rate of interest on farm loans, had provided valuable services to private banks and to state departments and industries, had established a uniform rate of interest for current funds of political subdivisions on deposit, on which many had received no interest before, had been able to transfer money to areas where it was needed from those which had an oversupply, and so on, the I.V.A. insisted that the Bank was actually losing money and that local governments had previously averaged twice as much interest as they were now receiving.[35]

The *Red Flame* attacked repeatedly and at length the inefficiency of the state Hail Insurance Department, claiming that there were many duplicate payments and payments to persons who had withdrawn, and that the adjusters showed favoritism to League members. Indemnities were paid too late, it said, and the League accounts of savings achieved did not take into account the cost to the counties of assisting in the administration of the system.[36]

The League, however, announced proudly that 72.78 per cent of the cropped area of the state had been insured with the state, with a risk of $84,376,196 carried. An indemnity tax of twenty-five cents added to the three-cent acreage tax had been adequate to pay the losses, amounting to approximately three and one-half million dollars. As compared with this twenty-eight cents, the average rate with private companies was seventy-seven cents, so that on the 12,000,000 acres insured there was claimed to be a saving of $5,400,000. Furthermore, while losses were paid later, farmers had to give cash or a note for premiums to private companies at the time of purchase, but the state tax did not fall due until the following March.[37]

On April 7 the Industrial Commission awarded the contract for construction of a 1,600,000-bushel elevator and a flour mill with a daily capacity of 3000 barrels, designed to be the most modern and best equipped then in existence. The total cost, exclusive of machinery and power plant was to be $922,850.[38] The citizens of Grand Forks subscribed the necessary one million dollars' worth of bonds, and work was to be started just as soon as the hands of the Industrial Commission were freed by the courts.

To keep company with the "42 taxpayers' suit," which was going through the federal courts, five Burleigh County farmers brought suit of a similar nature in the state courts, generally recognized to be a "friendly suit," or "test case." [39] On January 2 the state Supreme Court held that the amendments permitting the industrial program were not in conflict with the United States Constitution, and that the subsequent laws effectuating the program contravened neither the United States nor the state constitutions. The enterprises, it said, four justices concurring, were clearly for a public purpose, for which taxes might be laid and bonds issued. Mr. Justice Christianson dissented, still contending that the amendments had never been properly adopted, and also on the grounds that this was a "friendly suit" not presenting a justiciable controversy.[40]

On April 19 the appeals from both *Scott v. Frazier* and *Green v. Frazier*, since they involved almost identical issues, were heard together in the United States Supreme Court. Attorneys for the "42 taxpayers" were Judge N. C. Young, counsel for the Northern Pacific and several milling corporations, Tracy Bangs, counsel for the Red River Power Company, Western Union, and several telephone companies, and C. J.

Murphy, counsel for the Great Northern. For the state Attorney General Langer sent his two assistants, attorneys Nuchols and Lauder, while the Industrial Commission sent William Lemke and Frederick A. Pike. The defense having been allotted two hours, the four attorneys agreed to divide the time evenly, whereupon Nuchols and Lauder took up three fourths of the time, and Pike felt called upon to devote a good part of his twenty-five minutes to clearing up what he considered to be the false impressions created by the assistant attorneys general.

The appellants contended that the requirement of "due process" meant that taxation must be for a public purpose, and that mills, elevators, banks, and home building were by their nature private enterprises which under no conditions could be made public, even by constitutional amendment. There was active questioning of Young from the bench, after it had been twice suggested that he engage in less oratory on revolution and tell the court what the laws he was contesting were about.

"Why shouldn't the state operate a bank?" Young was asked.

"It might properly do so for bona fide banking purposes of its treasury," he responded, "but this bank is started merely to finance these industries."

"Well," replied Justice McReynolds, "and why should not the state go into business?"

"Why, that is taking money from the taxpayer without due process," answered Young.

"That is merely words," responded the justice sharply. "We are interested in reasons."

Mr. Pike, for the defense, argued that the state had full authority over its own affairs except as limited by the United States or state constitutions. The state constitution had been amended to make the various enterprises possible, and the people had repeatedly approved them. To invalidate the actions the court would have to find a specific surrender of the power of the state and its people to make decisions of this nature. "The people," Pike concluded, "have full authority, and the people of North Dakota have spoken." [41]

On June 1 decisions were handed down in both cases. In a memorandum opinion, the court agreed with Judge Amidon in dismissing the "42 taxpayers' suit" for want of jurisdiction, noting that on its merits the case was nearly identical with *Green v. Frazier*.[42] In the latter case a unanimous court held, in an opinion that was to become a landmark in American constitutional law, that since the people, the legislature, and the highest court of the state were agreed that the acts in question were for a public purpose, there was no deprivation of property without due process of law within the meaning of the Fourteenth Amendment:

. . . if the State sees fit to enter upon such enterprises as are here involved, with the sanction of its constitution, its legislature, and its people, we are not prepared to say that it is within the authority of this Court, in enforcing the observance of the Fourteenth Amendment, to set aside such actions by judicial decision.[43]

While many persons may have disliked the result, they could hardly argue with the fact that, as the *Cincinnati Post* put it, "the decision merely permits the people of a State to do what the majority wants done, and which is not in conflict with the Federal Constitution." [44] Whether or not the I.V.A. ever expected to win its suit, delay had at least been accomplished. Although more delay was occasioned by a shortage of cement, caused by a nationwide strike, by early summer construction on the state mill and elevator was at long last under way.

The decision of the Supreme Court gave impetus to the League's primary campaign. Enthusiasm was again stirred, the legal blocks had been cleared away, and the last and originally most important enterprise was about to begin. Campaign techniques had changed little, except that Townley now toured the state by airplane, the very novelty of which perhaps helped to draw crowds. Walter Davenport reported overdramatically: "From roundup to roundup he flew, swooping from the skies upon startled audiences, who, properly coached by livelier imaginations, hailed Mr. Townley as a winged messenger from heaven. Gabriel over the wheat fields. Michael putting Wall Street to the sword." [45]

The crowds were good, but for the most part they were slightly smaller, and the old crusading spirit was less in evidence. League-elected state officials, now in power, were forced to defend themselves and their record—no longer could they simply carry the attack. Moreover, to many it seemed that the fight had been won. The League program had been enacted into law, and much of it was already in operation. Why continue to pay dues and to spend valuable time in political activity? Things would probably go along reasonably well whoever was in office. This, to be sure, was not yet by any means a general attitude and most Leaguers were convinced of the need for holding the ground that had been gained, but it had made its appearance and the League was becoming aware that maintaining a high level of support was likely to be fully as great a problem as surmounting the original obstacles.

William Langer, moreover, was a different type of opponent. Whereas others had usually attacked both the League and its program, Langer loudly proclaimed his undying support of the original principles of the League and the enterprises established thereunder, though the support of the anti-League newspapers detracted somewhat from his claims. The "corrupt leadership" was the object of his attack, as he reiterated in speech after speech: "When I'm elected governor of North Dakota, the day after I am inaugurated there will not be a socialist left in the employ of the state and I will wire the President 'North Dakota is again back in the United States.'" [46]

The voters were also to have before them on referendum the state sheriff, investigation committee, and absent voters laws, plus the initiated law prohibiting the public display of red or black flags. Though it contended that there was nothing wrong with the laws of the special session and that the "anti-red-flag law" was quite unnecessary, the League made no significant campaign on these issues, devoting itself to the contest for offices. The organization was far from united on the laws at any rate—Judge Robinson, for example, had commented that the "smelling committee" savored of the Spanish Inquisition—and they were not worth a battle.

The issue of the election was clear to the *Grand Forks Herald*: "Shall A. C. Townley continue to rule North Dakota?" Throughout June it carried a daily series of articles in a page one box entitled "Will North Dakota Succumb to Socialized Schools and Churches, Socialized Business and Farms?" Meanwhile the I.V.A. was carrying on a tremendous speaking campaign. One of the most colorful of the troupe was the Reverend Allen O. Birchenough from St. Thomas, billed as the "fighting parson," a spellbinder who rarely talked for less than two hours at a stretch. "The fight, men," he would conclude in booming tones, "is between Jesus Christ and Karl Marx; between the philosophy

of the Christian religion and the materialistic philosophy of Socialism
. . . between Peter, James and John, the old apostles, and Trotzky,
Townley and Walter Thomas Mills." [47]

If Birchenough's analysis was correct, North Dakota apparently favored the new apostles, for although the opposition papers, seemingly
unable to learn by experience, on July 1 headlined a Langer victory,
Lynn Frazier once again emerged victorious with a lead of 5414 votes.
Almost all the races were extremely close, Lemke and Poindexter having majorities of only 2400 and 2700 respectively over Gallagher and
Kositzky. Hall was more successful than the other two "rebels," defeating Cahill by 4500, while Steen edged out Walker for treasurer by
a mere 881 votes. John N. Hagan and Minnie Nielson, on opposite sides
of the fence, proved to be the best vote-getters, leading their opponents
by 10,000 votes. The League nominated candidates for all other state
offices except one railroad commissioner. It was less successful, however,
in the congressional races, only Sinclair winning nomination; John Baer
at last lost to Olger Burtness by 2460 votes. [48]

Senator A. J. Gronna, a Roosevelt Progressive, had been instrumental
in deposing the McKenzie ring. In revenge, when the League endorsed
Dr. Ladd for the Senate seat, the McKenzie-McCumber forces put up
Frank White, later treasurer of the United States, who ran on his war
record as an American Legion aspirant, and diverted enough votes to
ensure the nomination of Ladd. [49] The I.V.A. thenceforth insisted that
the League and McKenzie were working in complete alliance, though
most of the evidence adduced would not bear too close inspection. It
was still a case of the McKenzie group liking the Progressives least, as
later events were to prove.

Although the League claimed that the results constituted perhaps its
greatest victory considering the terrific fight which had been made
against it, and it was true that Frazier's vote was higher than in 1918
although his majority was much less, yet it was obvious that the I.V.A.
had made extremely significant progress. The three referred laws were
defeated by majorities of from ten to sixteen thousand, while the "anti-
red-flag law" carried 74,634 to 41,009. [50] There had been no contest
in the Democratic primary, and with the I.V.A. newspapers continuously urging Democrats to vote in the Republican primaries O'Connor
received only about one third of the 9134 votes needed to keep the

party legally alive. The statute on this matter was, however, shortly declared unconstitutional, and he stayed on the ballot without the necessity of filing as an independent.[51]

The League remained a relatively much weaker force in the other states in which it had been organizing, and the degree and nature of political action in each of course depended on the local situation. Significant victories were scored in the Democratic primaries of Colorado and Montana. In the latter state Burton K. Wheeler had a two to one plurality in gaining the nomination for governor. In Wisconsin the League secured the cooperation of the LaFollette forces and was generally successful with its candidates for major state offices and the Congress in the Republican primary.

In South Dakota a change in the primary law forced abandonment of customary tactics, and the League had to operate under the cumbersome name "Nonpartisan League and Labor Party." In Idaho and Washington also it operated as a separate party, and its endorsed candidates therefore faced no primary contests. A failure in the Nebraska Republican primaries was followed by the nomination of an independent slate by petition, despite very dim hopes for success. In all instances legislative candidates were endorsed wherever the level of organization seemed to warrant it, and a good percentage were subsequently nominated. In Kansas and Texas the state organizations confined themselves to the legislative contests. There were beginnings of alliances with organized labor in all these states, with well-established cooperative agreements existing in Colorado, Idaho, and Montana.[52]

In all states where the League had had any significant measure of success, there were immediate movements to line up Republican-Democratic coalitions in opposition. This was of course an obvious situation in North Dakota and Minnesota, but it met with varying success in other states. In Montana Senator Walsh and the defeated candidate for governor both backed Wheeler and his running mates, but Senator H. F. Myers later announced that he would vote the Republican ticket. There were limited actions along this line in Wisconsin, but no really significant developments; an attempt to get together an anti-League Republican convention failed completely.[53] These coalitions had, of course, taken time to "jell" in North Dakota, and in the other states the opposition forces had not yet gotten themselves completely adjusted to the idea of living with a new political power which was actually strong enough to elect its candidates to office.

The Nonpartisan League did not formally participate in the convention in Chicago the week of July 12 which formed the national Farmer-Labor party and nominated Parley Parker Christensen for President and Max Hayes for Vice President. A few Leaguers were present and seated as "fraternal delegates," and the Nonpartisan League party of South Dakota was represented, but there were no official delegates from the national organization. It was rumored that the League planned to affiliate with the new third party, just as similar rumors had been prevalent regarding the National party in 1918, but they were promptly denied. The League had no intention of abandoning its successful system and turning itself over to a poorly organized group which could not even achieve a show of unity at its founding convention and had not the slightest chance of success. The *Leader* did, however, find itself in general sympathy with the platform of the new party, remarking that while the hopes of most of the delegates for a LaFollette ticket were not realized, the groundwork had been laid "for the ultimate formation of a truly progressive third political party in the United States." While thus holding out some hope for the future of the Farmer-Labor party, the current position of the League was made quite clear:

. . . the League has never and never will merge, amalgamate or affiliate with any other organization or party. It might be that the League would indorse candidates running on a third party ticket, but . . . it would be only in the sense that it has in the past indorsed other party candidates . . .[54]

As a matter of fact the League never did endorse Christensen or even recommend him to the membership. It took no position upon the presidency other than to pronounce "a plague on both your houses" in regard to the major party candidates:

A question frequently asked these days is: "Which is the better man, Harding or Cox?" The best answer is along the old Yankee line of answering one question with another: "What difference does it make?" . . . Have either of these men shown, by any of their campaign speeches, the slightest grasp of the problems confronting the United States today? . . . Don't think that this election isn't an important one. It is. But the chief importance doesn't lie in who is elected president of the

United States. The chief importance lies in who is elected governor in the various League states.[55]

Fifteen hundred Leaguers were in the Minneapolis auditorium on July 7 to decide the future course of the state organization now that another primary defeat had been sustained. Expenses of campaigning in many states had been high and the national organization was in no position to bear the burden of a second major effort in Minnesota in one year. At about this time, in fact, the National Executive Committee ordered that because of high costs the national and state *Leaders* be published biweekly instead of weekly, alternating with each other so that members would receive a paper each week. Townley spoke bluntly to the assembled delegates, asking them at the outset if they wanted to quit. The response was a thundered "No!" In that case, he said, there must be plenty of hard work and money: "This is not going to be a sixteen dollar fight." His impassioned pleas brought forth dozens of emotional pledges of devotion, often from men unused to public utterance, and many a farmer caught up in the swelling spirit of self-sacrifice came forward with brimming eyes to contribute hard-earned savings to the cause.[56]

The convention readily agreed to file by petition the same candidates that had run in the primaries, though subsequently Miss Anderson, then qualified to run, was returned to her original position as candidate for secretary of state. Cyrus M. King, who had filed on the Farmer-Labor ticket to keep it "alive," was importuned by various anti-Leaguers to stay in the race, but he withdrew and stumped for Shipstead. Those who had run in the primary as Republicans now filed as independents, but Miss Anderson filed as a Farmer-Laborite, as did congressional candidates in the first, fifth, and tenth districts. All other congressional candidates, now including Charles A. Lindbergh in the sixth district, were independents except Carss and Keller, who of course were on the Democratic and Republican tickets respectively.[57]

In the effort to woo the rural vote, leading anti-League Republicans in Minnesota suddenly became ardent proponents of cooperative marketing enterprises, while the Sound Government Association played at the theme of "socialism" with all the stops out. Three years later Harry C. Wilbur, general manager of the Minnesota Employers' Association who had served as head of the Sound Government Association in 1920, testified before a Minnesota Senate investigating committee that the organization had spent approximately $225,000 to defeat the League in the 1920 campaign. The bulk of this sum, contributed by "certain public spirited men" for "educational purposes," went for the printing and circulation of "anti-Socialist" literature. Since the money had not been used in behalf of any candidate, said Mr. Wilbur, presumably with tongue in cheek, its expenditure could not be subject to the corrupt practices act. The organization, he insisted with fascinating logic, was "non-political and non-factional" since it included both Republicans and Democrats, and its fight "was directed solely on . . . the Nonpartisan League." [58]

The Twin Cities newspapers pleaded continually with the Democrats to support Preus. The Hodgson candidacy was hopeless, they said, and the Democrats stood as arbiters between the two Republican factions. The *Minneapolis Journal* was certain that if the situation were reversed all good Republicans would now be supporting Hodgson:

There is no real issue here dividing Republicans and Democrats. The great issue is between Preus with his sane and responsible program of state development on one side, and Shipstead with his Nonpartisan League program of state socialism, higher taxes, and a whole flock of visionary schemes on the other. [59]

Throughout the state huge posters proclaimed "Help Save Minnesota from Socialism" and "Don't Exchange Old Glory for the Red Flag of Socialism." Full-page advertisements screamed from the newspapers. As election day neared, Jacob Preus was still on his original theme, tugging at the heartstrings with his plea: "Let us not permit the destruction of property rights; let us not permit the destruction of religion; let us not cease to sing 'Home, Sweet Home'." [60]

In North Dakota the I.V.A., after losing in its primary bid, promptly endorsed J. F. T. O'Connor and the other Democratic candidates for offices for which Leaguers had secured the Republican nomination, and in several cases Democrats who would have been contesting with I.V.A. Republicans considerately withdrew. The resources of the "Joint Campaign Committee" were then thrown behind the entire "anti-Townley ticket." It was also agreed to initiate five measures to be voted upon at the November election: making optional the deposit of local government funds in the Bank of North Dakota; providing for an audit of the state enterprises; specifying that only items that state and county officials were required to publish need be placed in official newspapers; restoring duties to the state superintendent of public instruction; and altering the procedure of the Bank of North Dakota in making loans to individuals.[61]

A special League convention at Fargo subsequently endorsed candidates to run as independents for those offices which had been lost in the primary. The selections included Alfhild Alfson, daughter of a Bismarck minister, for secretary of state; Ole Kaldor, treasurer of Traill County, for state treasurer; F. G. Hildebrand, president of a farmers' bank at Kulm for railroad commissioner; John Baer, "drafted" after previously stating that he would not run, for first district congressman; and Ole Olson, state senator from Eddy County, for second district congressman.[62]

The League organization was rocked with more internal difficulties in mid-August when J. R. Waters and J. W. Brinton, both of whom had in effect been eased out in the process of the long overdue "housecleaning," issued savage attacks on the League leadership, principally Townley and Lemke. The reputations of these gentlemen were such that the I.V.A. could scarcely take them to its bosom, but the anti-League newspapers gave a vast amount of space to their claims of misappropriations of League funds by Townley and Lemke. The *Grand Forks Herald* subsequently published a series of articles by Brinton entitled "A. C. Townley, Dreamer, Promoter, Boss Politician," carefully indicating that it did not vouch for the truth of what he said.[63]

Townley and Lemke retaliated in kind, and it seems likely that the League papers did not help the cause by publishing numerous stories of the nefarious activities of Brinton and Waters. It was perhaps well enough to disown them, but the fact remained that higher officials presumably bore some of the responsibility for the acts of men who had been with the organization almost from the beginning, frequently in high-level positions. The *North Dakota Leader* shortly published letters and telegrams from Brinton to Townley indicating that he had sought League endorsement for Congress and had become incensed when he was not even considered. It also printed a letter from Waters to the state manager of the League threatening to "start fireworks" if not given $1000.[64]

The *Leader* announced with more bravado than accuracy that the attacks of these men were "causing amusement among League farmers." [65] The fact was that affairs of this sort were extremely damaging, even though they did not shake the faith of the truly stanch devotees of the organization. The defection of individuals like Teigen, Maxwell, and Quigley was of relatively little significance, but the Langer-Hall-Kositzky break had had strong repercussions, and it could not be denied that Waters and Brinton had long been high in the councils of the League. Whether or not their charges were true was in many ways of less importance than the simple fact that major rifts were occurring in the organization, and repeated similar charges from many sources began to have the effect of creating doubts if not convictions.

The League campaign was based largely on claims of successes for the enterprises already established, and a request that the League administration be given a chance to prove itself now that the entire program was at last under way. Its campaign was vigorous, but much of the old fire was lacking. A. C. Townley had been in North Dakota but little, though he made a brief speaking tour the latter part of October, among other things reportedly promising townspeople in some localities that if they beat the League candidates he would return to North Dakota and organize farmers' boycotts which would ruin local businessmen.[66] The I.V.A., on the other hand, sensed victory in the air, and by November 1 was ready to forecast a 10,000-vote majority, perhaps 15,000 to 20,000 if the weather were good.[67]

The farmers of North Dakota, however, were not ready to sell the League short. O'Connor held a commanding lead for the first twenty-four hours, but as the returns came in from rural areas and the iron-clad League third district it rapidly melted away. The League elected every one of its candidates who had secured the Republican nomination, but none of its independents. Complete control of the Industrial Commission was particularly important. Ladd was elected to the Senate with a majority of more than 42,000, but majorities for the state offices were for the most part between five and ten thousand, Frazier winning over O'Connor by 117,118 to 112,488.[68] All five initiated measures carried by majorities ranging from 7000 to 16,000; the highest majority was received by the law providing for an audit of state industries and the lowest by that making deposits of local government funds in the Bank of North Dakota no longer mandatory.[69]

At the same time that the newspaper law was being amended, the voters were electing official papers for the first time. Although League papers had had the designation for seventeen months and thus presumably possessed a considerable advantage, only thirty-three survived, and twenty were defeated. Whereas after the system had first been put into effect in 1919 a number of non-League papers had failed, following the 1920 election there were from one to five sales, suspensions, mergers, or foreclosures of League papers monthly for more than a year.[70]

In Minnesota the League salvaged nothing by its post-primary efforts. The vote for governor was Preus 415,805, Shipstead 281,402, and Hodgson 81,293, and the results of the contests for the other state offices were not greatly different. Oscar Keller was an easy winner in the fourth district congressional race, but all other League congressional candidates were defeated, O. J. Kvale in the seventh and W. L. Carss in the eighth by narrow margins.[71] The Democratic vote for Preus was again highly significant, but here as in other states one of the most important factors was the feminine vote, strong in the cities and weak in the rural areas, which both sides conceded went heavily in favor of conservative candidates. Nevertheless, while the total Minnesota vote increased 109 per cent over 1918, Shipstead's vote increased 151 per cent over that polled by Evans. Evans had had 29 per cent of the total vote, while Shipstead received 35 per cent.[72]

In Wisconsin John J. Blaine was elected governor, George Comings lieutenant governor, and Elmer Hall secretary of state, while five congressmen favorable to the League were sent to Washington. Though anti-League publications claimed that these were really LaFollette candidates, the fact is that they were both, and Blaine throughout the campaign had stood unequivocally upon the League platform. His plurality over the Democratic candidate, McCoy, was 118,501.[73]

In no other states were the League state tickets successful; even Montana and Colorado, normally Democratic states where the League had taken over the Democratic column, were lost in the nationwide Republican landslide. However, both Wheeler and Collins, the gubernatorial candidates, ran well ahead of Cox. In Washington and South Dakota the state Farmer-Labor parties were placed in the same column with the national Farmer-Labor party, yet in both cases the former ran second to the Republican party. The direct primaries were saved in referendums in Nebraska and Montana, where the legislatures had endeavored to block the League by abolishing or severely restricting the primary system.[74]

From the standpoint of actually securing the League program, of course, the control of state legislatures was more significant than the election of state officials, and here the picture was perhaps even more dismal. Representation in most states was not materially changed, and in Wisconsin it had in fact increased, but it was in North Dakota that the axe had fallen. In the seventeenth legislative assembly the League was to control the Senate by one vote, while the I.V.A. would dominate the House by a four-vote margin, though it varied from one to five on different measures.* This situation, combined with the fact that the nation was wallowing further and further into an economic depression, clearly presaged a stormy voyage ahead.

* The representation by states is given by Henry G. Teigan, "The National Nonpartisan League," *American Labor Year Book, 1921–1922*, p. 426, as follows:

	Senate	House
North Dakota	25	54
Minnesota	11	33
Wisconsin	6	31
Nebraska	2	16
Montana	5	5
Idaho	4	2
South Dakota	2	5
Colorado	3	3
Washington	1	2

A Legislature without Legislation

GOVERNOR FRAZIER eyed the composition of the North Dakota legislature and made his biennial message concise. No new major legislation was needed, he said, although it would be desirable to improve the rural schools, raise the soldiers' bonus levy to one mill, provide for state operation of a lignite mine to furnish fuel for state institutions, and memorialize the Congress to develop a St. Lawrence seaway, to permit the states to regulate interstate corporations doing intrastate business, and to guarantee an honest market in farm products. The shorter the session the better, he suspected:

During the past four years the legislative assemblies of North Dakota have enacted much progressive legislation . . . There is but little new legislation needed at this time. Not laws, but cooperation and an earnest, helpful endeavor of all our people to test and try out that which we have, is what is needed . . . It is our duty, as public officials, to economize and conserve. Needless legislation means needless expense. The greatest service you can confer is by making essential adjustments and speedily providing for the necessary appropriations and then adjourning.[1]

The House, however, was in no mood to temporize, and after electing L. L. Twichell as speaker it promptly defeated a joint resolution from the Senate which would have provided for a joint committee of ten to plan major legislation, particularly with reference to the industrial program. The I.V.A.'s House majority appeared to be two votes, since one representative, Lawrence Bjorge of Grand Forks County, who claimed to be independent of both factions, voted with the League on

303

most matters other than organization. The League's twenty-five to twenty-four majority in the Senate, plus the vote of the lieutenant governor if needed, was threatened when the election of Gust Wog, from the thirty-ninth district in the western part of the state, was contested on the grounds of irregularities in the process of assistance to non-English-speaking voters by election officials. The vote in the Senate on the seating of Wog was a straight factional affair, with Lieutenant Governor Wood casting the deciding ballot.[2]

Immediately after the 1920 election Arthur LeSueur, who had been a League attorney and adviser for several years, and was now practicing in Minneapolis, renewed his battle against control of the state enterprises by a commission of state officials. Opening his campaign on November 30 with a thirty-one-page letter to the governor and all members of the legislature, LeSueur argued as he had in 1919 when the Industrial Commission was created that the state industries must be "kept out of politics." If left in the hands of a board constituted as at present, subject to turnover every two years, the industries, he said, would become political footballs and were bound to fail. Instead, the present Industrial Commission should be given authority to appoint boards of directors for the bank, the mill and elevator, and so on, to have long, overlapping terms but to be subject to popular recall. Only thus, he contended, could a stable management by full-time experts be secured.[3]

It was natural that such action by a former League official should receive widespread publicity in the anti-League press, especially since Townley and LeSueur were at loggerheads. Nevertheless, his plan received a large measure of support from both Leaguers and I.V.A.'s, but the legislature, with other things on its mind, took no action.

For the first three weeks both houses were virtually marking time, waiting for reports to be submitted by the Bishop-Brissman Company, a Twin Cities auditing firm. The old State Auditing Board of Langer, Hall, and Kositzky, under the provisions of the law initiated at the general election, had engaged the Bishop-Brissman Company to audit the state enterprises, but since the Industrial Commission was unable and unwilling to pay the cost out of its appropriation it was necessary for I.V.A. sympathizers to raise $12,000 for the purpose. Though the full audit was nowhere near complete, the legislature received partial reports on January 25 which covered the Bank of North Dakota and unfinished statements on the Drake mill and the Home Building Association. The auditors disagreed with some of the policies of the Bank and were highly critical of several of the statutes relating to the industrial program, but they found nothing seriously wrong with the Bank. Even though the reports were not complete on the Drake mill and the Home Building Association, however, it was evident that here all was not well. The *Grand Forks Herald* announced that the Bishop-Brissman reports indicated gross mismanagement, but conceded that there was no implication of dishonesty.[4]

The Equitable Audit Company, which always handled all League auditing and could be counted upon not to publicize unfavorable information, had been working on the same three institutions for some time, but its complete report was never published. The *Leader*'s account of the report, which covered the period up to January 1, 1921, reiterated claims of profits and indicated that everything was in order.[5] The League leaders and the Industrial Commission, however, knew that such was not the case, and toward the end of January it was announced that J. J. McGovern's resignation as manager of the Mill and Elevator Association had been accepted, and that William Anderson, as secretary to the Industrial Commission, was temporarily in charge.[6]

Since the Bishop-Brissman report was incomplete and nothing incriminating had been found concerning the Bank of North Dakota, the House voted by a majority of one to conduct a special investigation. A nine-member committee was appointed for that purpose, of which three were Leaguers, but after sitting for several days the three withdrew, terming the hearings a "mockery" of an impartial investigation.[7]

The Industrial Commission instructed all officials and employees to cooperate with and assist the committee, but directed them not to turn over "papers, books, files, or other papers" to the committee except upon order of the commission, since compliance with a demand for such material would stop all operations and destroy the industries. The committee was to be given full access to the records in the offices in which they were kept, but it was carefully specified that changes, alterations, or removals must not be permitted.[8] To counteract the efforts of the House, the League-controlled Senate promptly established its own investigating committee, which examined the Bishop-

Brissman Company as well as the state industries, and the major interest of the session centered around the two investigations.

Meanwhile, economic difficulties continued to multiply.

A gradual price recession had begun in May 1920, and prices continued to drop steadily. The cost of producing that year's crop had been high, but by harvest time prices were below cost, despite the fact that there was no oversupply. Both the Bank of North Dakota and most local bankers urged the farmers to hold onto their wheat as long as possible in the expectation of a subsequent price rise, and a so-called sellers' strike began. Nevertheless, the price kept dropping. Credit conditions rapidly became extremely serious, yet the farmers by now could not meet their obligations at the banks even if they sold their crops. For four consecutive years the western part of the state particularly had had poor crops, and most farmers were heavily in debt. Bank after bank began to close its doors, and in the face of this precarious financial situation the law had been initiated which permitted treasurers of local government units to deposits funds wherever they wished.

One of the functions of the Bank of North Dakota was to render temporary help to financially distressed areas of the state by the deposit of public funds in local banks. It was the practice to redeposit the great bulk of all funds in the sections from which they came, with the rest distributed on the basis of need. Operating on this principle the Bank had deposited in the western part of the state more than $1,000,000 over the amount that had come from that area.[9] If large amounts were withdrawn from the Bank of North Dakota as a result of the initiated law, it would be forced to call in these redeposits and dozens of banks that were continuing to carry loans to farmers on the strength of this help in "tiding them over" would be ruined.

In order to forestall a "run" on the Bank by hostile local treasurers, the Industrial Commission, immediately after the initiated law went into effect, interpreted it by resolution as not being retroactive. In other words local treasurers might in the future deposit elsewhere if they so desired, but they could not withdraw funds already deposited with the Bank of North Dakota simply in order to deposit them in another bank, and the Bank was instructed not to honor checks for wholesale withdrawals.[10] But, since many local treasurers deposited new funds in other banks while at the same time continuing to draw checks on the Bank of North Dakota for current expenditures, the Bank was gradually forced to recall some of its redeposits. As a result eighteen private banks closed in the first three weeks.[11]

Part of the reason for the strain on the Bank was the difficulty encountered in marketing the bonds for the state industries, which had forced the Bank to make large loans to the industries in order that they might begin operations. There was genuine fear on the part of the large financial houses that the enterprises and the League regime might be unstable, but some were also strongly averse to aiding and abetting these "socialistic schemes." In September of 1919 Wm. R. Compton and Company of Chicago had agreed to purchase $3,000,000 worth of bonds, subject to approval of counsel for the syndicate. The counsel, however, advised against the purchase until the suits testing the constitutionality of the industries were finally settled, and the company indicated in its letter to the Industrial Commission that it had been given to understand that the fight against the League would be kept up, making it difficult for the syndicate to dispose of the bonds.[12] By the time the suits had been decided the recession had set in, and the situation became even more difficult.

Having decided that recommendations were getting nowhere, the Industrial Commission passed a resolution instructing the Bank of North Dakota to discontinue until further notice honoring the checks of local treasurers who had ceased depositing with the Bank. The reasons given were the continued practice of withdrawing funds for deposit elsewhere and the fact that many local banks were unable to meet the demands of the Bank for redeposit money.[13] With the first of the new year the Industrial Commission also ordered the temporary suspension of work on the state mill and elevator and Home Building Association projects, because the initiated law had "crippled" the Bank.[14]

On January 7 the North Dakota Bankers Association, which had previously pledged cooperation in this crisis, offered to "undertake to sell" North Dakota bonds to eastern financiers, but it specified certain conditions: (1) that the Bank of North Dakota's operations be limited to state, state institution, and state industry finances, farm loans, and farm loan bonds; (2) that a new law be secured making every "going" bank a public depository for local governments and fixing a required rate of interest; (3) that assurance be provided that the industrial program would be limited to the Bank of North Dakota, the Drake mill, and the Grand Forks mill and elevator, and that no state indebtedness other than that authorized for those enterprises be created during the term of the current administration; and (4) that the Industrial Commission confer with attorneys for the bond buyers and grant any needed orders or secure any needed legislation to make the bonds more readily marketable.[15]

The Industrial Commission, however, was not yet ready to admit that it was this "hard up," and it haughtily rejected the offer, insisting that the bonds were good and could be sold without abandoning the "farmers' programs":

The proposition . . . cannot honorably be considered by the commission for the reason that it is a plain attempt on the part of financial interests, presumably Wall Street financiers, to dictate the political, financial, and industrial policies of the State of North Dakota, and requiring a surrender of the sovereign powers of the state to manage its own affairs . . .[16]

The House of Representatives thereupon promptly passed a bitterly contested resolution calling upon the governor and the Industrial Commission either to provide an immediate remedy for the state's financial condition or to explain in reasonable fashion why the bankers' offer had been refused.[17] Aside from the political animus behind this move, it was to a degree evidence of a tendency common in North Dakota at the time, because of the struggle which was in progress, to overlook the fact that the economic crisis was nationwide and that North Dakota was on the whole no worse off than other states.

The fact that the bankers had not really become "converts" was further evidenced by the fact that shortly after the refusal the secretary of the association gave out publicity casting doubt on the soundness of the state sinking funds, and the annual association convention in Grand Forks July 2 issued a broadside stating their position:

That their [the bankers'] indorsement and support of the sale of the state bonds then being offered by the administration, was in the belief, and with the assurance that the administration and the people responsible for it had recovered from the financial debauch of the past four years, had abandoned the extravagant and impractical and socialistic theories and plans which propaganda had so persistently and insidiously instilled into their minds, and which were responsible for the wrecking of the state's credit.[18]

308

The fact that less than a year before the same organization had assigned depressed wheat prices as the reason for the plight of the state seemed to be overlooked. The League insisted that no one ever gave the assurances claimed and that they would not even be considered. Moreover, it said, if the Bank of North Dakota had wanted to be ruthless in carrying out the results of the I.V.A.-initiated law, it could simply have called in all public funds, met its demands, and let the private banks smash. Instead it "saved these loan-sharks in the banking business from the results of their own supreme, brainless folly"—for which it was then denounced, despite the fact that the private banks at the time had pleaded for help.[19]

Since it was obvious that the House investigating committee was seeking political ammunition and that despite all efforts the level of public deposits in the Bank of North Dakota was continuing to drop, the Industrial Commission on February 10 announced that it would be forced to collect the approximately $3,000,000 in redeposits and overdue loans from local banks. Many, of course, were unable to pay, but in that case it was assumed that at least part of the blame for the crisis could be placed on the local bankers. At this point the bankers hastily urged Twin Cities investment firms to handle the North Dakota bonds, and a conference between their representatives and state officials was arranged.

The Minneapolis bankers offered to market $6,000,000 worth of bonds, but stipulated much the same conditions that the Bankers Association had previously proposed. Some League leaders were tempted to agree in part, but Townley failed to convince the League caucus that compromise was necessary, and at any rate the I.V.A. hinted that it would block approval of any agreements in the legislature unless Lemke were to resign, the Bank go out of business, and control of the Industrial Commission be transferred to I.V.A. state officials. If the bonds were purchased, it was indicated, recall proceedings would be started and the state kept in such a turmoil that it would be difficult for anyone to dispose of the bonds. The conference therefore ended without agreement, the Industrial Commission still stoutly maintaining that the bonds could and would be sold.[20]

Following the breakdown of these negotiations the Bank commenced two new programs in addition to the recall of deposits as a part of its attempt to ride out the crisis successfully. It started a big campaign to secure individual deposits, both checking and savings, from within as well as outside the state, and then launched a drive to sell small denomination bonds to individual investors throughout the country. Citizens of North Dakota were circularized, widespread advertising was utilized, and Chicago and New York offices were eventually established. Agents were put on the road at salaries from $50 to $150 per week; plus commissions and expenses, much as if it were League memberships being sold. The Public Ownership League, which naturally had an interest in the success of the North Dakota enterprises, volunteered its services and devoted much time and effort to both campaigns.

On February 23, Governor Frazier went to Washington, D.C., to lay the case before the executive council of the American Federation of Labor, citing the labor record of the League-controlled legislature as reason for aid. The conference formally recommended to all labor organizations that they give "friendly consideration" to the purchase of North Dakota bonds, and the Illinois Federation of Labor later went further by placing sizable time deposits in the Bank of North Dakota. July 23 was proclaimed by the governor as "North Dakota Bond Selling Day," the active work of various clubs was enlisted, provision was made whereby bonds might be purchased at 10 per cent down and the balance in October, and canvassing was undertaken much in the fashion of the war bond drives.[21] All this activity was reasonably successful, to the extent of five or six million dollars (the exact amount was never stated), but it constituted an expensive method of selling bonds, and while enough was secured to carry the Bank along, major sales were still badly needed.

Meanwhile, banks were not the only enterprises failing as the depression progressed. The *Grand Forks American* had suffered an advertising boycott from the beginning in its predominantly anti-League area, and it suspended publication on January 3, less than eighteen months after it had been established. Four days later a receiver was appointed, and though the stockholders voted a 10 per cent assessment on capital stock and laid plans to resume publication, the new building and much expensive equipment were ultimately sold in a foreclosure sale at a fraction of the original cost. In mid-March a receiver was appointed for the Consumers' United Stores Company, which went into bankruptcy owing $16,000 to the Drake mill, $100,000 to the Scandinavian-American Bank of Fargo, and various amounts to a number of other

League banks.[22] Several League weeklies and other subsidiary enterprises also experienced difficulties, and it can be safely assumed that many who lost investments in that manner became less steadfast League supporters.

In January a League convention in Bismarck nominated ten men from which the membership was to choose a new five-man state committee. All were farmers and most were members of the state legislature, but the *Grand Forks Herald* contended that the most radical Socialist elements controlled the nominations.[23] As the result of a mail vote conducted by the *North Dakota Leader*, Walter Maddock, R. H. Walker, Ole Kaldor, Christ Levang, and A. A. Liederbach were selected.

Meanwhile, with the investigations stealing the show, the legislature remained deadlocked on all major legislation. The House was particularly turbulent. Parliamentary wrangling was standard fare, and the sergeant-at-arms was frequently called upon to quiet the members, who at times almost came to blows. The Senate passed an appropriation for a state-owned lignite mine, and the House countered with a bill to change the personnel of the Industrial Commission to the secretary of state, the treasurer, and the commissioner of agriculture and labor, which would thus make it I.V.A. controlled at least for the present.[24] Senate bills of any importance were either killed or studiously ignored in the House, and the favor was of course returned by the upper chamber. The Senate passed sizable appropriations for the various state departments, and the House slashed many of them down to almost nothing.

I.V.A. members of the House took particular pleasure in cutting out entirely the appropriation for the Immigration Department, which they charged was nothing more than a League propaganda agency.[25] The department claimed to have published and distributed more than 350,000 bulletins and other pieces of literature descriptive of the state and its opportunities for immigrants. In addition it had published numerous articles in magazines and newspapers, and had maintained twelve to fifteen deputies in adjoining states who promoted immigration through lectures and the use of motion pictures.[26] Ultimately a compromise was reached whereby the department secured a meager appropriation which reduced its functions largely to correspondence.

When the new attorney general had taken the oath he discovered that very little of the previously slashed appropriation for his office, which was presumably to last through June 30, remained. Lemke, therefore, laid claim to having collected $1,233,880 in back taxes from the railroads and sought an additional appropriation of $12,000 to fight other such cases. The request, as might be expected, met with well-restrained enthusiasm in the House and never left committee.[27]

As the allotted time for the session came to an end, the House and Senate investigating committees filed their reports. The Senate report commended the Industrial Commission and spoke favorably of the condition of the state industries. Expressing its preference for the findings of the Equitable Audit Company, the committee attacked the accuracy of the Bishop-Brissman report, and indicated that certain discharged League employees (Brinton and Waters, who had given much testimony to the House committee) were seeking revenge by attempting to discredit the farmers' program. A minority report by Senators Murphy and Ployhar condemned the majority statement as a "cover up," pointing out that the investigation had been largely conducted by attorneys for the Industrial Commission, which was supposedly being investigated. The committee, they said, had devoted itself for the most part to endeavoring to impeach the testimony of the witnesses who had appeared before the House committee, rather than investigating the state industries. The report, nevertheless, did contain a considerable amount of constructive argument, whatever the validity of its information.[28]

The House committee report was concerned almost entirely with what it had set out to prove, that "political considerations" had entered into the management of the state's industries. A fairly good case was made out for this contention, but the analyses of the various industries were rather brief, and comprehensive statements were not available for nearly ten months. The committee somewhat overplayed its hand in a set of conclusions designed for future campaign documents, which were embellished with considerable invective:

These impractical theorists have launched the state into an orgy of financial excesses and delirium of socialistic experimentation, born in hate and nurtured in prejudice . . .

North Dakota is a pitiful object lesson to the world as to what greed, dishonesty and faithlessness to a public trust, combined with misguided theories of government, can accomplish . . .

The committee recommends that the state confine its business activities to those matters which are, in their nature at least, quasi-governmental in character, that it awake from its socialistic dream of empire . . . that it brand as "quack" the remedies for industrial injustice that have been recommended as the panacea for all ills . . . that it divorce itself from the false prophets . . .[29]

While the House committee was preparing its attack, the Industrial Commission was paying $1740 per week for full-page advertisements in newspapers around the state defending the industrial program and charging that the House investigation was all part of a "political conspiracy to wreck the state." The advertisements carried such titles as "Every Business in State Is Endangered" (by the conspiracy), "State Bank Stands Sound as Gibraltar," and "Where Blame Rests for Credit Collapse," while across the bottom of this last were the words "Don't Let Any One Induce You to Sign Any Recall Petition—We Have Troubles Enough—See!"[30]

Although the Senate refused to agree to a House bill for appropriation of $12,000 to pay the cost of the Bishop-Brissman audit, it did approve payment of the expense of the House investigation committee in return for similar consideration for the expense of its committee.[31] The House would have been happy to continue its investigations after the end of the session, but that could be accomplished only by joint resolution, which of course was impossible to secure. On the last day the I.V.A. leadership temporarily lost control of the House, which overruled Speaker Twichell on an appeal from a decision of the chair and approved several bills of minor significance passed by the Senate. Both houses accepted the actions of conference committees on the appropriations bills, which generally split the difference. By this time much of the bitterness of the session had waned, and I.V.A.'s and Leaguers joined in singing while waiting for the reports of conference committees to come in.[32]

The concluding night of the seventeenth legislative assembly, however, was a scene of turmoil containing elements of an old-fashioned melodrama. Crowds, predominantly anti-League, surged through the corridors of the capitol searching for excitement. Fist fights were common and the galleries were almost impossible to control. The Senate demanded that attorneys Murphy and Sullivan, who had conducted the examinations for the House investigating committee, appear before it for questioning, but the House insisted that the Senate had no power to investigate the activities of the other chamber. The Senate thereupon issued warrants for the arrest of the attorneys, and the sergeant-at-arms apprehended them in a downtown theater.

Brought before the Senate, each named the other as his counsel and a long period of fruitless wrangling ensued. Murphy refused to submit to an oath as a witness on the grounds that he was under arrest and a prisoner. Accordingly the Senate passed a resolution dismissing the warrants for arrest, and Murphy at once dodged out the rear door of the chamber. The sergeant-at-arms was ordered to pursue him, but he escaped in the crowd and a melee was precipitated in the corridors, Carl Kositzky, the former state auditor, emerging from one brawl nursing a black eye and cut cheek. Lieutenant Governor Wood ordered all doors closed and secured and did his utmost to maintain order in the chamber itself. Sullivan then informed the Senate that he would answer no questions whatsoever, and, his Irish temper aroused, added that "all the Nonpartisans between Hudson Bay and Hell" couldn't make him. Senator Baker promptly moved to cite Sullivan for contempt of the Senate, and tension in the chamber mounted to fever pitch. Several I.V.A.'s voted for the action so that they could move to reconsider, but in the end he was cited and placed under arrest.

Not wanting to take the risk of facing the crowd in attempting to take Sullivan to the county jail, the sergeant-at-arms spirited him into the attorney general's office and locked the doors. I.V.A. members, who had seen Justice Birdzell in the gallery, quickly got him to sit in chambers long enough for a writ of habeas corpus to be prepared, but having secured the writ they at first could find neither the sergeant-at-arms nor the prisoner. Locating them finally, they could not convince the sergeant-at-arms that this was anything more than an attempt to kidnap his prisoner, and the door was nearly torn off the attorney general's office before he opened it and allowed service of the writ. At seven o'clock in the morning, as dawn was breaking, the weary legislators decided to call a halt, and the seventeenth assembly came to a stirring if inconclusive end.[33]

The Recall Imbroglio

SCARCELY a year after the passage of the League-sponsored constitutional amendment making possible the recall of public officers petitions were being circulated for the recall of League-elected state officials. Such action had been talked of almost since the election of 1920, but it was given new impetus at the I.V.A. meeting in Bismarck on February 12, 1921, when a general recall was threatened unless the League acceded to the previously mentioned demands that control of the Industrial Commission be transferred to the I.V.A., the Bank of North Dakota reduced to a farm loan agency, and so on. Two days before the end of the legislative session the I.V.A. members of both houses approved a proposal of the "Committee of 21" for a recall election to be held between June 15 and June 30.

It was hoped that the Industrial Commission might be recalled on the grounds of poor management of the state industries, Lieutenant Governor Wood for his vote to seat Senator Wog, and Supreme Court Justices Grace, Bronson, and Robinson for their decision in the Scandinavian-American Bank case. Even State Auditor Poindexter and a number of League legislators were not to be overlooked. It was also agreed that laws should be initiated to limit or abolish the various state enterprises.[1] A League meeting immediately after the close of the session declared that if a recall were attempted the farmers of the state should let their farms lie idle and devote themselves to the battle—"summer fallow and fight" was adopted as the slogan.[2] Both sides at once set about the task of raising the largest possible campaign funds.

The *Bismarck Tribune*, which generally took the view of the "old

315

guard" Republicans, had no use for the I.V.A. and its advocacy of carrying out most of the League program under new management. The I.V.A. leadership, consisting of "outlaw Leaguers," it said, was doing no more than making a "drive for the pie counter"; the real need was to do away with the entire League program and start afresh: "The people should not be asked to share the expense of another election if we are merely going to swap our radical socialists for the mild variety who stagger at a million but would dabble with the public funds just to 'try out socialism'." [3]

As a matter of fact there were many prominent in the I.V.A., such as John Steen, who considered the movement for recall a mistake. Why not let the League run the industries into the ground, they argued, and then "clean house" completely in the 1922 primaries? Why take over in midstream, assuming that a recall could be successful, which was not at all certain, and run the risk of being blamed for failures? Nevertheless, the "hotheads" had their way.

An I.V.A. state convention was called for March 30 and 31 at Devils Lake, with district conventions the preceding week to elect delegates on a basis of one for each two hundred votes cast for the initiated law providing for an audit of state industries. The convention voted in favor of a recall, but, concluding that a June date was not feasible, it agreed on the fall, sometime before November 8. It also decided not to attack too many officials and to concentrate upon the Industrial Commission.

Rangvold A. Nestos of Minot, earnest, hard-working, and possessed of a good Norwegian name, was selected to contest the governorship with Lynn Frazier. For the office of attorney general the Republican Nestos was balanced with Sveinbjorn Johnson, chairman of the Democratic State Central Committee and law partner of J. F. T. O'Connor. [4] No endorsement was made for commissioner of agriculture and labor, but a committee later picked Joseph A. Kitchen, a state legislator from the strongly pro-League western part of the state. The convention also agreed upon the general content of a constitutional amendment and six laws to be initiated, with the purpose of watering down the League program, and set a goal of 80,000 signatures for the recall petitions. [5]

As one of its first major steps in fighting the recall movement, the Industrial Commission on June 1 published *The North Dakota Indus-*

trial Program, a progress report to December 31, 1920, which was a well-written account of the origin and development of the Nonpartisan League and a statement on the organization and operation of each of the industries. It presented ably the League case and claims of success. Neither the League nor the I.V.A., when it had the opportunity, had any particular scruples against using state publications for thinly veiled political propaganda. Shortly after the appearance of this official report, the League itself published a pamphlet entitled *Townleyism*, designed to point out the benefits to the state that had arisen from what the opposition sneeringly termed "Townleyism."

In the face of the I.V.A.'s charges of great losses on the various enterprises, inefficiency, and tremendous cost to the taxpayers, the Industrial Commission's report boldly announced that there existed a surplus of more than $217,000 above all appropriations made for the state industries. While it admitted that a loss of $17,668.31 had been sustained at the Drake mill, and noted that initial expense of the Home Building Association and the Mill and Elevator Association would not be paid back until the enterprises had been in operation for some time, it stated that the Bank of North Dakota had earned a surplus of $176,681.84, thus making a total net profit for the state industries of $117,111.09.[6] On the question of taxes the report pointed out that the per capita tax for state and local purposes in 1919 had been $36 in North Dakota as compared with $46 in Minnesota, while the state tax per capita was $6.20 in North Dakota and $11.40 in Minnesota. In comparing nine League states, it found that only Kansas, Oklahoma, and Wisconsin had lower per capita taxes than North Dakota. But most important, it said, appropriations for the state industries constituted only a very small portion of the total amount and would be paid back out of earnings.[7]

The claims of achievement made by the League for the Bank of North Dakota were numerous. In addition to the fact that a surplus had been accumulated over and above reserves for repayment of the initial appropriation, interest on bonds, and depreciation, it had financed the state industries to the extent of more than $1,000,000 at a time when they would otherwise have had to be abandoned. It had made almost $3,000,000 worth of loans to farmers at an interest rate 2½ per cent below the previous average, and in so doing had reduced and stabilized the commercial rate. Though hampered by the initiated depository law, the Bank, it was claimed, was still doing much to place surplus funds in areas where most needed. By the end of February twenty-one counties, three fourths of the school districts, and one half of the cities and villages were continuing to deposit their funds in the Bank even though free to put them elsewhere, and the initiated measure had simply reduced the volume of redeposit activity. It was admitted that many of the Bank's outstanding loans could not be rapidly liquidated. The controversy over whether or not the Bank had really earned a profit revolved largely around the ultimate recoverability of the loans to farmers and state enterprises and the loans and redeposits of $1,484,000 in closed banks.[8]

Dr. Ladd, as state grain inspector, estimated that the state grain-grading law had saved the farmers of the state in its two years of operation between twelve and fifteen million dollars.* Payments for dockage amounted to nearly $4,000,000 on the 1919 crop alone, and producers were also being protected against unfair grading and short weight. The power to specify the margin of profit in elevator charges had been invoked after the national government ceased fixing the price of grain, in order to foil the attempt of the buyers to pay farmers the December option price instead of the current market quotations, which were from ten to twenty-three cents higher.[9]

The cream-testing law operated in much the same manner as the grain-grading act, with buyers being licensed by the state and required to retain samples for twenty-four hours, during which time they might be tested by state inspectors. This, it was claimed, served both the seller and the honest buyer, since the former was certain of a fair price for his cream and the latter was not forced to compete with dishonest buyers. Tests made at the time the law went into effect indicated that 51.8 per cent of all cream sold was undertested, with an average of 2.13 pounds of butterfat being taken from each purchase without compensation. A sample check at the end of the first year's operation showed that only 18 per cent was being undertested and that to the extent of only .71 pound per purchase. At an average rate of fifty cents per pound the savings were estimated to be $286,962 annually, for an administrative cost of a mere $2000.[10]

---

* In 1922 a divided United States Supreme Court declared the act unconstitutional on the grounds that it imposed a direct burden on interstate commerce, reversing a 1919 decision by Judge Amidon. Lemke v. Farmers' Grain Co. of Embden, 258 U.S. 50, 42 S.Ct. 244.

Confident claims were also made as to the advantages of the state hail insurance system, still providing insurance at 55 per cent less than the private companies, the State Fire and Tornado Fund, the workmen's compensation system, and others. The statements concerning the Home Building Association were more restrained, but it was maintained that despite unfavorable conditions it had built houses at approximately 20 per cent under current replacement costs. In the first year fifty-eight houses had been constructed or were under construction in four cities. Eight were for business or professional men and the remainder for wage earners; no farm homes had been undertaken. After the 1921 legislative session its activities had been largely restricted to the completion of buildings already under way, owing to a heavy slash in its appropriation.[11]

The internal struggle for control of the League organization broke out into the open when on July 6 the *Fargo Courier-News* published an attack on the majority members of the state committee. Following the election in early 1921, this committee had come into the control of men eager for personal power. Liederbach had promised Kaldor and Levang salaried jobs in return for his election as chairman of the committee, and they subsequently employed themselves as state manager, cashier, and state organizer, at salaries of $250 per month and expenses, discharging the trained employees. The *Courier-News*, controlled largely by Lemke at the time, now charged the misuse of contributions to the recall campaign by Liederbach and Kaldor, saying that $50,000 had been raised but none seemed to be available. "Distasteful as the task is," it said, calling for a new election and instructing members to send contributions to State Auditor Poindexter instead of to the Fargo headquarters of the League, "it is the duty of the *Courier-News* to present the facts as they exist."[12]

Actually only a relatively few copies of that day's *Courier-News* ever went on sale, for word of what was to be published had gotten out through a printer. Early in the morning Liederbach and Kaldor with ten or twelve men entered the newspaper's offices, forcibly ejected editor C. K. Gummerson, and ordered the destruction of the forms. Five thousand copies of the issue were burned. The next day's *Courier-News* glossed over the incident with the statement that it was all the work of a few disgruntled employees who had been subsequently discharged for incompetency. The state committee met in Fargo that day, and Liederbach and Kaldor claimed to be able to account for all the money and threatened to sue Gummerson and business manager George Totten, Jr., for libel. Ultimately William Lemke served as peacemaker, Gummerson and Totten retracted their charges, the libel suit was dropped, and the *Courier-News* continued under the supervision of the majority members of the state committee.[13]

The fact that a million-dollar note held by the Merchants Loan and Trust Company of Chicago fell due on March 15, 1921, was one of the reasons for the Industrial Commission's February 10 order to the Bank of North Dakota to force collections from local banks. At the same time it had ordered the Bank to register the checks of the state treasurer except those in payment of the ordinary expenses of the state educational, charitable, and penal institutions, feeling that it was best to maintain a good credit rating outside the state even at the risk of worsening the situation within. The note was paid when due, but it had been necessary also to restrict payment on the checks of the treasurers of local governments to certain specified objects, others being registered and bearing 6 per cent interest. The Bank itself termed this "a drastic policy to meet a temporary situation." It was justified as the only means of averting a statewide financial catastrophe, and on the grounds that since the state itself could register warrants for future payment, anticipating future revenue, a state bank could logically do likewise in an emergency. It was noted that New York banks had followed a similar procedure in 1907 and at that time they had not even paid interest.[14]

By September 27 the liquidation of many previously frozen loans and redeposits, the increase of individual deposits, progress in bond sales, and the securing of a $500,000 loan in the East enabled the Bank of North Dakota to announce that it was again in a position to pay all registered checks and other obligations, and one of the I.V.A.'s chief objects of attack was thereby removed. The Industrial Commission insisted that this method of weathering the financial storm had been easiest on all concerned, since it had made it possible for scores of banks which were on the verge of collapse to continue to function. Otherwise the Bank would have been forced to demand payment from all, rather than being able to avoid pressing those which found themselves in especially weak positions.[15]

On September 15 the I.V.A. filed petitions containing 74,000 signatures calling for a recall election to be held on October 28. Accompanying this were petitions for the initiation of a constitutional amendment and six laws. The amendment would establish a state debt limit and set specific limits on bond issues for the Bank of North Dakota, the Mill and Elevator Association, and the Home Building Association. The initiated laws would provide for the following:

The nomination and election of state officers without party designation

Separate party ballots for primaries for other offices and a single ballot for general elections, with the primaries moved from June to March

Requiring the deposit of all public funds in state and national banks

Re-enactment of the Industrial Commission law (a) in order to have that body consist of the secretary of state, the state treasurer, and the commissioner of agriculture and labor until the first following legislative assembly, when it should become a board of three members appointed by the governor with the consent of the senate, to serve for overlapping terms, (b) to dissolve the Home Building Association upon the completion of existing contracts, and (c) to limit mill and elevator projects to those at Drake and Grand Forks

The establishment of a rural credits system under a separate rural credits board

Dissolution of the Bank of North Dakota [16]

Obviously the I.V.A. could secure most of its objectives if these measures passed, even if the recall should prove unsuccessful.

With the petitions filed, both sides settled down to the final stages of the campaign in earnest. The I.V.A. had planned its tactics more shrewdly than had the League opposition in North Dakota at any previous time. Its candidates professed to be supporters of the original League program, or at the least to be willing to give it a "fair trial"; it was only the deviations from the original program and the administration of the enterprises that were under attack. This was a plausible kind of argument, which it was difficult to assert was just a further attempt of the "interests" to beat down the farmer, though the *Leader* assured its readers continuously that the I.V.A. protestations of love for the farmers' program were mere camouflage.

The *Grand Forks Herald* was willing to accept this type of ap-

A Mother's Prayer

An I.V.A. view of the Nonpartisan League "threat."

proach, with reservations, but the *Bismarck Tribune* would still have nothing to do with these "compromises with Socialism." It repudiated completely the "renegade Nonpartisan Leaguers" and "discarded socialists" who were stumping the state for Nestos, and insisted that there was no merit in "swapping one breed of Socialists for another." The I.V.A., it said, simply wanted offices and patronage, and in the process it was ruining party government. "No true Republican or Democrat can support such a measure to break down party lines completely," the *Tribune* editorialized. "What mandate do these men and their associates hold from the people of North Dakota to plunge them into another bitter fight?"[17] The entire League program was a fallacy, it said, and it was foolish to support anyone who believed in it, whether Leaguer or I.V.A.:

If there has been any dishonesty, any stealing of State funds, why does not the IVA come to Bismarck and file the information with State's Attorney McCurdy and demand the arrest and removal from office of the offending officials through the courts? Why resort to a

recall a few months ahead of a primary election to place in power another coterie which professes to believe in the same thing and which
seeks to gain the reins of power under the disguise of salvage? The
IVA program spells anything but salvage however cleverly that intent
is camouflaged . . . It seems beyond the realm of reason that any fair-
minded people would challenge a State administration on such a flimsy
program.[18]

It was natural that with such an attitude from the *Tribune* the I.V.A.
should charge that there existed a conspiracy between the League and
Alexander McKenzie. The League, however, maintained that both were
out to kill the League, but the *Tribune* was honest about its objectives
while the I.V.A. sought to fool the people. It did concede that undoubtedly the McKenzie forces would like to see the I.V.A. lose out
in the recall, because that might end it as a political factor, making
it possible for the "old guard" to return to power by defeating the
League in 1922.[19] This analysis was probably not too far from the
mark, and it was also true that the McKenzie group feared trouble
from the Progressives in McCumber's coming bid for re-election to the
Senate.

The I.V.A. press of course gave tremendous publicity to every aspect of the Nestos campaign and indicated that the little remaining
League support was rapidly fading away. Representative Burtness returned from Washington to stump the state for ten days. Governor
Preus, "the man who beat the League in Minnesota," made a brief tour
of the principal cities. Former Senator A. J. Gronna conducted one
of the most vigorous campaigns of his life, and his opinions were highly
valued by many. Nor were those to whom the *Bismarck Tribune* referred to as the "renegade Leaguers" inactive; Arthur LeSueur, for
example, toured the state making "revelations" on the "dictatorship"
of the League organization, and J. W. Brinton gave lectures illustrated
with lantern slides of miscellaneous documents relating to the Consumers' United Stores, the Scandinavian-American Bank, the Sisal Trust,
and so on.[20]

One of the most persistent and annoying thorns in the side of the
League during this campaign was a house which the Home Building
Association had built for William Lemke in Fargo. I.V.A. pamphlets
claimed that it had cost $24,000 of "public money" and played it up
to such an extent that it came near being the central issue of the cam-

paign. It would seem merely a matter of common political sense that the Home Building Association should never have been used to build homes for state officials, yet a duplex was also built for George Totten, and a small home was constructed for John N. Hagan, which he flatly refused to accept when it developed that it had cost more than he had agreed to pay and more than the $5000 maximum allowed by statute.

Yet it was the Lemke house which drew the real fire, and the *North Dakota Leader* was finally forced to issue a statement that the house had cost $14,000 instead of $24,000, of which the state had advanced but $4000, secured by a first mortgage on the property.[21] Nevertheless, the I.V.A. continued to run a free taxi service from the Fargo depot so that visitors might view the Lemke house, and Townley never lost his conviction that that "scandal" was a deciding factor in the election. It was at this juncture that he had occasion to wish devoutly that he had insisted that Lemke completely divorce himself from the organization if he wished to run for public office, for he felt that the League might then have disowned the attorney general rather than having to suffer from the attempt to defend him.[22]

A succession of poor crop years followed by a depression meant of course that the farmers had little money for political campaigns, and the League solicited contributions from all states to save the North Dakota program. A number of liberally inclined speakers, as for example John Skelton Williams, former comptroller of the currency, volunteered their services. Charges were rife that bankers throughout the state were letting it be known among those persons indebted to them that immediate collection would be demanded if the League won in the recall election, and there were thinly veiled hints in the publication of the Bankers Association that out-of-state creditors might force payment from banks if socialism continued.[23]

A. C. Townley had virtually nothing to do with the campaign, in large measure because he was not wanted by the North Dakota state committee, and his famous "revival meetings" were keenly missed. In the effort to give a final week's prodding to the League membership, the weekly *North Dakota Leader* was abandoned on October 22 and it was announced that henceforth all members in the state would receive instead the daily *Fargo Courier-News*. In its last issue, however, the *North Dakota Leader* raised a storm with charges of "wholesale fraud" in the petitions the I.V.A. had filed. Commissioner of Agriculture and Labor Hagan was said to have discovered twenty-eight names duplicated on two petitions from the precinct next to his in McHenry County, and it was claimed that this was standard practice. It was insinuated that the I.V.A. had deliberately fostered such action, and much was made of the I.V.A. instructions to petition circulators: "If there is any doubt about them having signed before, have them sign yours. It is better to have some sign twice than not at all. The petitions will be checked for duplicates before they are filed." [24]

During the first week of October, less than a month before the recall election, the Industrial Commission triumphantly announced the sale of $6,100,000 worth of North Dakota bonds to Spitzer, Rorick, and Company of Toledo, at last breaking the long-standing bond boycott. This, claimed the League, would put an end to the state's financial crisis; other bonds could now be sold easily, and the credit of the state was proven to be good.[25] The *Grand Forks Herald* screamed that this was a "fake sale," which was not the case, but it was true that a rather questionable transaction was involved. Since the statutes provided that sales must be made at par, the Industrial Commission had nominally sold the bonds to the Bank of North Dakota at par, which in turn sold them to Spitzer, Rorick, and Company at a discount in the form of a commission.

Once again the I.V.A. resorted to the courts, and on October 18 Governor Frazier was served with a restraining order signed by Judge J. A. Coffey of Jamestown which was so sweeping that if obeyed it would virtually have tied up the entire state government as well as the Bank of North Dakota. Issued without any notice to the Bank or opportunity for it to be heard, the order prohibited the Bank from accepting deposits from either state or local officials or the proceeds of bond sales, and calmly adjudged it insolvent. The temporary injunction was made returnable November 3, well after the recall election, to show cause why it should not be made permanent.

The move was unexpected, but the League promptly rushed its judicial forces to the fore. William Lemke left his speaking tour at Hatton and hastened to Bismarck, where on October 20 he secured a writ from the Supreme Court ordering Judge Coffey to certify the proceedings to the Supreme Court and directing that the restraining order be vacated until the further order of that court. The order of the Stutsman County District Court had been secured by means of assertions that

I.V.A. state Treasurer John Steen testified before the Supreme Court were false, and there were many I.V.A.'s who were displeased with the action. Ultimately the Supreme Court, in a unanimous decision written by Judge Christianson, held that the order of the lower court had been erroneous.[26]

With this incident out of the way, the voters of North Dakota went to the polls with assurances from the *Fargo Courier-News* that the bond sale had been made, that Spitzer, Rorick, and Company would take all real estate bonds of the state as fast as they were issued, that all frozen loans of the Bank of North Dakota had been liquidated, and that the Bank was again ready to make farm loans as rapidly as the applications could be examined and approved.[27] Nevertheless, the air was far from clear.

On October 29 a goat, led from Douglas by a gentleman named Gust Larson, was met on the outskirts of Minot by a brass band and a new governor-elect. "The Goat That Can't Be Got" had been "got." Although the vote was so close that for some time absolute certainty was impossible, for the first time in the history of the nation a governor of a state had been recalled, and with him went the other two members of the Industrial Commission.* Yet curiously enough every one of the initiated measures, on the basis of which in large part the campaign had supposedly been fought, was defeated by majorities approximately equivalent to those which elected the I.V.A. candidates.[28] Thus, ironically, R. A. Nestos was assigned the task of carrying out the program which his faction had aimed to curtail. "The fact is," commented the *Minneapolis Tribune*, "the voters are mildly amazed at what they did and are wondering what is going to be the real result of what happened Friday, October 28 . . . the mandate of the next administration is vague and contradictory . . . Smashed in the recall election, the Nonpartisan League numerically is still the strongest faction in North Dakota politics." [29]

The third congressional district, comprising the western part of the state, remained in the League column as usual, and the League had a very slight edge in the second, but the heavy I.V.A. vote in the eastern

* The vote for governor was Nestos, 111,434, Frazier, 107,332; for attorney general, Johnson, 112,361, Lemke, 105,575; for commissioner of agriculture and labor, Kitchin, 111,249, Hagan, 105,914 (*Compilation of Election Returns, National and State, 1914–1928* (N.D.), p. 48).

first district tipped the balance. The success of the recall might be and has been ascribed to many things, such as the money poured into the state by opposition elements, the rather poor campaign run by the League state committee, the absence of A. C. Townley, the Lemke house, increased taxation, overconfidence on the part of many League voters, the inability of the farmers to finance the campaign adequately, the failure of various subsidiary enterprises, the fact that after six years of struggle there was still no state mill and elevator, the confusion resulting from both sides' claiming to be the real farmers' party. All these had doubtless played a part, but more important was the lack of confidence resulting from the disclosures of mismanagement. Clearly the people were not willing to abandon the League program. The I.V.A. had promised to give it a "fair trial" and had managed to convince enough voters of its sincerity to win the day.

Perhaps the most fundamental cause, however, was one that has always plagued movements of reform. It is a herculean and well-nigh impossible task to keep a large mass of people sufficiently excited over a "cause" for them to exert themselves actively in its behalf over a long period of time. Especially when a part or all of the original objectives have been achieved does it become much easier to "let George do it." In many respects, therefore, the recall is less surprising than that after six years of bitter strife and a tremendous opposition campaign the League program should be sustained and its candidates defeated by only a narrow margin.

Joy in the ranks of conservatism was unconfined, as headlines from coast to coast proclaimed that socialism had failed again.[30] Most of the newspapers close to the scene, however, were aware that the obituaries were premature and that with the program still intact considerable life remained in the corpse. Yet there was no shadow of a doubt in the mind of the *Grand Forks Herald*, at the time unaware that the initiated measures had failed, which maintained its record as a poor prophet:

The change which the people of North Dakota have decreed in their state government is a permanent one. There is not the slightest prospect that in any conceivable circumstances there will be a return to the policy and the program that have come to be known as Townleyism. That system has been discarded and its official ministers voted into retirement because of the conviction that the system was unsound and that the men administering it were not to be trusted . . . [It was] a vote so decisive that the verdict cannot be questioned.[31]

The *Leader*, on the other hand, while naturally unhappy over the recall, gave its headlines to the "victory" of the League program, and expressed its hope for the future:

The test of permanency of a political program is its ability to become established in the laws and constitution and to remain to be carried out regardless of changes in State administrations. The Nonpartisan League program has stood this test . . .

League leaders made many mistakes in North Dakota—mistakes which undoubtedly had their effect in convincing a certain number of friends of the program that it was better to have a change of administration, while at the same time retaining the League program . . .

This vote ought to be, and will be, a lesson to the farmers of North Dakota and their leaders. Set backs are often good in the long run. If properly taken advantage of by Leaguers the recall of Governor Frazier may yet not prove to have been without benefit . . . It will force the reorganization of the League on a broader, more substantial, more effective basis . . . It will be a benefit if it has taught the lesson of sticking together better, of fighting harder, of not becoming overconfident, of keeping their organization intact and well financed. These things are paramount.[32]

It was proposed by a few Leaguers to challenge the validity of the election on grounds of fraudulent and duplicating signatures on petitions, and though the state committee, the *Leader*, and President Townley all opposed the action, such a suit was brought. The *Leader* maintained that if there had been a desire to do this it should have been undertaken before the election, since the vote of the people cured any irregularity. Moreover, it said, the program had been saved and the League did not exist to keep any particular men in office.[33] The Supreme Court agreed completely with the *Leader*'s analysis, shortly ruling that the secretary of state had performed his functions correctly and that the court could not review such a matter after the people had spoken.[34]

After the sale of bonds to Spitzer, Rorick, and Company, a suit had been brought contesting the legality of the sale at less than par by the Bank of North Dakota. With this case also the Supreme Court, in recent months far more harmonious than before, had no difficulty. The statutes clearly forbade the sale at less than par, it said in sustaining an injunction issued by the District Court, and the Bank did not actually buy the bonds from the Industrial Commission, but merely acted as custodian and agent.[35]

328

While the suit was pending, however, the Industrial Commission signed a new contract with the Toledo firm replacing the old one and providing that all issues not yet sold be sold at par. This was announced on November 22, the day before the new administration took office. Lemke stated that the total of bonds now sold amounted to $15,000,000.[36] Lynn Frazier could say, in his farewell message as governor, that the Bank of North Dakota, the "keystone" of the industrial program, had been left in excellent shape. The fight, he concluded, must be continued until the success of the entire program was assured:

I leave office "with malice toward none and charity for all," and with the abiding conviction that the people of North Dakota will not only settle the grave problems that confront them, but will, in the future as in the past, be in the front trenches of the forces that are now struggling to establish economic freedom for the producing classes of the world.[37]

The League program was now in the hands of its enemies, pledged, however, to give it a fair trial. Indeed, compared with the struggle which the League administration had faced for five years, the I.V.A. administration started with the odds all in its favor. The program was now cleared through the courts, the majority of the people were behind it, the enterprises were under way, and the bonds were sold so that money was available to push them to completion. Yet it was not surprising that the new administration was at least as much concerned with discrediting both the League program and its administration as with the "fair trial."

That it found much confusion is hardly open to question, but it lost no time in publishing as soon as possible after the end of the year an official report on the industrial program which, like the last report of the League administration, was primarily a political campaign document. Although they suffered in authoritativeness because of the general character of the publication, the analyses of the enterprises, based largely on the Bishop-Brissman reports, deserve attention as the first comprehensive statement upon them by other than League sources. The primary purpose of the report was well indicated by what the new Industrial Commission termed its "general deductions":

When a government gets out of its domain it loses efficiency, multiplies leaks and gives an opportunity for controlling the electorate by inflated payrolls . . . For several years we have been dominated by fly-by-nights who flared out of obscurity for a brief spell and will be remembered only by the havoc they have wrought. However meritorious a cause may be, there is none so worthy as to sanctify waste . . . We have been bled white by official extravagance picturesque in its boldness.

During the reign of the so-called League industrial program, under which the state has been staggering, nothing is lacking but success—not one oasis in the dreary desert of failure . . .

Many causes have contributed to the disastrous results that confront us; among which, may be named, false theories; lack of training on the part of those named as managers; the newness of the work; ill-defined duties; wide powers under the laws and lack of judicial interpretation; but most of all official incompetency and a failure, either through inability or overconfidence on the part of the former Commission, to exercise adequate supervision . . . Bad as are some of the so-called "program laws," it is not in the laws themselves as much as in their administration that their seamy side shows so obtrusively.[38]

A number of the causes listed were quite correct, but, carried away by its own eloquence, the I.V.A. Industrial Commission alleged and insinuated far more than it was actually prepared to prove. In fact, little of real significance was found wrong with the results of most of the "program laws," and the attack was concentrated largely on the Bank of North Dakota, the Drake mill, and the Home Building Association, with the Bank not faring too badly if differences of opinion on certain policies are discounted. Perhaps worthy of note is the fact that it was found impossible to keep the campaign promises that League state officials would be jailed for dishonest practices as soon as an I.V.A. administration gained access to the records.

That McGovern had mismanaged the Drake mill even the League administration had cautiously admitted, but the I.V.A. report contended that the loss sustained on the project by the end of 1920 was $41,098.26 rather than the $17,668.31 indicated by the Equitable Audit Company, and that by December 31, 1921, it had mounted to $74,379.12. The losses therefore, according to the I.V.A., had run an average of more than $100 per day of operation or $1.58 per barrel of flour ground. The mill had, of course, been a poor investment in the first place; it had also frequently purchased unwisely; and it had suffered considerably in the failure of the Consumers' United Stores Company. The report did, however, admit that "outside of the unjustifiable policy of sending out consignment goods during the first year of its operation and the losses thereby incurred, the mill's losses have been such as may come to any business enterprises." [39]

There was a note of pride evident in the comments on the state mill and elevator now under construction at Grand Forks, as the commission pledged an efficient administration of this enterprise. The closing of the Fargo office of the Mill and Elevator Association on February 1, 1921, was commended, but the previous cost of that office and the expenses incurred by Mr. McGovern came in for sarcastic censure:

The Manager of the Mill and Elevator Association used in the Fargo office mileage equal to about once and a half around the world. To make clear the phenomenal feat performed let us say that a man could have started in the southeast corner of the state on the Red River and gone westward on the southern tier of townships to the Montana line, then turned back on the next tier of townships to the north and continued back and forth from the Montana line to the Red River, covering every tier of townships to the Canadian line, then turned at the northwest corner of the state and covered every tier of ranges from Canada to the South Dakota line backwards and forwards till the Red River was reached. Following this, one could have made ten round trips from Fargo to Bismarck and a like number of trips from Fargo to Minneapolis and had mileage enough left to have taken a good vacation on either coast. Through all this active wandering the record does not disclose a meal missed, or one that cost less than eighty cents, whether in hamlet or city.

This is commended to the notice of the taxpayers as a test of physical endurance seldom equalled. [40]

It was the Home Building Association, however, which presented the truly sorry picture. Both Manager Blakemore and his assistant proved completely unfitted for their jobs, and though the fundamental idea of the association was good they had made a miserable record. The Equitable Audit Company's report of May 31, 1921, indicated that it had endeavored to train two successive chief accountants recommended by Blakemore, but both had proved quite incompetent in even the simplest procedures, despite the fact that a system and forms had been carefully devised for them. There were virtually no records on the first three months of construction work. Invoices were filed in no order at all, and it took auditors hours to trace items for which checks had been issued. A number of duplicate and some triplicate payments were discovered; the bank account was not in balance and the statements were not even reconciled monthly.

The auditors found that material slips were not being made out for the various construction projects, but were informed that a record had been kept on separate forms. When examined, these disclosed such items as seven loads of sand used in the construction of one house and forty-two in another of identical model. The officials admitted that they did not know how much had been used, and it finally developed that the material slips were "fakes" based on guesses as to the amounts of materials used. There were many instances of cash sales from stocks of materials with the only record a bank deposit and a credit to stock sales, but no information on the amount or kind of material sold or to whom sold. A sizable quantity of material was claimed to be of undesirable dimensions or otherwise unusable, as for example caked sacks of plaster and cement, but the surplus supplies were later sold without loss.

The requirements of membership in a Home Buyers' League and a 20 per cent down payment had been almost completely ignored, and only a few of the owners were making regular payments. Fifty-three houses and one barn had been built and five other houses had been purchased through the association, yet there existed no contracts on fifty-one of them—nothing but oral agreements. Moreover, not one had been built within the statutory cost limit of $5000, which was of course too low for this period, and a number of the buyers refused to accept them at their book value. Although the association was supposedly permitted to use only funds derived from appropriations, sale of bonds, or income from deposits or payments on houses, officers had executed notes in the name of the association to the extent of $416,322.81.

To date, the I.V.A. Industrial Commission said, office overhead had amounted to $1400 a month, a figure which required payments would just about equal. Even if every home owner paid the amount charged against him, the loss statement at the time, it was claimed, was $133,256.76, and the commission was justifiably harsh in its condemnation of the administration of this project, though the law was not really fundamentally at fault:

The handling of this Association is a picture of the most dismal failure . . . The whole scheme has not enough substantial merit in it to form the basis of a fatuous dream. In all its varied activities this Association measured up to its opportunities in only one particular and that was by using every dollar in sight regardless of where that dollar came from. Even a careful study does not reveal one single instance where the management missed an opportunity to blunder, and in the blundering the Industrial Commission, the Manager of the Association and the Bank of North Dakota are alike culpable, though not in equal degree.[41]

The retiring Industrial Commission had passed a resolution on its last day in office urging those who had supported the Bank of North Dakota to continue to do so and expressing faith in its worth to the state, but the new administration had no intention of letting this important element of the League program escape unscathed. Contrary to the League's claims of profits for the Bank, the I.V.A. commission insisted that it had lost $255,088.14 since its opening in 1919. It maintained that the various industries had "ridden" the Bank too freely, stated that the Bank was tremendously overstaffed, and blasted what it termed political favoritism in its loan and redeposit policies.[42] As to whether the Bank had made a profit or sustained a loss, much depended upon one's evaluation of the book item "interest earned and not collected." The Bank should probably have made more allowances for possible loss, and it appears that it actually made little if any profit, though the I.V.A. studiously overlooked the fact that it was set up for service rather than for profit.[43]

A large part of the difficulties of the Bank of North Dakota arose from the failure of banks in which it had redeposited public funds. It had made little prior examination of depository banks, considering the needs of the community and the banks more important. There was frequently an attempt to rehabilitate weak banks, and many were chosen unwisely when in fact the greatest care should have been exercised to ensure that the public funds were always safe and available.[44]

The Bank was quickly reorganized and new officials appointed, but it was not long before it was again under attack, from a number of sources in addition to the League. The principal complaints were lodged against the extreme conservatism of its farm loan policies, which were such that the Bank was of relatively little help to farmers. The situation, economist Alvin S. Tostlebe says, "has led careful observers both in North Dakota and elsewhere to the conclusion that the Independent administration has had as its main aim discredit, sabotage and destruction of the Bank," and while this may be too harsh, despite the most favorable conditions in the history of the Bank "the record of loans is on the whole unsatisfactory."[45] Even if Governor Nestos did desire a "fair trial," there were many in and behind the I.V.A. who were eager for the Bank to fail, thus "proving" the undesirability of public ownership.

Tostlebe, after a careful and comprehensive study of the Bank of North Dakota, concluded that there was no exaggeration of the need for cheaper rural credit and that in a state largely composed of farmers a state bank was probably the best solution. Likewise there was a meritorious objective of using public money only for the public good, but it was his contention that it was a mistake to have the Bank under the control of a board constituted as was the Industrial Commission. The mortgage and reserve banking functions, he felt, should be separated, and the legislature should have prescribed more definite rules and standards of operation for the guidance of the administrative officers.[46]

It seems clear that the picture of the state enterprises as a whole was not by any means as horrible as the I.V.A. Industrial Commission quite naturally endeavored to paint it. The Bank was not really in bad shape, though there was certainly room for honest differences of opinion over some of its policies. It weathered the depression and helped many other banks to do so, providing at the same time a number of useful services to private banks, lowering farm credit rates, and financing the state industries in their formative stages. The hail insurance and the fire and tornado insurance systems were undeniably successful. Though there were minor flaws which took time to work out, a more progressive scheme of taxation had been established. The various aspects of the state grain inspection program had proven extremely valuable, and though the state mill and elevator had been held up by many vicissitudes, both sides now professed to look forward eagerly to its completion. On the other hand there was no question of the mismanagement of the Drake mill, which was uneconomical to start with, and the Home Building Association under Blakemore had been a complete fiasco.

The failure of one major and one minor project did not, as so often claimed, by any means prove the unworkability of the League program. It proved little more than a pair of truisms—that inexperienced leaders can easily make mistakes, and that the utmost care must be exercised in the selection of professionally trained and experienced managers for any enterprise, public or private, to succeed. There was more than a little merit in Arthur LeSueur's contention that the management of the industries should be vested in an appointive body free to select

334

professional managers and responsible for their success, rather than in a board of officials elected to other jobs and able to give only part of their attention to these matters.

Occasional mistakes do not invalidate such a program any more than the existence of occasional political corruption completely negates the values of democracy. Nevertheless, it is certainly true that mistakes can readily be fatal at the outset of such a bitterly contested experiment as this. The League administration had made too many mistakes, and they came at the wrong time—the very beginning of what was proclaimed to be a new order. Even so, much had been accomplished, most of the errors were such that they could be remedied, and the "program" was far from dead, although the I.V.A. Industrial Commission eagerly led the obsequies with a sanctimonious statement overflowing with magnanimity:

The doomsday bugle has time and time again sounded across the graves of political theories—few having left a more burdensome aftermath than ours. Our people have gone out after strange gods and returned chastened. We cannot forget but we must forgive. The truceless jarrings of the past few years, let us grant, were mistakes of the head and not the heart. The mass of our people are sincere and honest but neither sincerity nor honesty in a mistaken cause will make a wrong right or lighten the penalty of folly. We must pay; there is no evasion. Our financial loss will not have been in vain if it serves as a signpost to our future. For the erring we ask forbearance; from our critics patience, as we grope towards the ideal where each will reap without tribute to any other the full results of his toil.[47]

The Tide Ebbs

TROUBLES rarely come singly, and the League's problems were no exception to the old maxim. On April 29, 1921, the Minnesota Supreme Court at last ruled on the appeal of Townley and Gilbert from their conviction in Jackson County in 1919 on charges of conspiring to discourage enlistments. The court quoted at length from the speeches of the defendants introduced at the trial by the prosecution and concluded that this circumstantial evidence, combined with the direct evidence based on the testimony of Ferdinand Teigen, clearly established the defendants' guilt. "Granting that he is a man of doubtful veracity and the defendants' enemy," it said, the jury had heard Teigen subjected to cross-examination and believed him. The court examined in some detail a few of what it conceived to be the most important of the 102 errors alleged by the appellants to have occurred in the proceedings of the trial court, and, without denying that errors may have existed, it found the principal ones not substantial enough to warrant overruling the verdict of the jury. In general, it said, the rule would be applied that "a criminal conviction will not be reversed for technical errors where the substantial rights of the accused have not been so violated as to make it reasonably clear that a fair trial was not had, where, as here, the guilt of the accused is clearly established." [1]

Just four days before the recall election in North Dakota the United States Supreme Court denied certiorari in the case, and the long legal battle was over. [2] Townley had gone to Fargo the day before the recall to get the election returns at first hand and to close up some of his private affairs before serving his sentence. He was there when the Jackson

County court was officially notified of the refusal of the Supreme Court to review the conviction, and Judge Dean immediately issued commitment papers. A number of Leaguers had planned a big demonstration in the form of a special train or an auto parade across the state to Jackson, but the commitment papers were issued too quickly and County Attorney Nicholas threatened to have Townley's bond forfeited unless he appeared at once. Even so, when Townley arrived at Jackson on the afternoon of November 2, there were between two and three hundred friends present to greet him and escort him to the jail.

A dozen or more representatives of national news services, special correspondents, photographers, and even a newsreel cameraman were present to witness the jailing, and although Townley had asked that the formality be waived, the sheriff insisted on reading the commitment papers to the crowd from the steps of the jail, and as the door closed a fireman in the adjoining building turned on a siren. As befitted a prominent guest, the small cell had been freshly whitewashed. It was not a heavily populated county and the only other involuntary inhabitants were a "bootlegger" and a youth who was serving thirty days because of his inability to raise a twenty-five-dollar fine imposed for stealing an old automobile tire. It was reported that one of Townley's first acts was to pay the boy's fine and give him money for a railroad ticket home.

E. H. Nicholas dropped in to inform the prisoner charitably that he no longer felt any bitterness toward him, and Townley, shaking hands, replied that he realized it was the prosecutor's duty to "do his best to get a conviction and make it stand up on appeal." Several hundred letters from all over the country were awaiting the League president, and the national office arranged to provide a secretary to help him with correspondence. It was announced that on visiting days he would confer with League officials and farmers and that his time would be spent in "studying and forming plans for the future of the farmers' organization." [3] During his stay in jail he prepared an editorial for each issue of the *Leader*, the main theme of which was advocacy of revival of the United States Grain Corporation for the purpose of guaranteeing minimum prices to farmers. Townley found the incarceration not too unpleasant, terming it the first real rest he had had in seven years.[4] Joseph Gilbert was at the time still serving his term in the Goodhue County jail, and did not transfer his residence to Jackson until shortly after Townley had completed his ninety-day sentence.

In the early years the League organization, as we have seen, was based on what it called "democratic centralization." The movement for greater state autonomy, however, had steadily gained force and had had its effect upon the 1919 national convention, when county organizations had been provided for and a reallocation of dues made. Many sincere men thought it best that the League should be a cooperative federation of state units, and there were always others in the various states who sought power for themselves. The pressure rapidly increased, and neither Townley nor the *Leader* vigorously opposed the trend toward decentralization, though they made clear their fears that the organization would lose its effectiveness as a fighting machine.

Long strides were taken by the meeting of the national committee at Minneapolis on March 8 and 9, 1921. It unanimously re-elected William Lemke to a six-year term as a member of the National Executive Committee, approved the books of the League, and authorized the *Leader* to reduce its subscription rate from $2.50 to $1.50 per year and to commence a drive for wider circulation outside the League membership. Its really significant actions, however, were the changes in the relationships between the national and state organizations:

The states were henceforth to receive $14 and the national League $4 of the biennial membership fee, half of the latter amount going to the support of the *Leader*.

The states rather than the national organization were to pay for and determine the policies of their own newspapers.

The keeping of books and accounts was transferred to the states, with the national League to receive summaries and conduct a periodic audit.

The national staff was to be reduced about one third and the state staffs increased as needed.

State committees were to direct all state activity, pay all expenses, and appoint the state manager, subject to national approval.

State conventions were to have full power to frame their political and economic programs, endorse state candidates, and decide whether to operate in the traditional fashion or as independent parties, while the national convention was to determine national political and economic policy.[5]

These changes, with the exception of the last item, clearly indicated a tremendous departure from the past, although to a considerable degree they were but a recognition of a power shift which had already occurred or was well under way. The convention indicated its desire that a huge new membership drive be undertaken, both for new members and to re-enroll the old ones, yet there was little League activity in the states other than North Dakota during most of 1921. In August the *Leader* announced plans for a big organizational and educational campaign throughout the winter months, but only very limited action along these lines ever developed. The fact was that League revenues had dwindled to a point where the large-scale operations of former days were virtually impossible. With the organizing activities now in the hands of the state Leagues, many of the national staff of lecturers and supervisors moved into the work in individual states or drifted away from the League entirely.

The situation was accurately indicated by a sudden change in the policy of the *Leader*. In the six years of its existence it had never pressed its subscribers on the matter of renewals. Since the League had wanted the *Leader*'s message to get out to as many as possible, no one was ever cut off the circulation list except at his own request, a practice which doubtless contributed to the difficulty of re-enrolling members since many naturally felt that they received all the benefits of the organization, including the paper, without the necessity of paying dues. In October of 1921 the *Leader* announced that subscriptions must be renewed if it were to continue. Hundreds were then running out, the paper said, and it was essential that they be renewed at once without waiting for an organizer to come around. Sales representatives to work on a commission basis in every township were also sought. On November 14 the League organ appeared as the *National Leader* instead of the *Nonpartisan Leader*, with no reason given for the change, and on May 1, 1922, it became a monthly rather than a semimonthly publication and further reduced its subscription rate to one dollar per year.

A. C. Townley stepped out of the Jackson County jail in time to attend a state conference of the leaders of the North Dakota League held in Bismarck in mid-February, which was to be followed by the state convention in Fargo a month later. As he left the jail, however, he was promptly arrested by North Dakota authorities and taken to Fargo, where he was charged with having in 1919 influenced J. J. Hastings, then vice president of the Scandinavian-American Bank of Fargo, to embezzle $3000 and invest it in the United States Sisal Trust, in which Townley was alleged to be personally interested. I.V.A. heads had promised the jailing of League leaders and were in need of results. Townley was released on bail, and three days after the state convention the case was dismissed on motion of the prosecuting attorney, the court having found that no embezzlement had taken place—there was merely a loan to the Sisal Trust which had been repaid three months later.[6]

Townley's jail-cell meditations had led him to the conclusion that the best future for the Nonpartisan League lay in the "balance of power" role, in supporting the desirable candidates of any political party in much the traditional fashion of the American Federation of Labor. The system would work best, he felt, if League endorsements were held off until just before elections, forcing candidates to seek its support, after which they would be considered pledged to the League program. The suggestion found many supporters but did not by any means meet with unmixed enthusiasm. The principal battles at both the conference and the state convention in North Dakota were fought first over the issue of control of the state organization and second over the "balance of power" proposal.

The real struggle of the convention revolved around the question of whether the North Dakota League was to continue to be dominated by the Liederbach-Kaldor-Levang faction, currently in control of the state committee and the *Fargo Courier-News*, or by the Townley-Lemke faction, represented on the state committee by Maddock and Walker. Feelings ran high, and the *Courier-News* sounded almost as if it had returned to its pre-League status as it announced that A. C. Townley was endeavoring to re-establish himself as "the supreme autocrat of the state." The delegates to the convention were almost evenly divided.

Fearing that the fight over leadership might disrupt the entire organization, Townley took a momentous step. He announced that in order that his personal leadership might not be an issue, he would offer his resignation as president of the National Nonpartisan League as soon as the national committee could be assembled. The minority members of the state committee then offered to resign if the majority would, in order that a new committee might be elected. The majority members were furious and begged that they be retained, but the convention accepted both proposals. Townley and Lemke, in a sense victorious in this encounter, did not put up a fight for the "balance of power" scheme, merely suggesting it as a possibility, and after a lengthy wrangle the convention decided to continue with the familiar tactics which had proved their worth, endorsing a full slate headed by state Senator Bert F. Baker, for governor and Lynn J. Frazier for United States senator.[7]

It had become clear to Arthur Townley long before he began his jail sentence that the reins of the organization, for the birth and development of which he had been so largely responsible and of which the anti-League forces still claimed that he was absolute dictator, had to a very real degree slipped from his hands. Upon his release he found that in several states, though not in all, even his advice was looked upon as "bossing" or "butting in," and he concluded that his usefulness as League president was past. The belief was confirmed by the events of the North Dakota state convention, which precipitated his decision to resign. The national committee met in May and somewhat unhappily accepted his resignation, replacing him on the National Executive Committee with H. F. Samuels of Idaho, and in July F. B. Wood was named national president.[8]

Townley had no plans for the future—his life had been wholly devoted to the League for more than seven years. Nevertheless, he accepted the situation philosophically, feeling that what he had set out to do had largely been accomplished. In 1915 he had anticipated that with luck the League he intended to organize might have some influence in one state election, at least forcing more consideration of the farmers' demands, and its subsequent successes had exceeded even his wildest dreams. Now the original program had been adopted, had been referred to the people repeatedly and approved, and for the most part was in operation. While the organization had not succeeded in controlling other states, he was certain that it had greatly liberalized the politics of those in which it had worked, and the efforts had therefore not been in vain.[9]

When the national committee accepted his resignation, Townley agreed to stay on as head of organization work, which was to be separated from the management of political campaigns. His argument was that in striving to elect candidates to office, the League had lost sight of the need for a solid, active membership base, essential to either political or economic success. It was also announced that he would continue to write a regular column for the *Leader*. He knew full well, however, as did most of the top leaders, that the League as such, barring a miracle, was on the downgrade.

A few weeks before the 1922 North Dakota primary election Attorney General Johnson secured an indictment from a Fargo grand jury of Townley, Lemke, Cathro, and H. A. Paddock, a former secretary to the Industrial Commission, for conspiring to have the Bank of North Dakota make advances to the Scandinavian-American Bank of Fargo when they knew it to be insolvent, for misusing the funds of the Scandinavian-American Bank, for concealing alleged insolvency, and for otherwise violating the state banking code. Since it was impossible for the trial to be held before the primaries, the League wailed that this was simply another attempt to hang charges over the heads of League leaders during a campaign. As a matter of fact the case dragged through the fall elections too, and it was not until April 12, 1923, that it was finally dismissed.[10]

The most interesting battle of the primaries pitted Lynn Frazier against Porter J. McCumber for the seat in the United States Senate. McCumber, a powerful figure in the Senate for some years, was possessed of an extremely cold and aloof personality, and from the day of his election in 1899 by the state legislature he had remained a faithful errand boy for the McKenzie group. The Progressive Republicans had long had a thorough distaste for McCumber, and the final straw came in 1921 when the return of a Republican national administration made available a bit of patronage. McCumber and Ladd both made recommendations to the President for United States marshal, district attorney, and a district judge to occupy the bench jointly with Judge Amidon until his retirement, but the former's recommendations naturally bore more weight.

When Harding's appointment of Andrew Miller of Bismarck as district judge was announced, there was an immediate torrent of protest, as he was felt to be a political "hack" completely unqualified for the position. McCumber was asked to come before a meeting of Progressives to answer questions, but he replied that while he would appear to read a prepared statement he would under no conditions submit to questioning.

The Progressives were in a difficult position, since they had no use for either McCumber or Frazier. A. J. Gronna would have liked nothing better than the opportunity to unseat McCumber, whom he detested personally and blamed in large measure for his own defeat in 1920, but he died before the primaries. It was clear that endorsement of anyone else would simply ensure the nomination of McCumber, and that there was in fact only one way to beat him. Reluctantly, therefore, though they were poles apart in philosophy from Leaguers, even such stanch conservatives as N. C. Young turned to the support of Lynn Frazier, whom despite their disagreements they knew to be honest and upright.[11] Many persons felt that Frazier had been done an injustice and treated too harshly in the recall, and he profited from this natural reaction.

Though there were a number of I.V.A.'s who contended that the senatorship was a minor issue compared with the welfare of the state, neither faction conducted the active kind of campaign which had become so familiar in recent years. Both sides, said the *Grand Forks Herald* on the day before the election, were puzzled by the silence of the voters.[12] There was, however, nothing ominous about it—"normalcy" had simply come to North Dakota as to the rest of the nation. Frazier emerged victorious over McCumber by better than 10,000 votes, while Nestos received the gubernatorial nomination by a similar majority over Baker. The League nominated its candidates for state auditor, commissioner of insurance, and the three railroad commissioners, while all others were I.V.A.[13] The Democratic nominee for senator was their perennial favorite, J. F. T. O'Connor, who in a later day was to be appointed comptroller of the currency by Franklin Roosevelt.

In Minnesota the Nonpartisan League and the Working People's Nonpartisan League once again held separate conventions at the same time, but sentiment in both conventions was strong for a third party rather than attempting to operate through the old parties. Thus the Farmer-Labor party, nominally in existence for almost four years, was at last formally activated, and though the Minnesota branch of the Nonpartisan League elected a new state committee and maintained a separate existence for a short time, it had in effect been superseded. A full slate of candidates was endorsed, headed by Henrik Shipstead for United States senator and Magnus Johnson, one of the first and most faithful Leaguers in Minnesota, for governor. There was, of course, no primary contest.[14]

Despite the obvious signs of decline of the League organization, branches had been started in three new states in the fall of 1921. In all three cases, however, the new Leagues were promoted by either local enthusiasts or former workers with the national League, rather than by the parent organization itself. In Oregon the League was looked upon as the political arm of the other farmers' organizations, and before the end of the year it had already endorsed C. E. Spence, master of the state Grange, for governor.[15] In Wyoming the League was overshadowed by the existence of a branch of the national Farmer-Labor party, and its activities were so limited as to attract almost no attention. The California League, organized in the winter of 1921–22 by D. C. Dorman, one-time manager of the organization department of the National Nonpartisan League, and Walter Thomas Mills, listed A. C. Townley on its letterhead as national president but really had little connection with the national organization. It was based on an entirely different plan of organization, involving representation by groups, such as farmers, housewives, factory workers, and professional workers; the letterhead proclaimed that its purpose was "to work for an administration of public affairs through proportional representation of all the useful occupations." [16] In none of these states did the League ever develop into a significant political factor.

The Nebraska and Montana Leagues both accepted the "balance of power" role advocated by Townley, though in the latter case the organization was from the beginning behind the candidacy of Burton K. Wheeler for the United States Senate.[17]

In Wisconsin Robert M. LaFollette was up for re-election, as was Governor John J. Blaine, and the campaign was a LaFollette affair from beginning to end. The League of course supported him wholeheartedly, and it soon was absorbed by the LaFollette progressive movement. In Colorado the League was largely taken over by the Democratic party, while in the weakly organized states of Iowa, Kansas, Texas, and Oklahoma there was a gradual drifting back to former allegiances. The South Dakota and Washington Leagues, had, of course, operated as third parties in 1920 and they did so again in 1922. In the summer of 1922 Idaho followed suit, a new Progressive party having been formed at Boise in June by a coalition of the League, organized labor, and the "Committee of 48." [18]

On October 30, 1922, just in time for the I.V.A. to use it in the campaign as a claim of achievement, the machinery of the first unit of the North Dakota state mill at Grand Forks was set in motion by Governor Nestos, with some two hundred persons standing in a drizzling rain to watch the ceremony.[19] Eight years after the demands for such a mill had helped give rise to the Nonpartisan League, this last of the League enterprises was finally under way.

With Frazier opposing O'Connor for the senatorial seat, the *Grand Forks Herald* was in a quandary. Either North Dakota must send a man "little in accord with what North Dakota really stands for," it said, or it must face the apparently odious necessity of sending a Democrat "in order to escape that fate." [20] The I.V.A. slate now included O'Connor and the Democratic candidates for the state offices won by Leaguers in the Republican primary, and the *Herald* shortly came to its support. A vote for Frazier, it indicated, was simply inconceivable.[21] Along with this expected opposition, however, came unexpected assistance as Senator LaFollette took time off from his activities in Wisconsin to campaign briefly in both North Dakota and Minnesota for Frazier and Shipstead.[22]

In the general elections all the North Dakota Leaguers who had won the Republican nomination were successful. Frazier, only a year before recalled as governor, won over O'Connor 101,312 to 92,464. Governor Nestos, however, swamped William Lemke, who had run as an independent with League support after the defeat of Baker in the primary, by a vote of 110,321 to 81,048.[23] In Minnesota third-party tactics at last proved successful, at least in part—Henrik Shipstead was elected to the Senate with a plurality of 83,539 over Senator Frank B. Kellogg. Magnus Johnson, however, lost to Preus for the governorship by a margin of 14,000 votes. Farmer-Labor-backed candidates Oscar Keller, O. J. Kvale, and Knud Wefald were elected to Congress from the fourth, seventh, and ninth districts respectively, although only Wefald was technically running as a Farmer-Laborite.[24] The League now controlled neither house of the North Dakota legislature, but the new party in Minnesota managed to elect no fewer than twenty-four senators and forty-six representatives, materially increasing its legislative strength.[25]

A year later Magnus Johnson had his revenge when he overwhelmed Jacob Preus 290,165 to 195,319 in the contest for the seat in the United States Senate left vacant by the death of Senator Knute Nelson.[26]

In addition to Frazier and Shipstead the League laid claim to a number of other successes, including Senator LaFollette, Senator Wheeler of Montana, Senator Smith W. Brookhart of Iowa, Senator R. B. Howell of Nebraska, Senator C. C. Dill of Washington, three congressmen in Minnesota, one in North Dakota, ten in Wisconsin, two in Nebraska, one in Montana, and seven in Oklahoma. State Leagues had also endorsed successful candidates for governor in Wisconsin, Nebraska, Colorado, and Kansas, plus scattered other state officers.[27] In all cases outside North Dakota and Minnesota, however, with the possible exception of Wheeler in Montana, these men were not primarily League candidates, and it is impossible to determine to what extent League votes were significant factors in their success.

Despite these "successes," however they might be interpreted, it was more than clear that the League in its original form was rapidly on its way out. The Publishers' National Service Bureau had planned in February of 1920 to reorganize on a cooperative basis in order to make the project self-supporting,[28] but with the coming of the depression it, too, found itself in financial difficulties. By 1921 its activities had declined to a point where it was virtually inoperative, and in November 1922 it went into receivership.[29] The *Fargo Courier-News* carried on manfully until early 1923, when the incorporators sold it to a private publisher. Like the *Grand Forks American*, though not to such a great extent, it had been the victim of a serious advertising boycott, and throughout most of its existence it had been something of a drain on the League treasury.[30]

Finally, with the July 1923 issue, the *Leader* breathed its last, suspended because no funds were available for further publication. The national office, it said, no longer was receiving any share of the fees from state organizations, if indeed they were receiving any themselves. In October the North Dakota League formally severed connections with the virtually nonexistent national body in order to continue on its own. The last great farmers' crusade had ground to a halt.

In its eight years of existence the League had accumulated nearly $2,000,000 worth of unpaid postdated checks. The system made possible the rapid building of membership, but when they were not paid the League suffered not only the loss of that anticipated revenue—it also lost the organizer's commission, the cost of trying to collect on the check, and the expense of the newspapers sent to the "member," often for a long period of time.[31] Some persons, of course, had at various times stopped payment on their checks, and in some instances there had been difficulties with bankers, but it was also true that the postwar deflation had been a serious blow, and even though biennial dues had been reduced to $6.50 at the end of 1922 many farmers were unable to contribute any amount to political activity.

In February of 1923 Townley founded the National Producers' Alliance, in which organization he held the position of "national organizer." The final issue of the *Leader* was largely devoted to this new organization, which was intended to involve no political action whatsoever. Once the farmers of the nation were organized, paying a $4.50 membership fee and $2.00 per year dues, which was to include a subscription to a national paper, the three-step program was simplicity itself: (1) determining costs of production, (2) demanding a return of the cost of production plus a "reasonable" profit, and (3) holding products off the market when prices offered were below the cost of production, marketing them gradually so that there would at no time be an oversupply. Farmers, it was argued, must fix prices just as others do. The technical problems involved in such an undertaking apparently were to be worried about when they arose. The *Leader*, in commenting on the new affiliation of the League's former president, indicated in a rather cryptic statement that he still had faith in political activity—but for someone else:

Mr. Townley wishes all Leaguers to be assured that he has not abandoned in the least his belief in political action by farmers . . . He expects the farmers to continue their political movement. But Mr. Townley has been brought by his study and his experience to the very definite conclusion that farming can not be made to pay by politics alone. Mr. Townley is, therefore, turning politics over to those who want to deal with politics.[32]

In subsequent years, after giving up the short-lived National Producers' Alliance, A. C. Townley drifted haphazardly from one activity to another. For a short time he promoted the financing of gas-well drilling at Robinson, North Dakota, occasionally he was an unsuccessful candidate for nomination for public office, including those of con-

347

gressman and governor of Minnesota, and during the depths of the depression of the 1930s he devoted months of a hand-to-mouth existence to the profitless task of traveling about the state of North Dakota telling impoverished farmers how they might save their farms from foreclosure under the provisions of the Frazier-Lemke Act.

It is a striking commentary on the fortunes of politics that the man who once made governors and legislators, whose word was law to tens of thousands of faithful followers, whose speaking swayed multitudes as but few men have ever done, known at once as a savior and a demon, acknowledged foremost leader of one of America's great movements of protest, should today be a virtually penniless traveling salesman, lonely, unknown to most who meet him, wandering aimlessly through the states in which he once knew fame and honor. The Nonpartisan League was Arthur Townley's one great work; never again did he find a niche where his talents could be utilized and in which he could feel content.

The amazingly rapid success of the League in North Dakota is attributable to a number of factors. Although the League at times tended to exaggerate them, friend and foe alike agree that there existed in 1915 serious evils in the marketing system which handled the principal product of the state and thus directly affected the lives of a great majority of the population. It is hardly surprising that this, coupled with the fact that for many years the dominant economic interests had had a most important hand in the politics of the state, created a situation in which the farmers of North Dakota were ready for a spectacular type of remedy. This state had been but little beyond the frontier stage at the time of the Granger and Populist movements, and their impact had been slight. In a sense Populism came late to North Dakota, yet the League was unique on the political scene. A strong persecution complex had developed over the years, and there was a motive akin to revenge in many hearts, tied in with the desire for greater returns from crops. These farmers, indeed, were almost pathetically eager to become the dominating political force in this state in which they constituted so great a majority. They needed only a leader to show them the way.

A. C. Townley could have seized upon no more opportune time for the launching of his new political movement than when the accumulated resentment of the farmers reached the boiling point with the defeat of the terminal elevator bill at the 1915 legislative session. The League capitalized on this resentment and mushroomed in strength. Initially it appealed with almost equal facility to all farmers, well-to-do and impoverished alike, for all had grounds for dissatisfaction with existing conditions, but though many of the former remained in the organization its strongest hold was always upon the economically less fortunate. It was in the western portion of North Dakota, where the land was poorest, climatic conditions most hazardous, transportation costs highest, and credit conditions most rigorous, that the League was completely invincible, and much the same situation was evident in other states. The national origin of the population seems to have been of little significance in determining the areas in which the League was strong or weak.

Even as we recognize the fortuitous conditions under which the movement started, it would, however, be hard to overestimate the importance of Townley's organizing tactics. The principles of applied psychology and high-pressure salesmanship were applied to politics with outstanding success, and the organization was "sold" to the members as no other political movement has ever been. It is perfectly true that the farmers did not organize themselves into the League; they were organized *by* the League. Unique indeed was the use of highly trained professional organizers and lecturers, but the system was based on sound politics—organization from the bottom up and the establishment of the broadest possible base of support before entering upon campaign activity. Financing the organization by means of dues had the dual advantage of keeping the League reasonably independent of "outside" elements and giving the members an additional stake in its success, so that they would be more likely to participate actively.

No single item was of greater importance to League success than the maintenance of its own newspapers for the dissemination of information and propaganda and the guidance of the actions of the members. Without the *Nonpartisan Leader*, later the state *Leaders*, and to a lesser degree the standard-type dailies and weeklies which took the League point of view, coordinated action and unity of such a scattered membership would have been impossible. Had the farmers been dependent upon the opposition press for information about the organization it would not have lasted six months. Instead, they were told to believe nothing except what they read in their own publications, and thousands obeyed those instructions to the letter. In many areas the faith in the League, the *Leader*, and Townley was implicit—the common saying that "the farmers would vote for a yellow dog if he were endorsed by the Nonpartisan League" was only a mild exaggeration.

The League was acutely aware of the reputation of farmers for inability to "stick together," and it placed unending emphasis on "organization" as the only road to the achievement of desired objectives. The farmers were the only unorganized group, it said, and by united action alone could they expect to combat the highly organized "interests" they opposed. In getting a large body of farmers to "stick" to an organization and a program the League had success unparalleled before or since. Yet in the end the League died in large part because the farmers ceased paying dues and actively working at politics.

While this would seem on the surface fairly significant evidence against the possibility of long-continued political unity of farmers, the fact remains that the League itself was in no small degree responsible for the decline of support. Who can say what the result might have been had the North Dakota League administration been more wise in its selection of managers for state industries, had the League not become involved in the various subsidiary enterprises—and had a depression not intervened at a crucial moment? Nevertheless, it is obvious that to bear the stamp of permanency a movement must be able to overcome and outlive adversity. In North Dakota to a degree the League has done so, but elsewhere, at least in its original form, it has not.

The gradual acceptance of many of the reforms it advocated meant, as it has for most third-party movements in America, a lessened drawing power and a drift of the membership back to more conventional political paths. Also, the League learned painfully as have many other movements and parties that it is vastly easier to whip up enthusiasm while carrying the attack than it is to maintain unified support when charged with the responsibility of government. In politics at least the offense is simpler than defense.

The tremendously important role of A. C. Townley in the founding, building, and early years of operation of the League led to the oft-reiterated charges that he was the "autocrat" of the organization, and to a considerable degree this was true. There is no doubt that for years his decisions largely determined the policies of the League and that he personally directed much of its activity, yet he was not by any means the absolute dictator that he was frequently alleged to be. He held his position of pre-eminence because of his unquestioned ability as an organizer, a speaker, and a leader of men. The farmers had confidence in him, and he was, after all, the only head the organization had had throughout most of its existence.

Townley had, it is true, what was in a sense a controlled press, though there was no shortage of opposition papers, but the other appurtenances of dictatorship were missing. He had no hold on either the membership or the officers and employees of the League except their belief in the cause which he represented, and their conviction that he was the most able leader that could be found. The advice of his circle of lieutenants was influential, perhaps in some cases too much so, and there were many times when he did not have his way. The national committee, over whose members he had no unusual control, could have dispensed with his services at any time had they wished to do so, and the fact that he had far from an absolute grip on the organization could be no more adequately illustrated than by the manner in which his power waned between 1920 and 1922.

Nevertheless, for the first four years the League certainly was characterized by highly centralized power. It seriously endeavored to maintain the utmost democracy in its political action, and in the selection of candidates and delegates the membership undoubtedly had a greater voice than they had ever had in their earlier political party affiliations. Internally, however, there was a considerable degree of one-man rule. The League always contended that in order to fight battles it needed a commander, but it stoutly insisted that its strong central power was derived from and subject to the membership.

During the formative period there was a real need for a strong hand at the controls and without Townley's driving force organization would never have been accomplished. Yet the League would probably have been in a stronger position, particularly from the standpoint of public reaction, if greater internal democracy had been introduced after stability was achieved. The truth is that the League membership, on the whole, apparently had little if any objection to conditions as they existed—the complaints of "dictatorship" came from other sources. It was criticized, it seems, largely because it got results, as is not uncommon in politics; the hard-working farmers themselves clearly had no desire for additional time-consuming duties and were more than willing to leave the day-to-day work of a political organization to professional leaders.

The introduction of more election processes into the League might have had the advantage of making possible the development of other topnotch leaders, but during these years Townley would have been an overwhelming victor in any contest for the presidency. The results when the League actually did decentralize were far from favorable, it is true, but this occurred when the organization was already breaking up and too many other factors were involved to make possible a judgment on the effect of this change. What the results might have been had "democratization" been brought about in 1918, for example, is of course purely a matter of speculation.

Certainly one of the most interesting and significant features of the Nonpartisan League was its objective of the destruction of "blind party loyalty," and the substitution of the reality of economic interests for inherited traditions and catchword issues. The words of Jay Gould were quoted as a pertinent example of the attitude of the powers the farmers were fighting: "In Democratic states I am a Democrat; in Republican states I am a Republican; but I am always for the Erie Railroad." [33] Although it never completely accomplished the objective, the League professed to stand for the complete ignoring of old party lines and the backing of men who would best serve the farmers' interests regardless of their party affiliations.

It did not ignore, however, the importance of party labels in winning elections, especially since the votes of many persons other than members must be secured, and its technique of utilizing the direct primary to take over the dominant party of a state was both novel and highly effective. Its election successes were normally achieved by adding the straight-ticket votes of the majority party to its own fairly solid bloc. As Samuel P. Huntington points out, the League once again illustrated the power of a well-organized minority,[34] and the opposition in North Dakota was most successful when it copied League tactics.

Candidates for public office were supposedly always to be "drafted," and persons who sought endorsement were to be avoided. Once elected, the individual, it was assumed, would in no way concern himself with personal glory, but would devote himself to unselfish service to the farmers and to the state as a whole—that was the kind of men who were to be selected. It might have been anticipated, however, that the system of selection would not be infallible, and it was only natural that many should come to enjoy the prominence of public office. Though in the early years the League achieved a remarkable freedom from self-seeking on the part of candidates and officeholders, the human love of power and prestige proved too great. Many came actively to seek endorsements and positions of power in the organization, and the League steadily weakened as the spirit of selflessness deteriorated.

The argument of those who contended that there was no fundamental difference between the two major parties in the United States was appreciably strengthened by the appearance, especially in North Dakota and Minnesota, of strong Democratic-Republican alliances against the League, both in campaigns and within state legislatures, though such an argument always boils down to one's definition of "fundamental." The League itself found it virtually impossible to maintain complete nonpartisanship over a long period of time. Eventually in all states it either became a separate party or was submerged in the existing parties. In some it had been compelled almost from the beginning to function as a third party. Even in North Dakota where it nominally continues to operate in the traditional manner, as early as 1919 it had become in effect one party of a new two-party alignment, and was adhering strictly to its own members and elected officials, defending them against attack whether right or wrong. At various times and places, especially where weakly organized, it resorted to a "balance of power" role.

The most persistent charge against the League, and one which continued to dog its footsteps, was that the leaders were Socialists and that its program was socialism and therefore bad. Proof of the inevitable dire consequences of a socialist experiment was not considered necessary and was rarely offered except in exaggerated instances. A careful distinction must here be drawn between the League membership and the officers and employees of the organization. The great bulk of the former were not, of course, Socialists, though many in time developed essentially similar points of view on many issues under the influence of the League press and the extremely able League lecturers. For most of the farmers the purpose of the League was simply the reform of the marketing system toward the end of securing a greater return from farm products.

On the other hand, a large percentage of the officers and employees were or had been members of the Socialist party, and they did not abandon their beliefs. Without them the organization would probably never have been built, for they were the crusaders—men who would work for the cause without compensation, if necessary. Townley, as previously mentioned, had no use at this time for the Socialist party even though he retained much of its basic philosophy. For him the League was an end in itself, but for many of those with whom he surrounded himself the League was but a means toward the ultimate achievement of a socialist society. This did not mean, however, as so often claimed, that these men had no real interest in the farmers. With but few exceptions they were genuinely interested in the success of the League as such and in the improvement of the lot of the midwestern farmer. Public ownership, they were convinced, was the only road to the achievement of that improvement.*

Although many Socialists worked with the League, the official attitude of the Socialist party was generally antagonistic, despite the fact that the *Call* referred to the League enthusiastically in 1917:

The farmers are after the source of the trouble—the profit system—and their aim is one with that of the Socialists, even if they are mostly oblivious of our existence.

Good for Townley and the North Dakota farmers! If they are mad we want to see them bite the agriculturalists of all other states and infect them too. We do not look upon their effort as a competitor or rival of Socialism, but a movement converging on the same road, and with the same object—the abolition of the profiteer . . . We shall indulge in no envious feelings if they send a score of their representatives to Congress before we do. Nor do we care much about the name. While their main object remains the extirpation of the profit system they are Socialists, whatever other name they may call themselves, and are working for the realization of Socialism.[35]

This was not the view of the more doctrinaire members who largely controlled both the national and state parties. Socialists were subsequently warned against opportunism of the League variety, and a war-

---

* "Regardless of party names," says William Lemke, "the leaders of the League were interested in making North Dakota and the nation a better place to live in. They were interested in the underprivileged. They did not wish to destroy the social order but to improve it . . . A. C. Townley was sincerely attempting and did improve the conditions of agriculture. If you knew Townley at his best you would have known him as a genius, and, of course, a genius is never satisfied with his accomplishments. Usually a genius wants to change the world overnight . . ." (Letter to the author, Aug. 27, 1947.)

time Socialist year book pictured the League as an organization of "landowners made rich by the recent high level of prices, who are now thirsting for political power for themselves."[36] Showing a fine disdain for political office, the year book pointed out that Socialists who joined the League were mistaking the mission of the party, while state organizations were reminded that fusion or compromise meant being swallowed up and destroyed. The power of the Socialist party, it was said, rests "in its clear cut, specific declaration of political and economic principles, rather than in the number of votes cast for party candidates." State units were urged to

. . . maintain the revolutionary position of the Socialist Party and maintain in the utmost possible vigor the propaganda of Socialism, unadulterated by association of office seekers, to the end that the solidarity of the working class, the principles of international Socialism, may continue to lay the foundation for the social revolution.

The social revolution, not political office, is the end and aim of the Socialist Party. No compromise, no political trading.[37]

But what of the "socialism" of the League program? Obviously, in advocating state credit facilities, state insurance systems, public ownership of certain means of distribution, and the like, the program involved a degree of state socialism. It meant turning to the state to remedy undenied evils in the private enterprise system, and in those particular areas of endeavor attempting to substitute the public good for private profit. To those whose pocketbooks were adversely affected this was of course nothing short of the first step in the decay of civilization, but the producers had begun to ask themselves why the state, as the representative of all the people, should not serve the people in whatever way the majority deemed best, whether politically or economically.

The League professed to consider its program as a "middle way," an alternative to revolution. It accepted some elements of socialist theory and rejected others, as for example the collectivization of land. While the demands for state action were radical, they represented no vital departure from the farmer's traditional views on property rights. The basic philosophy of the Nonpartisan League was eloquently summed up in the final report of the League Industrial Commission in North Dakota:

They [the farmers of North Dakota] have undertaken the great and noble work of their own emancipation, and thereby the saving of the country from industrial disaster. They have arrived at the conclusion that this can be done by the simple method of applying to this situation the machinery of democracy which has worked so well for more purely political and social purposes . . .

They conceive that this democratic system of government of ours was established for the purpose of securing to all individuals, communities and interests the equal right to life, liberty, and the pursuit of happiness . . . They hold that one of the purposes of the establishment of government is that of promoting the general welfare of the people . . .

They hold that where necessary it is as consistent with the principles of the Declaration and the Constitution to promote that welfare directly, through government operation, as indirectly, by restriction or regulation. In other words, they hold that the government has a positive as well as a negative function. And in so holding they do not mean that the government should take over all activities; that industry should be socialized; that individual enterprises should be curtailed or discouraged. What they hold is that when in the course of the development of private enterprises power concentrates in the hands of certain groups and is so used as to prevent or to curtail the equal opportunity of other groups or individuals, and where that cannot be prevented by regulation, then the government should take and exercise that power. They hold that where there are certain services which must be supplied to all in order that equal industrial opportunity may be enjoyed, and that individual energy may be applied so as to secure the maximum production, government may, and sometimes must, supply that service.[38]

The first two decades of the twentieth century were not only the period of the greatest strength of the Socialist party; reform was the watchword in many areas of American life. It was the era of the direct primaries, of the initiative, referendum, and recall, of the "muckrakers," of the promotion of municipal government reorganization and research, of public ownership leagues, popular government leagues, proportional representation leagues, of prohibition, of "trust busting," and of expanded government regulation of business. A nation whose economy had for some years been growing steadily more and more under the domination of an expanding monopoly capitalism had begun to fear the monster it had created. Attacks on the "trusts" were one of the most popular items on the political bill of fare, and it was only natural that "Wall Street," always a handy and frequently logical whipping boy, should be an immediate target of the League, which never ceased to excoriate "Big Biz" in any form.

That the League was definitely in part a product of its times is evident from the nature of many of the proposals which it espoused, such as the short ballot, progressive taxation, direct legislation measures, woman suffrage, council-manager government for cities, and workmen's compensation systems. In large measure these were the ideas advocated by contemporary reform groups, with which many of the League leaders were closely connected. The League was sufficiently sincere in its belief in the general desirability of these reforms to foster actively even those, as for example the referendum and the recall, which it knew full well would promptly be used against it. Convinced that they contributed to greater political democracy, it supported them regardless of the ultimate cost.

Much has frequently been made of the idea that in a federal system of government the states may serve as "political laboratories." Experiments found valuable in one state may be adopted by other states or by the nation, and in like manner those which prove undesirable may be avoided. Numerous examples have been adduced, and in a sense the spread of the League from North Dakota to other states may be said to be another. Yet though it is true that there was much demand from those states for expansion of the League, the actual building of the organizations came largely as a result of the sending in of trained organizers and speakers by national headquarters to do the job *for* the farmers of the area.

Where such a violently controversial program as this was involved, there was little chance of agreement in adjoining states on relative desirability or undesirability, and the same battles were fought over and over again in virtually every state the League entered. Despite the fact that the League program was designed to operate primarily at the state level, the existence of state boundaries in a very real sense hindered its spread. North Dakota had been taken by storm, almost before an organized opposition could develop, but the opposition was prepared in advance for the entry of the League into other states. Though there were many reasons, previously discussed, for the lesser degree of success in other states, as for example the existence of widely different conditions, the incorrect assumption that the North Dakota program and tactics could simply be transplanted, less thorough organizing activity, and Governor Norbeck's highly effective procedure in South Dakota of taking over much of the program, of major significance was the well-organized opposition, forewarned and armed with charges of "bolshevism" and "disloyalty" and an endless supply of counterpropaganda.

The League, despite its novel character among "third-party" movements, did have its roots in the earlier movements of agrarian protest. There were many in the League ranks who were veterans of the Grange, the Alliance, and Populism, and they entered upon League activity already well grounded in much of the dogma they were to hear from the lips of a new generation of orators. The League differed from its predecessors in numerous important respects, such as its manner of organizing, its method of financing, its emphasis on absolute solidarity and on the essentiality of its own press, its Socialist leadership, its use of the direct primary, and in a considerable degree its very success. It provided striking evidence of the value of strong organization at the precinct level, an important aspect of political action in which third parties have always been disastrously weak.

Nevertheless, it is possible to point out many similarities between the Nonpartisan League and the Populist movement of a quarter-century before. Both were born of adversity and injustices among midwestern farmers, and feeding upon these accumulated grievances both grew almost overnight. The all-day picnics used with such success by the League had been utilized by the Populists in the early 1890s. There was even a ring of familiarity to the speeches. "It is a struggle between the robbers and the robbed!" cried the famous "Sockless Jerry" Simpson, and League speakers reiterated the cry. The targets of both were the railroads, the marketing system, and the financial interests—the League's charges that Wall Street owned and ran the country were the stock-in-trade of the redoubtable Mary Ellen Lease, who had audaciously advised Kansas farmers to "raise less corn and more hell." Public ownership and operation was to a large degree the answer both saw for the elimination of the evils of the "middleman."

While the Populists had operated as a national third party, the Grange and Alliance primarily as pressure groups, and the Equity and other cooperatives at least nominally outside the political sphere, the League endeavored to engage in direct political action without acquiring the disabilities common to third parties. It was one of the most striking attempts to use the primary to make an existing party express the will of the majority of the party voters, however that will might deviate from past practice, and to secure the benefits arising from voter habit and tradition as well.

Was the Nonpartisan League the last of the great farmers' crusades? On such a matter no one, of course, can claim to prophesy, but the odds are heavy that it was. As the farmer has become more and more a hopeless minority in relation to urban population, the chances of successful independent political action have steadily waned. Even the League found necessary an alliance with organized labor in virtually every state aside from North Dakota, and there it was not by any means spurned. In combination with other groups farm elements may at some time enter again into third-party activity, but another purely agrarian movement seems now almost inevitably foredoomed to insignificance.

Moreover, as the League had begun to do in 1922, the farmers have long since turned to Washington for the solutions to their economic problems, and have found well-organized pressure group activity to be highly effective. Farm group lobbies have a potent voice in the nation's capital, and the rural areas have learned to make good use of their overrepresentation both in the Congress and in the legislatures of many states. With the rural vote still an important factor in a goodly number of states neither major party is likely to sell the farmer short.

In evaluating the League program in general one must conclude that it possessed a measure of real merit. Though poorly administered in some instances and operating in its early stages under the terrific handicaps of a depression, war hatreds, and unremitting bitter opposition, it nevertheless brought significant benefits to the farmers of North Dakota. Cheaper credit and more adequate credit facilities were provided, vastly more economical hail insurance was made available, a more equitable system of taxation was established, railroad rates were lowered and improved services secured, fair weights and payment for dockage were achieved, and an important contribution was made toward gradual abolition of other evils in the marketing system. In addition to its own direct achievements, the League gave considerable impetus to cooperative marketing and to much national and state legislation directed toward the improvement of agricultural conditions.

In itself one of the most fascinating political movements in the history of the United States, the Nonpartisan League also laid much of the foundation of modern midwestern liberalism. It helped develop some of the most independently minded electorates in the country. It built one of the first successful alliances between farmers and organized labor, and gave birth to Minnesota's Farmer-Labor party, which was to control that state through the years of the great depression and which continues powerful in a fusion as the Democratic Farmer Labor party.[39] In the 1948 elections in the states of the Upper Midwest such divergent groups as Americans for Democratic Action and the Progressive party of Henry Wallace both claimed League paternity and drew upon its experiences and methods as a guide for their own actions.

The North Dakota League, after its defeat in 1922, surged forward again two years later to capture the governorship and control of the lower house. It also elected governors in 1926, 1932, and 1936, and a League lieutenant governor assumed the office of governor in 1934 after the disqualification of the Democrat who had been elected. League votes put Gerald Nye and William Langer in the United States Senate as successors to Ladd and Frazier, and repeatedly sent William Lemke (though no longer under the League banner), James Sinclair, and Usher Burdick to the House.

Since the early days of the depression the North Dakota League has been dominated to a considerable degree by William Langer, and though its strength varies somewhat with economic conditions it remains at or near the top of the political heap. State offices are commonly divided quite evenly between Leaguers and members of the other Republican faction, the so-called Republican Organizing Committee, and their relative strengths in the legislature are nearly equal as well. Leaguers are still Republicans for the sake of expediency in normally heavily Republican North Dakota, but aside from contesting the Republican primaries the League has little in common with the Republican Organizing Committee. It still on occasion runs Democrats in Republican primaries, and in some areas cooperates with the Democratic party. It flatly refused to form a "united front" with the Republican Organizing Committee after an even split in the 1948 primaries. In many respects, certainly, it is close to being a third party.

Opinion in North Dakota is sharply divided as to the value of the state mill and elevator to the state, but there is general agreement today on the part of both friends and foes of the League that the other enterprises and reforms that it instituted have served North Dakota well. Only the Home Building Association no longer exists. Although the Nonpartisan League underwent many changes after 1921, its basic philosophy has been altered surprisingly little. Still looked upon as the furthest to the left of any major element in North Dakota politics, its views no longer give rise to charges of anarchy and bolshevism. The bitter antagonism of forty years ago is gone. The radicalism of 1916 is in large measure the accepted practice of today.

FOOTNOTES, BIBLIOGRAPHY, AND INDEX

Footnotes

Chapter 1

[1] John H. Worst in a speech before the Tri-State Grain Growers Association Convention, Fargo, Jan. 20, 1916. Text in the *Nonpartisan Leader* (hereafter cited simply as *Leader*), Jan. 20, 1916, pp. 4, 13. Cf. H. G. Teigan to Jacob Vogel, Trimmer, N.D., Aug. 8, 1916 (National Nonpartisan League Papers).

[2] *Statistical Abstract of the United States, 1915*, pp. 32, 39. The Census Bureau sets the rural population at 89 per cent, but this includes villages of less than 2500 population.

[3] *Thirteenth Census of the United States, 1910*, Vol. 1, *Population*, pp. 149, 730–34.

[4] Andrew A. Bruce, *Non-Partisan League*, pp. 23–24. Bruce was violently anti-League, but there is general agreement of both sides as to this political situation.

[5] Lewis F. Crawford, *History of North Dakota*, I, p. 420.

[6] On this "Revolution of 1906" see Bruce, pp. 28–31.

[7] *Thirteenth Census of the United States, 1910*, Vol. 7, *Agriculture: Reports by States*, pp. 273–74. See also *Leader*, Nov. 4, 1915, p. 9.

[8] These facts are developed in great detail in the *Report of the Special Committee of the Minnesota House of Representatives for Investigation of the Grain Trade, 1913*, and in *Hearings on House Bill 14493*, 63 Cong., 1, 2, 3 Sess., 1915. See also Charles E. Russell, *The Story of the Nonpartisan League*, p. 168 and *passim*.

[9] This practice is also treated in the publications cited in note 8. It is developed briefly by William Langer, *The Nonpartisan League: Its Birth, Activities and Leaders*, pp. 17–18.

[10] Scott v. Frazier, 258 F. 669 (1919).

[11] *Leader*, Aug. 17, 1916, pp. 5–6. This article contains an interesting account of the whole terminal market grading process.

[12] E. F. Ladd, "Is the Present System of Grading Wheat Equitable?" *Special Bulletin No. 14*, Vol. III (Food Department), North Dakota Agricultural College Experiment Station, Jan. 1915, p. 238. See also the *Grand Forks Herald*, Feb. 21, 1916, p. 4.

[13] E. F. Ladd, "Chemical and Physical Constants for Wheat and Mill Products," *Bulletin No. 114*, North Dakota Agricultural College Experiment Station, Jan. 1916. These findings were later borne out by facts reported in Thomas Sanderson,

"The Bread Value of Wheat," *Bulletin No. 137*, North Dakota Agricultural College Experiment Station, May 1920.

¹⁴ E. F. Ladd, "Chemical and Physical Constants for Wheat and Mill Products," *Bulletin No. 114*, North Dakota Agricultural College Experiment Station, Jan. 1916, p. 274.

¹⁵ Quoted in *Leader*, Nov. 23, 1915, p. 7.

¹⁶ F. Lauriston Bullard, "The People's Czar in North Dakota," *Independent*, 98:148 (April 26, 1919).

¹⁷ E. F. Ladd, "Chemical and Physical Constants for Wheat and Mill Products," *Bulletin No. 114*, North Dakota Agricultural College Experiment Station, Jan. 1916, p. 276.

¹⁸ John H. Worst in a speech before the Tri-State Grain Growers Association Convention, Fargo, Jan. 20, 1916. Text in *Leader*, Jan. 20, 1916, pp. 4, 13.

¹⁹ Charles Edward Russell, *Bare Hands and Stone Walls*, p. 343.

²⁰ Melvin D. Hildreth, "The Farmers Capture North Dakota," *World's Work*, 32:687 (Oct. 1916).

²¹ *Ibid.*, p. 688. Cf. Russell, *Nonpartisan League*, pp. 56–57.

²² *Minneapolis Journal*, Feb. 19, 1913, p. 8. See also *Hearings on House Bill 14493*, 63 Cong., 1, 2, 3 Sess., 1915, Vol. 1, p. 464 and *passim*; and Langer, pp. 18–19.

²³ *Duluth News Tribune*, Feb. 5, 1913.

²⁴ Quoted in *Leader*, June 8, 1916, p. 7.

²⁵ John Thompson, "The National Nonpartisan League," *Review of Reviews*, 57:397 (April 1918). Robert H. Bahmer, "The Economic and Political Background of the Nonpartisan League" (Ph.D. Thesis), pp. 252–53, gives some further data on this practice. Cf. *Redwood Falls Sun*, March 28, 1913.

²⁶ Bahmer, p. 257.

²⁷ Quoted in Langer, p. 12.

²⁸ A. C. Townley to Herbert C. Hoover, food administrator of the United States, Nov. 26, 1917 (LeSueur Papers).

²⁹ *Leader*, Sept. 23, 1915, p. 6.

³⁰ Quoted in *Leader*, Sept. 30, 1915, p. 6.

³¹ *Leader*, Sept. 30, 1915, p. 11.

³² Quoted in *Leader*, Feb. 23, 1916, p. 5.

³³ *Leader*, Jan. 6, 1916, p. 11.

³⁴ Scott v. Frazier, 258 F. 669 (1919).

³⁵ *Leader*, Aug. 31, 1916, p. 10.

³⁶ Lynn J. Frazier in Fargo Labor Day Address, 1916; quoted in *Leader*, Sept. 14, 1916, p. 3. The idea was put similarly by Senator McCumber in a speech before the Grain Growers Convention in 1909 (*Fargo Forum*, Jan. 22, 1909, p. 11).

³⁷ *Leader*, Aug. 10, 1916, p. 4; March 24, 1919, p. 5.

³⁸ *Leader*, Sept. 7, 1916, p. 16.

³⁹ Arthur LeSueur, "The Nonpartisan League," ms. in LeSueur Papers.

⁴⁰ *Leader*, Oct. 14, 1915, pp. 2, 9.

⁴¹ *Leader*, April 20, 1916, pp. 5, 11.

⁴² Meyer Jacobstein, "Farm Credit in a Northwestern State," *American Economic Review*, 3:598–605 (Sept. 1913).

⁴³ *Leader*, Dec. 30, 1915, p. 6. General discussions of the grievances of the farmers in this period may be found in Eugene W. Burgess, *La "Nonpartisan League": Une Expérience Américaine de Socialisme d'Etat Agraire*, pp. 33–69; Bruce, pp. 34–50; Herbert E. Gaston, *The Nonpartisan League*, pp. 15–40; and Alvin S. Tostlebe, *The Bank of North Dakota: An Experiment in Agrarian Banking*, pp. 36–37. It is interesting to note that with one exception, John Steen, even the stanchest anti-Leaguers agree completely on the existence and nature of these

grievances, although some contend that they were subsequently exaggerated by the League.

⁴⁴ See Robert H. Bahmer, "The American Society of Equity," *Agricultural History*, 14:33–63 (Jan. 1940); Theodore Saloutos, "The Rise of the Equity Cooperative Exchange," *Mississippi Valley Historical Review*, 32:31–62 (June 1945); Bruce, pp. 54–58. Bahmer also includes considerable material on the earlier movements.

⁴⁵ Bruce, p. 57.

⁴⁶ The report is summarized in the *Journal of the North Dakota House of Representatives*, 1915, pp. 165–189. See also *Leader*, March 9, 1916, pp. 4, 6; Gaston, p. 42; Russell, *Nonpartisan League*, pp. 105–6.

⁴⁷ Theodore Saloutos, "The Rise of the Nonpartisan League in North Dakota, 1915–1917," *Agricultural History*, 20:44–45 (Jan. 1946).

⁴⁸ Interview with Chief Justice A. M. Christianson of the North Dakota Supreme Court, Sept. 1, 1948; *Grand Forks Herald*, Feb. 3, 1915, pp. 1, 6–7; *Bismarck Tribune*, Feb. 3, 1915, p. 1.

⁴⁹ Speech before the Producers and Consumers Convention, St. Paul, Sept. 20, 1917. J. I. Levine's Reports, 3rd Installment (copy in LeSueur Papers).

Chapter 2

¹ *National Cyclopedia of American Biography*, Vol. A, p. 514; Burgess, p. 72.

² Interview with Mrs. Ruth Townley (Mrs. Covert F.) by William Watts Folwell, March 12, 1925 (recorded in Folwell Papers).

³ Willis Williams in the *St. Paul Dispatch*, Sept. 13, 1917; Gaston, pp. 45–50. For a pseudo-fictionalized and overly dramatic though basically accurate account of this entire story, see O. M. Thomason, *The Beginning and the End of the Nonpartisan League*, Chs. I through XIII, pp. 11–87.

⁴ See for example "North Dakota State Platform, Socialist Party, February 27, 1911" (copy in LeSueur Papers). The *Iconoclast*, a Socialist paper published at Minot, continually urged the farmers to organize as a class to promote their own interests.

⁵ This account is taken largely from Arthur LeSueur, "The Nonpartisan League," ms. in LeSueur Papers.

⁶ William Watts Folwell, *A History of Minnesota*, III, p. 542. Joseph Gilbert says Townley was never an active Socialist and knew little of the principles. "He became a Socialist because he needed a job." (Interview, July 19, 1947.)

⁷ Interview with A. C. Townley, Sept. 23, 1948. Bowen claimed that Townley had taken over his idea, but recognizing Townley's abilities as an organizer he agreed to his leadership. See Davis Douthit, *Nobody Owns Us*, pp. 94–95.

⁸ Interview with A. C. Townley, Sept. 23, 1948; Howard R. Wood to the author, Jan. 14, 1948.

⁹ Gaston, pp. 57–58.

¹⁰ *Ibid.*, p. 60.

¹¹ See *Leader*, March 9, 1916, p. 3.

¹² Jan. 4, 1917, p. 10.

¹³ *Leader*, Oct. 14, 1915, p. 6.

¹⁴ Gaston, p. 58. A new member paid the same amount whether he entered early or late in the two-year period, since he was considered to receive the same benefits as a result of the campaigns (*Correspondence Course for Organizers*, VI, p. 15).

¹⁵ Quoted in James Manahan, *Trials of a Lawyer*, p. 218.

¹⁶ Interview with A. C. Townley, Sept. 23, 1948; "North Dakota's Farmer Revolt," *Literary Digest*, 54:115 (Jan. 20, 1917).

¹⁷ Interview with John N. Hagan, Aug. 28, 1948.

¹⁸ Arthur LeSueur, "The Nonpartisan League," ms. in LeSueur Papers.

[19] The average default over a period of several years was about 15 per cent (Gaston, p. 71).

[20] John E. Pickett, "A Prairie Fire," *Country Gentleman*, 83 (No. 20):4 (May 18, 1918).

[21] Copies of this course, prepared by Mrs. Marian LeSueur, may be found in the LeSueur Papers. On instructions to organizers see also Bruce, p. 72n.

[22] *Correspondence Course for Organizers*, IV, pp. 10–12, 14–15.

[23] *Ibid.*, VI, p. 16.

[24] John E. Pickett, "A Prairie Fire," *Country Gentleman*, 83 (No. 20):4 (May 18, 1918); cf. *Leader*, June 28, 1917, p. 18.

[25] *Correspondence Course for Organizers*, VI, p. 9.

[26] Manahan, pp. 219–20.

[27] Interview with A. C. Townley, Sept. 23, 1948.

[28] John E. Pickett, "A Prairie Fire," *Country Gentleman*, 83 (No. 20):4 (May 18, 1918).

[29] Ray McKaig, "The Nonpartisan Champion," *Public*, 22:518 (May 17, 1919). William Lemke comments, "I will say that as I knew him he was one of the great men of the Nation. I have met few men who are his equal in ability, on the platform and as an organizer." (Letter to the author, Aug. 27, 1947.)

[30] Ray McKaig, "The Nonpartisan Champion," *Public*, 22:518–19 (May 17, 1919).

[31] *Leader*, April 6, 1916, p. 7.

[32] Fargo weekly, quoted in *Leader*, Jan. 6, 1916, p. 6.

[33] *Leader*, Jan. 6, 1916, p. 7.

[34] See Arthur LeSueur, "The Nonpartisan League," ms. in LeSueur Papers.

[35] James Frost, *Townley and Co. and the Nonpartisan League*, p. 31.

[36] J. Wells Brinton, *Wheat and Politics*, p. 34. The story is probably apocryphal, as Townley recalls only that he was required to present a membership list (interview, Sept. 23, 1948). Cf. *Leader*, Sept. 22, 1919, p. 4.

[37] Quoted in *Leader*, Sept. 23, 1915, p. 10.

[38] Rural weekly quoted in Thomason, p. 106.

[39] Quoted in *Leader*, Sept. 23, 1915, p. 11.

[40] *Leader*, Sept. 23, 1915, p. 9.

[41] Thomason, pp. 108–9.

[42] Interview with Joseph Gilbert, July 19, 1947.

[43] Charles Edward Russell, *In and Out of the Yoke*, p. 24.

[44] Sept. 23, 1915, p. 6.

[45] *Leader*, Sept. 23, 1915, p. 7.

[46] *Leader*, Nov. 4, 1915, p. 8.

[47] *Leader*, Oct. 21, 1915, p. 1.

[48] *Leader*, Feb. 23, 1916, p. 6.

[49] Feb. 23, 1916, p. 6.

[50] See for example *Leader*, Feb. 23, 1916, p. 6; Feb. 17, 1916, pp. 6–7.

[51] Nov. 23, 1915, p. 4.

[52] *Leader*, Dec. 16, 1915, p. 8.

[53] Bruce, p. 72n.

[54] Quoted in *Leader*, Jan. 20, 1916, pp. 3–4.

[55] Reported in *Leader*, Feb. 23, 1916, p. 9.

[56] *Fargo Forum*, Jan. 24, 1916, p. 1.

[57] Quoted in Gaston, p. 86.

[58] For the text of a speech embodying this idea, see *Leader*, April 5, 1917, pp. 5, 14.

[59] J. Edmund Buttree, *The Despoilers*, p. 8.

[60] Quoted by Willis Williams in the *St. Paul Dispatch*, Sept. 22, 1917.

[61] Sept. 23, 1915, p. 12.

[62] Interview with A. C. Townley, Sept. 23, 1948.

[63] Jan. 27, 1916, p. 16.

Chapter 3

[1] Lynn Frazier, quoted in Arthur Warner, "The Farmer Butts Back," *Nation*, 111:240 (Aug. 28, 1920).

[2] Nov. 23, 1915, p. 7.

[3] Feb. 10, 1916, p. 2.

[4] "North Dakota's Farmer Revolt," *Literary Digest*, 54:115 (Jan. 20, 1917). Cf. *Leader*, March 2, 1916, pp. 3–4.

[5] *Leader*, March 2, 1916, p. 4.

[6] *Leader*, Jan. 20, 1916, p. 6. It was necessary to reiterate this stand frequently. It was of course obvious that local affairs would be greatly influenced, but there were to be no official endorsements or recommendations.

[7] Feb. 3, 1916, p. 6.

[8] *Grand Forks Weekly Times-Herald*, May 18, 1916, p. 4.

[9] Feb. 3, 1916, p. 6.

[10] The list was published in the *Leader* for March 30, 1916, p. 6, and almost weekly thereafter until November.

[11] Gaston, p. 99.

[12] Quoted in *Leader*, March 30, 1916, p. 5.

[13] Gaston, p. 101.

[14] Feb. 10, 1916, p. 1.

[15] See for example an editorial on Dec. 2, 1915, p. 6.

[16] *Fargo Forum*, March 31, 1916, p. 1; *Leader*, April 6, 1916, pp. 3–4.

[17] Interview with John N. Hagan, Aug. 28, 1948; Thomason, pp. 114–15; Gaston, pp. 102–6.

[18] *Leader*, April 6, 1916, p. 3.

[19] Bruce, p. 68; Gaston, pp. 108–9.

[20] *Fargo Forum*, March 31, 1916, p. 1.

[21] *Grand Forks Weekly Times-Herald*, April 6, 1916, p. 8; *Grand Forks Herald*, April 1, 1916, p. 4.

[22] *Fargo Forum*, March 31, 1916, p. 1.

[23] April 6, 1916, p. 7.

[24] Quoted in *Leader*, April 13, 1916, p. 7.

[25] Quoted in Brinton, p. 37.

[26] Russell, *Nonpartisan League*, p. 210.

[27] Louis Levine, "Farmers Causing Political Upheaval in West," *New York Times Magazine*, Feb. 25, 1917, Sec. V, p. 4.

[28] Quoted in *Leader*, April 6, 1916, p. 6.

[29] *Leader*, April 27, 1916, p. 7.

[30] The following biographical data is taken from the *Leader*, April 6, 1916, pp. 5–6.

[31] Interview with George E. Wallace, July 16, 1947. "In all my acquaintants," says William Lemke, "I have never known a person in whose steadfastness of purpose I had more confidence. Frazier was sound in judgment. He was always willing to listen but was fearfully blunt at times." (Letter to the author, Aug. 27, 1947.)

[32] Frederick M. Davenport, "The Farmers' Revolution in North Dakota," *Outlook*, 114:327 (Oct. 11, 1916).

[33] Quoted in *Leader*, April 13, 1916, p. 7.

[34] May 18, 1916, p. 11.

[35] Address before the Producers and Consumers Convention, St. Paul, Sept. 19, 1917. J. I. Levine's Reports, 3rd Installment (LeSueur Papers).

[36] *Leader*, April 6, 1916, p. 2.

[37] April 6, 1916, p. 15.

[38] For examples see *Leader*, April 6, 1916, p. 4; May 18, 1916, p. 6.

[39] *Leader*, April 6, 1916, p. 29.

[40] *Leader*, May 18, 1916, p. 6. John M. Baer says that the absence of dictation is evidenced in that "Townley and the leaders did not get their choices in many, say one-half, the cases" (letter to the author, Oct. 2, 1948).

[41] *Fargo Courier-News*, May 12, 1916, p. 1.

[42] *Leader*, June 29, 1916, p. 14.

[43] *Grand Forks Weekly Times-Herald*, April 6, 1916, p. 8.

Chapter 4

[1] Arthur M. Evans in undated newspaper clipping in LeSueur Papers.

[2] Apparently printed in Grand Forks about 1918.

[3] *Grand Forks Herald*, April 6, 1916, p. 4; *Grand Forks Weekly Times-Herald*, April 13, 1916, p. 4. The *Times-Herald* was the weekly edition of the *Herald*, and consisted largely of reprints of the daily *Herald* material.

[4] A fairly large collection of correspondence on this subject, largely handled by Henry G. Teigan, may be found in the National Nonpartisan League Papers.

[5] Correspondence files of Henry G. Teigan in the National Nonpartisan League Papers.

[6] See *Leader*, April 13, 1916, p. 2; April 20, 1916, pp. 3-4.

[7] *Grand Forks Herald*, April 1, 1916, p. 4.

[8] Teigan correspondence in the National Nonpartisan League Papers. A good example is Edward Braseth, Caledonia, N.D., to A. C. Townley, May 15, 1916.

[9] May 18, 1916, pp. 2-3; May 25, 1916, p. 10. See also Arthur LeSueur to A. C. Townley, May 10, 1916 (LeSueur Papers).

[10] Sec. 6386, Rev. Code of 1913.

[11] Sec. 6388, Rev. Code of 1913.

[12] Arthur LeSueur to A. C. Townley, May 10, 1916 (LeSueur Papers).

[13] June 1, 1916, p. 7.

[14] The statement was printed in the *Leader*, May 18, 1916, p. 11.

[15] *Leader*, April 13, 1916, p. 3.

[16] April 13, 1916, p. 5.

[17] *Leader*, April 27, 1916, p. 5.

[18] June 8, 1916, p. 5.

[19] *Leader*, April 27, 1916, p. 12; May 4, 1916, p. 22.

[20] *Leader*, May 4, 1916, p. 22.

[21] *Leader*, June 8, 1916, p. 9.

[22] *Leader*, May 18, 1916, p. 9.

[23] *Leader*, June 22, 1916, p. 1.

[24] John E. Pickett, "A Prairie Fire," *Country Gentleman*, 83(No. 20):4 (May 18, 1918).

[25] Quoted in *Leader*, June 1, 1916, p. 7.

[26] *Leader*, June 8, 1916, p. 1.

[27] One such letter was reproduced in the *Leader*, June 15, 1916, p. 10.

[28] *Leader*, June 22, 1916, p. 11. This was reprinted as a political advertisement in the *Fargo Forum*, June 26, 1916, p. 9.

[29] *Fargo Courier-News*, June 28, 1916, p. 4.

[30] *Grand Forks Weekly Times-Herald*, June 8, 1916, p. 8.

[31] A letter from the North Dakota Bankers' Association to its members was reproduced in the *Leader*, June 22, 1916, p. 4.

[32] *Leader*, June 8, 1916, p. 6.

[33] *Fargo Courier-News*, June 25, 1916, p. 4.

[34] Letter from North Dakota Bankers' Association to its members, reproduced in the *Leader*, June 22, 1916, p. 4.

[35] *Fargo Forum*, June 16, 1916, p. 4. See also the *Forum*, June 20, 1916, p. 4.

[36] June 22, 1916, p. 7.

[37] *Fargo Forum*, June 22, 1916, p. 4.

[38] *Leader*, June 8, 1916, p. 13.

[39] *Fargo Courier-News*, June 27, 1916, p. 2.

[40] See *Leader*, June 15, 1916, p. 8; June 29, 1916, p. 8.

[41] Manahan, pp. 221–22.

[42] *Grand Forks Weekly Times-Herald*, June 22, 1916, p. 3. This was probably the one thing he should not have attacked.

[43] Usher L. Burdick, *History of the Farmers' Political Action in North Dakota*, p. 84.

[44] A number of these charges and refutations were taken up by the *Leader*, June 22, 1916, p. 5.

[45] June 25, 1916, p. 1.

[46] June 27, 1916, p. 1.

[47] The letter is reproduced in English translation in the *Fargo Courier-News*, June 27, 1916, p. 1.

[48] June 25, 1916, p. 2.

[49] June 28, 1916, p. 4.

[50] June 22, 1916, p. 1.

[51] June 29, 1916, p. 1.

[52] For some interesting comparisons and stories of "banner precincts," see *Leader*, July 13, 1916, pp. 20–21.

[53] See Frederick M. Davenport, "The Farmers' Revolution in North Dakota," *Outlook*, 114:325 (Oct. 11, 1916).

[54] *1919 Legislative Manual, State of North Dakota*, pp. 240–42, 246, 252–53.

[55] *Leader*, July 13, 1916, p. 8. Joseph Gilbert says that the best the League leaders had hoped for was control of the legislature, and that the total success was beyond their wildest dreams (interview, July 19, 1947). In view of Frazier's immense popularity the statement is questionable as far as he is concerned.

[56] Quoted in *Leader*, July 13, 1916, p. 19.

Chapter 5

[1] Aug. 24, 1916, p. 3.

[2] Gaston, p. 82. Gaston edited the *Courier-News* for some time after this.

[3] *Grand Forks Herald*, June 28, 1916, p. 4.

[4] *Leader*, July 6, 1916, p. 5.

[5] Quoted in *Leader*, Aug. 17, 1916, p. 11.

[6] Aug. 10, 1916, p. 4.

[7] Quoted in *Leader*, Aug. 31, 1916, p. 10.

[8] *Leader*, Aug. 24, 1916, p. 13; Aug. 31, 1916, p. 20; Sept. 14, 1916, p. 16; Sept. 21, 1916, pp. 2, 11; Oct. 5, 1916, p. 21.

[9] *Leader*, Sept. 7, 1916, pp. 3, 5–6.

[10] Burgess, p. 103.

[11] Paul F. Sharp, *The Agrarian Revolt in Western Canada*, pp. 77–78, 83–84.

[12] See *Grand Forks Weekly Times-Herald*, Aug. 31, 1916, p. 8.

[13] For accounts of this meeting see *Leader*, Sept. 14, 1916, pp. 12, 20; and *Fargo Courier-News*, Sept. 7, 1916, p. 1; Sept. 8, 1916, p. 2. Townley looked upon this "capture" as a defensive move, necessary to prevent the party machinery from being used against the League (interview, Sept. 23, 1948).

[14] *Fargo Courier-News*, Sept. 8, 1916, p. 2; *Leader*, Sept. 14, 1916, p. 20.

[15] Sept. 8, 1916, p. 4.

[16] See *Leader*, Sept. 7, 1916, p. 6.

[17] Quoted in *Leader*, Aug. 10, 1916, p. 8.

[18] E. F. Ladd, "North Dakota Wheat for 1916," *Bulletin No. 119*, North Dakota Agricultural College Experiment Station, Nov. 1916, pp. 55-56.

[19] *Ibid.*, p. 57. Even if Ladd ignored some factors or used poor samples, as later claimed, his general point was apparently not successfully challenged.

[20] Henry G. Teigan to J. Brooks Atkinson, Cambridge, Mass., Jan. 23, 1917 (National Nonpartisan League Papers).

[21] *Leader*, Oct. 5, 1916, p. 4.

[22] See, for example, discussions of the tax law cases and the capital removal case in the *Leader*, Sept. 21, 1916, p. 15 and pp. 7, 19; Sept. 28, 1916, pp. 5, 20.

[23] Quoted in Paul R. Fossum, *The Agrarian Movement in North Dakota*, p. 122.

[24] Constitution of North Dakota, Sec. 202, Subdivision 2, which reads as follows: "Any amendment or amendments to this constitution may also be proposed by the filing with the secretary of state, at least six months previous to any general election, of an initiative petition containing the signatures of at least 25 per cent of the legal voters in each of not less than one-half of the counties of the state."

[25] State *ex rel.* Linde v. Hall, 35 N.D. 34, 159 N.W. 281 (1916).

[26] See for example *Leader*, Sept. 21, 1916, p. 7.

[27] Sept. 7, 1916, pp. 4, 21; Sept. 28, 1916, pp. 8, 20; Oct. 19, 1916, p. 9.

[28] Oct. 26, 1916, p. 5.

[29] See for example *Leader*, Sept. 28, 1916, p. 19. Lemke insists that ". . . whatever I did was in full accord with the League's viewpoint." He then begs the question of the theory of nonpartisanship by concluding, ". . . that one exception [Steen] was not so bad. In fact, he had considerable following for the office which he held in the League convention." (Letter to the author, Aug. 27, 1947.) Townley says that while this was inconsistent, Lemke apparently felt obliged as state chairman to do it, and that he acted entirely on his own (interview, Sept. 23, 1948).

[30] *Leader*, Oct. 5, 1916, pp. 3-4.

[31] Correspondence files for this period are in Teigan Papers.

[32] Theodore Saloutos, "The Rise of the Nonpartisan League in North Dakota, 1915-1917," *Agricultural History*, 20:53 (Jan. 1946). This statement appears in the *New International Yearbook*, 1916, p. 496.

[33] Interview, Sept. 23, 1948.

[34] *Fargo Forum*, Nov. 2, 1916, pp. 1, 7.

[35] Henry G. Teigan to M. L. Amos, May 26, 1917 (National Nonpartisan League Papers).

[36] Speech by E. R. Meitzen, Nonpartisan League lecturer, printed by the Texas branch of the National Nonpartisan League, 1918 (National Nonpartisan League Papers).

[37] *1919 Legislative Manual, State of North Dakota*, p. 263.

[38] *Leader*, Nov. 16, 1916, p. 3.

[39] *Leader*, Nov. 23, 1916, p. 4. Stories of other exceptional precincts may also be found in this issue.

[40] *1919 Legislative Manual, State of North Dakota*, pp. 256-66.

[41] *World Almanac, 1947*, p. 170 (Wilson, 55,206; Hughes, 53,471). The *New York Times* (Dec. 6, 1916, p. 5) gave the official plurality as 2620.

[42] Ray McKaig, "The New Minnesota Despotism," *Public*, 21:467 (April 13, 1918). There was hope at the time he wrote that the national government might take over the packing industry, oil production, etc.

[43] *Leader*, Nov. 30, 1916, pp. 5, 12. None of the three League candidates running on the Socialist ticket were successful.

[44] Quoted by Willis Williams in the *St. Paul Dispatch*, Sept. 22, 1917.

[45] *Leader*, Aug. 10, 1916, p. 3.

[46] Austin P. Haines, "An Adjournment of Common Sense," *New Republic*, 16:158 (Sept. 7, 1918).

Chapter 6

[1] Reprinted in *Leader*, Jan. 4, 1917, p. 2.
[2] Feb. 22, 1917, p. 3.
[3] On this controversy see Bruce, pp. 190–98.
[4] Jan. 3, 1917, p. 3.
[5] His statement was printed in the *Leader*, Jan. 18, 1917, p. 16.
[6] *Message of Governor Lynn J. Frazier Delivered to the Fifteenth Legislative Assembly of the State of North Dakota* (Bismarck, 1917).
[7] Interview with A. C. Townley, Sept. 23, 1948. The opposition later circulated excerpts from these speeches under such headings as "What Townley Really Thinks of the Farmers."
[8] See for example *Grand Forks Herald*, Jan. 5, 1917, p. 1.
[9] Charles Merz, "Political Revolt in the Northwest," *New Republic*, 13:44 (Nov. 10, 1917).
[10] Feb. 16, 1917, p. 1.
[11] Interview with John N. Hagan, Aug. 28, 1948; interview with A. C. Townley, Sept. 23, 1948.
[12] An account of these so-called "bologna banquets" may be found in M. G. Franklin, "A Farmer-Governed State," *Farm and Fireside*, June 1918 (reprinted in *Leader*, July 1, 1918, p. 19).
[13] *Leader*, Jan. 25, 1917, p. 2. Cf. *Grand Forks Herald*, Jan. 8, 1917, pp. 1, 5.
[14] *Leader*, Jan. 25, 1917, p. 20.
[15] The *Grand Forks Herald* for Jan. 4, 1917 (p. 1) stated that Bowen had announced agreement on the calling of a convention, with drafts to be submitted by the legislature.
[16] Jan. 11, 1917, pp. 3–4.
[17] House Bill 44, Fifteenth Legislative Assembly (copy in LeSueur Papers).
[18] Ferdinand A. Teigen, *The Nonpartisan League: Its Origin, Development and Secret Purposes*, p. 42.
[19] *Leader*, April 5, 1917, p. 14.
[20] *Grand Forks Herald*, Jan. 24, 1917, p. 10. See also Gaston, pp. 145–46.
[21] Jan. 18, 1917, p. 7.
[22] A detailed account of these events may be found in *Leader*, Feb. 1, 1917, p. 5.
[23] Feb. 1, 1917, p. 7.
[24] *Grand Forks Herald*, Jan. 31, 1917, p. 1.
[25] Feb. 8, 1917, p. 4.
[26] *Grand Forks Herald*, Jan. 8, 1917, p. 1; *Leader*, Jan. 11, 1917, p. 11.
[27] Jan. 10, 1917, p. 4.
[28] *Leader*, Feb. 15, 1917, p. 2.
[29] *Leader*, Feb. 22, 1917, pp. 7, 9.
[30] Crawford, I, pp. 426–27; *Leader*, March 8, 1917, p. 8.
[31] *Leader*, March 8, 1917, p. 7; Gaston, p. 154.
[32] *Leader*, March 22, 1917, p. 14. The League apparently hated to part with the only existing state-owned utility.
[33] *Grand Forks Herald*, March 3, 1917, p. 3.
[34] *Leader*, March 8, 1917, p. 5.
[35] Gaston, p. 149.

Chapter 7

[1] *Leader*, Aug. 30, 1917, p. 7.
[2] Gaston, pp. 177–78.
[3] July 5, 1917, p. 7.
[4] Quoted in *Leader*, July 26, 1917, p. 14.

[5] Quoted in *Leader*, Aug. 2, 1917, p. 4.
[6] *Leader*, July 5, 1917, p. 11.
[7] Nov. 29, 1917, p. 4.
[8] May 31, 1917, p. 5.
[9] Interview with Judge A. M. Christianson, Sept. 1, 1948. See Bruce Nelson, *Land of the Dacotahs*, p. 296.
[10] Interview with Judge A. M. Christianson, Sept. 1, 1948.
[11] Crawford, I, p. 420.
[12] April 12, 1917.
[13] *Leader*, April 26, 1917, p. 16.
[14] National Nonpartisan League Papers.
[15] Nelson, p. 285.
[16] J. D. Bacon, *A Warning to the Farmer against Townleyism as Exploited in North Dakota*, p. 29.
[17] Gaston, p. 242.
[18] A sample is reproduced in Brinton, p. 57.
[19] Interview with F. A. Vogel, Aug. 25, 1948; interview with John N. Hagan, Aug. 28, 1948; Buttree, p. 152.
[20] On the Consumers' United Stores generally see the *Minneapolis Journal*, Jan. 22, 1918, p. 3; *Red Flame*, June 1920, p. 34; Brinton, pp. 56–68; Gaston, pp. 241–42; Teigen, pp. 56–61.
[21] Brinton, p. 44; Gaston, p. 303.
[22] See the advertisement in *Leader*, April 26, 1917, p. 13.
[23] Tostlebe, pp. 96–97.
[24] Gaston, p. 304; Teigen, pp. 62–63.
[25] Brinton, pp. 48–49.
[26] Teigen, p. 33.
[27] For the following information I am indebted primarily to Joseph Mader, "The Political Influence of the Nonpartisan League on the Press of North Dakota" (M.A. Thesis), especially pp. 23–26. This is a comprehensive and fairly satisfactory study of the entire story of the Nonpartisan League press, though based largely on anti-League sources.
[28] See Brinton, pp. 68–69.
[29] Interview with A. C. Townley, Sept. 23, 1948.
[30] On the Sisal Trust see Buttree, pp. 165–69; Brinton, p. 69.
[31] Dozens of such letters may be found in the National Nonpartisan League Papers.
[32] *Leader*, Jan. 11, 1917, p. 22.
[33] *Leader*, Feb. 22, 1917, p. 6.
[34] Gaston, pp. 165–66.
[35] *Ibid.*, p. 167.
[36] *Leader*, Aug. 2, 1917, p. 18.
[37] *Leader*, Sept. 6, 1917, p. 9. See also Douthit, pp. 100–1.
[38] *Leader*, April 26, 1917, pp. 8, 13.
[39] *Leader*, May 3, 1917, p. 15.
[40] *Leader*, Aug. 23, 1917, p. 4.
[41] Correspondence in the National Nonpartisan League Papers gives considerable evidence of the extent of this influence.
[42] For a large measure of the following information on South Dakota I am indebted to Gilbert Fite, "Peter Norbeck and the Defeat of the Nonpartisan League in South Dakota," *Mississippi Valley Historical Review*, 33:218–22 (Sept. 1946). See also *Leader*, March 15, 1917, p. 5; Dec. 17, 1917, p. 11.
[43] Sharp, pp. 91–93.
[44] *Ibid.*, pp. 93–98, 103.
[45] *Leader*, Jan. 18, 1917, p. 22.

⁴⁶ *Leader*, June 28, 1917, pp. 10, 18.

⁴⁷ Reprinted in *Leader*, Aug. 16, 1917, p. 11.

⁴⁸ Douthit, p. 105; *Leader*, July 19, 1917, p. 4.

⁴⁹ *Leader*, March 29, 1917, p. 9; April 19, p. 9.

⁵⁰ Quoted in *Leader*, March 29, 1917, p. 9.

⁵¹ *Leader*, May 10, 1917, p. 3.

⁵² Quoted in *Leader*, April 5, 1917, p. 20.

⁵³ *Leader*, June 9, 1919, p. 4. For the entire "exposé" of the "fake league" see *Leader*, June 9, 1919, pp. 4–5, 13; June 16, pp. 8–9; June 23, pp. 8–9; June 30, pp. 8–9.

⁵⁴ *Leader*, July 5, 1917, p. 4.

⁵⁵ *Leader*, Aug. 9, 1917, p. 4.

⁵⁶ *Leader*, June 7, 1917, p. 7. Cf. Gaston, pp. 171–72.

⁵⁷ *Leader*, June 14, 1917, p. 7.

⁵⁸ *Leader*, June 28, 1917, p. 9.

⁵⁹ *Grand Forks Herald*, June 22, 1917, p. 4; *Leader*, June 28, 1917, p. 9.

⁶⁰ State *ex rel*. Burtness v. Hall, 37 N.D. 259, 163 N.W. 1055 (1917).

⁶¹ June 7, 1917, p. 7.

⁶² July 6, 1917, p. 4.

⁶³ June 29, 1917, p. 10; June 30, p. 1.

⁶⁴ July 5, 1917, p. 2.

⁶⁵ *Leader*, July 12, 1917, p. 6.

⁶⁶ *Leader*, July 19, 1917, p. 4.

⁶⁷ *Leader*, July 26, 1917, p. 3. Congressman P. D. Norton stoutly defended Baer and the League on the floor of the House, vigorously attacking the news stories (*Leader*, Aug. 16, 1917, p. 18).

⁶⁸ "A New National Party," *Literary Digest*, 55:13–14 (Aug. 11, 1917).

⁶⁹ *Red Flame*, June 1920, p. 29. Everyone, including McArthur, of course knew that he had no chance whatsoever in 1916.

⁷⁰ See for example *Leader*, Sept. 6, 1917, p. 3.

⁷¹ Interview with O. B. Herigstad, Aug. 27, 1948. *Grand Forks Herald*, Feb. 23, 1917, p. 3.

⁷² Interview with A. C. Townley, Sept. 23, 1948.

⁷³ *Leader*, June 7, 1917, p. 6.

⁷⁴ *Grand Forks Herald*, June 30, 1917, p. 1.

⁷⁵ Quoted in Bruce, p. 144.

⁷⁶ *Grand Forks Herald*, July 6, 1917, p. 7.

⁷⁷ Bruce, p. 144.

⁷⁸ Gaston, p. 212.

⁷⁹ *Leader*, Aug. 16, 1917, p. 7.

⁸⁰ On the writing of these statements see Douthit, pp. 101–3.

⁸¹ *Leader*, June 14, 1917, p. 9.

⁸² *Leader*, May 13, 1918, p. 9.

⁸³ *Leader*, June 14, 1917, pp. 5–6, 15.

⁸⁴ *Fargo Forum*, June 9, 1917, p. 4. It was reprinted in full in the *Grand Forks Herald*.

⁸⁵ *Leader*, June 28, 1917, p. 3.

⁸⁶ Quoted in J. D. Bacon, *Townleyism Unmasked; Now Stands before the World in Its True Light as Radical Socialism*, p. 27. Cf. Buttree, pp. 132–33.

⁸⁷ *Leader*, Sept. 6, 1917, pp. 4–5.

⁸⁸ Sept. 6, 1917, p. 4.

⁸⁹ Aug. 23, 1917, p. 6.

⁹⁰ *Leader*, Sept. 13, 1917, pp. 4–6; Sept. 27, pp. 4–6; *Minneapolis Journal*, Sept. 18, 1917, p. 6.

⁹¹ *Leader*, Sept. 13, 1917, p. 5.

⁹² *Leader*, Oct. 4, 1917, pp. 8–9, 17–19 (stenographic transcript).

⁹³ The text of the resolutions is printed in full in the *Leader*, Sept. 27, 1917, pp. 15–17.

⁹⁴ On this incident see Belle C. and Fola LaFollette, *Robert M. LaFollette*, pp. 761–72; *Minneapolis Journal*, Sept. 21, 1917, pp. 1, 26; *Leader*, Sept. 27, 1917, p. 11; Edward N. Doan, *The LaFollettes and the Wisconsin Idea*, p. 87; Gaston, pp. 209–11; Robert Kingsley, "Recent Variations from the Two Party System as Evidenced by the Nonpartisan League and the Agricultural Bloc" (M.A. Thesis), p. 19; Frank O'Hara, "The Grievance of the Spring Wheat Growers," *Catholic World*, 106:381–82 (Dec. 1917); Austin P. Haines, "The Nonpartisan League and the Loyalty Issue," *New Republic*, 16:187 (Sept. 14, 1918).

⁹⁵ Sept. 23, 1917, p. 12.

⁹⁶ Doan, pp. 87, 90.

⁹⁷ Sept. 21, 1917, p. 18.

⁹⁸ Oct. 4, 1917, p. 6.

⁹⁹ Oct. 11, 1917, p. 6; Oct. 18, p. 6.

¹⁰⁰ Doan, p. 90; *Leader*, Dec. 16, 1918, p. 7.

¹⁰¹ The story is reprinted in the *Leader*, Nov. 1, 1917, pp. 17–18. Only the Duluth paper carried it, though the Twin City papers had abbreviated versions the next day.

¹⁰² Quoted in *Leader*, Nov. 1, 1917, p. 17.

¹⁰³ *Leader*, Nov. 29, 1917, p. 5.

¹⁰⁴ *Leader*, Nov. 11, 1917, pp. 12–13, 22.

¹⁰⁵ The letter is reproduced in *Memorial to the Congress of the United States Concerning Conditions in Minnesota, 1918*, pp. 5–6. See also *Leader*, Dec. 17, 1917, p. 9; *St. Paul Pioneer Press*, March 8, 1918.

¹⁰⁶ Interview with Judge William A. Anderson, April 28, 1949.

¹⁰⁷ The versions of her remarks are varied but are mostly in a similar vein. See for example the quotation on the cover of J. D. Bacon, *Sovietians, Wreckers of Americanism*. J. D. Bacon, *Warning to the Farmers*, pp. 64–79, reprints Mrs. O'Hare's final statement to the court and Judge Wade's remarks at the time of sentencing.

¹⁰⁸ *Leader*, June 14, 1917, p. 15.

¹⁰⁹ *Leader*, Nov. 29, 1917, p. 9.

¹¹⁰ Quoted in *Leader*, Dec. 17, 1917, pp. 4–6.

¹¹¹ *Leader*, Dec. 17, 1917, p. 4.

¹¹² *Leader*, Dec. 17, 1917, p. 9.

¹¹³ See for example *Leader*, Dec. 10, 1917, p. 16.

¹¹⁴ *Leader*, Dec. 31, 1917, p. 17.

Chapter 8

¹ *Leader*, Oct. 11, 1917, p. 11; Oct. 18, p. 4.

² *Leader*, Oct. 18, 1917, pp. 4–5.

³ *Leader*, Oct. 18, 1917, p. 5.

⁴ *Leader*, Oct. 18, 1917, pp. 5, 16.

⁵ *Memorial to the Congress Concerning Conditions in Minnesota, 1918*, p. 28.

⁶ A photo copy of this letter may be found in the National Nonpartisan League Papers.

⁷ *Leader*, Nov. 1, 1917, p. 5.

⁸ Letter from Sam G. Wallace, Perham, Minnesota, to the editor of the *Leader*, Nov. 1, 1917, p. 5.

⁹ The *Minnesota Leader* reported in some detail incidents of this sort regularly

throughout the fall and winter. One of the most comprehensive collections of data on this terrorism is to be found in the *Memorial to the Congress Concerning Conditions in Minnesota, 1918*, which consists largely of notarized statements of persons subjected to violence or witnesses to the incidents. A number of cases are briefly related in Howard E. Bloom, "Violence against the Nonpartisan League in Minnesota during the World War," thesis submitted in the Funk Prize Contest, Macalester College, 1931 (manuscript in the Minnesota Historical Society Library). Photo copies of several local orders forbidding League activity are available in the National Nonpartisan League Papers. See also George Creel, "Our 'Aliens'—Were They Loyal or Disloyal?" *Everybody's Magazine*, 40:71–72 (March 1919); "Lawlessness in Minnesota," *Public*, 21:876–78 (July 13, 1918); Ray McKaig, "The New Minnesota Despotism," *Public*, 21:465–67 (April 13, 1918); Gaston, pp. 222–30. It is interesting that the Twin City dailies rarely mentioned these incidents, and then only briefly, though they reported fully all arrests of League speakers.

[10] Quoted in *Leader*, Feb. 18, 1918, p. 9.

[11] Quoted in Bloom, "Violence against the Nonpartisan League in Minnesota," p. 22. In justice to the *Post* it should be said that it later changed its attitude on this matter.

[12] The *Minnesota Leader* for Feb. 23, 1918, carried a list of meetings prevented up to that time.

[13] *Leader*, May 20, 1918, p. 5. Accompanying the article is a picture of the upper half of Hokstad's body covered with tar and feathers.

[14] A photo copy of the letter may be found in the National Nonpartisan League Papers. See also the *Minneapolis Journal*, Jan. 24, 1918, p. 2; *Leader*, Feb. 11, 1918, p. 14.

[15] For a detailed account of this incident see Douthit, pp. 117–25. Cf. *Leader*, March 4, 1918, pp. 11, 17.

[16] *Leader*, July 28, 1919, p. 3.

[17] *Leader*, March 4, 1918, pp. 11, 17.

[18] May 6, 1918, pp. 6–7.

[19] Numerous samples of these may be found in the *Memorial to the Congress Concerning Conditions in Minnesota, 1918*, pp. 70–93.

[20] *Ibid.*, pp. 97–101. See also *Minneapolis Journal*, Feb. 19, 1918, p. 1; *Minneapolis Tribune*, Feb. 20, 1918.

[21] *Minneapolis Journal*, March 2, 1918, p. 1.

[22] Quoted in Lynn and Dora B. Haines, *The Lindberghs*, p. 281.

[23] This correspondence may be found in the National Nonpartisan League Papers. See also *Memorial to the Congress Concerning Conditions in Minnesota, 1918*, pp. 94–97.

[24] See the series of telegrams in *Memorial to the Congress Concerning Conditions in Minnesota, 1918*, pp. 115–19.

[25] George Creel, "Our 'Aliens'—Were They Loyal or Disloyal?" *Everybody's Magazine*, 40:72 (March 1919).

[26] Quoted in Russell, *Nonpartisan League*, pp. 245–46.

[27] March 18, 1918, p. 5.

[28] Quoted in Haines, pp. 281–82. Versions with slightly varying wording, but essentially similar, appeared in the *Leader*, May 6, 1918, pp. 5, 23, and the *Grand Forks Herald*, April 19, 1918, p. 8.

[29] *Leader*, May 13, 1918, p. 6.

[30] May 6, 1918, p. 5.

[31] Reprinted in *Leader*, July 1, 1918, p. 12, from the *Arvard* (Okla.) *Tribune*.

[32] *Leader*, April 22, 1918, p. 11.

[33] *Leader*, July 22, 1918, p. 3.

[34] Quoted in *Leader*, March 25, 1918, p. 15. See also *St. Paul Daily News*, March 10, 1918.

[35] *Leader*, March 17, 1919, pp. 11–12. For Gilbert's account of this incident, see Douthit, pp. 128–33.

[36] *Leader*, April 1, 1918, p. 3.

[37] State v. A. C. Townley and Another, 140 Minn. 413, 168 N.W. 591 (1918).

[38] *St. Paul Pioneer Press*, July 6, 1918, p. 1.

[39] *Minneapolis Journal*, Dec. 20, 1918, p. 1.

[40] Accounts of this trial may be found in *Leader*, May 27, 1918, p. 6, and Douthit, pp. 106–8, 137–43.

[41] Gilbert v. Minnesota, 254 U.S. 325, 41 S.Ct. 125 (1920).

[42] Zechariah Chafee, Jr., *Free Speech in the United States*, p. 295.

[43] *Ibid.*, pp. 285–86.

[44] *Leader*, March 25, 1918, p. 12.

[45] *Leader*, May 6, 1918, p. 13.

[46] Quoted in *Leader*, March 25, 1918, p. 12.

[47] *Leader*, Feb. 25, 1918, p. 13.

[48] Quoted in *Leader*, May 13, 1918, p. 13.

[49] *Leader*, May 13, 1918, p. 13; May 27, p. 7.

[50] April newsletter of the State Council, quoted in *Leader*, May 13, 1918, p. 21.

[51] *Leader*, May 27, 1918, p. 5.

[52] *Leader*, May 27, 1918, pp. 5, 23.

[53] *Leader*, Feb. 25, 1918, p. 12.

[54] *Leader*, July 29, 1918, pp. 7, 10.

[55] *Leader*, April 1, 1918, p. 8.

[56] *Leader*, April 1, 1918, p. 23.

[57] *Leader*, April 1, 1918, p. 8.

[58] *Leader*, Sept. 16, 1918, pp. 10–11.

[59] *Leader*, May 20, 1918, pp. 4–5, 23.

[60] The statements of the three men were published in the *Leader*, April 29, 1918, pp. 3–4.

[61] *Leader*, April 29, 1918, p. 3.

[62] This editorial was reprinted in the *Leader*, April 29, 1918, pp. 3–4.

[63] Quoted in *Leader*, Aug. 12, 1918, pp. 6, 8–9.

[64] George Creel, "Our 'Aliens'—Were They Loyal or Disloyal?" *Everybody's Magazine*, 40:72 (March 1919); George Creel, "What Do These Senators Want?" *Colliers*, 71:10 (March 10, 1923); *Grand Forks Herald*, Jan. 17, 1921, p. 4.

[65] Quoted in Russell, *Nonpartisan League*, pp. 244–46.

Chapter 9

[1] *Leader*, April 15, 1918, pp. 11–12; *Grand Forks Herald*, March 27, 1918, p. 1.

[2] *1919 Legislative Manual, State of North Dakota*, pp. 285–87; *The New Day in North Dakota*, pp. 129–32.

[3] Teigan to Judson King, March 9, 1917 (National Nonpartisan League Papers).

[4] Bruce, pp. 103–4.

[5] *Leader*, April 15, 1918, p. 6.

[6] *Grand Forks Herald*, May 7, 1918, p. 3.

[7] *Leader*, July 15, 1918, pp. 5–7, 21.

[8] *Leader*, July 15, 1918, pp. 5, 21.

[9] June 26, 1918, p. 4.

[10] June 24, 1918, p. 4.

[11] June 27, 1918, p. 4.

[12] *1919 Legislative Manual, State of North Dakota*, pp. 272–80.

[13] Feb. 18, 1918, p. 12.
[14] *Leader*, April 1, 1918, p. 11.
[15] *Leader*, April 1, 1918, pp. 11-12.
[16] *Leader*, April 8, 1918, p. 13.
[17] *Leader*, March 25, 1918, p. 5.
[18] *Leader*, April 8, 1918, p. 6.
[19] Quoted in *Leader*, April 8, 1918, p. 14.
[20] Quoted in *Leader*, April 8, 1918, p. 11.
[21] *Leader*, April 1, 1918, pp. 10, 20-21.
[22] *Minneapolis Journal*, March 21, 1918, p. 12.
[23] Quoted in Haines, p. 279.
[24] *Leader*, April 8, 1918, p. 14.
[25] The pledge was printed in the *Leader*, June 3, 1918, p. 6.
[26] Quoted in Haines, p. 267.
[27] His earlier book, *Banking and Currency and the Money Trust* (1913), had already marked him for the financial interests as a man to be beaten.
[28] March 20, 1918, p. 2.
[29] Jan. 12, 1918, p. 4.
[30] Gaston, p. 219.
[31] Jan. 21, 1918, pp. 6-7, 23.
[32] Teigen, p. 37.
[33] *Leader*, May 13, 1918, p. 6.
[34] *Leader*, May 27, 1918, p. 7.
[35] *Leader*, Sept. 9, 1918, p. 12.
[36] *Leader*, Aug. 19, 1918, pp. 8-9, 15.
[37] *On the Square*, May 1918, p. 4.
[38] *Leader*, Aug. 19, 1918, pp. 9, 15.
[39] The recommendations are reproduced in full in S. R. Maxwell, *The Nonpartisan League from the Inside*, pp. 31-36. Cf. Douthit, pp. 143-49.
[40] Haines, p. 281.
[41] *Leader*, July 8, 1918, p. 12.
[42] *Minneapolis Journal*, June 11, 1918, p. 1.
[43] Haines, pp. 282-83.
[44] Quoted in Haines, p. 293.
[45] *Duluth News-Tribune*, May 29, 1918, p. 6.
[46] June 10, 1918, p. 7.
[47] June 10, 1918, p. 6.
[48] June 1, 1918, p. 4.
[49] June 14, 1918, p. 20; June 15, p. 4.
[50] June 17, 1918, p. 1.
[51] *1919 Legislative Manual, State of Minnesota*, p. 252.
[52] Kingsley, p. 30.
[53] *Leader*, July 29, 1918, p. 2.
[54] *1919 Legislative Manual, State of Minnesota*, p. 252.
[55] July 8, 1918, p. 6.
[56] June 18, 1918, p. 16.
[57] *Leader*, July 1, 1918, p. 5.
[58] Orville M. Kile, *The Farm Bureau through Three Decades*, p. 62.
[59] *Leader*, April 8, 1918, p. 7.
[60] Gilbert C. Fite, "Peter Norbeck and the Defeat of the Nonpartisan League in South Dakota," *Mississippi Valley Historical Review*, 33:222 (Sept. 1946).
[61] *Leader*, May 20, 1918, p. 16.
[62] *Leader*, July 29, 1918, pp. 3, 13.

[63] Ray McKaig, "The Farmers Mob the Mobbers," *Public*, 21:1241–42 (Sept. 28, 1918).

[64] Sept. 23, 1918, pp. 3, 7.

[65] *Leader*, Sept. 30, 1918, p. 4.

[66] *Leader*, Oct. 14, 1918, p. 10.

[67] Annabelle McDonald, "A History of the Nonpartisan League in Colorado" (M.A. Thesis), p. 43.

[68] *Leader*, Sept. 16, 1918, p. 12.

[69] *Leader*, July 7, 1919, pp. 4–5; July 14, pp. 8–9, 13; July 21, pp. 8–9; July 28, pp. 8–9; Aug. 4, pp. 8–9. A great deal of documentary evidence was reproduced along with the articles.

[70] Reproduced in *Leader*, Sept. 9, 1918, p. 3.

[71] *Leader*, June 24, 1918, pp. 9–10; July 1, pp. 15–16.

[72] *Leader*, Aug. 19, 1918, p. 6.

[73] The articles were quickly printed in book form (Maxwell, *Nonpartisan League from the Inside*).

[74] Sept. 16, 1918, p. 3.

[75] Folwell, III, p. 548.

[76] *Townleyism's Future in North Dakota*, issued by the Independent Voters' Association, p. 96.

[77] *Leader*, Sept. 9, 1918, p. 12.

[78] State *ex rel.* Twichell v. Hall, 44 N.D. 459, 171 N.W. 213 (1918).

[79] *The Truth about the Constitutional Amendments*, issued by the Republican State Central Committee.

[80] Nov. 2, 1918, p. 3.

[81] Oct. 23, 1918, p. 14.

[82] *1919 Legislative Manual, State of North Dakota*, p. 498.

[83] Henry G. Teigan, "The National Nonpartisan League," *American Labor Year Book, 1919–1920*, p. 284; Henry G. Teigan to Arthur W. Macmahon, New York City, Nov. 28, 1919 (National Nonpartisan League Papers); *Leader*, Nov. 25, 1918, p. 4. These sources vary slightly and the figures given are the best possible reconciliation.

[84] *Leader*, Nov. 25, 1918, p. 4; Henry G. Teigan, "The National Nonpartisan League," *American Labor Year Book, 1919–1920*, p. 284.

[85] *Leader*, Dec. 30, 1918, p. 4; *Grand Forks Herald*, Jan. 2, 1919, p. 1; *Minneapolis Journal*, Dec. 10, 1918, p. 14. The vote of the canvassing board was Langer, Kositzky, and MacDonald for; Hall and Steen against. The vote on the amendments is given in the *1919 Legislative Manual, State of North Dakota*, pp. 285–87. The five highest in order were (1) Number of Judges to Declare Law Unconstitutional, (2) Two hail insurance amendments, (3) Voting Privileges of Cooperative Corporations, (4) Initiative and Referendum.

[86] State *ex rel.* W. E. Byerley and Theodore G. Nelson v. State Board of Canvassers, 44 N.D. 126, 172 N.W. 80 (1919). The decision was based on a 1908 precedent in which the Court construed similar language in a case involving a vote on changing a county boundary, State *ex rel.* McCue v. Blaisdell, 18 N.D. 31, 119 N.W. 360 (1908).

[87] *Leader*, Aug. 19, 1918, pp. 3, 14.

[88] Peter Norbeck, *Message to the People of South Dakota*.

[89] Quoted in *Leader*, June 9, 1918, p. 8.

[90] Gilbert C. Fite, "Peter Norbeck and the Defeat of the Nonpartisan League in South Dakota," *Mississippi Valley Historical Review*, 33:230–31 (Sept. 1946); *Leader*, Nov. 4, 1918, p. 10.

[91] *Leader*, Nov. 4, 1918, p. 14.

[92] Quoted in Gilbert C. Fite, "Peter Norbeck and the Defeat of the Nonparti-

san League in South Dakota," *Mississippi Valley Historical Review*, 33:231 (Sept. 1946).

⁹³ *Leader*, Nov. 25, 1918, p. 4; Teigan to Macmahon, Nov. 28, 1919.

⁹⁴ Quoted in Gilbert C. Fite, "Peter Norbeck and the Defeat of the Nonpartisan League in South Dakota," *Mississippi Valley Historical Review*, 33:236 (Sept. 1946).

⁹⁵ Quoted in *ibid.*, p. 225.

⁹⁶ *Leader*, Nov. 25, 1916, p. 4; Teigan to Macmahon, Nov. 28, 1919.

⁹⁷ Teigan to Macmahon, Nov. 28, 1919.

⁹⁸ Nov. 25, 1918, p. 6.

⁹⁹ Minnesota 50,162; North Dakota 35,062; South Dakota 24,669; Montana 21,550 (Henry G. Teigan, "The National Nonpartisan League," *American Labor Year Book, 1919–1920*, p. 285).

¹⁰⁰ Gaston, pp. 238–40.

¹⁰¹ This is attributed to Townley by Maxwell (*Nonpartisan League from the Inside*, p. 56).

¹⁰² Maxwell, *Nonpartisan League from the Inside*, pp. 54–57.

¹⁰³ *Leader*, Nov. 25, 1918, p. 2; Dec. 16, 1918, pp. 3–4.

¹⁰⁴ *Leader*, Dec. 23, 1918, pp. 3–4.

¹⁰⁵ *The Fighting Program of the National Nonpartisan League, Unanimously Adopted in Annual Meeting, St. Paul, Minn., Dec. 3, 1918.*

¹⁰⁶ Dec. 16, 1918, p. 4.

¹⁰⁷ The following discussion is based on "The Articles of Association of the National Nonpartisan League," published in *Leader*, Dec. 16, 1918, pp. 4, 11.

¹⁰⁸ *Leader*, Dec. 23, 1918, p. 6.

¹⁰⁹ Walter Thomas Mills, *The Articles of Association of the National Nonpartisan League, Together with a Discussion of the Democracy of the League's Purposes, the Democracy of Its Form of Organization, the Democracy of the Measures Supported by the League, and the Ending of the Autocratic Monopolies and the Triumph of Democracy.*

¹¹⁰ Quoted in *Leader*, Dec. 23, 1918, p. 3.

¹¹¹ Dec. 23, 1918, p. 7.

¹¹² The vote by states is given in *Leader*, Jan. 27, 1919, p. 5.

¹¹³ Quoted in *Leader*, Jan. 13, 1919, pp. 4, 14. The creditor still contended that Townley had an interest in at least the Nonpartisan Publishing Company, the property of which could be attached. On Aug. 23, 1920, the Circuit Court of Appeals upheld the District Court, holding that a "mere suspicion" of such proprietary interest was not enough to prevent discharge, McCutcheon v. Townley, 266 F. 985 (1920). Neither at that time nor since has Townley lived in other than an extremely modest fashion.

Chapter 10

¹ Quoted in *Leader*, Feb. 3, 1919, p. 5.

² Feb. 4, 1919, p. 1.

³ Jan. 4, 1919, p. 4. The *Herald* did later recognize that it was the spirit which was important, and that the people were unlikely to rush into voiding the Declaration.

⁴ *Grand Forks Herald*, Jan. 7, 1919, p. 1; *Leader*, Feb. 3, 1919, p. 6.

⁵ *The North Dakota Industrial Program*, issued by the Industrial Commission, pp. 19–20.

⁶ State *ex rel.* Langer v. MacDonald, 41 N.D. 389, 170 N.W. 873 (1919).

⁷ MacDonald v. Nielson, 43 N.D. 346, 175 N.W. 361 (1919). See also *Grand Forks Herald*, Jan. 6, 1919, p. 6; Jan. 10, p. 1; Jan. 23, p. 1.

⁸ William MacDonald, "North Dakota's Experiment," *Nation*, 108:420 (March

22, 1919). Doubtless the I.V.A. would have maintained that he looked in the wrong places for the individuals he thought missing.

[9] See Langer, pp. 123-24.

[10] The fifteen caucus rules, mostly relating to such matters as parliamentary procedure, were published in the *Grand Forks Herald*, Feb. 21, 1919, p. 3.

[11] Quoted in Russell, *Nonpartisan League*, p. 253.

[12] Feb. 6, 1919.

[13] *Grand Forks Herald*, Jan. 18, 1919, p. 1.

[14] Interview with A. C. Townley, Sept. 23, 1948; *Red Flame*, Nov. 1919, p. 29. In 1920 the I.V.A. printed and circulated leaflets containing Townley's "instructions" to Mees.

[15] Interview with A. C. Townley, Sept. 23, 1948.

[16] Jan. 16, 1919, p. 3.

[17] See for example *Red Flame*, June 1920, p. 5.

[18] Feb. 7, 1919, p. 4.

[19] Interview with John N. Hagan, Aug. 28, 1948.

[20] *North Dakota Session Laws, 1919*, Ch. 151.

[21] *Ibid.*, Ch. 147. For a thorough discussion of the creation and legal basis of the Bank of North Dakota see Tostlebe, pp. 65-75.

[22] *North Dakota Session Laws, 1919*, Ch. 152.

[23] *Ibid.*, Ch. 150. For a good summary of this setup see *The North Dakota Industrial Program*, pp. 53-56.

[24] *North Dakota Session Laws, 1919*, Ch. 160.

[25] *Ibid.*, Chs. 138, 241. See also *Leader*, March 17, 1919, pp. 5, 13.

[26] *North Dakota Session Laws, 1919*, Ch. 223.

[27] *Grand Forks Herald*, March 3, 1919, p. 2.

[28] *Grand Forks Herald*, Feb. 28, 1919, p. 6.

[29] These arguments and others are summarized in Mader, pp. 41-43. Mader gives a detailed coverage of the entire process of passage, including committee actions and excerpts from debates, pp. 29-49.

[30] *Grand Forks Herald*, March 3, 1919, p. 6.

[31] *Grand Forks Herald*, Feb. 18, 1919, pp. 1, 2.

[32] Those of which the League was most proud are briefly described following the text of major acts in *The New Day in North Dakota*. The *Grand Forks Herald* summarized those it considered important on March 3, 1919, p. 2.

[33] *Grand Forks Herald*, March 3, 1919, p. 2; *Minneapolis Journal*, March 2, 1919, pp. 1, 10. The minority letter, which had been issued on facsimile state stationery, is reprinted on pp. 50-51, and the House resolution on p. 49 of J. D. Bacon, *Townleyism Unmasked; Now Stands before the World in Its True Light as Radical Socialism*.

[34] March 3, 1919, p. 2.

[35] July 17, 1919, p. 4.

[36] March 3, 1919, p. 4.

Chapter 11

[1] *Leader*, March 17, 1919, p. 7.

[2] Quoted in *Leader*, May 26, 1919, p. 13; *Grand Forks Herald*, May 10, 1919, pp. 1, 4.

[3] The statement was made to Judge William A. Anderson (interview, April 28, 1949).

[4] On this episode see Langer, pp. 67-75; Buttree, pp. 162-65; Brinton, p. 49. The *Fargo Courier-News* at the time struggled with the defense for several weeks.

[5] *Grand Forks Herald*, March 1, 1919, p. 1; April 15, p. 3.

[6] Quoted in *Leader*, April 14, 1919, p. 7.

[7] Quoted in Buttree, pp. 180–81.

[8] April 14, 1919, p. 7.

[9] Scott v. Frazier, 258 F. 669 (1919). For other interesting views voiced by the court in this case see *supra*, p. 7.

[10] On the League campaign see Leader, June 23, 1919, pp. 4–5; Judson King, "The Nonpartisan Victory," *Public*, 22:706–8 (July 5, 1919).

[11] *Leader*, July 14, 1919, p. 12.

[12] June 23, 1919, p. 4.

[13] June 26, 1919, p. 4.

[14] *1919 Legislative Manual, State of North Dakota*, pp. 288–89.

[15] June 27, 1919, p. 4.

[16] *Leader*, April 21, 1919, p. 3; May 19, p. 12.

[17] Tostlebe, pp. 81–82.

[18] *Ibid.*, pp. 80–81. A good statement of the purposes and methods of operation of the Bank may be found in *The North Dakota Industrial Program*, pp. 21–24.

[19] Tostlebe, pp. 85–86; Charles Merz, "The Nonpartisan League; A Survey," *New Republic*, 22:335–36 (May 12, 1920).

[20] See Fossum, pp. 113–15; Langer, p. 100.

[21] Russell, *Nonpartisan League*, p. 300. Langer claimed that a 5 per cent interest rate would have been possible had a simple rural credit system been set up rather than a bank with large overhead (*Nonpartisan League*, p. 101).

[22] *Leader*, Aug. 25, 1919, p. 6; Sept. 1, p. 3.

[23] *The North Dakota Industrial Program*; Lynn J. Frazier, "Governor Frazier's Own Story of the Nonpartisan League," *New York Times*, May 16, 1920, Sec. XX, p. 3.

[24] See Russell, *Nonpartisan League*, pp. 319–20.

[25] For a summary of this situation see Fossum, pp. 112–13.

[26] *Leader*, June 16, 1919, p. 3.

[27] *Townleyism: A True Story of the Operation of the Nonpartisan League Program in North Dakota, as Told in Official Reports of the Various Departments of the State Government*, pp. 17–18.

[28] *Townleyism*, pp. 18–20; *The New Day in North Dakota*, p. 30.

[29] Interview with Governor Fred G. Aandahl, Aug. 23, 1948.

[30] State *ex rel.* Amerland v. Hagan, 44 N.D. 306, 175 N.W. 372 (1919).

[31] *Leader*, May 26, 1919, p. 3.

[32] *Leader*, June 9, 1919, p. 3.

[33] *Leader*, July 28, 1919, p. 10.

[34] *Leader*, May 26, 1919, p. 3.

[35] Interview with Judge William A. Anderson, April 28, 1949.

[36] Mader, pp. 84–86. The fifty papers chosen were listed in the *Grand Forks Herald*, Aug. 10, 1919, p. 1.

[37] Mader, pp. 100–2.

[38] *Ibid.*, pp. 92–94, 103–4.

[39] Minnie J. Nielson, *A Message to Minnesota Womanhood*, p. 6.

[40] On this whole affair see Langer, pp. 201–10; Nielson, especially pp. 6–8; *Red Flame*, Nov. 1919, pp. 30–31.

[41] *Annual Report, North Dakota Board of Administration, 1919*, p. 34.

[42] Nielson, p. 8.

[43] State *ex rel.* Langer v. Totten, 44 N.D. 557, 175 N.W. 563 (1919).

[44] Bacon, *Sovietians; Wreckers of Americanism*, pp. 18–19.

[45] Charles E. Selden, "Terrorism and Fraud of the Nonpartisan League," *New York Times Magazine*, Jan. 4, 1920, Sec. IX, pp. 1, 10. The article includes a complete list of the periodicals, which may also be found in *Annual Report, North Dakota Board of Administration, 1919*, p. 122.

⁴⁶ Teigan to Stanley, Feb. 6, 1919 (National Nonpartisan League Papers).
⁴⁷ Stanley to Teigan, March 1, 1919.
⁴⁸ Teigan to Stanley, March 6, 1919.
⁴⁹ See Bacon, *Sovietians; Wreckers of Americanism*, p. 18.
⁵⁰ See *Leader*, June 23, 1919, pp. 1, 6.
⁵¹ Interview with Nelson A. Mason, Sept. 3, 1948.
⁵² *Leader*, July 28, 1919, p. 4.
⁵³ Judson King, "The Prosecution of Mr. Townley," *Nation*, 109:143 (Aug. 2, 1919). The names and addresses of the jurors selected are given in Douthit, p. 156n.
⁵⁴ *Leader*, July 28, 1919, p. 4.
⁵⁵ This account of the trial is based largely upon the following general sources except where otherwise noted: State v. A. C. Townley and Another, 149 Minn. 5, 182 N.W. 773 (1921); *Leader*, July 28, 1919, pp. 4–7; Douthit, pp. 153–60; C. R. Johnson, "The Conviction of Townley," *New Republic*, 20:18–20 (Aug. 6, 1919); Judson King, "The Prosecution of Mr. Townley," *Nation*, 109:143–44 (Aug. 2, 1919); Ray McKaig, "The Townley Mistrial," *Public*, 22:855–57 (Aug. 9, 1919).
⁵⁶ Quoted in the opinion of the court, State v. A. C. Townley and Another, 149 Minn. 5, 182 N.W. 773 (1921). Teigen's past history is reviewed in some detail in the *Leader*, Aug. 4, 1919, pp. 4–5.
⁵⁷ *Leader*, Aug. 4, 1919, pp. 4–5.
⁵⁸ *Minneapolis Journal*, July 10, 1919, p. 26.
⁵⁹ *Minneapolis Journal*, July 13, 1919, p. 1.
⁶⁰ July 15, 1919, p. 14.
⁶¹ *Leader*, Sept. 29, 1919, p. 7.
⁶² July 11, 1919, p. 1.
⁶³ See for example the *Minneapolis Journal*, July 15, 1919, p. 14.
⁶⁴ July 14, 1919.

Chapter 12

¹ Quoted in *Leader*, Aug. 4, 1919, p. 3.
² *Leader*, Aug. 4, 1919, p. 12. For some details of this organization see Henry G. Teigan, "Minnesota's Political 'Why'," *Labor Age*, Feb. 1923, p. 11.
³ *Grand Forks Herald*, Sept. 1, 1919, p. 11; *Leader*, Sept. 22, 1919, p. 12.
⁴ *Leader*, Oct. 13, 1919, pp. 3, 14.
⁵ The letter is reprinted in Langer, pp. 185–86. See also the *Minneapolis Tribune*, Sept. 28, 1919.
⁶ State *ex rel*. Lofthus v. Langer, 46 N.D. 462, 177 N.W. 408 (1919). On the Scandinavian-American Bank affair see Tostlebe, pp. 96–105; Langer, pp. 76–87, 115–18; *Leader*, Oct. 20, 1919, pp. 4, 7, 13, 14; Oct. 27, pp. 4, 12; Nov. 10, pp. 3–4, 13; Gaston, pp. 306–9; *Red Flame*, Nov. 1919, pp. 15, 24–25, 29–30; Nelson, p. 286; Buttree, pp. 267–75; Bacon, *Sovietians; Wreckers of Americanism*, pp. 34–58; "Townley and Fargo's Bank Blow-up," *Literary Digest*, 63:44–50 (Nov. 1, 1919); "That Unsuccessful Bank 'Blow-up' in Fargo," *Literary Digest*, 63:48, 52 (Dec. 20, 1919); "Politics, Bank Explosions, Lawsuits and Other Live Matters in North Dakota," *Literary Digest*, 64:62–66 (March 20, 1920). The daily newspapers all of course carried running accounts.
⁷ *Leader*, Oct. 20, 1919, p. 11; Nov. 3, pp. 4–5, 18; *Grand Forks Herald*, Oct. 22, 1919, p. 1.
⁸ *Red Flame*, Nov. 1919, pp. 3, 37.
⁹ J. D. Bacon, *North Dakota's Reward for Electing Nonpartisan League Officers*, p. 12.
¹⁰ Quoted in Buttree, p. 192; *Red Flame*, Nov. 1919, pp. 36–37.
¹¹ P. 192.
¹² Fossum, pp. 109–11. Cf. Gaston, p. 302.

[13] Oct. 21, 1919, p. 1.

[14] *Leader*, April 5, 1920, p. 9.

[15] Quoted in *Leader*, Feb. 2, 1920, p. 5.

[16] *Message of Governor Lynn J. Frazier Delivered to the Sixteenth Legislature of the State of North Dakota, Assembled in Special Session, November 25, 1919* (Bismarck, 1919).

[17] That part of Burtness' remarks which the House stenographer transcribed may be found in the *Journal of the House of the Special Session of the Sixteenth Legislative Assembly, 1919*, pp. 347–60. See also the *Red Flame*, April 1920, p. 19; *Leader*, Dec. 15, 1919, p. 12; Bacon, *Sovietians; Wreckers of Americanism*, pp. 19–25; Langer, pp. 189–92.

[18] *Journal of the House of the Special Session of the Sixteenth Legislative Assembly, 1919*, pp. 252–56.

[19] Quoted in the *Grand Forks Herald*, Dec. 15, 1919, p. 1.

[20] Harold S. Quigley, "The Nonpartizan League," *Unpartizan Review*, 14:71–72 (July 1920); Gaston, pp. 297–98.

[21] *Minneapolis Journal*, Dec. 12, 1919, p. 14; Gaston, p. 297.

[22] *Minneapolis Journal*, Dec. 12, 1919, p. 14.

[23] *Grand Forks Herald*, Dec. 19, 1919, p. 6.

[24] *Minneapolis Journal*, Dec. 16, 1919, p. 4.

[25] Dec. 15, 1919, p. 4.

[26] Bacon, *Sovietians; Wreckers of Americanism*, p. 17. See also Buttree, pp. 302–3; *Red Flame*, June 1920, pp. 5, 11.

[27] *Red Flame*, June 1920, p. 10.

[28] *The Despoilers*, p. 300.

[29] Ch. 41, *Special Session Laws*, 1919.

[30] June 1920, pp. 3–5.

[31] The full text of this act is printed in Langer, p. 7. His book was written in challenge to the act, which, however, was never enforced.

[32] State *ex rel.* Langer v. Olson, 44 N.D. 614, 175 N.W. 528 (1920).

[33] *Leader*, Dec. 29, 1919, pp. 5, 14.

[34] Gaston, p. 318.

[35] *Leader*, Dec. 29, 1919, p. 4.

Chapter 13

[1] *Leader*, April 12, 1920, p. 3.

[2] "Minutes of the 1st Biennial Convention of the Working People's Nonpartisan League of Minnesota, St. Paul, March 24 and 25, 1920" (copy in Teigan Papers). Those considered for all offices are listed.

[3] *Leader*, April 12, 1920, pp. 3–4, 14.

[4] *Leader*, May 31, 1920, p. 12.

[5] *Leader*, June 14, 1920, p. 5.

[6] *Leader*, Feb. 24, 1919, pp. 11, 14.

[7] *Leader*, April 12, 1920, p. 6.

[8] *Leader*, March 29, 1920, p. 9; May 31, p. 12.

[9] *Leader*, April 26, 1920, p. 5.

[10] *Leader*, April 12, 1920, p. 8; April 19, p. 10; May 3, p. 12.

[11] *Leader*, May 31, 1920, p. 4.

[12] Quoted in the *Minneapolis Tribune*, May 4, 1920.

[13] June 14, 1920, p. 5; June 28, p. 6.

[14] June 7, 1920, p. 16.

[15] *1921 Legislative Manual, State of Minnesota*, pp. 100–1.

[16] *Leader*, July 12, 1920, p. 4.

[17] The official vote was Hilton, 118,932; Sullivan, 117,799 (*1921 Legislative Manual, State of Minnesota*, pp. 100-1).

[18] C. R. Johnson, "Is the Nonpartisan League Declining?" *New Republic*, 24:88 (Sept. 22, 1920).

[19] *Grand Forks Herald*, Feb. 6, 1920, p. 1.

[20] *Grand Forks Herald*, Feb. 18, 1920, p. 1.

[21] *Grand Forks Herald*, March 1, 1920, p. 4.

[22] *Grand Forks Herald*, March 16, 1920, p. 1; March 20, p. 1; *Leader*, April 5, 1920, p. 9.

[23] State *ex rel.* Kositzky v. Waters, 45 N.D. 115, 176 N.W. 913 (1920). Interview with Judge William A. Anderson, April 28, 1949.

[24] Langer, p. 29.

[25] *Grand Forks Herald*, April 22, 1920, p. 4.

[26] *Grand Forks Herald*, March 1, 1920, p. 1. The letter is printed in Langer, pp. 46-47.

[27] *Grand Forks Herald*, May 13, 1920, p. 1.

[28] The platform may be found in the *Red Flame*, June 1920, pp. 11-15.

[29] *Grand Forks Herald*, May 20, 1920, p. 1.

[30] *Leader*, May 31, 1920, pp. 6-7.

[31] Interview with A. C. Townley, Sept. 23, 1948.

[32] April 1920, p. 36.

[33] Quoted in *Leader*, April 26, 1920, p. 6.

[34] Sample I.V.A. arguments on this matter may be found in the *Red Flame*, May 1920, pp. 20-21, and Langer, pp. 135-59. Comprehensive statements of the League contentions are presented in the *Fargo Courier-News*, May 23, 1920, p. 10, and *Townleyism*, pp. 22-24.

[35] See the *Fargo Courier-News*, May 23, 1920, p. 9; *Red Flame*, April 1920, pp. 5-7.

[36] See for example the *Red Flame*, June 1920, pp. 6-8.

[37] *Townleyism*, pp. 12-15.

[38] *Leader*, April 26, 1920, pp. 3-4. A detailed description of the proposed layout, together with estimates of the benefits to be obtained, may be found in *The North Dakota Industrial Program*, pp. 40-52.

[39] See *Leader*, Jan. 26, 1920, p. 8; *Grand Forks Herald*, June 1, 1920, p. 1.

[40] Green v. Frazier, 44 N.D. 395, 176 N.W. 11 (1920).

[41] This account of the hearing is taken from "State Socialism Constitutional," *Literary Digest*, 65:20-21 (June 26, 1920), and *Leader*, April 26, 1920, p. 4; May 17, p. 4.

[42] Scott v. Frazier, 253 U.S. 243 (1920).

[43] Green v. Frazier, 253 U.S. 233, 40 S.Ct. 499, 64 L.Ed. 878 (1920).

[44] Quoted in "State Socialism Constitutional," *Literary Digest*, 65:21 (June 26, 1920).

[45] Walter Davenport, "Mr. Lemke Stops to Think," *Collier's*, 98:8, 25 (Oct. 17, 1936).

[46] Quoted in the *Grand Forks Herald*, May 24, 1920, p. 13.

[47] Quoted in Bacon, *Sovietians; Wreckers of Americanism*, pp. 26-27.

[48] *Compilation of Election Returns, National and State, 1914-1928* (Bismarck, 1930), p. 36. The vote for governor was Frazier, 59,355; Langer, 53,941.

[49] Interview with Judge A. M. Christianson, Sept. 1, 1948; Chester H. Rowell, "Political Cyclone in North Dakota," *World's Work*, 46:266-67 (July 1923). The vote was Ladd, 54,957; Gronna, 51,142; White, 5477 (*Compilation of Election Returns, National and State, 1914-1928* (N.D.), p. 36).

[50] *North Dakota Blue Book, 1942*, p. 142.

[51] *Leader*, Aug. 9, 1920, p. 12.

[52] Detailed accounts of the primary developments in these states may be found in the *Leader* for March 8, March 15, March 22, April 12, May 17, May 31, June 7, June 28, July 12, Aug. 23, Sept. 6, Sept. 20, Oct. 4, Oct. 18, and Nov. 1, 1920.

[53] *Leader*, Oct. 4, 1920, p. 8.

[54] *Leader*, Aug. 9, 1920, pp. 5-6.

[55] *Leader*, Oct. 18, 1920, p. 3.

[56] See *Leader*, July 26, 1920, pp. 4, 10.

[57] *Leader*, Nov. 1, 1920, p. 6.

[58] *Minneapolis Tribune*, April 4, 1923.

[59] Oct. 18, 1920, p. 16.

[60] M. H. Hedges, "Where Democrats Vote Republican," *New Republic*, 23 :334 (Aug. 18, 1920); "Continued Political Upheaval in the Northwest," *Outlook*, 125 :208 (June 2, 1920).

[61] *Grand Forks Herald*, July 20, 1920, p. 13; July 24, p. 1; July 27, p. 7.

[62] *Leader*, Sept. 20, 1920, p. 8.

[63] The series commenced Oct. 5, 1920.

[64] *Leader*, Sept. 6, 1920, p. 9.

[65] Sept. 6, 1920, p. 9.

[66] *Grand Forks Herald*, Oct. 20, 1920, p. 9; *Minneapolis Journal*, Oct. 29, 1920, p. 8.

[67] *Grand Forks Herald*, Nov. 1, 1920, p. 1.

[68] *Compilation of Election Returns, National and State, 1914-1928* (N.D.), pp. 42, 44.

[69] *North Dakota Blue Book, 1942*, p. 142.

[70] Mader, pp. 108-9, 118-19.

[71] *1921 Legislative Manual, State of Minnesota*, pp. 526-27.

[72] *Leader*, Nov. 29, 1920, p. 9.

[73] *Leader*, Dec. 13, 1920, p. 13.

[74] *Leader*, Dec. 27, 1920, p. 5.

Chapter 14

[1] *Message of Lynn J. Frazier, Governor of North Dakota, to the Seventeenth Legislative Assembly, January 5, 1921* (Bismarck, 1921).

[2] *Grand Forks Herald*, Jan. 19, 1921, pp. 4, 8.

[3] His original letter and a vast amount of correspondence and newspaper clippings on the subject may be found in the LeSueur Papers.

[4] *Grand Forks Herald*, Jan. 26, 1921, p. 1. On the hiring of the company and their initial reports see the *Report of the North Dakota Industrial Commission for the Year Ending December 31, 1921* (Bismarck, 1922), pp. 6-7, and *Leader*, Feb. 21, 1921, p. 3.

[5] *Leader*, Feb. 21, 1921, p. 5.

[6] *Grand Forks Herald*, Jan. 28, 1921, p. 1.

[7] *Leader*, Feb. 21, 1921, p. 3.

[8] *Grand Forks Herald*, Feb. 2, 1921, p. 1.

[9] *Leader*, Dec. 13, 1921, p. 3.

[10] Tostlebe, p. 131.

[11] *Leader*, Dec. 13, 1920, p. 3.

[12] *Leader*, March 7, 1921, p. 5.

[13] Tostlebe, p. 132.

[14] *Leader*, Jan. 10, 1921, p. 16.

[15] *Grand Forks Herald*, Jan. 8, 1921, p. 1.

[16] The reply is quoted in full in Burgess, pp. 156-57.

[17] *Grand Forks Herald*, Jan. 14, 1921, p. 5.

[18] Quoted in *Townleyism*, p. 85.

[19] *Townleyism*, p. 87.

[20] Tostlebe, pp. 133–35; *Leader*, March 7, 1921, p. 20; *Grand Forks Herald*, Feb. 14, 1921, p. 1.

[21] Tostlebe, pp. 139–47; *Leader*, March 21, 1921, p. 5; May 2, p. 4; May 30, p. 12; June 13, pp. 3, 5.

[22] *Grand Forks Herald*, Jan. 4, 1921, p. 1; Jan. 7, p. 10; Jan. 12, p. 8; March 21, p. 3; Mader, p. 110.

[23] Jan. 15, 1921, p. 1.

[24] *Grand Forks Herald*, Feb. 7, 1921, p. 1; Feb. 16, p. 1.

[25] *Grand Forks Herald*, Feb. 7, 1921, p. 8.

[26] *Townleyism*, p. 29.

[27] *Leader*, Feb. 21, 1921, p. 3.

[28] *Journal of the Senate of the Seventeenth Session of the Legislative Assembly: State of North Dakota.* The report of the investigating committee may be found at pp. 752–98; the minority report, pp. 799–807; exhibits and transcript of hearings, pp. 808–2530.

[29] *Journal of the House of the Seventeenth Session of the Legislative Assembly: State of North Dakota.* The report of the investigating committee may be found at pp. 925–78 and the transcript of hearings at pp. 979–1484. It is interesting that this report was privately published in the fear that it would not fare well at the hands of the state administration.

[30] *Divide County Farmers Press*, Feb. 18, 1921; *McCluskey Gazette*, March 11, 1921; *Cando Record*, March 3, 1921.

[31] *Grand Forks Herald*, March 5, 1921, p. 1.

[32] *Minneapolis Journal*, March 5, 1921, p. 3; *Leader*, March 21, 1921, p. 5.

[33] The account of the final night of the session is taken largely from reports in the *Bismarck Tribune*, March 5, 1921, pp. 1, 6, and the *Minneapolis Journal*, March 5, 1921, pp. 1, 2. See also *The Nonpartisan League in North Dakota*, pp. 72–73.

Chapter 15

[1] *Grand Forks Herald*, March 2, 1921, p. 1.

[2] *Leader*, March 21, 1921, p. 5.

[3] Feb. 17, 1921, p. 4.

[4] *Grand Forks Herald*, April 1, 1921, p. 1; *Leader*, April 18, 1921, p. 4.

[5] *Leader*, April 18, 1921, p. 4.

[6] *The North Dakota Industrial Program*, pp. 57–60.

[7] *Ibid.*, pp. 61–78.

[8] *Ibid.*, pp. 21–37; *Townleyism*, pp. 68–71.

[9] *Townleyism*, pp. 46–49.

[10] *Ibid.*, pp. 62–64.

[11] *The North Dakota Industrial Program*, pp. 53–56; *Townleyism*, pp. 54–57.

[12] *Fargo Courier-News*, July 6, 1921, p. 1.

[13] *Grand Forks Herald*, July 7, 1921, p. 1; July 11, p. 6; July 13, p. 1.

[14] *Bank of North Dakota Bulletin*, June 1921; Tostlebe, pp. 137–38.

[15] *Leader*, Oct. 17, 1921, p. 6; Tostlebe, p. 139.

[16] *North Dakota Publicity Pamphlet: Constitutional Amendment and Initiated Measures to Be Submitted to the Electors at the Recall Election October 28, 1921.*

[17] Oct. 25, 1921, p. 4.

[18] "North Dakota's Political Twister," *Literary Digest*, 71:13 (Oct. 22, 1921).

[19] *Leader*, Oct. 3, 1921, pp. 10, 14.

[20] *Grand Forks Herald*, Oct. 18, 1921, p. 1; Oct. 25, p. 1; *Mandan Daily Pioneer*, Oct. 19, 1921, p. 1.

[21] *Leader*, Oct. 22, 1921, p. 3. On the houses built for state officials see the *Grand Forks Herald*, Jan. 27, 1921, p. 1.

[22] Interview with A. C. Townley, Sept. 23, 1948.

[23] *North Dakota Leader*, Oct. 22, 1921, p. 1.

[24] Quoted in *North Dakota Leader*, Oct. 22, 1921, pp. 2, 4.

[25] *Leader*, Oct. 17, 1921, pp. 6–7.

[26] State *ex rel.* Lemke v. District Court of Stutsman County; Yaeger v. Frazier, 49 N.D. 27, 186 N.W. 381 (1921). On these events see also *Leader*, Oct. 31, 1921, p. 13; *Mandan Daily Pioneer*, Oct. 19, 1921, p. 1; *North Dakota Leader*, Oct. 22, 1921, p. 1.

[27] Oct. 26, 1921, p. 1.

[28] *North Dakota Blue Book, 1942*, pp. 142–43.

[29] "North Dakota's 'Recall' Puzzle," *Literary Digest*, 71:10 (Nov. 19, 1921).

[30] Typical samples were collected by the *Literary Digest* in *ibid.*

[31] Oct. 31, 1921, p. 1.

[32] Nov. 14, 1921, pp. 3–5.

[33] Nov. 28, 1921, p. 13.

[34] State *ex rel.* Laird v. Hall, 49 N.D. 11, 186 N.W. 284 (1921).

[35] Currie v. Frazier, 48 N.D. 600, 186 N.W. 244 (1921).

[36] Tostlebe, p. 156.

[37] Quoted in *Leader*, Dec. 12, 1921, p. 7.

[38] *Report of the North Dakota Industrial Commission for the Year Ending December 31, 1921*, pp. 9–10.

[39] *Ibid.*, pp. 31–37.

[40] *Ibid.*, pp. 60–61.

[41] *Ibid.*, pp. 43–58.

[42] *Ibid.*, pp. 19–30.

[43] Tostlebe, pp. 121–22.

[44] *Ibid.*, pp. 106–7.

[45] *Ibid.*, pp. 172–73.

[46] *Ibid.*, pp. 180–95.

[47] *Report of the North Dakota Industrial Commission for the Year Ending December 31, 1921*, p. 10.

Chapter 16

[1] State v. A. C. Townley and Another, 149 Minn. 5, 182 N.W. 773 (1921).

[2] 257 U.S. 643 (1921).

[3] For accounts of the jailing episode see *Leader*, Nov. 14, 1921, pp. 7, 9; *Grand Forks Herald*, Nov. 3, 1921, p. 2.

[4] Interview with A. C. Townley, Sept. 23, 1948.

[5] *Leader*, March 21, 1921, p. 8.

[6] *Leader*, April 17, 1922, p. 7.

[7] *Leader*, April 17, 1922, p. 6; *Minneapolis Tribune*, March 23, 1922.

[8] *Leader*, May 1922, p. 7; Aug. 1922, p. 7.

[9] Interview with A. C. Townley, Sept. 23, 1948.

[10] *Leader*, June 1922, p. 6; May 1923, p. 3.

[11] Interview with Judge A. M. Christianson, Sept. 1, 1948.

[12] June 27, 1922, p. 1.

[13] *Compilation of Election Returns, National and State, 1914–1928* (N.D.), pp. 50–51. The vote for senator in the Republican primary was Frazier, 91,387; McCumber, 80,821.

[14] *Leader*, April 17, 1922, pp. 6–7.

[15] *Leader*, Dec. 12, 1921, p. 7.

[16] Virtually the only evidence of the existence of the Wyoming and California

leagues, which were never mentioned by the *Leader*, is a very limited amount of correspondence on stationery bearing the letterheads of the organizations in the National Nonpartisan League Papers.

[17] *Leader*, March 20, 1922, p. 6; Sept. 1922, pp. 8–9.

[18] *Leader*, June 1922, p. 6; Aug. 1922, p. 7.

[19] *Leader*, Nov. 1922, p. 6.

[20] July 1, 1922, p. 4.

[21] Nov. 6, 1922, p. 4.

[22] Doan, p. 107.

[23] *Compilation of Election Returns, National and State, 1914–1928* (N.D.), p. 54.

[24] *1923 Legislative Manual, State of Minnesota*, pp. 452–53. For senator: Shipstead (F-L), 325,372; Kellogg (R), 241,833; Oleson (D), 123,624. For governor: Preus (R), 309,756; Johnson (F-L), 295,479; Indrehus (D), 79,903.

[25] Kingsley, p. 40.

[26] *1925 Legislative Manual, State of Minnesota*, p. 301.

[27] *Leader*, Nov. 1922, p. 7.

[28] *Leader*, March 8, 1920, p. 9.

[29] Mader, pp. 119–22.

[30] *Ibid.*, p. 111.

[31] *Leader*, July 1923, p. 3.

[32] *Leader*, July 1923, p. 3. On this new organization see Theodore Saloutos, "The National Producers' Alliance," *Minnesota History*, 28:37–44 (March 1947).

[33] *Nonpartisan League Methods and Principles*, p. 10.

[34] Samuel P. Huntington, "The Election Tactics of the Nonpartisan League," *Mississippi Valley Historical Review*, March 1950, pp. 613–32.

[35] *Call*, Sept. 20, 1917.

[36] Quoted in *Leader*, May 13, 1918, p. 7.

[37] "Report of the Resolutions Committee on the Relation of the Socialist Party to the National Nonpartisan League" (n.d.; LeSueur Papers).

[38] *The North Dakota Industrial Program*, p. 14.

[39] On the Minnesota Farmer-Labor party see Arthur E. Naftalin, "A History of the Farmer-Labor Party of Minnesota" (Ph.D. Thesis); George H. Mayer, *The Political Career of Floyd B. Olson*.

Bibliography

Books

Brinton, J. Wells. *Wheat and Politics*. Minneapolis, 1931.

Bruce, Andrew A. *Non-Partisan League*. New York, 1921.

Burdick, Usher L. *History of the Farmers' Political Action in North Dakota*. Baltimore, 1944.

Burgess, Eugene W. *La "Nonpartisan League": Une Expérience Américaine de Socialisme d'Etat Agraire*. Paris, 1928.

Buttree, J. Edmund. *The Despoilers*. Boston, 1920.

Chafee, Zechariah, Jr. *Free Speech in the United States*. Cambridge, Mass., 1941.

Christianson, Theodore. *Minnesota: A History of the State and Its People*. 5 vols. Chicago and New York, 1935.

Crawford, Lewis F. *History of North Dakota*. 3 vols. Chicago and New York, 1931.

Doan, Edward N., *The LaFollettes and the Wisconsin Idea*. New York, 1947.

Douthit, Davis. *Nobody Owns Us: The Story of Joe Gilbert, Midwestern Rebel*. Chicago, Washington, D.C., New York, 1948.

Fine, Nathan. *Labor and Farmer Parties in the United States, 1828-1928*. New York, 1928.

Fite, Gilbert C. *Peter Norbeck: Prairie Statesman*. Columbia, Mo., 1948.

Folwell, William Watts. *A History of Minnesota*. 4 vols. St. Paul, 1926-1931.

Fossum, Paul R. *The Agrarian Movement in North Dakota*. Baltimore, 1925.

Gaston, Herbert E. *The Nonpartisan League*. New York, 1920.

Haines, Lynn and Dora B. *The Lindberghs*. New York, 1931.

Haynes, Fred E. *Social Politics in the United States*. New York, 1924.

Holbrook, Franklin F., and Livia Appel. *Minnesota in the War with Germany*. 2 vols. St. Paul, 1932.

Holzworth, John M. *The Fighting Governor: The Story of William Langer and the State of North Dakota*. Chicago, 1938.

Kile, Orville M. *The Farm Bureau through Three Decades*. Baltimore, 1948.

LaFollette, Belle C. and Fola. *Robert M. LaFollette*. New York, 1953.

Langer, William. *The Nonpartisan League: Its Birth, Activities and Leaders*. Mandan, N.D., 1920.

Lindbergh, Charles A. *Why Is Your Country at War and What Happens to You after the War and Related Subjects*. Washington, D.C., 1917.

Lindstrom, David E. *American Farmers' and Rural Organizations*. Champaign, Ill., 1948.

McConnell, Grant. *The Decline of Agrarian Democracy.* Berkeley, Calif., 1953.
MacKay, Kenneth C. *The Progressive Movement of 1924.* New York, 1947.
Manahan, James M. *Trials of a Lawyer.* Minneapolis, 1933.
Martin, Boyd A. *The Direct Primary in Idaho.* Palo Alto, Calif., 1947.
Maxwell, S. R. *The Nonpartisan League.* New York, 1920.
————. *The Nonpartisan League from the Inside.* St. Paul, 1918.
Mayer, George H. *The Political Career of Floyd B. Olson.* Minneapolis, 1951.
Nelson, Bruce. *Land of the Dacotahs.* Minneapolis, 1946.
Nye, Russell B. *Midwestern Progressive Politics.* East Lansing, Mich., 1951.
Rice, Stuart A. *Farmers and Workers in American Politics.* New York, 1924.
Russell, Charles Edward. *Bare Hands and Stone Walls.* New York, 1933.
————. *The Story of the Nonpartisan League.* New York, 1920.
Saloutos, Theodore, and John D. Hicks. *Agricultural Discontent in the Middle West, 1900–1939.* Madison, Wis., 1951.
Sharp, Paul F. *The Agrarian Revolt in Western Canada.* Minneapolis, 1948.
Stedman, Murray S. and Susan W. *Discontent at the Polls.* New York, 1950.
Steinel, Alvin T. *History of Agriculture in Colorado.* Ft. Collins, Colo., 1926.
Surface, Frank M. *The Grain Trade during the World War.* New York, 1928.
Thomason, O. M. *The Beginning and the End of the Nonpartisan League.* St. Paul, 1920.
Tittemore, James N., and A. A. Vissers. *The Nonpartisan League vs. the Home.* Milwaukee, 1922.
Tostlebe, Alvin S. *The Bank of North Dakota: An Experiment in Agrarian Banking.* In Columbia University Studies in History, Economics, and Public Law, Vol. 114. New York, 1924.
Wiest, Edward. *Agricultural Organization in the United States.* In University of Kentucky Studies in Economics and Sociology. Lexington, Ky., 1923.
Witham, James W. *Fifty Years on the Firing Line.* Chicago, 1924.

Government Publications

MINNESOTA

Record of Testimony before the Senate Committee to Investigate Grain Exchanges, 1913. (Typewritten.)
Report of Hearings before the Senate Committee to Investigate Grain Exchanges, 1913. (Typewritten.)
Report of the Special Committee of the Minnesota House of Representatives for Investigation of the Grain Trade, 1913. St. Paul, 1913.

NORTH DAKOTA

Annual Report of the Board of Administration, 1919. Bismarck, 1920.
Constitution, Laws and Amendments Thereto Authorizing the North Dakota Industrial Program. Bismarck, 1921.
Constitutional Amendments and Initiated Measures to Be Submitted to the Electors at the Recall Election October 28, 1921. (North Dakota Publicity Pamphlet.) Bismarck, 1921.
Ladd, E. F. *Chemical and Physical Constants for Wheat and Mill Products.* Bulletin No. 114, North Dakota Agricultural College Experiment Station, Jan. 1916.
————. *Is the Present System of Grading Wheat Equitable?* Special Bulletin No. 14 (Vol. III), North Dakota Agricultural College Experiment Station (Food Department), Jan. 1915.
————. *North Dakota Wheat for 1916.* Bulletin No. 119, North Dakota Agricultural College Experiment Station, Nov. 1916.

Measures Enacted by the Sixteenth Legislative Assembly and to Be Referred to the Electors at a Special Election June 26, 1919. (North Dakota Publicity Pamphlet.) Bismarck, 1919.

Message of Governor Lynn J. Frazier Delivered to the Fifteenth Legislative Assembly of the State of North Dakota. Bismarck, 1917?

Message of Governor Lynn J. Frazier Delivered to the Sixteenth Legislative Assembly of the State of North Dakota, January 8, 1919. Bismarck, 1919.

Message of Governor Lynn J. Frazier Delivered to the Sixteenth Legislature of the State of North Dakota, Assembled in Special Session, November 25, 1919. Bismarck, 1919.

Message of Lynn J. Frazier, Governor of North Dakota, to the Seventeenth Legislative Assembly, January 5, 1921. Bismarck, 1921.

The North Dakota Industrial Program. (Industrial Commission, Office of the Commissioner of Immigration.) Bismarck, 1920.

The North Dakota Industrial Program. (Industrial Commission.) Bismarck, 1921.

Report of the North Dakota Industrial Commission for the Year Ending December 31, 1921. Bismarck, 1922.

Sanderson, Thomas. *The Bread Value of Wheat.* Bulletin No. 137, North Dakota Agricultural College Experiment Station, May, 1920.

————. *The Milling and Baking Data for the 1915 Crop of Wheat.* Bulletin No. 122, North Dakota Agricultural College Experiment Station, June 1917.

UNITED STATES

Congressional Record, 74 Cong., 2 Sess., June 17, 1936, pp. 9695-9725. (Extension of the remarks of Rep. Ernest Lundeen of Minnesota on the history and platform of the Farmer-Labor party of Minnesota.)

Edwards, E. E. *A Bibliography of the History of Agriculture in the United States.* Miscellaneous Publications of the United States Department of Agriculture, No. 84, 1930.

Hearings before the Committee on Agriculture on H.R. 14493, To Provide for the Uniform Grading of Grain. United States House of Representatives, 63 Cong., 1, 2, 3 Sess. 2 vols. Washington, D.C., 1915.

List of References on the National Nonpartisan League. United States Library of Congress, Nov. 1, 1918.

Report of the Federal Trade Commission on the Grain Trade. 7 vols. Washington, D.C., 1920-1926.

Rich, John H. *The Problems of the Northwestern Farmer.* Report of the Federal Reserve Agent, Ninth Federal Reserve District, Minneapolis, to the Federal Reserve Board, November 10, 1922.

Surface, Frank M. *The Stabilization of the Price of Wheat during the War and Its Effect upon the Returns to the Producer.* United States Grain Corporation. Washington, D.C., 1925.

Pamphlets

ISSUED BY THE NONPARTISAN LEAGUE

Address of A. C. Townley at the Farmers and Workers Conference Held at St. Paul, Sept. 18-20, 1917. St. Paul? 1917?

Borner, Florence. *A Modern Hiawatha.* St. Paul? 1920?

Cathro, F. W. *How about Your Taxes?* Fargo, 1919.

Facts about North Dakota's New Laws, as Passed by the Sixteenth Legislative Assembly in Session at Bismarck, North Dakota, January and February, 1919. Fargo, 1919.

Facts for the Farmer. (Minnesota Handbook.) St. Paul, 1917, 1918, 1919.

Facts Kept from the Farmer. (General Handbook of the National Nonpartisan League.) St. Paul, 1917, 1918, 1919.

The Fighting Program of the National Nonpartisan League, Unanimously Adopted in Annual Meeting, St. Paul, Minn., Dec. 3, 1918. St. Paul, 1919.

Freedom for All Forever. (1918 Souvenir Rally Booklet.) Minneapolis, 1918?

How the Fake League Was Started. (Reprint from the *Nonpartisan Leader.*) St. Paul, 1919.

How to Finance the War. St. Paul, 1918?

Information for League Speakers and Boosters. (Compiled from Addresses Given at Bismarck, October 1920, by State Officials, League Officers, and League Candidates.) N.p., n.d.

Memorial to the Congress of the United States Concerning Conditions in Minnesota, 1918. (National and State Executive Committees of the National Nonpartisan League.) St. Paul, 1918.

Memorial to the President of the United States Concerning Conditions in Minnesota, 1918. (National and State Executive Committees of the National Nonpartisan League.) St. Paul, 1918.

Mills, Walter Thomas. *The Articles of Association of the National Nonpartisan League, Together with a Discussion of the Democracy of the League's Purposes, the Democracy of Its Form of Organization, the Democracy of the Measures Supported by the League, and the Ending of the Autocratic Monopolies and the Triumph of Democracy.* St. Paul, 1919?

Minnesota, the Problems of Her People and Why the Farmers and Workers Have Organized for Political Action. (Women's Nonpartisan Clubs.) Minneapolis, 1920?

The New Day in North Dakota. Bismarck, 1919.

The New Day in North Dakota: Synopses of the Laws Making It. St. Paul? 1919?

The New Day. What the Organized Workers and Farmers Have Done for Themselves in North Dakota. Madison, Wis., 1920?

The Nonpartisan League: Its Origin, Purpose and Method of Operation. Minneapolis, 1918.

Nonpartisan League: Methods and Principles. Waco, Texas, n.d.

The 116 Nonpartisan League Members of the 16th Legislative Assembly of North Dakota to the Farmers and Other Workers of America. Bismarck, 1919?

Platform and Declaration of Principles Adopted by Delegates to the State Convention of the Minnesota Branch of the National Nonpartisan League. St. Paul, 1918.

Political Patrioteers. St. Paul, 1918?

Resolutions Adopted by Farmers' and Workers' National Nonpartisan League Campaign Rally, St. Paul Auditorium, March 19–21, 1918. N.p., n.d.

Resolutions Adopted by the Nonpartisan League Conference Held at St. Paul, Sept. 18–19–20, 1917. N.p., n.d.

Russell, Charles Edward. *In and Out of the Yoke.* St. Paul, 1921.

Townleyism: A True Story of the Operation of the Nonpartisan League Program in North Dakota, as Told in Official Reports of the Various Departments of the State Government. Fargo, 1921.

The Truth about North Dakota Taxes. Minneapolis and Fargo, 1920.

The Truth about the Constitutional Amendments. (Republican State Central Committee.) Fargo, 1918.

Where the People Rule; North Dakota, A State Where Democracy Is Safe. St. Paul, 1918.

Why Should Farmers Pay Dues? St. Paul, 1918.

Winning the War. St. Paul, 1918?

394

ISSUED IN OPPOSITION TO THE NONPARTISAN LEAGUE

Are You Ready to Hand Over Your Farm to a Bunch of Socialist Adventurers: That Is What Townleyism Means, Mr. Farmer. Grand Forks? n.d.

Bacon, J. D. *A. C. Townley, Pretending to Be the Farmer's Friend, Plays into the Hand of the Socialists and IWW's by Assisting in Keeping the Price of Wheat Down.* Grand Forks, 1918?

————. *A. (After) C. (Cash) Townley Smoked Out.* Grand Forks, 1918.

————. *Carry the Truth to the People.* Grand Forks, 1918.

————. *The Farmer and Townleyism.* Grand Forks, 1917.

————. *North Dakota's Reward for Electing Nonpartisan League Officers.* Grand Forks, 1920?

————. *A Socialist Constitution for North Dakota.* Grand Forks, 1917.

————. *Sovietians; Wreckers of Americanism.* Grand Forks, 1920.

————. *Townleyism Unmasked: Now Stands before the World in Its True Light as Radical Socialism.* Grand Forks, 1919.

————. *A Warning to the Farmer against Townleyism as Exploited in North Dakota.* Grand Forks, 1918.

Brinton, J. W., and J. R. Waters. *A. C. Townley; Dreamer, Promoter and Boss Politician; His Failures and the Defeat of the Nonpartisan League.* Bismarck, 1920.

Declaration of Principles and By-Laws of the Minnesota Sound Government Association. St. Paul? 1920?

Farmers, Investigate! Shall We Be Governed by a League Affiliated with the I.W.W.? (Issued by the state committee of the Utah Farm Bureau.) N.p., 1919.?

Frost, James. *Townley and Co., and the Nonpartisan League.* Beach, N.D., 1918.

Governor Peter Norbeck Replies. Pierre, S.D., 1918.

The Great Conspiracy. (Issued by the Montana Loyalty League.) Helena, Mont., 1919.

How the Farmer Can "Get His." N.p., n.d.

Howard, Asher (comp.). *The Leaders of the Nonpartisan League; Their Aims, Purposes and Records Reproduced from Original Letters and Documents; with a Letter to the Public by Senator Ole O. Sageng, Ex-Senator J. E. Haycraft, and Capt. Frank E. Reed.* Minneapolis, 1920.

If You Are An-American—Read: Bolshevism Here at Home. N.p., n.d.

Legislative Purposes of the League Leadership and Procedure to Attain It. (Issued by the Joint Campaign Committee.) Grand Forks, 1920.

Miller, C. B. *The Poison Book of Lindbergh.* St Paul, 1918.

Mr. Frazier: Please Answer! N.p., n.d.

The National Nonpartisan League: Its Aims and Purposes. N.p., n.d.

The New Day in North Dakota. (Issued by the Montana Loyalty League.) Helena, Mont., 1919.

Nielson, Minnie J. *A Message to Minnesota Womanhood.* (Issued by the Minnesota Sound Government Association.) St. Paul, 1920?

The Nonpartisan League in North Dakota. (Issued by the Canadian Reconstruction Association.) Toronto, 1921.

Norbeck, Peter. *Message to the People of South Dakota.* Redfield, S.D., 1918.

Please Bear in Mind: Non-Partisan League Is Only Another Name for "Socialism." (Issued by the Republican State Committee of Minnesota.) N.p., n.d.

Report of House Audit Committee Investigating Bank of North Dakota and Other State Industries, 1921. Minority Report of Senate Audit Committee Investigating Bank of North Dakota, 1921. St. Paul, 1921.

Richter, D. E. *Weeds; An Exposition of Arthur C. Townley.* N.p., 1919.

Sir Rufus Wallingford Has Thrown up His Hands! Truth Is Stranger Than Fiction. N.p., n.d.

Socialism Is Real Menace in Our State Now. N.p., n.d.

Teigen, Ferdinand A. *The Nonpartisan League: Its Origin, Development and Secret Purposes.* St. Paul, 1918.

Townleyism's Future in North Dakota. (Issued by the Independent Voters Association.) Fargo, 1919.

A Typical Townley Trick. N.p., n.d.

Who's Who in the Nonpartisan League; Also a Compilation of Quotations from Persons and Publications Friendly to the League. (Issued by the Montana Loyalty League.) Helena, Mont., 1919.

MISCELLANEOUS

Goldberg, Ray. *The Nonpartisan League in North Dakota.* (Undergraduate Honors Thesis, Harvard University, 1948.) Fargo, N.D., n.d.

Kurtz, Dan W. B., Jr. *The Good and the Bad; Facts about North Dakota State Owned and Operated Flour Mill and Elevator; Also of Kindred Matters.* Minot, 1940.

Youmans, Grant. *Justice Held for Ransom.* Minot? 1920.

Magazines Issued in Opposition to the Nonpartisan League

America First. (St. Paul.) April–Oct. 1919.

Minnesota Issues. (St. Paul.) Feb. 1920–March 1921.

The Non-Partisan. (St. Paul.) March–July, 1917.

Northwest Warriors Magazine. (St. Paul.) Aug. 1919–March 1920.

On the Square. (St. Paul.) May–June 1918.

Pan-American Anti-Socialist. (St. Paul.) 1918. (Exact dates uncertain, copies not available.)

The Red Flame. (Bismarck.) Nov. 1919–Oct. 1920.

Articles

"Address by A. C. Townley on the Organization of Farmers," American Federation of Labor, *Proceedings,* 1917, pp. 237–40.

Anderson, Douglas. "Revolt of a State," *LaFollette's Magazine,* 9:6–7 (Aug. 1917).

"Arthur C. Townley, the Radical Autocrat of North Dakota," *Literary Digest,* 61:62–64 (April 19, 1919).

Bahmer, Robert H. "The American Society of Equity," *Agricultural History,* 14:33–63 (Jan. 1940).

Bailey, Thomas A. "The West and Radical Legislation, 1890–1932," *American Journal of Sociology,* 38:603–11 (Jan. 1933).

"The Bar and the Nonpartisan League," *Public,* 22:974 (Sept. 13, 1919).

Boyle, James E. "The Agrarian Movement in the Northwest," *American Economic Review,* 8:505–21 (Sept. 1918).

————. "The Drive against 'Big Biz'," *Nation's Business,* April 1920, pp. 24–26.

Bullard, F. Lauriston. "The People's Czar in North Dakota," *Independent,* 98:138 (April 26, 1919).

"Class Movements in Politics," *Public,* 21:38–39 (Jan. 11, 1918).

Colegrove, Kenneth. "The Farmer and the Socialists," *Unpopular Review,* 8:287–301 (Oct. 1917).

"Confusing the Issue," *Public,* 22:814–15 (Aug. 2, 1919).

"Continued Political Upheaval in the Northwest," *Outlook,* 125:207–8 (June 2, 1920).

Creel, George. "Our 'Aliens'—Were They Loyal or Disloyal?" *Everybody's Magazine*, 40(No. 3):36–38, 70–71 (March 1919).

————. "What Do These Senators Want?" (Interview with Senator Lynn J. Frazier), *Collier's*, 71:9–10 (March 10, 1923).

Currie, B. W. "A Great Upheaval," *Country Gentleman*, 82:675–76, 760–61, 798–99, 830–31 (April 7–May 12, 1917).

Davenport, Frederick M. "The Farmers' Revolution in North Dakota," *Outlook*, 114:325–27 (Oct. 11, 1916).

————. "Radicalism in the Making," *Outlook*, 122:599–600 (Aug. 20, 1919).

Davenport, Walter. "Mr. Lemke Stops to Think," *Collier's*, 98:7–8, 25 (Oct. 17, 1936).

Davies, W. P. "The North Dakota Nonpartisan League," *American Cooperative Journal*, 11:922 (May 1916).

Devine, Edward T. "North Dakota—The Laboratory of the Nonpartisan League," *Survey*, 43:684–89 (March 6, 1920).

"Eye-Witness." "A 'Gold Brick' from North Dakota," *Weekly Review*, 2:621–23 (June 16, 1920).

————. "The Nonpartisan League," *Weekly Review*, 1:207–9 (July 19, 1919).

"The Farmer and the War," *New Republic*, 13:8–9 (Nov. 3, 1917).

Fite, Gilbert C. "Peter Norbeck and the Defeat of the Nonpartisan League in South Dakota," *Mississippi Valley Historical Review*, 33:217–36 (Sept. 1946).

Frazier, Lynn J. "Governor Frazier's Own Story of the Nonpartisan League," *New York Times*, Sec. XX, p. 3, May 16, 1920.

————. "Marketing Problems of the Northwestern Farmer," Fourth National Conference on Marketing and Farm Credits, *Proceedings*, 1916.

Frederick, John T. "A Legislature That Works," *New Republic*, 14:105–7 (Feb. 23, 1918).

Gaston, Herbert E. "Farmer versus Labor," *New Republic*, 40:10–12 (Sept. 3, 1934).

Gilbert, A. B. "The Farmers' Experiment in Democracy," *The World Tomorrow*, Aug. 1918, pp. 201–5.

————. "The Farmers in the Northwest," *Intercollegiate Socialist*, 7:21–23 (Feb. 1919).

————. "Out for a 'Solid West'; The Coming Political Battle of the Nonpartisan League," *Forum*, 60:727–37 (Dec. 1918).

————. "Who Killed the Nonpartisan League?" (Letter to editor), *Nation*, 123:151 (Aug. 18, 1926).

Gillette, John M. "Agrarian Political Movements with Special Reference to the Nonpartisan League," American Sociological Society, *Proceedings* ("Trend of Population"), 18:194–98 (1924).

————. "The North Dakota Harvest of the Nonpartisan League," *Survey*, 41:753–60 (March 1, 1919).

Gordon, F. G. R. "Farmers' Nonpartisan League," *American Industries*, 18:14–15 (Feb. 1918).

Gregg, William C. "North Dakota Resents?" *Outlook*, 129:382–83 (Nov. 9, 1921).

————. "The Political Storm in North Dakota," *Outlook*, 129:220–23 (Oct. 12, 1921).

Haines, Austin P. "An Adjournment of Common Sense," *New Republic*, 16:158–60 (Sept. 7, 1918).

————. "The Nonpartisan League and the Loyalty Issue," *New Republic*, 16:187–90 (Sept. 14, 1918).

Harger, Charles M. "Farmers Organizing Politically," *Financial World*, 30:10 (March 23, 1918).

Hedges, M. H. "Where Democrats Vote Republican," *New Republic*, 23:334–35 (Aug. 18, 1920).

Hicks, John D. "The Third Party Tradition in American Politics," *Mississippi Valley Historical Review*, 20:3–28 (June 1933).

Hildreth, Melvin D. "The Farmers Capture North Dakota," *World's Work*, 32:678–89 (Oct. 1916).

Horwill, A. K. "The Nonpartisan League," *New Republic*, 18:303–6 (April 5, 1919).

Huntington, Samuel P. "The Election Tactics of the Nonpartisan League," *Mississippi Valley Historical Review*, 36:613–32 (March 1950).

"Ideal State in the Northwest," *World's Work*, 37:495–96 (March 1919).

"Industrial Program of the Nonpartisan League Upheld by Supreme Court of North Dakota," *Law and Labor*, 2:68–71 (March 1920).

Jacobstein, Meyer. "Farm Credit in a Northwestern State," *American Economic Review*, 3:598–605 (Sept. 1913).

Joachim, Leo H. "Populism Today and Yesterday," *Public*, 22:234–36 (March 8, 1919).

Johnson, C. R. "The Conviction of Townley," *New Republic*, 20:18–20 (Aug. 6, 1919).

————. "Is the Nonpartisan League Declining?" *New Republic*, 24:88–90 (Sept. 22, 1920).

————. "Minnesota and the Nonpartisan League," *New Republic*, 20:290–93 (Oct. 8, 1919).

————. "The Nonpartisan League Defeated," *Nation*, 111:614 (Dec. 1, 1920).

————. "Struggle in North Dakota," *New Republic*, 26:42–44 (March 9, 1921).

King, Judson. "Banking and Steel Interests and the Townley Trial," *Public*, 22:1089–90 (Nov. 22, 1919).

————. "Big Business and the Background of the Townley Trial," *Public*, 22:1071–73 (Nov. 15, 1919).

————. "Millers, Packers, Politicians, and the Townley Trial," *Public*, 22:1113–15 (Nov. 29, 1919).

————. "The Nonpartisan Victory," *Public*, 22:706–8 (July 5, 1919).

————. "The Prosecution of Mr. Townley," *Nation*, 109:143–44 (Aug. 2, 1919).

"Lawlessness in Minnesota," *Public*, 21:876–78 (July 13, 1918).

LeSueur, Arthur. "The Nonpartisan League; A Criticism," *Socialist Review*, Nov. 1920, pp. 193–95.

Levine, Louis. "Farmers Causing Political Upheaval in West," *New York Times Magazine*, Feb. 25, 1917, Sec. V, p. 4; March 4, 1917, Sec. V, p. 4; March 18, 1917, Sec. VII, p. 10.

Locke, Walter. "The Irrepressible Farmer," *New Republic*, 25:99–101 (Dec. 22, 1920).

Lundberg, George A. "The Demographic and Economic Basis of Political Radicalism and Conservatism," *American Journal of Sociology*, 32:719–32 (March 1927).

MacDonald, William. "North Dakota's Experiment," *Nation*, 108:420–22 (March 22, 1919).

McFadden, W. C. "How North Dakota's League Reacted on the Banks," *Banker's Monthly*, Aug. 1921, pp. 16–17+.

McKaig, Ray. "The Farmers Mob the Mobbers," *Public*, 21:1241–42 (Sept. 28, 1918).

————. "The New Minnesota Despotism," *Public*, 21:465–67 (April 13, 1918).

————. "The Nonpartisan Champion," *Public*, 22:518–20 (May 17, 1919).

————. "The Nonpartisan League and Its Independent Press," *Public*, 22:13–15 (Jan. 4, 1919).

————. "The Townley Mistrial," *Public*, 22:855–57 (Aug. 9, 1919).

McNally, Winnifred. "The History of the Nonpartisan League with Specific

Reference to the Direct Primary," *Ariston* (St. Catherine's College Quarterly), Spring 1923?

Mader, Joseph. "The North Dakota Press and the Nonpartisan League," *Journalism Quarterly*, 14:321–23 (Dec. 1937).

Merz, Charles. "The Nonpartisan League; A Survey," *New Republic*, 22:333–38 (May 12, 1920).

——. "Political Revolt in the Northwest," *New Republic*, 13:15–17, 44–46, 71–73, 121–23 (Nov. 3, 10, 17, Dec. 1, 1917).

Mikolasek, V. F. "Cooperation under the Nonpartisan League," *Co-operation*, 9:35 (Feb. 1923).

Miller, Elisabeth. "Farmers Their Own Legislators," *Social Progress*, Feb. 1919.

"Minnesota, The Nonpartisan League, and the Future," *Nation*, 117–22 (Aug. 1, 1923).

Moorhead, Frank G. "The Nonpartisan League in Politics," *Nation*, 107:364–65 (Oct. 5, 1918).

Morris, Oliver S. "The Nonpartisan League" (Letter to editor), *Nation*, 111:733 (Dec. 22, 1920).

——. "The Nonpartisan League and the Cooperative Movement" (Letter to editor), *New Republic*, 25:229–30 (Jan. 19, 1921).

——. "The Vote of the North Dakota Farmers," *Nation*, 113:535–36 (Nov. 9, 1921).

——. "What Is Happening in North Dakota," *Nation*, 112:367–69 (March 9, 1921).

"The National Non-Partisan League," *American Labor Year Book, 1923–1924*, pp. 153–54.

Neal, W. S. "North Dakota Returns to Sanity," *Nation's Business*, March 1926, pp. 13–17.

"A New National Party," *Literary Digest*, 55:13–14 (Aug. 11, 1917).

Nicholas, E. H. "Mr. Creel and the Nonpartisan League," *Weekly Review*, 1:101 (June 14, 1919).

"The Nonpartisan League," *Bellman*, 24:314 (March 23, 1918).

"The Nonpartisan League Fights On," *Nation*, 114:711 (June 14, 1922).

"Nonpartisan League Plague," *Industry*, March 15, 1920, pp. 9–10.

"Non-Partisan Partisanship," *Outlook*, 123:411–12 (Dec. 3, 1919).

"Non-Partizan League Gains," *Literary Digest*, 67:21–22 (Dec. 11, 1920).

"North Dakota Farmers," *Public*, 22:318–19 (March 29, 1919).

"North Dakota Five Years After," *New Republic*, 46:292–93 (April 28, 1926).

"North Dakota Nears the Rocks," *Outlook*, 127:328 (March 2, 1921).

"North Dakota Wins Her Fight," *Nation*, 113:438 (Oct. 19. 1921).

"North Dakota's Farmer Revolt," *Literary Digest*, 54:115–16 (Jan. 20, 1917).

"North Dakota's Financial Crisis," *Literary Digest*, 68:13–14 (March 5, 1921).

"North Dakota's Political Twister," *Literary Digest*, 71:12–13 (Oct. 22, 1921).

"North Dakota's Rash Adventure," *Outlook*, 122:396–97 (July 9, 1919).

"North Dakota's 'Recall' Puzzle," *Literary Digest*, 71:10 (Nov. 19, 1921).

"North Dakota's Revolution," *Literary Digest*, 60:11–14 (March 29, 1919).

"North Dakotaism's Victory," *Literary Digest*, 62:15–16 (July 19, 1919).

O'Hara, Frank. "The Grievance of the Spring Wheat Growers," *Catholic World*, 106:380–87 (Dec. 1917).

"Oliver and Son," *New Republic*, 92:75 (Aug. 25, 1937).

Packard, F. E. "Farmers' Movement in North Dakota and Taxation," National Tax Association, *Proceedings*, 1917, pp. 266–74.

Patterson, R. G. "North Dakota: A Twentieth Century Valley Forge," *Nation*, 117:134–36 (Aug. 8, 1923).

Pickett, John E. "A Prairie Fire," *Country Gentleman*, 83(No. 20):3-4, 30-31; (No. 21):13-15, 31; (No. 22):13-14; (No. 23):13-14, 23; (No. 24):13-14, 22; (No. 25):13-14, 23 (May 18, 25, June 1, 8, 15, 22, 1918).

Plachy, Frank, Jr. "The Nonpartisan League," *Nation*, 107:92-93 (July 27, 1918).

"Politics, Bank Explosions, Lawsuits and Other Live Matters in North Dakota," *Literary Digest*, 64:62-66 (March 20, 1920).

Preus, Jacob A. O. "A Government Experiment vs. Life Insurance Principles, with Special Reference to the Rights of the Nonpartisan League" (Address delivered at the 15th Annual Convention of the Association of Life Insurance Presidents, New York City, Dec. 9, 1921), *Economic World*, 22:885-89 (Dec. 17, 1921).

Quigley, Harold S. "The Nonpartizan League," *Unpartizan Review*, 14:55-75 (July 1920).

Ratliff, Beulah A. "The 'Cream Lady'," *New Republic*, 28:240-42 (Oct. 26, 1921).

"Revolt of the Farmers: The National Nonpartisan League," *Social Service Bulletin*, 9:1-2 (July 1919).

Rockwell, J. E. "Struggle in North Dakota" (Letter to editor), *New Republic*, 26:238-39 (April 20, 1921).

Rowell, Chester H. "Political Cyclone in North Dakota," *World's Work*, 46:265-74 (July 1923).

Roylance, W. G. "Americanism in North Dakota," *Nation*, 109:37-39 (July 12, 1919).

Russell, Charles E. "The Farmers' Battle," *Pearson's Magazine*, 33:516-27 (May 1915).

————. "Grain and the Invisible Government," *Pearson's Magazine*, 34:515-27 (Dec. 1915).

————. "The Nonpartisan League," *Publications of the American Sociological Society*, Vol. XI ("Sociology of Rural Life"), 1917, pp. 31-36.

————. "Origin and Aim of the Farmers' Nonpartisan League," *Community Center*, 3:20-21 (March 17, 1917).

————. "The Revolt of the Farmers," *Pearson's Magazine*, 33:417-27 (April 1915).

Saby, Rasmus B. "The Nonpartisan League in North Dakota: The Story of America's Most Remarkable Farmers' Political Movement," *North Star*, 2:11-15 (Jan. 1920).

Saloutos, Theodore. "The Expansion and Decline of the Nonpartisan League in the Western Middle West, 1917-1921," *Agricultural History*, 20:235-52 (Oct. 1946).

————. "The National Producers' Alliance," *Minnesota History*, 28:37-44 (March 1947).

————. "The Rise of the Equity Cooperative Exchange," *Mississippi Valley Historical Review*, 32:31-62 (June 1945).

————. "The Rise of the Nonpartisan League in North Dakota, 1915-1917," *Agricultural History*, 20:43-61 (Jan. 1946).

Schrader, F. F. "Nonpartisan League Wins," *Issues and Events*, 7:35 (July 21, 1917).

Selden, Charles E. "Terrorism and Fraud of the Nonpartisan League," *New York Times Magazine*, Jan. 4, 1920, Sec. IX, pp. 1, 10.

"State Socialism Constitutional," *Literary Digest*, 65:20-21 (June 26, 1920).

Steele, H. H. "Tax Program of the Nonpartisan League of North Dakota," National Tax Association, *Proceedings*, 1919, pp. 517-27.

Taylor, Eleanor. "Farmer and Factory Hand," *Survey*, 38:564-65 (Sept. 29, 1917).

Teigan, H. G. "Fight in North Dakota," *Socialist Review*, 10:55-58 (April 1921).

————. "Minnesota's Political 'Why'," *Labor Age*, Feb. 1923, pp. 10-12.

————. "The National Nonpartisan League," *American Labor Year Book,*
1919–1920, pp. 280–89; *1921–1922*, pp. 421–26.

"That Unsuccessful Bank 'Blow-up' in Fargo," *Literary Digest,* 63:48, 52 (Dec. 20,
1919).

"The Third Party Is Born," *Nation,* 115:541 (Nov. 22, 1922).

Thompson, John, and W. H. Hunter. "The National Nonpartisan League," (Pro
and Con), *Review of Reviews,* 57:397–401 (April 1918).

"Townley and Fargo's Bank Blow-up," *Literary Digest,* 63:44–50 (Nov. 1, 1919).

"Townley in Kansas," *Literary Digest,* 68:17–18 (March 12, 1921).

"The Trial of Townley and Gilbert," *Weekly Review,* 1:230 (July 26, 1919).

Tryon, W. S. "Agriculture and Politics in South Dakota," *South Dakota Historical Collections,* 1926.

Vontrees, Ross. "A Farmer Speaks," *New Republic,* 20:291–93 (Feb. 4, 1920).

Warner, Arthur. "The Farmer Butts Back," *Nation,* 111:240–41 (Aug. 28, 1920).

————. "When Farmers Turn Politicians," *Nation,* 111:183 (Aug. 14, 1920).

"Why the Nonpartisan League Started," *Farmers' Open Forum,* Jan. 1920, pp.
15–16.

Wilcox, Benton H. "An Historical Definition of Northwestern Radicalism," *Mississippi Valley Historical Review,* 26:377–94 (Dec. 1934).

Willis, Hugh E. "North Dakota's Industrial Program and the Law," *Survey,* 45:
418–19 (Dec. 18, 1920).

Theses and Other Unpublished Writings

Anderson, Robert D. "Charles A. Lindbergh, Sr., Progressive." Special Honors
thesis, Hamline University, 1937. (Ms. in library of Minnesota Historical Society.)

Bahmer, Robert H. "The Economic and Political Background of the Nonpartisan
League." Ph.D. Thesis, University of Minnesota, 1941.

Beyer, Carlyle. "The People's Lawyer. A Study of the Life of James Manahan
and His Part in the Progressive Movement in the Northwest." Special honors
thesis, Hamline University, 1937. (Ms. in library of Minnesota Historical Society.)

Bloom, Howard E. "Violence against the Nonpartisan League in Minnesota during the World War." Thesis submitted in the Funk Prize Contest, Macalester
College, 1931. (Ms. in library of Minnesota Historical Society.)

Hofland, Carl J. "The Nonpartisan League in South Dakota." M.A. Thesis, University of South Dakota, 1940.

Hudson, Edwin E. "A Comparison of the Farmers' Alliance and the Nonpartisan
League in Minnesota." Term Paper, Department of History, University of
Minnesota, 1924. (Ms. in library of Minnesota Historical Society.)

Kingsley, Robert. "Recent Variations from the Two Party System as Evidenced
by the Nonpartisan League and the Agricultural Bloc." M.A. Thesis, University
of Minnesota, 1923.

McDonald, Annabelle. "A History of the Nonpartisan League in Colorado." M.A.
Thesis, Colorado State Teachers College, 1930.

Mader, Joseph H. "The Political Influence of the Nonpartisan League on the
Press of North Dakota." M.A. Thesis, University of Minnesota, 1937.

Merritt, Howard A. "The Farmer Labor Party of Minnesota." M.A. Thesis, University of Wisconsin, 1937.

Naftalin, Arthur E. "A History of the Farmer-Labor Party of Minnesota." Ph.D.
Thesis, University of Minnesota, 1948.

Phillips, E. B. "The Nonpartisan League in Nebraska." M.A. Thesis, University
of Nebraska, 1931.

Quigley, Walter E. "Out Where the West Begins." (Ms. in library of Minnesota Historical Society.)

Saloutos, Theodore. "Farmer Movements since 1902." Ph.D. Thesis, University of Wisconsin, 1940.

Wilcox, Benton H. "Character and Economic Basis of Northwestern Radicalism." Ph.D. Thesis, University of Wisconsin, 1933.

Collections of Papers and Manuscripts

All of the following are housed in the library of the Minnesota Historical Society.

The Committee of 48: Minnesota State Central Committee Papers, 1920–1924. Correspondence dealing for the most part with organization work and solicitation of funds. Contains limited information on relations with the National Nonpartisan League and the Farmer-Labor Party of Minnesota.

Drake Papers. Correspondence and other papers of Benjamin Drake, an attorney for the Equity Cooperative Exchange. Includes transcripts of hearings during the investigation of the grain trade by the Minnesota legislature in 1913, a report of the proceedings before the Federal Trade Commission in its study of the grain trade in September of 1922, and a report of the hearings on grain exchanges conducted by the rules committee of the United States House of Representatives in 1914.

Folwell Papers. Notes and correspondence of William Watts Folwell, much of the material having been collected during the preparation of his *History of Minnesota*. Contains a few items of interest on the history of the League in Minnesota and the early life of A. C. Townley.

Hall Papers. Correspondence and extensive clipping collection of E. George Hall, former president of the Minnesota Federation of Labor. Contains a limited amount of information on the Working People's Nonpartisan League of Minnesota.

LeSueur Papers. Correspondence, clippings, and other papers of Arthur LeSueur, for several years an attorney and adviser for the Nonpartisan League. Includes a set of correspondence lessons for League organizers.

Manahan Papers. Correspondence and scrapbooks of James Manahan, former congressman from Minnesota and attorney for the Nonpartisan League. Most of the material is contained in his *Trials of a Lawyer*.

National Nonpartisan League Papers. A miscellaneous collection, largely the correspondence of Henry G. Teigan, former executive secretary of the National Nonpartisan League. The most useful collection dealing with the League.

Nelson Papers. The voluminous papers of former Senator Knute Nelson of Minnesota contain a very limited amount of useful information on the 1918 and 1920 campaigns in that state.

Teigan Papers. Correspondence and other papers of Henry G. Teigan, mostly for other periods than during his affiliation with the Nonpartisan League. The League correspondence here contained is largely that of the Publishers' National Service Bureau.

Index

DATE DUE